NEUROBIOLOGY AND NEUROENDOCRINOLOGY OF AGEING

COVER ILLUSTRATION

Bildnis eines 92 jährigen by A. Dürer. Reproduced with permission from Graphische Sammlung Albertina, Vienna.

© 1993 by the *Journals of Reproduction and Fertility Ltd.*
22 Newmarket Road, Cambridge CB5 8DT, UK.

No part of this publication may be reproduced, stored in a retrieval system, or transmitted, in any form or by any means, electronic, mechanical, photocopying, recording or otherwise, without the prior permission of the copyright owner. Authorization to photocopy items for internal or personal use, or the internal or personal use of specific clients, is granted by Journals of Reproduction and Fertility Ltd for libraries and other users registered with the Copyright Clearance Center (CCC) Transactional Reporting Service, provided that the base fee of $02.00 per copy (no additional fee per page) is paid directly to CCC, 21 Congress St, Salem, MA 01970. This consent does not extend to other kinds of copying, such as copying for general distribution, for advertising or promotional purposes, for creating new collective works, or for resale.

$$0449\text{-}3087/93\ \$02.00+0$$

First published 1993

ISSN 0449-3087
ISBN 0 906545 24 2

JOURNAL OF REPRODUCTION AND FERTILITY

The *Journal* publishes original papers, reviews and bibliographies on the morphology, physiology, biochemistry and pathology of reproduction in man and other animals, and on the biological, medical and veterinary problems of fertility and lactation. Clinical subjects are welcome. The *Journal* is the official organ of the Society for the Study of Fertility.

The *Journal* also publishes Supplements which are distinct from the regular issues, are not associated with any particular volume and are known by their serial number and date.

Published by **The Journals of Reproduction and Fertility Ltd.**

Agents for distribution: **Portland Press, P.O. Box 32, Commerce Way, Whitehall Industrial Estate, Colchester, CO2 8HP, Essex, UK.**

Printed in Great Britain by
Henry Ling Ltd., at
The Dorset Press, Dorchester, Dorset

JOURNAL OF REPRODUCTION AND FERTILITY

SUPPLEMENT 46

Proceedings of the First International Symposium

on

NEUROBIOLOGY AND NEUROENDOCRINOLOGY OF AGEING

Bregenz

Austria

19–24 July 1992

Edited by R. Falvo, A. Bartke, E. Giacobini and A. Thorne

Journal of Reproduction & Fertility

1993

Sponsors

Land Vorarlberg, Austria

The President's Office and the Graduate School
Southern Illinois University at Carbondale
Carbondale, Illinois

School of Medicine
Southern Illinois University
Springfield, Illinois, USA

Sigma Tau Pharmaceuticals
Rome, Italy

CONTENTS

List of participants — vi

Foreword — viii

J. Meites. Anti-ageing interventions and their neuroendocrine aspects in mammals — 1–9

S. P. Kalra, A. Sahu & P. S. Kalra. Ageing of the neuropeptidergic signals in rats — 11–19

M. Isaeff, L. Goya & P. S. Timiras. Alterations in the growth and protein content of human neuroblastoma cells *in vitro* induced by thyroid hormones, stress and ageing — 21–33

P. M. Wise. Neuroendocrine ageing: its impact on the reproductive system of the female rat — 35–46

F. Piva, F. Celotti, D. Dondi, P. Limonta, R. Maggi, E. Messi, P. Negri-Cesi, M. Zanisi, M. Motta & L. Martini. Ageing of the neuroendocrine system in the brain of male rats: receptor mechanisms and steroid metabolism — 47–59

R. W. Steger, A. Bartke & M. Cecim. Premature ageing in transgenic mice expressing different growth hormone genes — 61–75

A. Mode. Sexually differentiated expression of genes encoding the P4502C cytochromes in rat liver—a model system for studying the action of growth hormone — 77–86

A. P. D'Costa, R. L. Ingram, J. E. Lenham & W. E. Sonntag. The regulation and mechanisms of action of growth hormone and insulin-like growth factor 1 during normal ageing — 87–98

E. E. Müller, S. G. Cella, V. De Gennaro Colonna, M. Parenti, D. Cocchi & V. Locatelli. Aspects of the neuroendocrine control of growth hormone secretion in ageing mammals — 99–114

R. Marcus, L. Holloway & G. Butterfield. Clinical uses of growth hormone in older people — 115–118

G. M. Gilad, R. Li, R. J. Wyatt & Y. Tizabi. Effects of genotype on age-related alterations in the concentrations of stress hormones in plasma and hypothalamic monoamines in rats — 119–130

D. M. Bowen, P. T. Francis, M. N. Pangalos & I. P. Chessell. Neurotransmitter receptors of rat cortical pyramidal neurones: implications for *in vivo* imaging and therapy — 131–143

A. Nordberg. Neuronal nicotinic receptors and their implications in ageing and neurodegenerative disorders in mammals — 145–154

G. Pepeu, F. Casamenti, I. Marconcini Pepeu & C. Scali. The brain cholinergic system in ageing mammals — 155–162

Author Index — 163

Subject Index — 165

LIST OF PARTICIPANTS

L. Angelucci	Pharmacology, University of Rome, La Saplenza, P. le A. Moro 5, 00185 Rome, Italy
M. Barcikowska	Neurology, Medical Research Institute, Warsaw, Poland
G. Barolin	Ludwig-Boltzmann Institute, Landes-Nervenkrankenhaus Valduna, A-6830 Rankwell, Austria
A. Bartke	Physiology, School of Medicine, Southern Illinois University, Carbondale, IL 62901, USA
D. M. Bowen	Neurochemistry, Institute of Neurology, 1 Wakefield St, London WC1N 1PJ, UK
A. Bratt	School of Pharmacy, University of Bradford, Bradford, BD7 1DP, UK
H. Budka	Neurological Institute, University of Vienna, Schwarzspanierstrasse 17, A-1090 Vienna, Austria
L. Calza	Neural Pathophysiology Laboratory, Via Arqua, 80/A, 41100 Modena, Italy
V. Chandrashekar	Physiology, School of Medicine, Southern Illinois University, Carbondale, IL 62901, USA
W. P. Dunlap	Fisons Pharmaceuticals, 755 Jefferson Road, Rochester, NY 14623, USA
D. Falvo	Rehabilitation and School of Medicine, Southern Illinois University, Carbondale, IL 62901, USA
R. Falvo	Graduate School, Physiology, School of Medicine, Southern Illinois University, Carbondale, IL 62901, USA
S. Feldman	Neurology, Hadassah University Hospital, P.O. Box 12000, Jerusalem, Israel
J. Friberg	680 N. Lake Shore Drive, Suite 1030, Chicago, IL 60611, USA
E. Giacobini	Pharmacology School of Medicine, Southern Illinois University, Springfield, IL 62702, USA
L. Giardino	Neural Pathophysiology Laboratory, Via Arqua, 80/A, 41100 Modena, Italy
G. Gilad	Division of Morphological Sciences, Terchnio-Israel Institute of Technology, Efron St, P.O. Box 9649, Haifa 31096, Israel
O. Hornykiewicz	Institute of Biochemical Pharmacology, University of Vienna, Borschkegasse 8 a, A-1090 Vienna, Austria
D. Hurley	Cell and Molecular Biology, Tulane University Medical School, 1430 Tulane Avenue, New Orleans, LA 70112, USA
P. Kaira	Gynecology, University of Florida, College of Medicine, Gainesville, FL 32610, USA
S. P. Kaira	Gynecology, University of Florida, College of Medicine, Gainesville, FL 32610, USA
E. Kitraki	National University of Athens, Medical School, P.O. Box 14224, Athens (GR 11510), Greece
H. J. Koch	Lautengasse 19, D-7900, Ulm, Germany
M. Kohn	Office of Mental Health, The Nathan S. Kline Institute for Psychiatric Research, Orangeburg, NY 10962, USA
T. Laasberg	Laboratory of Molecular Genetics, Estonian Academy of Sciences, 200026 Tallinn, Republic of Estonia
P. Liberski	Department of Oncology, Medical Academy, Lodz, Poland
P. Mandel	National Center for Scientific Research, 5 rue Bjaise Pascal, 67084 Strasbourg Cedex, France
B. Marchetti	Pharmacology, University of Catania, Viale Andrea Doria 6-95125 Catania, Italy
R. Marcus	Department of Veterans Affairs, 3801 Miranda Avenue, Palo Alto, CA 94304, USA
J. Meites	Physiology, Michigan State University, East Lansing, MI 48824, USA
A. Mode	Karolinska Institute, Department of Medical Nutrition, F60 NOVUM, S-141 86 Huddinge, Sweden
G. E. Morris Husbands	Wyeth-Ayerst Research, CN 8000, Princeton, NJ 08543-8000, USA
D. Müller	Pathology and Neurochemistry, 6900 Heidelberg, INF 220/221, Germany
E. E. Müller	Medical Pharmacology, University of Milan, Via Vanvitelli, 20129 Milan, Italy
T. Nippoldt	Mayo Clinic, 200 First StSW, Rochester, MN 55905, USA
A. Nordberg	Department of Pharmacology, Uppsala Biomedical Center, P.O. Box 591, S-751 24, Uppsala, Sweden
J. M. Ordy	Fisons Pharmaceuticals, 755 Jefferson Road, Rochester, NY 14623, USA
G. Pepeu	Pharmacology, University of Florence, Viale G.B. Morgagni, 65, 50134 Florence, Italy
C. Phelps	Anatomy, Tulane University Medical School, 1430 Tulane Avenue, New Orleans, LA 70112, USA
F. Piva	Department of Endocrinology, Via G Balzaretti 9, 20133 Milan, Italy
L. Robson	Department of Physiology and Pharmacology, Queen's Medical Centre, University of Nottingham, Nottingham NG7 2UH, UK

B. Schmidt	Biochemical Pharmacology, Troponwerke Gmbh & Co. KG, Berliner Strasse 156, D-5000 Koln 156, Germany
E. Schönbaum	Peelkensweg 4, 5428 NM Venhorst. N.B.R., The Netherlands
W. E. Sonntag	Physiology and Pharmacology, Bowman Gray School of Medicine, 300 South Hawthorne Road, Winston-Salem, NC 27103, USA
K. Sparring-Bjorksten	Psychiatry, University Hospital, S-501 85 Linkoping, Sweden
R. Steger	Physiology, School of Medicine, Southern Illinois University, Carbondale, IL 62901, USA
R. Summers	National Institute of Neurological Disorders, 7550 Wisconsin Avenue, Bethesda, MD 20892, USA
A. Thorne	Journals of Reproduction and Fertility, Ltd., 22 Newmarket Road, Cambridge CB5 8DT, UK
P. Timiras	Molecular and Cell Biology, University of California, Berkeley, CA 94720, USA
Y. Tizabi	Department of Pharmacology, College of Medicine, Howard University, Washington D.C. 20059, USA
M. Trabucchi	Experimental Medicine and Biochemistry, University of Rome, Via Orazio Raimondo, 00173 Rome, Italy
W. K. Waldhäusl	Clinical Endocrinology, 1 Medical University Klinik, Lazarettgasse 14, A-1090 Vienna, Austria
C. Watson	Department of Physiology and Pharmacology, Queen's Medical Centre, University of Nottingham, Nottingham NG7 2UH, UK
P. M. Wise	Physiology, School of Medicine, University of Maryland at Baltimore, 655 West Baltimore St, Baltimore, MD 21201-1559, USA

Foreword

This volume originates from a symposium focusing on neurobiology and neuroendocrinology of ageing processes and their relationship to degenerative diseases. In planning the programme we did not attempt to reach a comprehensive coverage of this vast and rapidly developing field, or to include contributions from all the key scientists working in this area. Instead, we selected a few topics for more detailed coverage. A fundamental aspect of ageing is the decline of the functional state of endocrine control mechanisms and the progressive impairment of this system. In the past, senility has been described as an 'epoch of gradual endocrine insufficiency' and, over the years, a diversity of more or less severe functional changes has been described in detail. The concept of stress and hormones and ageing neurones is updated and reviewed in several articles in this volume and, following specific descriptions of alterations in neuroendocrine mechanisms, the relationship between hormonal function, stress and behaviour is considered as a single phenomenon.

Hypothalamic mechanisms in ageing have been studied at various levels and with different models. Some of these mechanisms were discussed during the symposium, including the potential usefulness of transgenic animals in this type of research. Marked alterations of hypothalamic function, steroid receptors and steroid metabolism are evident during senility. The roles of growth hormone and of changes in growth hormone secretion and insulin-like growth factors are new areas of interest, the study of which has raised an exciting possibility of endocrine intervention into the ageing process in humans.

Particular emphasis is given to ageing of the cholinergic system in mammals, humans included. This is because the cholinergic system is central in several therapeutic approaches directed towards functional replacement in Alzheimer's disease. To what extent specific age-related changes may cause or contribute to degeneration of the nervous system in Alzheimer's and Parkinson's disease remains to be established. Several disorders common to old age have been considered to be an effect of cumulative 'metabolic' or 'hormonal' stress. A particular example of stress is the 'free radical accumulation' hypothesis, which bridges the concept of normal and pathological ageing.

In this volume age-related diseases are presented as an example of imbalance or desynchronization of neuroendocrine function that may result in an enhanced or accelerated degeneration of the nervous system. Alzheimer's disease could be an example of such a process. In general, the material presented in this volume supports the concept of ageing as a 'disease of neuroendocrine misadaptation'. Although this hypothesis still awaits experimental and clinical confirmation, the concept represents a useful framework for present and future research in neurobiology of ageing.

It is tentatively planned to organize the next *Symposium on Neurobiology and Neuroendocrinology of Ageing* in 1994 and to consider a possibility of meeting regularly every two years. This should provide an opportunity for covering the topics not included in the first symposium along with emerging new areas.

R. Falvo
A. Bartke
E. Giacobini

Anti-ageing interventions and their neuroendocrine aspects in mammals

J. Meites

Department of Physiology, Michigan State University, East Lansing, MI 48824, USA

Summary. A number of interventions for delaying or reversing declines in body functions due to ageing are critically reviewed here, including their relation to neuroendocrine function. Diets severely deficient in calories retard the ageing of body tissues, inhibit the development of disease and tumours, and significantly prolong the lifespan of rats and mice. Such diets also decrease hormone secretion, reduce the metabolism of the whole body, and lower gene expression. Administration of hormones, thymic peptides and other immune factors, and appropriate drugs can improve declining immune function in old rats and mice, thereby increasing resistance to infection, autoimmune disease and tumours. In old rats, correction of faults that develop in the neuroendocrine system with age—particularly in the hypothalamus—can restore oestrous cycles, increase the secretion of growth hormone, increase protein synthesis, inhibit development of disease and tumours, and prolong life. Antioxidants administered to rats and mice in an attempt to reduce damage to cells caused by free radicals, do not significantly retard ageing or prolong the lifespan of these animals. Regular, moderate exercise in elderly humans decreases incidence of heart disease, improves lung function, reduces bone loss, and produces other beneficial effects. Suitable drugs that will improve memory function in elderly humans remain to be developed, although a few have produced small improvements albeit with undesirable side effects. Overall, the neuroendocrine and immune approaches offer the best prospects for delaying and reversing declines in body functions due to ageing.

Keywords: ageing; neuroendocrinology; neuroendocrine interventions; ageing interventions; mammals

Introduction

The first report of how the endocrine system could be manipulated to intervene in the ageing process was made by the French physiologist Brown-Séquard, who is regarded as the father of endocrinology. He may also be regarded as the father of experimental gerontology. In 1889, at 72 years of age and feeling that he was declining in physical and mental vigour, which he attributed to a decrease in testicular function, he ground up dog and guinea pig testes, added a little distilled water, passed this through a Pasteur filter and then injected himself with the mixture. He reported that although it produced a slightly painful local reaction he was again able to work all day in his laboratory and, after going home in the evening and eating dinner, he could read and write and engage in other mental pursuits without falling asleep. Although his reports aroused considerable scepticism, his idea had considerable merit in light of present knowledge and led to many attempts to reverse ageing changes by hormonal interventions that continue to the present day.

More successful methods for retarding the ageing process have been developed in recent years as a result of the increase in knowledge of both the biological changes that occur over time and of the causes of some of these changes. Some of these methods will be reviewed with particular emphasis on those bearing a relation to the neuroendocrine system.

Methods of intervening with the ageing process

Dietary restriction

When normal daily food intake by rats or mice is reduced by 40 or 50%, many types of decline in body function due to ageing are inhibited: the incidence of disease and tumours is reduced; the decrease in immune function is retarded; and the lifespan is prolonged beyond the maximum length by 50% or more (McCay et al., 1935; Weindruch & Walford, 1988; Masoro, 1990). These anti-ageing effects do not depend on the percentage of fat, carbohydrate or protein in the diet, but rather on the number of calories consumed. The diet is otherwise adequate in vitamins and minerals. The anti-ageing effects of dietary restriction can be demonstrated in young and mature animals, but apparently not in old animals. In young animals dietary restriction results in a significant decrease in body growth, and in mature animals it results in loss of body weight. It also results in a decrease in whole-body metabolism, a reduction in body temperature, and lower blood glucose concentrations in old animals (Masoro, 1990). In young animals dietary restriction causes a delay in the onset of puberty, and in mature animals a decrease in reproductive functions.

The mechanisms by which dietary restriction produces its anti-ageing effects are not yet fully understood. The basal metabolic rate per unit of lean body mass in rats subjected to dietary restriction remains the same as in rats fed on a normal diet, but whole-body metabolism is reduced together with body weight (Masoro, 1990). The anti-ageing actions of dietary restriction have been attributed to the decreased incidence of disease, but this was found not to be the major explanation (Masoro, 1990). Various cellular mechanisms have also been proposed to explain the anti-ageing effects of reduced calorie intake (Weindruch & Walford, 1988).

The anti-ageing effects of dietary restriction are exerted mainly by reducing hormone secretions by the neuroendocrine system (Meites et al., 1987; Meites, 1990). There is considerable evidence that dietary restriction results in a decrease in hypothalamic secretion of peptide hormones such as growth-hormone-releasing hormone (GHRH), luteinizing-hormone-releasing hormone (LHRH) and thyrotrophin-releasing hormone (TRH), catecholamines, and all pituitary hormones and hormones secreted from target glands (thyroid, gonads, adrenals, pancreas) (Campbell et al., 1977). The sole exception occurs when dietary restriction is severe, such as during chronic starvation when adrenocorticotrophic hormone (ACTH) and adrenal glucocorticoid secretion are actually increased due to stress. There is evidence that hormone secretion evoked by dietary restriction remains low for the duration of dietary restriction. Thus, a 50% reduction in food intake by rats over 10 weeks resulted in a decrease in circulating growth hormone (GH), triiodothyronine (T_3) and tetraiodothyronine (T_4) when assayed at the end of the 10 weeks. Even after much longer periods on dietary restriction, the blood concentration of hormones in rats remained low. Reduced hormone values also were reported in humans on low food intake, such as during anorexia nervosa (Martin & Reichlin, 1987).

Administration of hormones to raise hormone concentrations in rats subjected to dietary restriction has been shown to counteract many of its effects. Among the organs that are reduced in size and function by dietary restriction are the ovaries and testes. Injection of gonadotrophic hormones into rats undergoing dietary restriction increased gonadal size, stimulated growth of follicles in the ovaries and spermatogenesis in the testes, and promoted steroid hormone secretion. Depressed thyroid size and decreased thyroid hormone secretion in such rats was counteracted by injection of thyroid-stimulating hormone. Injection of GH increased protein synthesis and reduced nitrogen loss in the urine. Leung et al. (1983) reported that regression in size of mammary adenocarcinomas produced by a 50% reduction in food intake was prevented by injecting the two hormones essential for mammary tumour growth in rats, oestrogen and prolactin.

Further evidence that dietary restriction exerts its anti-ageing effects mainly by reducing hormone secretion is provided by studies on the effects of chronic hypo- or hyperthyroidism.

Hypothyroidism was found to lengthen the lifespan, while hyperthyroidism was found to shorten it (Ooka & Shinkai, 1986; Ooka et al., 1983). Hypothyroidism also decreases secretion of GH, ACTH and gonadotrophic hormones, which contribute to the anti-ageing effects of this condition.

Although further studies are necessary to elucidate the mechanisms of the effects of dietary restriction, the evidence to date indicates that they are mediated primarily by reducing hormone secretion. This then results in reduced gene expression, decreased cellular growth, lower whole-body metabolism, decreased damage to DNA, and less 'wear and tear' on body organs and tissues.

Free radicals and antioxidants

The 'free radical theory of ageing' was first presented by Harman (1981). Free radicals may, for example, arise from air pollutants, pesticides, ozone, oxidation of lipids, radiation, drugs and toxins. Free radicals are believed to react with important biological molecules such as DNA, and result in damage to cells and their functions. The most common free radical in living cells is the superoxide anion, which reacts with hydrogen peroxide and other hydroperoxides to form highly reactive hydroxyl radicals. Antioxidants present in the body can prevent some of the damage caused by free radicals by scavenging for them and destroying them. Such antioxidants are mainly superoxide dismutase and glutathione peroxidase, which de-toxify superoxide radicals, hydrogen peroxide and lipid peroxides. Scavenging action for free radicals is also exerted by several sulfhydral compounds such as cysteine, methathionine, glutathione, and the enzyme catalase. Vitamins E, C and β-carotene are also important antioxidants (Balin, 1982).

Attempts have been made to supplement the intrinsic defence mechanisms against free radical damage and to prolong life by administration of antioxidants such as vitamins E and C. Harman (1981) tested five different antioxidants in Swiss albino mice, but none extended their lifespan. However, the lifespan was prolonged by several antioxidants in a short-lived mouse strain. Various antioxidants have also been tested in rats, guinea-pigs, fruit flies, and nematodes, but none was convincingly demonstrated to prolong life.

Damage to catecholamine neurones in the hypothalamus caused by free radicals may be partly responsible for many ageing developments in rats (see below). Catecholamines are metabolized mainly by monoamine oxidase, leading to formation of hydrogen peroxide, superoxide anions and hydroxyl radicals. These and other examples show that free radicals have a role in ageing processes.

Exercise

With age there is a general decrease in most body functions, including velocity and reaction time of nerve conduction, cardiovascular function, respiratory capacity, muscle strength, work capacity and bone maintenance (Shock, 1977). There is also less lean body mass and more body fat. There is evidence that regular exercise by older people can counteract some of these ageing effects, and will result in decreased incidence of heart disease, reduced bone loss and development of osteoporosis, and increased lung capacity. Exercise can also result in lower body fat, greater lean body mass and can promote a sense of well being.

In one study cited by Buskirk (1985), 15 elderly women and 9 elderly men engaged in regular exercise for a period of 19 weeks. Significant body weight loss occurred in both groups, more in men than in women, and both resting and exercise heart rate decreased as did systolic and diastolic blood pressure. In another study, 17 women aged between 52 and 79 years engaged in regular calesthenics, jogging and stretching for 1 h three times a week for three months. There was an increase in physical work capacity, aerobic capacity and oxygen pulse when these subjects were tested on riding a cycle. In another study, 110 sedentary healthy 60–71 year old men and women, about half of each sex, were placed on a regular regimen of jogging or walking for 40–50 min per day for one year. Cardiovascular function in both sexes improved by 20–25%, which was about the same as in young men and women on this exercise regimen. Older individuals can be physically conditioned in the same way as younger individuals (deVries, 1979), but the hazards are somewhat greater; a physician should therefore be consulted before a programme of exercise is initiated. There is no valid evidence as yet that regular exercise results in prolongation of the lifespan, despite its beneficial effects.

Relatively little is known of the effects of moderate exercise on the neuroendocrine system. However, it has been demonstrated that, in young and mature people, exercise results in a prompt increase in GH secretion (Martin & Reichlin, 1987). This may account in part for the increase in lean body mass and reduction in fat produced by exercise. Regular exercise has also been reported to result in a reduction in insulin secretion and in the ACTH–adrenal response to swimming tests (Buskirk, 1985).

Memory loss

Memory loss constitutes one of the greatest fears of individuals as they become older. The decline in short-term memory is usually much greater than in long-term memory. The causes for the decrease in memory function with age are not entirely clear. The hippocampus in the brain is believed to be the major memory-processing centre in the brain, and it has been found that a deficiency in acetylcholine (ACh) develops in this area with age (Bartus et al., 1983). Cholinergic drugs have therefore been tested in old rats, monkeys and humans to determine their effects on memory by a variety of tests. Physostigmine, which inhibits acetylcholinesterase (the enzyme that metabolizes ACh), and arecholine, an acetylcholine agonist, both significantly improve memory functions in old animals and humans. The precursors of ACh, dietary choline and lecithin were ineffective for reasons that are not yet clear. On the other hand, anticholinergic drugs such as atropine or scopolamine both produced memory impairment in animals and humans. A problem with the available cholinergic drugs is their undesirable effects on other body functions.

A number of pituitary hormones have been tested for their effects on memory function (Gispen et al., 1977). Arginine-vasopressin and a derivative of the first ten amino acids of ACTH were found to produce only minimal improvement in memory function, with no single dose more consistently effective than another. The role of catecholamines on memory function is not clear, although there is some evidence that they facilitate certain kinds of learning (Bartus et al., 1983). The effects of other neurotransmitters, peptides and hormones remain to be tested. Stimulants of the CNS (such as caffeine and methylphenidate) have not been shown to improve memory function. Drugs that can improve memory function while producing few side effects remain to be developed.

Immune competence

There is considerable evidence for a decline in immune competence with age. The thymus, considered to be the chief component of the immune system, exhibits a marked loss in size and function at about the time of puberty due to the rise in secretion of gonadal hormones. This is followed by a progressive decrease in secretion of thymic peptides such as thymosin 1, thymopoietin, and thymulin that are essential for production of mature T cells and other cells of the immune system (Fabris et al., 1988).

Hormones secreted by the neuroendocrine system have been shown to be important in regulating thymic function. Electrolytic lesions of the hypothalamus or reticular formation induce severe involution of the thymus (Isakovic & Jankovich, 1973), perhaps by decreasing the secretion of hormones by the hypothalamus and pituitary. GH, T_3 and T_4, prolactin, and possibly insulin promote immune function, whereas gonadal and adrenal glucocorticoid hormones depress immune function. The decrease in GH and thyroid hormone secretion in old rats is believed to contribute to the decline in immune function, as suggested by the correlation between the decrease in GH and T_4 secretion and the decrease in thymic and spleen function in old rats (Goya et al.,

1991). Administration of T_4 to old mice was reported to produce a youthful histological appearance of the thymus and resumption of thymulin secretion. Transplantation of the thymus from T_4-treated old mice to young thymectomized mice resulted in as much secretion of thymulin as by the young thymus (Fabris et al., 1988).

Sonntag & Meites (1988) reported that administration of GH significantly increases the weight of the thymus and spleen in old rats and mice. Kelley et al. (1986) found that GH not only restores thymus weight in old rats, but also restores full function of this gland as indicated by the results of five tests designed to challenge the immune system. Hypopituitary dwarf mice secrete very low amounts of GH, prolactin and ACTH, and this is associated with progressive involution of the immune tissues, accelerated greying of hair, general weakness and occasional cataracts; in addition, the mice die at 3–5 months of age. All of these effects were prevented by injecting GH and T_4 (Fabris et al., 1988).

The immune system has also been reported to stimulate secretion of hormones and, under some circumstances, may itself secrete hormones. Thus, the thymus secretes peptides that stimulate secretion of gonadotrophin-releasing hormone (GnRH), ACTH and luteinizing hormone (LH) (Fabris et al., 1988), whereas thymosin fraction 5 inhibits secretion of thyroid-stimulating hormone (TSH) in young but not old rats (Goya et al., 1991). Neonatal thymectomy in mice results in derangement of reproductive functions and reduced pituitary hormone secretion, which can be remedied by implantation of fetal thymic tissue (Fabris et al., 1988). Lymphocytes activated by disease were reported to secrete ACTH, TSH, and β-endorphin (Blalock et al., 1985). Whether administration of thymic peptides can favourably influence hormone secretion by the neuroendocrine system in old animals remains to be investigated.

Neuroendocrine interventions

Neuroendocrine interventions are based on many observations demonstrating that faults develop in the neuroendocrine system with age and that correction of these faults can delay or reverse some ageing developments (Meites et al., 1987; Meites, 1991). Dysfunctions have been demonstrated in the hypothalamus, pituitary, target glands and body tissues normally influenced by hormones. The most important faults occur in the hypothalamus. There is decreased release and loss of rhythm in release of some hypothalamic hormones that are associated with reduced neurotransmitter stimulation—particularly by the two catecholamines dopamine (DA) and noradrenaline. Hypothalamic noradrenaline is normally responsible for the release of GnRH, GHRH and TRH, whereas dopamine acts directly on the pituitary to inhibit prolactin secretion. Rhythmic release of these hormones is apparently controlled by the suprachiasmatic nucleus in the hypothalamus.

The reduction in release of GnRH results in decreased secretion of pituitary gonadotrophins, depressed ovarian function, loss of oestrous cycles in female rats and a reduction in secretion of testosterone in male rats. There is also evidence that the pituitary becomes less responsive to GnRH stimulation, the gonads become less sensitive to gonadotrophic stimulation, and target tissues (such as the uterus, vagina and prostate) do not respond as well to gonadal steroids. The decrease in GHRH release results in reduced GH and somatomedin (insulin growth factor 1) secretion, leading to diminished protein synthesis. The reduction in TRH release results in lower thyroid hormone secretion and decreased body metabolism, although body metabolism is not solely controlled by the thyroid. The decrease in hypothalamic dopamine activity results in increased prolactin secretion and development of numerous mammary and prolactin-secreting pituitary tumours. The reduction of GH and thyroid hormone secretion are believed to contribute to the decrease in immune function with age (Goya et al., 1991).

Administration of drugs that increase dopamine and noradrenaline activity in the hypothalamus of old rats has been shown to delay or reverse most of the ageing developments mentioned above. Daily administration of L-DOPA, the precursor of catecholamines, delays loss of oestrous cycles in ageing rats, and re-initiates oestrous cycles in old rats undergoing constant oestrus. Injection of iproniazid or deprenyl, monoamine oxidase inhibitors that reduce catabolism of catecholamines, also results in resumption of oestrous cycles in old constant-oestrus rats (Meites, 1991; Quadri, S.K. & Meites J., unpublished). Twice daily injection of L-DOPA into old rats increases GH secretion to that found in young rats, and partially restores protein synthesis in the diaphragm muscle of old male rats (Sonntag & Meites, 1988). Administration of catecholamine drugs to old rats also decreases prolactin secretion and induces regression of mammary and pituitary tumours.

In addition to the above, administration of catecholamine drugs to rats or mice was reported to inhibit development of disease and tumours, and to prolong the average lifespan. Thus, Walker et al. (1988) found that when ibopamine, a drug that stimulates catecholamine receptors, is given to rats 50 days old and is then continued for two years, the incidence of six neoplastic and five non-neoplastic diseases was significantly reduced. No significant effect on food intake or body weight was found in the drug-treated rats compared with the control rats, except for a slight reduction in weight of the rats given the highest dose of ibopamine.

Four different laboratories have reported that drugs that increase the concentration of brain catecholamines can prolong lifespan and promote reproductive functions. Cotzias et al. (1974) found that chronic addition of L-DOPA to the diet of Swiss albino mice increased the lifespan by about 50% and extended fertility. However, body weight was significantly reduced, suggesting that prolongation of the lifespan may have been due to reduced food intake. Clemens & Fuller (1978) observed that when female rats were fed legrotrile mesylate, a dopamine receptor agonist, for two years it significantly increased survival from 40–50% in control rats to 70–90% in the drug-treated rats without affecting food intake or body weight. Knoll (1988) reported that injection of deprenyl (a monoamine oxidase B inhibitor) into male rats initially two years of age, prolongs their lifespan by about one year compared with two-year-old control rats, and also increases sexual performance. The effects of deprenyl on prolongation of lifespan were partially confirmed in an inbred strain of two-year-old rats (Milgrim et al., 1990). Body weight was not reduced in these rats when compared with controls. It is of interest that when deprenyl, together with L-DOPA and a peripheral inhibitor of dopamine metabolism, were administered to patients with Parkinson's disease the patients lived longer than controls (Birkmeyer & Birkmeyer, 1989).

Discussion

A number of different interventions to delay or reverse ageing developments have been reviewed. Only a few have been applied to humans. Regular exercise improves many bodily functions in elderly as well as in young or mature individuals. Some of its beneficial effects may be exerted via the neuroendocrine system by increasing GH secretion and perhaps by reducing stress, leading to lower ACTH and glucocorticoid secretion. Probably very few individuals would accept a significantly restricted calorie diet for most of their adult life, particularly when there is no certainty that this will inhibit ageing processes or prolong the human lifespan. Indeed, there is some evidence that lean persons may not live as long as slightly overweight people (Andres, 1981), although some do not accept this view. There is ample evidence that calorie restriction in humans reduces hormone secretion, as it does in animals (e.g. anorexia nervosa). Thus far there is no definite proof that increased intake of antioxidants such as vitamins E and C, or β-carotene, can exert anti-ageing effects or prolong the lifespan in animals or humans, even though free radicals probably have a role in ageing processes. Although cholinergic and other drugs may produce positive effects on memory in old animals and people, their side effects make them much less than satisfactory. More suitable drugs to improve memory function remain to be developed.

The best anti-ageing possibilities appear to lie in interventions that can improve the functions of the neuroendocrine and immune systems. These two systems have been demonstrated to function coordinately in a bidirectional manner. They provide the most important mechanisms in the body for regulating and integrating body functions. They are probably the principal systems through which the genome and environment regulate ageing processes. It is the decline in these two systems that lead to many if not most declines in body function with ageing.

Research reported thus far on methods to improve immune function in ageing animals and humans appears promising, and requires further attention. In old humans and animals, there is an increased risk of infections, autoimmune diseases and tumours, all of which are associated with the decline in immune competence and probably with the decrease in neuroendocrine function. Some success in improving immune competence in old animals has been achieved by use of hormones such as GH and thyroid hormones, and by administration of thymic peptides or transplantation of immune tissues from fetal or young animals. The effects of central-acting neurotransmitters such as the catecholamines and other drugs that directly influence the hypothalamus or the thymus, remain to be tested.

The leading causes of death in the elderly are cardiovascular diseases, cancer and stroke. Kidney diseases also rank high. It has been estimated that if all cardiovascular diseases, stroke and kidney diseases were eliminated, about ten years would be added to the average human lifespan. Although ageing and disease are not the same, there is a relationship between the two. With time, the decline in the morphological and functional integrity of organs and tissues results in a more favourable environment for the development of disease. Thus, with normal ageing, there is a progressive decrease of dopamine neurones in the substantia nigra of the brain (McGreer *et al.*, 1989). If 80% or more of these neurones are lost, the individual develops Parkinson's disease. Normal lung function progressively declines with age and, therefore, infectious bacteria or viruses can more readily attack the lungs. The decrease in kidney function with age due to vascular occlusion, obstructions and trauma can lead to greater susceptibility to disease in this organ. The accumulation of extracellular material in arterial walls with time can result in increased blood pressure and vascular disease (Rowe & Minaker, 1985). It has been reported that injections of GH into old rats significantly increase the weight of the heart, kidneys, liver, spleen and thymus (Sonntag & Meites, 1988). If this also represents an increase in function as well as in size, and leads to strengthening these organs, then some of the diseases that can often develop may be delayed. Mention has already been made of the inhibitory effects on development of pathology and tumours by dietary restriction and of the effects of ibopamine on the incidence of neoplastic and non-neoplastic diseases in ageing rats (Walker *et al.*, 1988).

It would appear that the neuroendocrine approach offers the greatest possibilities for inhibiting or reversing ageing developments and perhaps for prolonging life. In view of the decline in the level of catecholamines in the rat hypothalamus with age and their important role in regulating release of peptide hormones that act on the pituitary, methods that serve to increase the levels of these substances in the hypothalamus need to be explored further. Drugs such as clonidine, a noradrenaline agonist, have been shown to increase GH secretion in humans as well as in animals (Martin & Reichlin, 1987). Is the decrease in hypothalamic noradrenaline activity in elderly humans responsible for the decline in GH secretion as has been shown in old rats (Sonntag & Meites, 1988)? The decrease in hypothalamic catecholamine activity with age is probably related in large part to the marked reduction of noradrenaline neurones in the locus coeruleus, a region of the brain that is a major supplier of noradrenaline to the hypothalamus. In addition to catecholamines, the role of other neurotransmitters that modulate pituitary hormone secretion needs to be investigated. Mention has already been made of the decline in ACh activity in the hippocampus, a brain area that has connections to the hypothalamus. ACh was reported to modulate release of several pituitary hormones, including gonadotrophins, GH and prolactin. Concentrations of 5-HT, which can modulate secretion of most pituitary hormones, apparently do not change significantly with age in the rat hypothalamus (Simpkins, 1984). Changes in other neurotransmitters in the hypothalamus with age also need to be studied. In addition, the question of reduced responsiveness with age to hormones and other stimuli by the pituitary, its target glands, and organs and tissues stimulated by the pituitary and target glands needs to be addressed. These defects are apparently due to loss of receptors or to postreceptor changes in cells with age. There are possibilities for developing methods to increase the responsiveness of these organs and tissues to hormones and other stimuli. The prospects are promising for the development in the future of many more and better interventions for delaying or reversing declines in body functions, for inhibiting disease and perhaps for prolonging the lifespan.

References

Andres, R. (1981) Aging, diabetes and obesity. *Mount Sinai Journal of Medicine*, New York **48**, 489.

Balin, A.K. (1982) Testing the free radical theory of aging. In *Testing the Theories of Aging*, pp. 137–182. Eds R. C. Adelman & G. S. Roth. CRC Press, Florida.

Bartus, R.T., Flicker, C. & Dean, R.L. (1983) Logical principles for the development of animal models of age-related memory impairments. In *Assessment in Geriatric Psychopharmacology*, pp. 263–299. Eds T. Crook, S. Ferris & R. Bartus. Mark Powley Associates, Inc., New Canaan, Connecticut.

Birkmeyer, W. & Birkmeyer, J.G.D. (1989) The L-dopa story. In *Parkinsonism and Aging*, pp. 1–7. Eds D. B. Calne, G. Comi, D. Crippa, R. Horowski & M. Trabucchi. Raven Press, New York.

Blalock, J.E., McMenamin, D.H. & Smith, E.M. (1985) Peptide hormones shared by the neuroendocrine and immunologic systems. *Journal of Immunology* **135**, 858–861.

Brown-Séquard, C.E. (1889) Des effets produit chez l'homme par des injections sous-cutanées d'un liquide retiré des testicules frais de cobaye et de chien. *Comptes Rendus Seances Societe de Biologie Series 9* **1**, 415–419.

Buskirk, E.R. (1985) Health maintenance and longevity: exercise. In *Handbook of the Biology of Aging (2nd edn)*, pp. 894–931. Eds C. E. Finch & E. L. Schneider. Van Nostrand Reinhold Co., New York.

Campbell, G.A., Kurcz, M., Marshall, S. & Meites, J. (1977) Effects of starvation on serum levels of follicle stimulating hormone, lutenizing hormone, thyrotropin, growth hormone, and prolactin; response to LH releasing hormone and thyrotropin releasing hormone. *Endocrinology* **100**, 580–587.

Clemens, J.A. & Fuller, R.W. (1987) Chemical manipulation of some aspects of aging. In *Pharmacological Intervention in the Aging Process*, pp. 187–206. Eds J. Roberts, R. C. Adelman, & V. J. Cristofalo. Plenum Press, New York.

Cotzias, G., Miller, S., Nicholson, A., Matson, W. & Tang, K. (1974) Levo-dopa, fertility, and longevity. *Proceedings of the National Academy of Sciences USA* **71**, 2466–2469.

deVries, H.A. (1979) Tips on prescribing exercise regimens for your older patient. *Geriatrics* **34**, 75–81.

Fabris, N., Mocchegiani, E., Muzzioli, M. & Provinciali, M. (1988) Immune–neuroendocrine interactions during aging. *Progress in Neuroendocrinimmunology* **1**, 4–9.

Gispen, W.H., Reith, M.E.A., Schotman, R.P., Wiegant, V.W., Zwiers, W.H. & de Wied, D. (1977) CN and ACTH-like peptides: neurochemical response and interaction with opiates. In *Neuropeptide Influences on the Brain and Behavior*, pp. 61–80. Eds L. H. Miller, C. A. Sandman & A. J. Kastin. Raven Press, New York.

Goya, R.G., Brooks, K., & Meites, J. (1991) A comparison between hormone levels and lymphocyte function in young and old rats. *Mechanisms of Aging and Development* **61**, 275–285.

Harman, D. (1981) The aging process. *Proceedings of the National Academy of Sciences USA* **78**, 7124–7128.

Isakovic, K. & Jankovich, B.D. (1973) Neuro-endocrine correlates of immune response II. Changes in the lymphatic organs of brain lesioned rats. *International Archives of Allergy* **45**, 373–384.

Kelley, K.W., Brief, S., Westly, H.J., Novakofski, J., Bechtel, P.J., Simon, J. & Walker, E.B. (1986) GH3 pituitary adenoma cells can reverse thymic aging in rats. *Proceedings of the National Academy of Sciences USA* **83**, 5666–5667.

Knoll, J. (1988) The striatal dopamine dependency of lifespan in male rats. Longevity study with (−) deprenyl. *Mechanisms of Aging and Development* **46**, 237–262.

Leung, F.C., Aylsworth, C.F. & Meites, J. (1983) Counteraction of underfeeding-induced inhibition of mammary tumor growth in rats by prolactin and estrogen administration. *Proceedings of the Society of Experimental Biology and Medicine.* **173**, 159–163.

McCay, C.M., Crowel, M.F. & Maynard, L.A. (1935) The effect of retarded growth upon the length of the lifespan and upon the ultimate body size. *Journal of Nutrition* **10**, 63–79.

McGreer, P.L., Itagaki, S., Akiyama, H. & McGreer, E.G. (1989) Comparison of neuronal loss in Parkinson's disease and aging. In *Parkinsonism and Aging*, pp. 25–34. Eds D. C. Calne, G. Comi, D. Crippa, R. Horowski & M. Trabucchi. Raven Press, New York.

Martin, J.B. & Reichlin, S. (1987) *Clinical Neuroendocrinology (2nd edn)*. F. A. Davis Co., Philadelphia.

Masoro, E.J. (1990) Assessment of nutritional components in prolongation of life and health by diet. *Proceedings of the Society of Experimental Biology and Medicine* **193**, 31–34.

Meites, J. (1990) Aging: hypothalamic catecholamines, neuroendocrine–immune interactions and dietary restrictions. *Proceedings of the Society of Experimental Biology and Medicine* **195**, 304–311.

Meites, J., Goya, R. & Takahashi, S. (1987) Why the neuroendocrine system is important in the aging process. *Experimental Gerontology* **22**, 1–15.

Milgrim, N. W., Racine, R. J., Nellis, P., Mendonca, A. & Ivy, G.O. (1990) Maintenance on L-deprenyl prolongs life in aged male rats. *Life Sciences* **47**, 415–420.

Ooka, H. & Shinkai, T. (1986) Effects of chronic hyperthyroidism on the lifespan of the rat. *Mechanisms of Aging and Development* **33**, 275–282.

Ooka, H., Feyita, S. & Yoshimoto, E. (1983) Pituitary–thyroid activity and longevity in neonatally thyroxine-treated rats. *Mechanisms of Aging and Development* **22**, 113–120.

Rowe, J.W. & Minaker, K.L. (1985) Geriatric medicine. In *Handbook of the Biology of Aging (2nd edn)*, pp. 912–959. Eds C. E. Finch & E. L. Schneider, Van Nostrand Reinhold Co., New York.

Shock, N. (1977) System integration. In *The Handbook of the Biology of Aging*, pp. 639–665. Eds C. E. Finch & L. Hayflick. Van Nostrand Reinhold Co., New York.

Simpkins, J.W. (1984) Regional changes in monoamine metabolism in aging constant estrous rats. *Neurobiology of Aging* **4**, 309–314.

Sonntag, W.E. & Meites, J. (1988) Decline in GH secretion in aging animals and man. In *Regulation of Neuroendocrine Aging*, pp. 111–124. Eds A. V. Everitt and J. R. Walton. Karger, Basel.

Walker, R.F., Weidman, C.A. & Wheeldon, E.B. (1988) Reduced disease in aged rats treated chronically with ibopamine, a catecholaminergic drug. *Neurobiology of Aging* **9**, 291–301.

Weindruch, R. & Walford R.L. (1988) *The Retardation of Aging and Disease by Dietary Restriction*. Charles C. Thomas, Springfield, Illinois.

Ageing of the neuropeptidergic signals in rats

S. P. Kalra, A. Sahu and P. S. Kalra

Department of Obstetrics and Gynecology, University of Florida College of Medicine, Gainesville, FL 32610, USA

Summary. With advancing age, subtle and progressive disintegration of several components of peptidergic signals that drive luteinizing-hormone-releasing hormone (LHRH) secretion contribute to diminished pituitary–gonadal function in both sexes of the rat. The results show that in female rats, ageing *per se* and unopposed exposure to oestrogen disrupt different loci in the transmission line to neurones that release LHRH. Ageing *per se* appears to abolish the restraint on the influence of inhibitory opioids induced by a neural clock – an event necessary for the preovulatory surge of luteinizing hormone to occur in young rats. By contrast, unopposed exposure to oestrogen disrupts the progression and transduction of information at hypothalamic loci downstream from the neural clock–opioid link. In male rats, the age-related diminution in pituitary–gonadal function is probably due to a gradual decrease in release of neuropeptide Y, an excitatory peptidergic signal to LHRH-expressing neurones. Further studies have revealed that this decline is a consequence of age-related acquisition of refractoriness to testosterone by neurones producing neuropeptide Y. Cumulatively, these findings underscore the key roles of hypothalamic peptidergic signals to LHRH-expressing neurones in the ageing process of the reproductive system in rats.

Keywords: neuropeptides; β-endorphin; neuropeptide Y; ageing; steroids; rat

Introduction

Despite the subnormal reproductive function in ageing rats, several lines of evidence indicate that neurones producing luteinizing-hormone-releasing hormone (LHRH) retain the secretory capacity required to sustain normal pituitary–gonadal function. On the other hand, it is evident that as these rats become older subtle and progressive disintegration of several components of neural signals that drive secretory function of LHRH neurones lead to diminished pituitary gonadotrophin secretion and cessation of oestrous cycles. In this context, the realization that there is a distinct hypothalamic circuitry to regulate basal and cyclic LHRH secretion in young rats has gained considerable significance (Kalra & Kalra, 1983; Kalra, 1986; Fig. 1). With the aid of a variety of experimental paradigms and anatomical techniques it has been possible to identify the core components of this circuitry and to understand how they operate in synchrony to release a quantum of LHRH episodically in the establishment of the basal secretion pattern of luteinizing hormone (LH), and to accelerate the rate of LHRH discharge with clock-like precision for the preovulatory LH surge during the critical period of pro-oestrus. Information to date also favours the notion that modulatory neural and hormonal inputs influence not only LHRH release *per se*, but also provide a permissive milieu for LHRH neurones to produce and discharge optimal amounts with inherent periodicity (Estes *et al.*, 1982; Kalra, 1986). Additionally, it appears that whereas catecholaminergic systems (especially the hypothalamic adrenergic innervations via α_1 adrenoreceptors) contribute only minimally to the regulation of LHRH secretion, a network of neuropeptidergic systems locally in the hypothalamus integrates the basal and cyclic modalities of the release of this hormone (Clifton & Sawyer, 1979; Kalra, 1985, 1986).

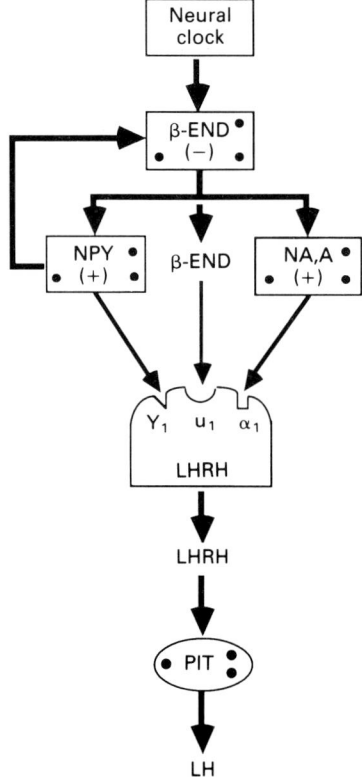

Fig. 1. Diagrammatic representation of the neural circuitry involved in the control of basal and cyclic luteinizing hormone (LH) release. The endogenous opioid peptide system, which is comprised mainly of neurones expressing β-endorphin (β-END) acting through μ_1 opiate receptors, maintains the basal secretion of luteinizing-hormone-releasing hormone (LHRH). However, at a certain point in the oestrous cycle (pro-oestrus), this inhibitory influence (−) is reduced and the excitatory influences (+) of neuropeptide Y (NPY) acting via Y_1 receptors and of adrenaline (A) and noradrenaline (NA) acting via α_1 adrenoreceptors are elicited. This leads to an increase in LHRH secretion necessary for the preovulatory release of LH from the pituitary (PIT). Neurones expressing NPY and β-END are also subject to regulation by gonadal steroids (■).

Our studies have shown that an inhibitory, endogenous opioid peptide (EOP) system, comprised primarily of the neurones expressing β-endorphin operating through μ_1 opiate receptors, and an excitatory, neuropeptide Y (NPY) neuronal system acting through Y_1 receptors, constitute the core network of the hypothalamic circuitry involved in the regulation of LHRH secretion (Kalra & Crowley, 1984; Kalra & Kalra, 1985; Leadem et al., 1985; Kalra, 1986; Kalra & Crowley, 1992; Fig. 1). Experimental evidence indicates that the EOP network restrains LHRH secretion to a basal range in male and female rats, but on the afternoon of pro-oestrus in regularly cycling female rats, a curtailment of this inhibitory tone results in augmentation of NPY and adrenergic transmitter discharge. This enhanced excitatory transmitter output then promotes the LHRH hypersecretion necessary for the preovulatory release of LH (Kalra, 1983; Kalra et al., 1989). The evidence that on the morning of pro-oestrus, experimentally induced restraint on inhibitory EOP influence advances the pre-ovulatory LH surge (Allen & Kalra, 1986; Allen et al., 1988), whereas prevention of the naturally occurring restraint by injecting β-endorphin blocks it (Leadem & Kalra, 1985a, b) strongly favours the suggested role of EOP in induction of ovulation. Similarly, the observations of increased neurosecretory activity in NPY-immunopositive axon terminals in the median eminence preceding and during the preovulatory LH surge, and blockade of the LH surge by immunoneutralization of NPY underscore the obligatory involvement of NPY in triggering LHRH hypersection on the afternoon of pro-oestrus (Crowley et al., 1985; Sutton et al., 1988; Sahu et al., 1989a).

The anatomical evidence is also in harmony with the idea that the hypothalamic EOP and NPY systems play a role in the control of LHRH secretion. Immunocytochemical and electron microscope studies have revealed that NPY and EOP neurones communicate with the LHRH-expressing network by axo–somatic or axo–dendritic synapses in the preoptic area (Leranth et al., 1988; Tsuruo et al., 1990), and by volume transmission modality in the median eminence (Leadem et al., 1985; Crowley & Kalra, 1987; Füxe & Agnati, 1991). It is also apparent that β-endorphin-releasing neurones are capable of regulating the release of NPY and adrenergic transmitters, which act synergistically to amplify LHRH output (Leadem et al., 1985; Allen et al., 1987; Sahu et al., 1990a). Our recent efforts have unravelled a new line of communication between hypothalamic NPY and β-endorphin neurones: NPY axon terminals synapse with β-endorphin-immunopositive dendrites and soma in the arcuate nucleus of the hypothalamus (Horvath et al., 1992), a finding suggestive of a potential regulatory role of NPY in governing the discharge of β-endorphin (Fig. 1).

Interestingly, information processing in neurones expressing NPY and β-endorphin is itself subject to modulation by gonadal steroids (Morrell et al., 1985; Kalra et al., 1987; Sar et al., 1990). It would seem that these interacting peptidergic systems, and not the LHRH-producing neurones (Kalra & Kalra, 1980; Shivers et al., 1984), are the neural substrates for gonadal steroid action (Kalra & Kalra, 1986; Kalra et al., 1987).

With this background in mind, it was hypothesized that a defect in the exquisite interplay between the inhibitory EOP and excitatory NPY afferents to LHRH neurones on the one hand, and feedback action of steroids on these peptidergic neurones on the other, may contribute to the age-related diminution of pituitary–gonadal function. Attempts to identify the loci of impairment in the interactions among EOP, NPY and steroids in aged rats of both sexes are summarized in this article.

Ageing, the EOP system and steroid action

The preovulatory release of LH occurs during the critical period between 14:00 h and 16:00 h on the day of pro-oestrus in regularly cycling, young female rats. Allen and colleagues observed that a prolonged restraint of the inhibitory opioid tone produced by infusion of the opiate receptor antagonist naloxone, on the morning of pro-oestrus, prematurely provoked LH hypersecretion, which resembled qualitatively and quantitatively the normal, spontaneous preovulatory LH surge (Allen & Kalra, 1986; Allen et al., 1988). This evidence *in vivo* and the observation that naloxone readily stimulates release of hypothalamic LHRH *in vitro* (Leadem et al., 1985) led to the proposal that the neural clock responsible for initiating the preovulatory gonadotrophin discharge normally curtails the existing inhibitory opioid tone in order that the LHRH–LH surge can occur during the critical period (Fig. 1). Several lines of evidence showing that secretion of β-endorphin (Sarkar & Yen, 1985), hypothalamic opiate receptor binding (Casulari et al., 1987; Jacobson & Kalra, 1989; Dondi et al., 1992), and the amount of pro-opiomelanocortin mRNA (Wise et al., 1990) decrease in association with the LH surge are in line with our hypothesis that "β-endorphin systems are interposed between the neural clock and LHRH neurones" (Allen et al., 1988; Fig. 1).

During ageing many rats develop irregular oestrous cycles, cycle length is increased and the preovulatory LH surge is delayed or attenuated. Eventually, LH surges cease and acyclicity ensues (Lu et al., 1979; Wise et al., 1991). Since the capacity of the pituitary to release the surge of LH and of the hypothalamus to release LHRH are largely unaffected in ageing rats (Zanisi et al., 1987; Sahu et al., 1988), it would seem that a progressive deficit or derangement in the link between the neural clock and opioid release caused by either ageing *per se* or an inappropriate ovarian oestrogen milieu results in the disappearance of the LHRH–LH surges in senescent rats. If this is true, it is possible that the absence of LH surges in old rats may be due to a loss of time-dependent restraint on inhibitory EOP tone. Since infusion of naloxone can mimic the naturally occurring decrease in opioid tone (Allen & Kalra, 1986), we examined the effects of naloxone infusion on LH release in 17–18-month-old rats with a history of acyclicity, as indicated by constant vaginal oestrus smears and an irregular cyclic pattern. These rats were ovariectomized and 4 weeks later received standard oestradiol treatment to evoke the LH surge (Masotto *et al.*, 1990; Sahu *et al.*, 1990a). The results showed that on the afternoon of pro-oestrus, the surge of LH occurred normally in young rats, but not in old rats treated with oestradiol (Fig. 2). Further, in agreement with previous studies (Masotto *et al.*, 1990; Sahu *et al.*, 1990a) infusion of naloxone advanced and amplified the LH surge in young rats. However, quite unexpectedly in old rats also, infusion of naloxone evoked LH surges that were equivalent in magnitude to that evoked by oestrogen alone in young rats (Sahu *et al.*, 1991). This observation implies that in response to an experimentally induced decrease in opioid tone with naloxone, LH surges can be reinstated in aged rats. Evidently, the spontaneous clock-induced restraint on inhibitory EOP influence that normally occurs in young rats fails to operate in aged rats; therefore, ageing, *per se*, is likely a key factor causing disruption in the time-dependent obligatory neural trigger for cyclic LH discharge (Sahu *et al.*, 1991).

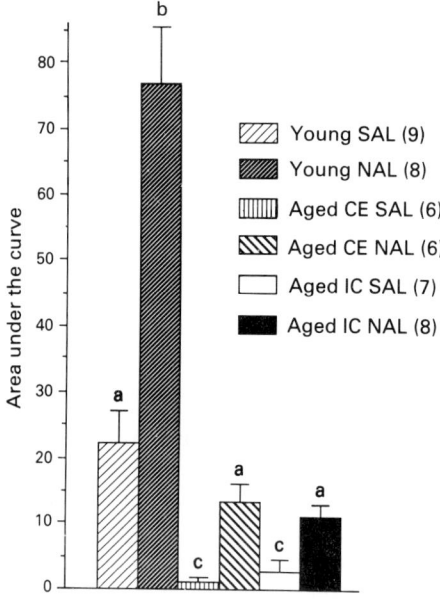

Fig. 2. Effect of naloxone (NAL) infusion on LH release in oestradiol-primed young (2–3 months) and aged (17–19 months) ovariectomized rats. Young and aged rats were ovariectomized and 4 weeks later received subcutaneous capsules filled with oil containing oestradiol. Rats were implanted with intrajugular cannula the next day. NAL (2 mg h^{-1}) or saline (SAL) was infused between 11:00 h and 14:00 h. Blood samples were collected at hourly intervals between 11:00 h and 18:00 h. The response made by LH between 11:00 h and 18:00 h is presented as area under the curve. Bars with similar superscripts are statistically not different with respect to each other ($P > 0.05$). Numbers in parentheses represent the number of rats per group. CE: constant oestrus; IC: irregular cycle.

Alternatively, it is possible that an unopposed oestrogen milieu, which normally occurs in ageing acyclic rats displaying constant vaginal oestrus, may abolish those neurosecretory events that should occur after the onset of clock-induced inhibition of opioid tone. The effects of short-term (3 days) and long-term (13 or 17 days) exposure to oestradiol on spontaneous LH surges, and naloxone- and progesterone-induced LH surges in young, ovariectomized rats were examined in a series of studies (Sahu *et al.*, 1991; Fuentes *et al.*, 1992). Continuous exposure to oestradiol for up to 13 days produced no deleterious effects on either the spontaneous or naloxone-induced LH surges. However, uninterrupted exposure to oestradiol for 17 days abolished the spontaneous LH surge and drastically impaired the ability of naloxone to reinstate the LH surge. In contrast, progesterone injection elicited undiminished LH responses in rats exposed to oestradiol either short or long term, indicating that the hypothalamic neural circuitry is fully responsive to appropriate stimuli even after prolonged exposure to oestrogen (Fig. 3). However, since naloxone failed to evoke LH surges in rats chronically treated with oestradiol, it is likely that progression and transduction of the message from the neural clock–EOP link are interrupted at loci downstream along the transmission line to the final destination – the LHRH-releasing neurones (Fig. 1). Since NPY-producing neurones are oestrogen target sites (Sar *et al.*, 1990), it seems likely that chronic oestrogen treatment, in the absence of progesterone, renders the NPY network unresponsive to messages emanating from the clock–EOP link. Further studies are underway to examine NPY neurosecretory function in aged rats displaying constant vaginal oestrus and in young rats chronically exposed to oestrogen. Nevertheless, the results already obtained suggest that the absence of an LH surge in ageing rats exposed to unopposed oestrogen may be due to a disruption at loci downstream of the neural clock–EOP link in the peptidergic transmission line to LHRH neurones.

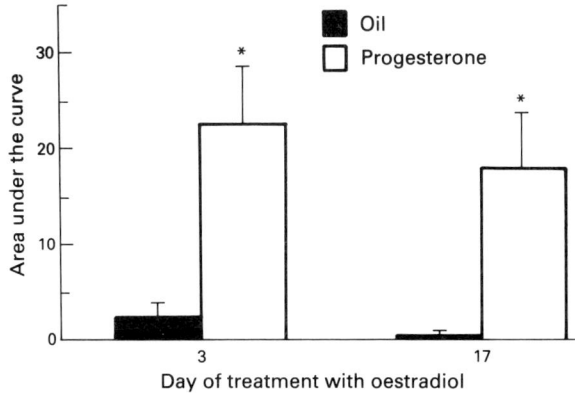

Fig. 3. Effect of 3 or 17 days of treatment with oestradiol on the progesterone-induced surge of luteinizing hormone (LH). Progesterone was administered at 11:00 h on the day of the test and blood samples were withdrawn at hourly intervals between 11:00 h and 17:00 h. The response of LH between 11:00 h and 17:00 h is presented as area under the curve. *($P < 0.05$) indicates a significant difference from oil-treated controls.

Ageing, the NPY system and steroid action

The disclosure that the intrinsic secretory capacity of LHRH neurones may not be impaired in aged male rats (Zanisi *et al.*, 1987; Sahu *et al.*, 1988) also led us to explore the possibility that diminution in LHRH and LH secretion may be due to a decreased excitatory NPY drive to LHRH neurones in aged rats (Kalra & Crowley, 1984; Crowley & Kalra, 1987; Crowley *et al.*, 1987). Indeed, it was observed that the medial basal hypothalamus of 13-month-old male rats releases significantly less NPY in response to K^+ *in vitro* compared with that of young 2·5-month-old rats (Sahu *et al.*, 1988). On the other hand, the K^+-induced LHRH release from the same tissue of young and aged rats was similar (Fig. 4), indicating that the observed diminution in hypothalamic NPY secretion is a result of decreased NPY stores in hypothalamic sites. Thus, it is possible that the secretory function of hypothalamic NPY neurones, which includes the production and processing of neuropeptides, is compromised with age. On the basis of results obtained from female rats (as alluded to in the preceding sections), we speculated further that endocrine factors as well as ageing *per se* contribute to the subnormal hypothalamic NPY function in aged male rats.

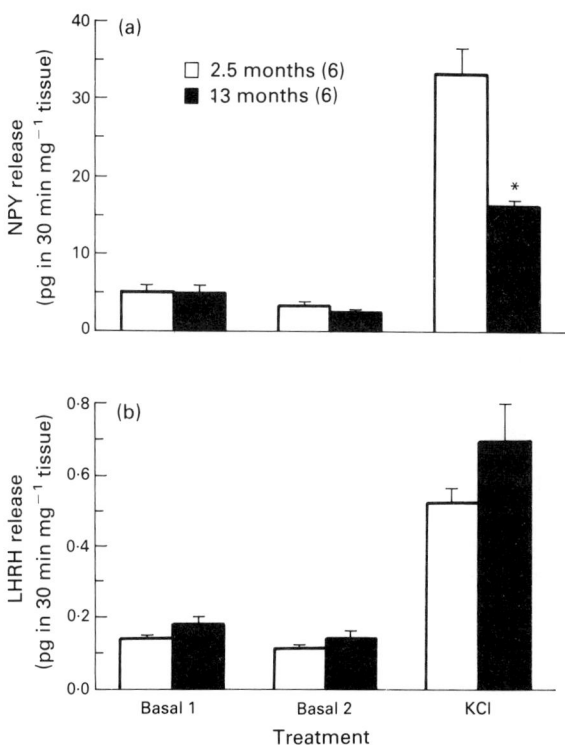

Fig. 4. Basal and KCl-induced release of (a) neuropeptide Y (NPY) and (b) luteinizing-hormone-releasing hormone (LHRH) *in vitro* from the medial basal hypothalamus of male rats 2·5 and 13 months old. Numbers in parentheses represent the number of rats per group. *($P < 0·05$) indicates a significant difference from the amount of NPY released from 2·5-month-old rats. The medial basal hypothalami were incubated for two 30 min sessions (Basal 1 and Basal 2) before addition of KCl (45 mmol l^{-1}) for 30 min.

Our studies showed that despite the widespread distribution of NPY in hypothalamic sites castration decreases the amount of NPY while testosterone replacement restores the amount of NPY selectively in the median eminence, arcuate nucleus and ventromedial nucleus of young rats (Sahu *et al.*, 1987, 1988). Maintenance by testosterone of NPY concentration in the arcuate nucleus and median eminence is interesting because these sites have long been implicated in the control of LHRH secretion by NPY (Crowley & Kalra, 1987; Kalra & Crowley, 1992). In fact, it has been documented that NPY release *in vitro* from the fragment of the medial basal hypothalamus containing these sites is decreased after castration and can be reinstated by testosterone replacement (Sahu *et al.*, 1989b). More recently, we have observed that NPY secretion *in vivo*, as estimated in perfusates collected with the aid of push–pull cannulae aimed at the pituitary, decreases after castration. Furthermore, the amount of preproNPY mRNA was found to be lower in castrated than in castrated, testosterone-treated rats (Sahu *et al.*, 1992). Since NPY-producing neurones in the hypothalamus are the apparent targets of steroid action (Sar *et al.*, 1990), these findings clearly

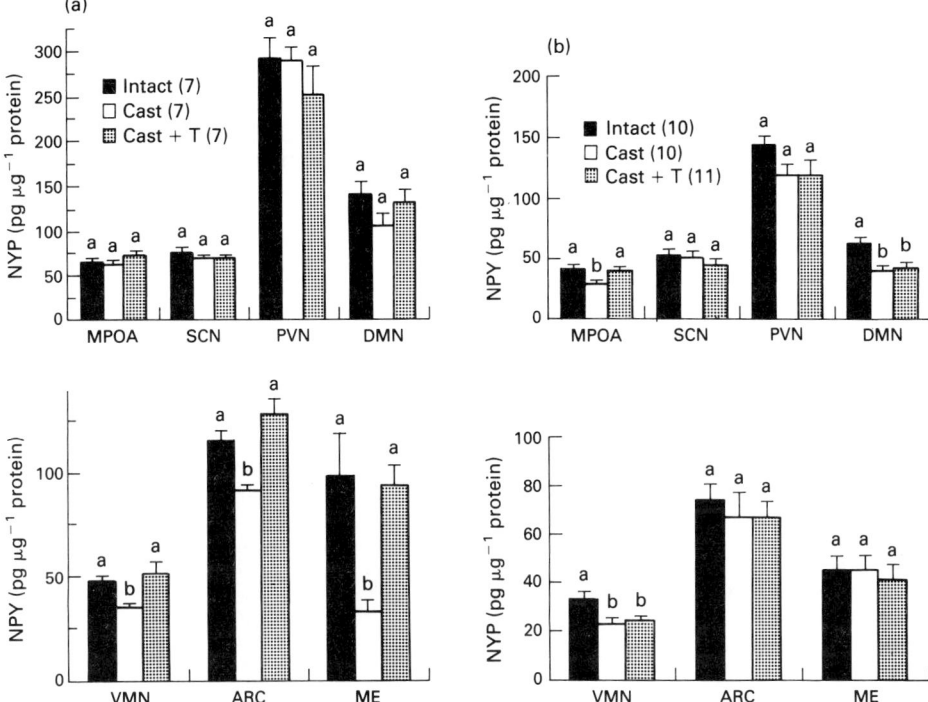

Fig. 5. Effects of castration (CAST) and testosterone (T) replacement on the amount of neuropeptide Y (NPY) in various hypothalamic sites of (a) young male rats and (b) aged male rats. ARC: arcuate nucleus; DMN: dorsomedial nucleus; ME: median eminence; MPOA: medial preoptic area; PVN: paraventricular nucleus; SCN: suprachiasmatic nucleus; VMN: ventromedial nucleus. Figures in parentheses denote number of rats. Bars with similar superscripts are not significantly different from each other for that nucleus ($P > 0.05$).

imply that gonadal steroids enhance the neurosecretory activity of hypothalamic NPY neurones by direct genomic activation.

The important question posed by these findings is whether the observed diminution in hypothalamic NPY secretory function is indeed due to a lack of testosterone support in aged rats. A comparative study of the effects of castration and testosterone replacement in aged and young rats has revealed intriguing facts (Sahu et al., 1990b). As expected, in young rats, castration reduces and testosterone replacement prevents the castration-induced depletion in NPY secretion in only three sites, i.e. the ventromedial nucleus, the arcuate nucleus and the median eminence (Fig. 5a). In contrast, castration in aged rats reduces NPY content not only in the ventromedial nucleus, as in young rats, but also in the medial preoptic area and dorsomedial nucleus (Fig. 5b). Surprisingly, the castration-induced reduction in the amount of NPY in the median eminence and arcuate nucleus that is consistently seen in young rats does not occur in aged rats (Fig. 5b). In addition, with the exception of the medial preoptic area, testosterone replacement in aged rats neither prevents the site-specific castration-induced decrease in the response of NPY, nor increases the concentration of NPY in any of the hypothalamic sites to the range seen in intact or castrated, testosterone-treated young rats (Fig. 5b).

The results of these studies have indicated that NPY secretory function is diminished in aged rats and that there is a disparate regional vulnerability to castration, which cannot be prevented by testosterone replacement therapy. Taken together with the previous demonstration that NPY readily stimulates LHRH release and potentiates the action of LHRH on pituitary LH release (Crowley & Kalra, 1987; Crowley et al., 1987; Kalra & Crowley, 1992), our results are in accord with the view that a gradual age-related diminution in hypothalamic NPY neuronal function, including the acquisition of refractoriness to testosterone action, may adversely affect the LHRH–LH axis and thereby contribute to reproductive ageing in the male rat.

Thanks are due to S. McDonell for secretarial assistance in preparation of the manuscript. The studies were supported by grants from the NIH, HD 08634 (SPK) and HD 11362 (PSK).

References

Allen, L.G. & Kalra, S.P. (1986) Evidence that a decrease in opioid tone may evoke preovulatory luteinizing hormone release in the rat. *Endocrinology* **118**, 2375–2381.

Allen, L.G., Crowley, W.R. & Kalra, S.P. (1987) Interactions between neuropeptide Y and adrenergic systems in stimulation of LH release in steroid-primed ovariectomized rats. *Endocrinology* **121**, 1953–1959.

Allen, L.G., Hahn, E., Caton, D. & Kalra, S.P. (1988) Evidence that a decrease in opioid tone on proestrus changes the episodic pattern of LH secretion: implications in the preovulatory LH hypersecretion. *Endocrinology* **122**, 1004–1013.

Casulari, L.A., Maggi, R., Dondi, D., Limonta, P., Piva, F., Motta, M. & Martini, L. (1987) Effect of oestrus cyclicity on the number of brain opioid μ receptors in the rat. *Hormone and Metabolic Research* **9**, 549–554.

Clifton, D.K. & Sawyer, C.H. (1979) LH release and ovulation in the rat following depletion of hypothalamic norepinephrine: chronic vs acute effects. *Neuroendocrinology* **28**, 441–449.

Crowley, W.R. & Kalra, S.P. (1987) Neuropeptide Y stimulates the release of luteinizing hormone-releasing hormone from medial basal hypothalamus *in vitro*: modulation by ovarian hormones. *Neuroendocrinology* **46**, 97–103.

Crowley, W.R., Tessel, R.E., O'Donohue, T.L., Adler, B.A. & Kalra, S.P. (1985) Effects of ovarian hormones on the concentrations of immunoreactive neuropeptide Y in discrete brain regions of the female rat: correlation with serum LH and median eminence LHRH. *Endocrinology* **117**, 1151–1155.

Crowley, W.R., Hassid, A. & Kalra, S.P. (1987) Neuropeptide Y enhances the release of luteinizing hormone induced by luteinizing hormone-releasing hormone. *Endocrinology* **120**, 941–945.

Dondi, D., Limonta, P., Maggi R. & Piva F. Effects of ovarian hormones on brain opioid binding sites in castrated female rats. *American Journal of Physiology* (in press).

Estes, K.S., Simpkins, J.W. & Kalra, S.P. (1982) Resumption of clonidine on pulsatile LH release following acute norepinephrine depletion in ovariectomized rats. *Neuroendocrinology* **35**, 56–62.

Fuentes, M., Sahu, A. & Kalra, S.P. (1992) Evidence that long-term estrogen treatment disrupts opioid involvement in the induction of pituitary LH surge. *Brain Research* **583**, 183–188.

Füxe, K. & Agnati, L.F. (1991) Two principal modes of electrochemical communication in the brain: volume vs wiring transmission. In *Volume Transmission in the Brain: Novel Mechanisms for Neurotransmission*, pp. 1–9. Raven Press, New York.

Horvath, T.L., Naftolin, F., Kalra, S.P. & Leranth, C. Neuropeptide Y innervation of β-endorphin-containing cells in the rat mediobasal hypothalamus. A light- and electromicroscopic double-immunostaining analysis. *Endocrinology* (in press).

Jacobson, W. & Kalra, S.P. (1989) Decreases in mediobasal hypothalamic and preoptic area opioid (^{3}H-naloxone) binding are associated with the progesterone-induced LH surge. *Endocrinology* **124**, 199–205.

Kalra, S.P. (1983) Opioid system – inhibitory neuronal systems in regulation of gonadotropin secretion. In *Role of Peptides and Proteins in the Control of Reproduction*, pp. 63–87. Eds S. M. McCann & D. S. Dhindsa. Elsevier, Amsterdam.

Kalra, S.P. (1985) Catecholamine involvement in preovulatory LH release: reassessment of the role of epinephrine. *Neuroendocrinology* **40**, 139–144.

Kalra, S.P. (1986) Neural circuitry involved in the control of LHRH secretion: a model for preovulatory LH release. *Frontiers in Neuroendocrinology* **9**, 31–75.

Kalra, S.P. & Crowley, W.R. (1984) Norepinephrine-like effects of neuropeptide Y on LH release in the rat. *Life Sciences* **35**, 1173–1176.

Kalra, S.P. & Crowley, W.R. (1992) Neuropeptide Y: a novel neuroendocrine peptide in the control of pituitary hormone secretion, and its relation to luteinizing hormone. *Frontiers in Neuroendocrinology* **13**, 1–36.

Kalra, P.S. & Kalra, S.P. (1980) Modulation of hypothalamic luteinizing hormone-releasing hormone levels by intracranial and subcutaneous implants of gonadal steroids in castrated rats: Effects of androgen and estrogen antagonists. *Endocrinology* **106**, 390–397.

Kalra, S.P. & Kalra, P.S. (1983) Neural regulation of luteinizing hormone secretion in the rat. *Endocrine Reviews* **4**, 311–351.

Kalra, P.S. & Kalra, S.P. (1985) Control of gonadotropin secretion. In *The Pituitary Gland*, pp. 189–220. Ed. H. Imura. Raven Press, New York.

Kalra, P.S. & Kalra, S.P. (1986) Steroidal modulation of the regulatory neuropeptides: luteinizing hormone releasing hormone, neuropeptide Y and endogenous opioid peptides. *Journal of Steroid Biochemistry* **25**, 733–740.

Kalra, S.P., Kalra, P.S., Sahu, A., Allen, L.G. & Crowley, W.R. (1987) The steroid-neuropeptide Y connection in the control of LH secretion. In *Regulation of Ovarian and Testicular Function: Advances in Experimental Biology and Aging*, pp. 65–83. Eds V. B. Mahesh, D. S. Dhindsa, E. Anderson & S. P. Kalra. Plenum Press, New York.

Kalra, S.P., Allen, L.G. & Kalra, P.S. (1989) Opioids in the steroid-adrenergic circuit regulating LH secretion: dynamics and diversities. In *Brain Opioid Systems in Reproduction*, pp. 95–111. Eds R. G. Dyer & R. J. Bicknell. Oxford University Press, Oxford.

Leadem, C.A. & Kalra, S.P. (1985a) Reversal of βE-induced blockade of ovulation and LH surge with PGE_2. *Endocrinology* **117**, 684–689.

Leadem, C.A. & Kalra, S.P. (1985b) The effects of endogenous opioid peptides and opiates on luteinizing hormone and prolactin secretion in ovariectomized rats. *Neuroendocrinology* **41**, 342–352.

Leadem, C.A., Crowley, W.R., Simpkins, J.W. & Kalra, S.P. (1985) Effects of naloxone on catecholamine and LHRH release from the perifused hypothalamus of the steroid-primed rat. *Neuroendocrinology* **40**, 497–500.

Leranth, C., MacLusky, N.J., Shanabrough, M. & Naftolin, F. (1988) Immunohistochemical evidence for synaptic connections between pro-opioimelanocortin-immunoreactive axons and LHRH neurons by the preoptic area of the rat. *Brain Research* **449**, 167–176.

Lu, K.H., Hooper, B.R., Vargo, T.M. & Yen, S.S.C. (1979) Chronological changes in sex steroid, gonadotropin and prolactin secretion in aging female rats displaying different reproductive states. *Biology of Reproduction* **21**, 193–203.

Masotto, C., Sahu, A., Dube, M.G. & Kalra, S.P. (1990) A decrease in opioid tone amplifies the LH surge in estrogen-treated ovariectomized rats: comparison with progesterone effects. *Endocrinology* **126**, 18–25.

Morrell, J., McGinty, F. & Pfaff, D.W. (1985) A subset of β-endorphin- or dynorphin-containing neurons in the medial basal hypothalamus accumulates estradiol. *Neuroendocrinology* **41**, 417–426.

Sahu, A., Kalra, S.P., Crowley, W.R., O'Donohue, T.L. & Kalra, P.S. (1987) Neuropeptide Y levels in microdissected regions of the hypothalamus and *in vitro* release in response to KCl and prostaglandin E_2: effects of castration. *Endocrinology* **121**, 310–315.

Sahu, A., Kalra, P.S., Crowley, W.R. & Kalra, S.P. (1988) Evidence that hypothalamic neuropeptide Y secretion decreases in aged male rats: implications for reproductive aging. *Endocrinology* **125**, 2199–2203.

Sahu, A., Jacobson, W., Crowley, W.R. & Kalra, S.P. (1989a) Dynamic changes in neuropeptide Y concentrations in the median eminence in association with preovulatory luteinizing hormone (LH) release in the rat. *Journal of Neuroendocrinology* **1**, 83–87.

Sahu, A., Kalra, S.P., Crowley, W.R. & Kalra, P.S. (1989b) Testosterone raises neuropeptide Y concentrations in selected hypothalamic sites and *in vitro* release from the medial basal hypothalamus of castrated male rats. *Endocrinology* **124**, 410–414.

Sahu, A., Crowley, W.R. & Kalra, S.P. (1990a) An opioid-NPY transmission line to LHRH neurons: a role in the induction of LH surge. *Endocrinology* **126**, 876–883.

Sahu, A., Kalra, S.P., Crowley, W.R. & Kalra, P.S. (1990b) Aging in male rats modifies castration and T-induced NPY response in various microdissected brain nuclei. *Brain Research* **515**, 287–291.

Sahu, A., Fuentes, M. & Kalra, S.P. (1991) Absence of LH surge in aged and young rats treated chronically with estradiol 17β (E_2) is due to impairment in different neural mechanisms. *73rd Annual Meeting of the Endocrine Society*, p. 140 (Abstract No. 438).

Sahu, A., Phelps, C.P., White, J.D., Crowley, W.R., Kalra, S.P. & Kalra, P.S. (1992) Steroidal regulation of hypothalamic neuropeptide Y release and gene expression. *Endocrinology* **139**, 3331–3336.

Sar, M., Sahu, A., Crowley, W.R. & Kalra, S.P. (1990) Localization of neuropeptide Y (NPY) immunoreactivity in estradiol concentrating cells in the hypothalamus *Endocrinology* **127**, 2752–2756.

Sarkar, D.K. & Yen, S.S.C. (1985) Changes in B-endorphin-like immunoreactivity in pituitary portal blood during the estrous cycle and after ovariectomy in rats. *Endocrinology* **116**, 2075–2079.

Shivers, B.D., Harlan, R., Morrell, J. & Pfaff, D.W. (1984) Absence of oestradiol concentration in cell nuclei of LHRH-immunoreactive neurons. *Nature* **304**, 345–347.

Sutton, S., Toyama, T., Otto, S. & Plotsky, P. (1988) Evidence that neuropeptide Y (NPY) release into the hypophyseal-portal circulation participates in priming gonadotropes to the effects of gonadotropin releasing hormone (GnRH). *Endocrinology* **123**, 1208–1210.

Tsuruo, Y., Kawano, H., Kagotani, Y., Hisano, S., Daikoku, S., Chihara, K., Zhang, T. & Yanaihara, N. (1990) Morphological evidence for neuronal regulation of luteinizing hormone-releasing hormone-containing neurons by neuropeptide Y in the rat preoptic area. *Neuroscience Letters* **110**, 261–266.

Wise, P.M., Scarbrough, K., Weiland, N.G. & Larson, G.H. (1990) Diurnal pattern of proopiomelanocortin gene expression in the arcuate nucleus of proestrous, ovariectomized and steroid-treated rats: a possible role in cyclic luteinizing hormone secretion. *Molecular Endocrinology* **4**, 886–892.

Wise, P.M., Scarbrough, K., Larson, G.H., Lloyd, J.M., Weiland, N.G. & Chiu, S. (1991) Neuroendocrine influences on aging of the female reproductive system. *Frontiers in Neuroendocrinology* **12**, 323–356.

Zanisi, M., Messi, E. & Martini, L. (1987) *In vitro* release of luteinizing hormone releasing hormone from the hypothalamus of old male rats. *Endocrinology* **120**, 49–54.

Alterations in the growth and protein content of human neuroblastoma cells *in vitro* induced by thyroid hormones, stress and ageing

M. Isaeff, L. Goya and P. S. Timiras

Department of Molecular and Cell Biology, University of California, Berkeley, CA 94720 USA

Summary. The effects of the thyroid hormone triiodothyronine (T_3), nerve growth factor (NGF) and stress (exposure to heat or aluminium sulfate) on growth, development and ageing of human neuroblastoma cells were studied *in vitro*. Differentiation of cells using retinoic acid and NGF inhibits cell growth and proliferation; simultaneously, it promotes acquisition of neuronal phenotype, down-regulation of T_3 receptors, and an increase in catecholaminergic tyrosine hydroxylase activity and microtubule assembly. The actions of T_3 on neuronal differentiation resemble those of NGF and suggest the existence of NGF–T_3 interactions. Exposure to stress inhibits cell growth and proliferation, increases immunoreactivity to the microtubule-assembling protein tau (which occurs in paired filaments of neurofibrillary tangles in the aged human brain), and facilitates formation of tau–ubiquitin complexes (which also occur in the aged brain). Stress does not prevent the inhibition of cell proliferation by high doses of T_3; however, T_3 doses that are equivalent to physiological levels reduce stress-induced inhibition of growth. Previous studies have shown that stress may also induce in these cells facsimile lesions of normal and abnormal ageing, such as accumulation of lipofuscin pigments, formation of paired helical filaments and increased immunoreactivity to tau, β-amyloid proteins, and ubiquitin. These lesions may represent cellular and molecular manifestations of increased vulnerability and susceptibility to genetic and extrinsic factors (e.g. hormones and environmental influences) with ageing. It is proposed that neuroblastoma cells may serve as a model to study mechanisms of neuronal ageing and to identify agents and conditions capable of preventing, delaying or reducing metabolic abnormalities leading to age-associated disorders.

Keywords: T_3; NGF; stress; neuroblastoma; ageing; humans

Introduction

This study assimilates a series of observations that provide a trail of phenomena leading to the idea that hormones and stress affect not only ontogenesis and maturation but also ageing of the CNS. The experiments described here have all been conducted in cultured neurones derived from human neuroblastoma and neurogenic teratocarcinoma cells grown in a manipulated environment. The use of tissue culture offers the opportunity of investigating the direct effects of a variety of agents and conditions on neurones. Cultured neurones may serve as a convenient model to understand CNS growth, development and ageing; they may also serve to screen rapidly and inexpensively for factors that are potentially beneficial in the promotion of neuronal growth, plasticity and regeneration. Although we have extrapolated our data to conditions *in vivo*, we are well aware of the limitations of this.

New data are presented here and are incorporated with previously collected and reported results, which altogether tell an interesting story. The parameters studied were cell proliferation and DNA synthesis, effects of triiodothyronine (T_3), effects of stress, microtubule tau proteins, and ubiquitin. Thyroid hormones, and particularly the major biologically active hormone T_3 are well-known promoters of normal CNS growth and development (see review by Timiras, 1988a). They also regulate some aspects of brain function and behaviour in the adult, and may affect ageing (Walker & Timiras, 1982; Ooka et al., 1983; Ooka & Shinkai, 1986) (Table 1) Stress and adrenal steroids induce neuronal loss and metabolic alterations in specific brain areas, and these may lead to disorders of homeostasis (Sapolsky et al., 1986; Timiras, 1991) (Table 2). Cellular stress (e.g. heat shock) or toxic substances (such as the anticarcinogen doxorubicin) that generate free radicals (Cole and Timiras, 1989; Argasinski et al., 1989) or that interfere with ion transport and microtubule dynamics [such as the cation aluminium (Al^{3+}), Mesco et al., 1991] induce in the cultured neurones alterations that resemble those in the aged brain in vivo. These alterations include accumulation of lipofuscin pigments (associated with ageing), the presence of paired helical filaments (the major component of neurofibrillary tangles), increased immunoreactivity to tau protein, to amyloid and amyloid precursor protein (the major component of neuritic plaques), and to the cytoplasmic protein ubiquitin (Cole et al., 1985; Cole & Timiras 1987a; Mesco et al., 1991; Mesco & Timiras, 1991). These and other lesions represent the major findings from the study of the pathology of Alzheimer's disease.

Table 1. The influence of thyroid hormones on brain development

Brain structure	Brain chemistry	Brain function
Size and weight	Energy metabolism (oxidation, glycolysis)	Electroencephalographs, evoked potentials
Cell proliferation and cell death	Proteins, DNA, RNA, receptors	Sensory and motor activity
Dendrites (number, length, spines)	Neurotransmitters (cholineric, monaminergic)*	Behaviour (cognitive, emotional)*
Axons (length, regeneration)	Microtubule system*	
Synapses	Myelinogenesis	
Cerebral capillaries		

*Also affected in the adult and perhaps in the ageing brain.

Table 2. The involvement of hormones in age-related alterations in the brain

Examples of age-related change	Hormone involved
Selected neuronal loss, hormonal receptor loss	Adrenal, sex steroids (in the hippocampus)
Decreased energy metabolism, neurotransmitter imbalance	Thyroid hormones (in the cortex)
Alterations in protein, DNA	Steroids, thyroid hormones
	Growth promoters and inhibitors (in neurones, glia)
Altered homeostasis, normal responses to stress	Adrenal, thyroid hormones (in the hypothalamus)

In this study the effects of T_3 on growth and differentiation of neuroblastoma cells are compared under 'normal', 'stressful' or 'aged' conditions. Results from these experiments have implications for the normally ageing brain. Additionally, some of the induced alterations (e.g. increased immunoreactivity to tau in neurofibrillary tangles, to neuritic plaques and amyloid precursor protein, and to changes in tau–ubiquitin conjugates) may be hallmarks of the abnormally ageing brain (as in dementia of Alzheimer's type).

Materials and Methods

Materials

Dulbecco's modified Eagle's medium (DMEM)/F-12 (50:50), fetal bovine serum (screened for viruses and mycoplasms, and trypsin-versene were supplied by Whittaker Bioproducts (Walkersville, MD, USA). The following were all obtained from Sigma (St Louis, MO, USA): 3,5,3'-triiodothyronine; aluminium sulfate; EDTA; Tris; all-*trans* retinoic acid; Dulbecco's phosphate-buffered saline; DNA (calf thymus type 1); 3,5-diaminobenzoic acid dihydrochloride (DABA); trichloroacetic acid; and antibiotic antimycotic solution (containing 10 000 iu penicillin, 10 mg streptomycin and 25 µg amphotericin B per ml). Lyophilized mouse NGF (26 kDa) was obtained from Promega, (Madison, WI, USA). [^{3}H]Thymidine (5 Ci mmol^{-1}) was obtained from Amersham Corporation, Arlington Heights, IL, USA, and Ready Safe liquid scintillation cocktail from Beckman Instruments Incorporated, Fullerton, CA, USA). All cells were obtained from the Tissue Culture Facility of the University of California, San Francisco, CA, USA.

Cells and methods of culture

Human neuroblastoma cells from the LAN-5 and SH-SY5Y lines (Sidell & Horn, 1985) were routinely grown in DMEM/F-12 (50:50) supplemented with 10% fetal bovine serum and 1% antibiotic antimycotic solution. All cells were grown on Corning tissue culture plates at 37°C in a humidified atmosphere of air and CO_2 (95:5), and the medium was changed every 3 days. Cells were allowed to reach 90% confluency and were harvested using trypsin-versene, re-plated in multiwells, and allowed to attach at least 24 h prior to any experiment.

Differentiation and ageing. To induce differentiation, retinoic acid (10 µmol l^{-1}) from a stock solution (10 mmol l^{-1}) was added to the medium every other day over a total of 6 days (Sidell & Horn, 1985; Cole & Timiras, 1987b).

To mimic some characteristics of neuronal ageing *in vitro* (e.g. accumulation of lipofuscin pigments, formation of paired helical filaments and immunoreactivity to amyloid), these cells as well as neuronal teratocarcinoma (NT2/D1) cells were 'aged' by exposing them to a variety of neurotoxic substances (Cole & Timiras, 1987b). In the experiments described here, the cells were exposed to physical (e.g. heat shock) and chemical (e.g. aluminium sulfate) stress. Heat shock was consistently performed in basal medium by floating the petri dishes on top of a water bath at 42°C for 1 h and then immediately returning the dishes to the humidified incubator. Heat-shocked cells were allowed to recover prior to addition of conditioned medium. Aluminium (as aluminium sulfate; 1 mmol l^{-1}) was added to the medium for 6–8 days; the sulfate vehicle, which was independently monitored, proved to have no effect.

Hormones and growth factors. The effects of T_3 and NGF were studied before and after differentiation. T_3 was also studied under both basal and stress conditions. Furthermore, to maintain consistent concentrations of experimental conditions in media, media containing T_3 or NGF were changed every 2 days. T_3 was added to the medium for 6–8 days from a stock solution of 3,5,3'-triiodothyronine (10 mmol l^{-1}) in increasing doses ranging from 10^{-10} mol l^{-1} to 10^{-4} mol l^{-1}. NGF was dissolved in DMEM/F-12 (50:50) and added to the medium to a final concentration of 2 nmol NGF l^{-1} for 8 days.

Protein and DNA assays

DNA levels and cell proliferation (growth curves), DNA synthesis, measured by [^{3}H]thymidine incorporation, tyrosine hydroxylase activity, T_3 nuclear receptors, tau protein and ubiquitin concentrations were all assayed. Some of these kinds of measurements had been conducted in previous experiments and have already been published; therefore, a summary is presented here.

Cell proliferation assays. LAN-5 cells were routinely plated at the density of 2.5×10^5 cells per cm^{-2}, which had been found to be best for cell proliferation. Cells were allowed to attach for 24 h prior to adjustment of conditions. At designated times, media was aspirated and the cells allowed to air-dry for 15 min before fixation with 70% ethanol. At the time of the assay the ethanol was aspirated, and the cells were allowed to dry under a slight vacuum for 1·5 h, after which 0·5 ml DABA (0·4 mol l^{-1}) was added to each well and the well incubated at 60°C for 1 h. The reaction was terminated with 1 mol HCl l^{-1}. Total DNA content was then determined using a Turner fluorometer (Hinegardner, 1971).

DNA synthesis assays. Cells were consistently plated and grown for 24 h in 96 multiwell dishes at a density of 5.0×10^5 cells cm^{-2}, after determining that the greatest incorporation of [^{3}H]thymidine occurred at this density, prior to adjustment of conditions. Cells were allowed to grow in conditioned medium for 24 h. During the last hour of growth, cells were incubated in [^{3}H]thymidine (6 µCi ml^{-1}) that was added directly to the well without replacing the medium. The fluid was then aspirated, and the cells washed and fixed three times with 10% trichloroacetic acid. Finally, cells were lysed using 0·5 mol NaOH l^{-1}. Individual wells were then harvested and placed in a water:scintillation (1:4) cocktail, and the radioactivity counted in a scintillation counter (Firestone et al., 1986).

Tyrosine hydroxylase activity. Tyrosine hydroxylase activity was measured according to Waymire *et al.* (1971), having been modified routinely for the frozen storage of cultured cells prior to assay, as first described by Safei & Timiras (1985).

T_3 nuclear receptors. The number of T_3 nuclear receptors was measured using Scatchard plots of the amount of T_3 bound per mg of DNA, and K_d value, as an index of the receptor affinity for the ligand, was calculated according to the methods previously used in our laboratory (Draves & Timiras, 1980; Goya & Timiras, 1991).

SDS-PAGE and immunoblotting. After protein determination, samples were electrophoretically separated in sodium dodecyl sulfate-polyacrylamide (SDS-PAGE) gels (Laemmli, 1970) and transferred to nitrocellulose membranes (Towbin *et al.*, 1979). Antibodies against tau protein (monoclonal Tau-1) were applied, localized with a second antibody (anti-immunoglobulin G), conjugated to alkaline phosphatase, and band-staining intensity was assessed by densitometry (for details, see Argasinski *et al.*, 1989; Lew *et al.*, 1990; John *et al.*, 1991; Mesco *et al.*, 1991; Mesco & Timiras, 1991).

Ubiquitin. Cell extracts were analysed by SDS-PAGE, immunoblot and immunoprecipitation techniques as summarized above (Mesco & Timiras, 1991). Ubiquitin–tau complexes were investigated using, in duplicate samples, the monoclonal antibody Alz-50 (which recognizes tau) (provided by Dr P. Davies), and an affinity-purified antiserum specific for ubiquitin (provided by G. Cole).

Statistical analysis

All data were subjected to statistical analysis according to Student's *t* test.

Results

Effect of differentiation on growth of neuroblastoma cells

Both LAN-5 and SH-SY5Y human neuroblastoma cells differentiate *in vitro* in the presence of retinoic acid ($10\,\mu mol\,l^{-1}$) for a minimum of 5 days. Dendritic production, neuritic extension and tyrosine hydroxylase activity have been used as markers for differentiation in these and other cells (Pennypacker *et al.*, 1989; Goya & Timiras, 1991). Observation of neuroblastoma cells under the microscope after a 6-day treatment with retinoic acid ($10\,\mu mol\,l^{-1}$) shows neurite outgrowth and dendritic spurs and other changes in cell shape characteristic of differentiated neurones (John *et al.*, 1991). When structural differentiation occurs, these cells present an increase in the activity of the catecholaminergic-synthesizing enzyme tyrosine hydroxylase (Ino *et al.*, 1986; Goya & Timiras, 1991; John *et al.*, 1991). Their neuronal-like phenotype and characteristics make these cells an interesting model in which neuronal ontogenesis is mimicked *in vitro*.

Differentiation using retinoic acid affected the growth of human neuroblastoma LAN-5 cells *in vitro*, as shown in Fig. 1. A growth curve measuring DNA levels with time showed a reduced rate of growth in differentiated cells compared with undifferentiated cells. Reduction of the growth rate (taken as an index of differentiation) was statistically significant 2 days after retinoic acid application ($P < 0.001$), and progressed further with time. After 8 days, undifferentiated cells had $89.5 \pm 1.0\,\mu g$ DNA per well, while differentiated cells had $46.4 \pm 0.5\,\mu g$ DNA per well—indicating that growth had been suppressed by about half in the differentiated cells.

Effect of T_3 on growth of neuroblastoma cells

T_3 receptors in the nuclei of human neuroblastoma cells have an affinity expressed as the dissociation constant K_d of $0.11 \pm 0.08\,nmol\,l^{-1}$. The amount of T_3 receptor protein decreases from $2.28 \pm 0.08 \times 10^{-16}$ mol of protein per µg DNA to $0.46 \pm 0.1 \times 10^{-16}\,mol\,\mu g^{-1}$ DNA after differentiation with retinoic acid for 4 days (Goya & Timiras, 1991). This decrease has been interpreted as a down-regulation of T_3 receptors in correlation with neuronal differentiation and parallels a similar response *in vivo* (Valcana & Timiras, 1978; Naidoo *et al.*, 1978; Margarity *et al.*, 1983). When human neuroblastoma cells were treated with doses of T_3 hormone (10^{-10}–$10^{-7}\,mol\,l^{-1}$), which are within the normal physiological range *in vivo*, suppression of

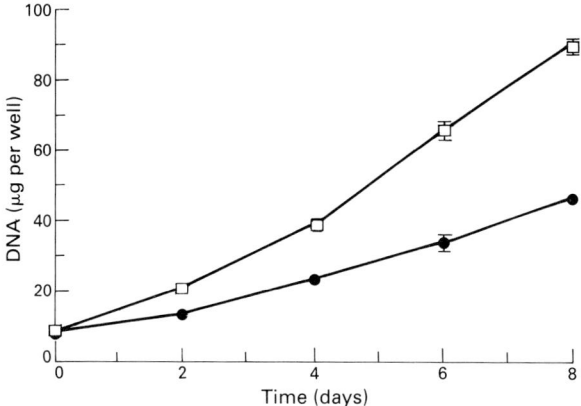

Fig. 1. Effect of differentiation with retinoic acid on the proliferation of human neuroblastoma LAN-5 cells *in vitro*. LAN-5 cells (—□—) undifferentiated and (—●—) differentiated were plated in multiwells and treated with retinoic acid (10 mmol l^{-1}) during the assay. At the indicated times, cells were fixed with 70% ethanol and DNA quantities measured by the 3,5-diaminobenzoic acid dihydrochloride (DABA) method. All the experimental time-points were measured in quadruplicate. Statistical analysis showed a significant difference between undifferentiated and differentiated cells at 2, 4, 6 and 8 days ($P < 0.001$).

growth was observed ($P < 0.01$) in undifferentiated cells at day 5 (Fig. 2a), but not in differentiated cells (Fig. 2b). However, when the dose of T_3 added to the medium was increased to 10^{-4} mol l^{-1}, growth was suppressed completely ($P < 0.001$) in all cells for the duration of treatment (Fig. 2a, b).

To study whether this suppression of growth was due to cell death or blocked proliferation, the effect of withdrawing 10^{-4} mol $T_3 l^{-1}$ from the medium was tested. Cell proliferation (Fig. 2a, b) and DNA synthesis (Fig. 3) recovered ($P < 0.001$) from the inhibitory effects of 10^{-4} mol $T_3 l^{-1}$, before and after differentiation. In the absence of the hormone, cells resumed their growth, indicating that the cells were alive but that proliferation had been inhibited.

Effect of NGF on growth of human neuroblastoma cells

NGF acts as a differentiating agent for several neuroblastoma cell lines *in vitro* (Pavelic *et al.*, 1987; Reynolds & Perez-Polo, 1989). Treatment with 2 nmol NGF l^{-1} induces differentiation in neuroblastoma cell lines, with extension of neurites and an increase in tyrosine hydroxylase activity showing a neuronal-like pattern. The number of T_3 receptors in the nucleus also decreases in human neuroblastoma cells after treatment with 2 nmol NGF l^{-1} for 6 days (Goya & Timiras, 1991) – an effect similar to that induced by other well-known differentiating agents for neuroblastomas *in vitro*, such as butyric acid (Prasad, 1980). When human neuroblastoma cells were treated with NGF for 8 days and assayed for cell proliferation on a growth curve, undifferentiated cells underwent a moderate growth reduction, with statistical differences at 6 ($P < 0.01$) and 8 ($P < 0.001$) days (Fig. 4a). Differentiated cells showed no changes in growth (Fig. 4b).

Effect of heat shock or aluminium sulfate on growth of human neuroblastoma cells

Heat shock (1 h at 42°C) and treatment with 10^{-3} mol aluminium sulfate l^{-1} for 6–8 days, either separately or together, slow down growth. As shown in Fig. 5a, growth is temporarily reduced 6 days after heat exposure in undifferentiated cells ($P < 0.001$), while after treatment with aluminium sulfate or a combination of both heat and aluminium sulfate, growth is reduced at both 6 and 8 days ($P < 0.001$). The effects of heat shock or aluminium sulfate or both acting together on differentiated cells resemble those on undifferentiated cells (Fig. 5b).

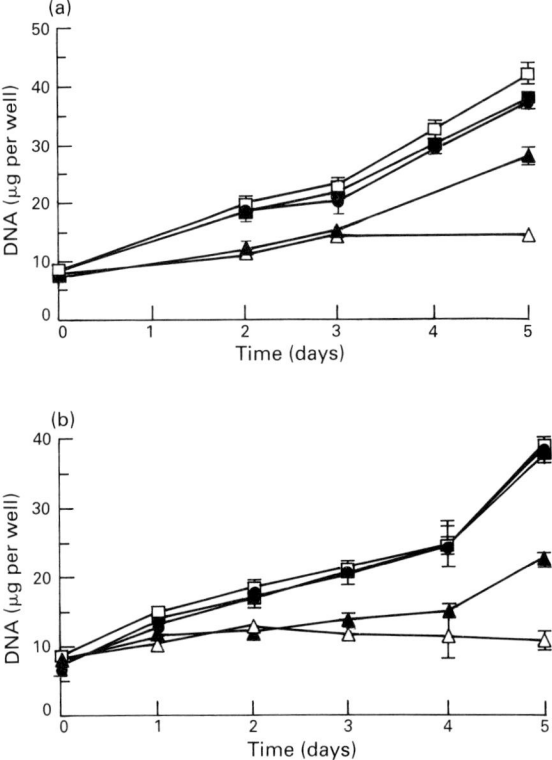

Fig. 2. Effects of T_3 on growth of undifferentiated and differentiated human neuroblastoma LAN-5 cells over a period of 5 days *in vitro*. Untreated cells (a) and cells that were differentiated using retinoic acid (10 mmol l^{-1}) (b) were plated in multiwells and treated with three different doses of T_3: (—□—) control; (—■—) 10^{-7} mol T_3 l^{-1}; (—●—) 10^{-10} mol T_3 l^{-1}; (—△—) 10^{-4} mol T_3 l^{-1} and (—▲—) 10^{-4} mol T_3 l^{-1} in the first 48 h. At the indicated times, cells were fixed with 70% ethanol, and the amount of DNA was measured by the 3,5-diaminobenzoic acid dihydrochloride (DABA) method. Four samples per condition were used in this assay. In undifferentiated cells, all T_3 doses inhibited growth on day 5 ($P < 0.01$ for undifferentiated cells versus those treated with T_3 at 10^{-7} and 10^{-10} mol l^{-1}, and $P < 0.001$ for undifferentiated cells versus those treated with T_3 at 10^{-4} mol l^{-1}). In differentiated cells, only T_3 at 10^{-4} mol l^{-1} evoked a significant reduction in growth ($P < 0.001$) from day 2 to day 5. Both in undifferentiated and differentiated cells, hormone withdrawal overcame growth suppression, with a significant difference at day 5 between cells treated with 10^{-4} mol T_3 l^{-1} constantly and those cells from which T_3 was withdrawn after 48 hours ($P < 0.001$).

Effect of physiological doses of T_3 on 'aged' neuroblastoma cells

To study the effect of physiological doses of T_3 on 'aged' neuroblastoma cell lines *in vitro*, undifferentiated and neuronal-like differentiated human neuroblastoma LAN-5 cells were 'aged' *in vitro* by a combined exposure to heat shock and 10^{-3} mol aluminium sulfate l^{-1}, and then treated with two doses of T_3 (10^{-7} and 10^{-4} mol l^{-1}) during the following entire experimental period. As already demonstrated, the combined heat shock and aluminium treatment significantly reduced cell growth before and after differentiation (Fig. 5a, b). In both groups of cells, 10^{-4} mol T_3 l^{-1} reduced growth ($P < 0.001$) by the same extent as in unstressed cells that had been treated with T_3 (Fig. 2a, b). T_3 administered in a 'physiological' dose (i.e. 10^{-7} mol l^{-1}) prevented the 'stress-induced' growth reduction on day 6 ($P < 0.001$) in undifferentiated (Fig. 6a) but not in differentiated (Fig. 6b) cells.

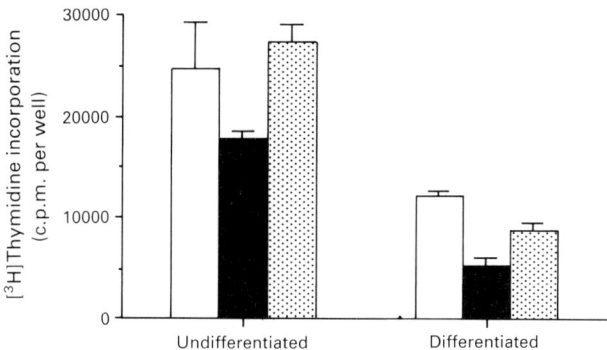

Fig. 3. Effect of T_3 treatment and T_3 withdrawal on [^{3}H]thymidine incorporation into human neuroblastoma LAN-5 cells. Undifferentiated LAN-5 cells and LAN-5 cells differentiated using 10 mmol retinoic acid l^{-1} were plated in multiwells and left untreated (□), treated with 10^{-4} mol T_3 l^{-1} for 24 h and then either (■) pulse-labelled with [^{3}H]thymidine for 1 h (T_3), or (▨) changed to a T_3-deprived medium for another 24 h and then pulse-labelled with [^{3}H]thymidine for 1 h (T_3 withdrawal). The incorporation of radiolabelled thymidine into DNA was determined by precipitation with 10% trichloroacetic acid. At least four samples were used per condition in this experiment. Statistical analysis showed significant differences between control and T_3-treated cells ($P < 0.001$), and T_3-treated cells and cells from which T_3 had been withdrawn ($P < 0.001$), for undifferentiated and differentiated cells.

Effects of aluminium sulfate on tau protein in neuroblastoma cells

Differentiated LAN-5 cells displaying a neuronal phenotype express tau proteins (Argasinski et al., 1989). Known functions of tau include the promotion and stabilization of microtubules. Microtubule assembly and distribution are dependent on thyroid hormones in vivo (Nunez et al., 1979) and in vitro (Draves et al., 1986), probably by T_3 action on tau proteins (Nunez, 1984). In the ageing brain, tau (which is located primarily in axons) is a structural element of the paired helical filaments – the characteristic component of neurofibrillary tangles that are the intracellular alterations related to the pathology of Alzheimer's disease. Addition of the trivalent metallic cation aluminium (Al^{3+}) to the medium for 6 days significantly increased the amounts of specific isomers of microtubule-associated tau proteins in LAN-5 cells (Mesco et al., 1991). Significant increases were seen in response to amounts of aluminium down to 100 μmol l^{-1}. The increases in the amounts of tau proteins were independent from that of total proteins.

Tau–ubiquitin conjugates in neuroblastoma cells

Ubiquitin is a constituent of neurofibrillary tangles and is increased in the brain of patients with Alzheimer's disease, where it is involved in the degradation of tau and other proteins (Cole & Timiras, 1987a). In LAN-5 cells, immunoreactivity to tau and ubiquitin is co-localized in specific gel bands that are predominantly located in cell membrane fractions (Mesco & Timiras, 1991). This relationship suggests that tau may be normally degraded by a ubiquitin-dependent mechanism, and alterations in this mechanism may contribute to the formation of neurofibrillary pathology.

Discussion

The CNS is not an uniform system. Ageing CNS components display a 'selective vulnerability' (similar to that occurring during ontogenesis), with some structures and molecules undergoing ageing processes earlier than others (Angelucci et al., 1991). Some changes that occur with ageing in the CNS are listed in Table 3. Neural cells differ in origin, structure, chemistry and function as well

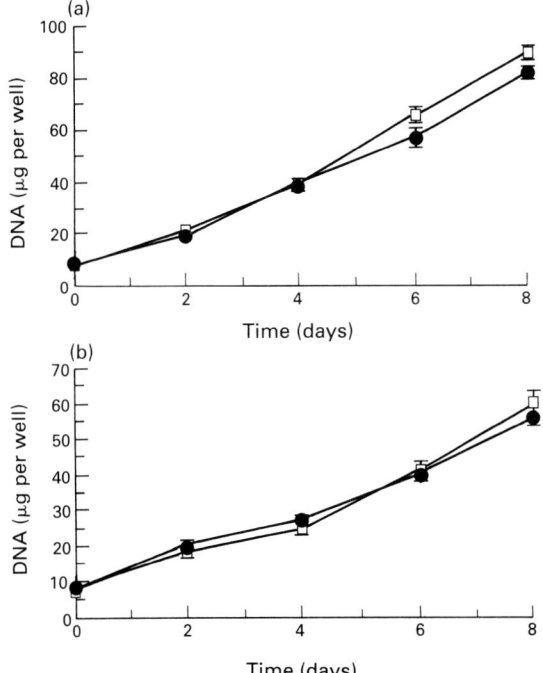

Fig. 4. Effect of nerve growth factor (NGF) on the proliferation of human neuroblastoma LAN-5 cells over a period of 8 days. Undifferentiated LAN-5 cells (a) and LAN-5 cells differentiated using 10 mmol retinoic acid l^{-1} (b) were plated in multiwells under (—□—) control conditions or (—●—) treated with 2 nmol NGF l^{-1} for 8 days. At the indicated times, cells were fixed with 70% ethanol and assayed for the amount of DNA by the 3,5-diaminobenzoic acid dihydrochloride (DABA) method. Four samples were used per condition in this experiment. Statistical differences were found in undifferentiated cells between untreated and NGF-treated cells at 6 ($P < 0.01$) and 8 ($P < 0.001$) days. No significant differences were found between untreated and NGF-treated differentiated cells.

as in susceptibility to ageing. Neurones are exquisitely designed for receiving and transmitting signals, while astrocytes provide supportive transport and metabolic functions. With ageing, neurones are lost in discrete brain areas whereas glial cells proliferate (gliosis) – perhaps in a compensatory attempt to provide stronger metabolic support to the remaining neurones (Brizzee et al., 1968).

Vulnerable sites to the ageing process are dendrites, axons and synapses. Lesions of blood vessels represent an extension of systemic atherosclerosis to CNS vasculature, and are partially responsible for the progressive CNS ischemia and hypoxia that affect the mitochondrion and energy metabolism. Studies of brain oxidative metabolism and of diseases caused by mitochondrial DNA mutations suggest that a variety of degenerative processes such as those that occur with ageing may be associated with defects of oxidative phosphorylation (Pettegrew et al., 1990; Blass & Gibson, 1991; Hoyer, 1992; Wallace, 1992).

Other mechanisms potentially responsible for CNS ageing include neurotransmitter imbalance, membrane and receptor alterations, intracellular neurofibrillary tangles (i.e. cytoskeletal alterations in the microtubule assembly protein tau and the formation of paired helical filaments) and the formation of neuritic plaques with deposition of β-amyloid protein in the extracellular matrix, especially around blood vessels. Catastrophic loss of neurones and accumulation of tangles and amyloid are taken as definitive diagnostic signs of Alzheimer's disease (Hardy & Higgins, 1992).

Functional consequences of ageing-associated changes are numerous. They involve sensory (including that of the five special senses) and motor functions as well as emotional and cognitive

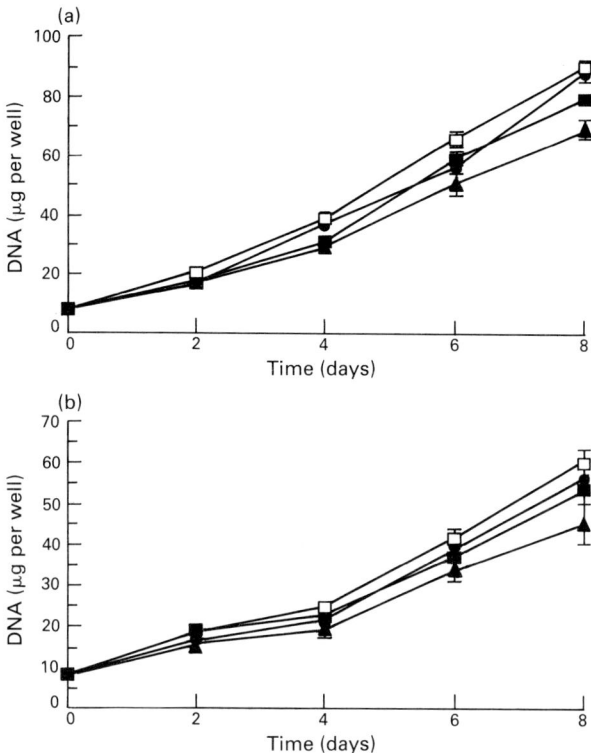

Fig. 5. Effects of stress by heat shock or aluminium sulfate treatment or both on growth of human neuroblastoma LAN-5 cells. (a) Undifferentiated LAN-5 cells and LAN-5 cells differentiated using 10 mmol retinoic acid l^{-1} (b) were plated in multiwells: (—□—) control; (—●—) treated at 42°C for 1 h (heat shock); (—■—) 10^{-3} mol aluminium sulfate l^{-1} (aluminium); or (—▲—) a combination of both (heat shock and aluminium), and grown for 8 days. At the indicated times cells were fixed with 70% ethanol and assayed for the amount of DNA by the 3,5-diaminobenzoic acid dihydrochloride (DABA) method. Four samples were used per condition in this experiment. Heat shock treatment significantly reduced growth in undifferentiated cells at 6 days ($P < 0.001$), while aluminium and a combination of both treatments reduced growth at 6 and 8 days ($P < 0.001$). In differentiated cells, only the combined treatment reduced growth at 6 and 8 days ($P < 0.001$).

types of behaviour; alterations in cognitive behaviour range from mild (e.g. benign forgetfulness) to extremely severe (e.g. dementia).

Results presented here show that human neuroblastoma cells may be induced to differentiate and then display a morphological and biochemical phenotype resembling adult neurones. Exposure of these cells to a variety of stressors induces alterations similar to those observed in aged neurones in vivo (Cole et al., 1985; Cole & Timiras, 1987b, 1989). Our data show that exposure to stress inhibits cell proliferation of neuroblastoma cells before and after differentiation. This inhibition may be related to the severity of the stress conditions: the effects of a combined treatment of heat shock and aluminium reduces growth more severely than either treatment administered alone (Fig. 5).

Theoretically, any hypothesis of neuronal ageing and age-related pathology must be placed against the background of the general response to specific types of damage. At the systemic physiological level, many investigators have noted an apparent relationship between stress, the hypothalamo–pituitary–adrenocortical system and ageing (see Meites, 1983; Timiras, 1991). The cellular response has not been so well studied. Heat shock involves the production of heat-shock proteins,

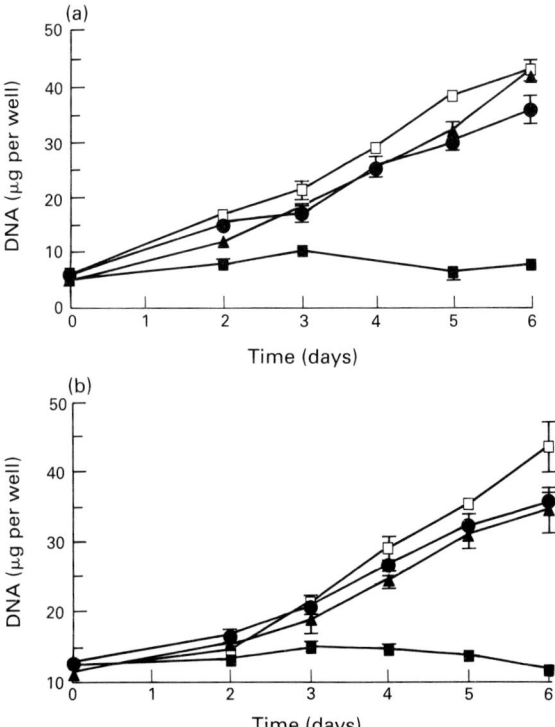

Fig. 6. Effect of T_3 on the stress-induced growth suppression of human neuroblastoma cells over a period of 6 days. Undifferentiated LAN-5 cells (a) and LAN-5 cells differentiated using 10 mmol retinoic acid l^{-1} (b) were plated in multiwells and treated at 42°C for 1 h (heat shock) ($\square$), or a combination of heat shock and 10^{-3} mol aluminium sulfate l^{-1} (heat shock and aluminium) ($\bullet$), and grown for 6 days in the absence or the presence of ($\blacktriangle$) 10^{-7} or ($\blacksquare$) 10^{-4} mol $T_3 \, l^{-1}$. At the indicated times, cells were fixed with 70% ethanol and DNA amounts were assayed by the 3,5-diaminobenzoic acid dihydrochloride (DABA) method. Statistical analysis showed that treatment with 10^{-7} mol $T_3 \, l^{-1}$ did not prevent stress-induced growth suppression in undifferentiated cells on days 1–5 but overcame this effect on day 6 [no difference between heat shock plus aluminium treatment and heat shock plus aluminium plus T_3 treatment on day 5, but there was a significant difference between the two treatments ($P < 0.001$) on day 6], whereas no effect was observed in differentiated cells. Growth of undifferentiated and differentiated cells was reduced by 10^{-4} mol $T_3 \, l^{-1}$ at all times tested.

Table 3. Changes that occur with ageing in the nervous system

Location	Mechanisms	Consequences
Regional selectivity	Neurotransmitter imbalance	Sensory and motor decrements
Neuronal loss or gliosis	Alterations in membranes or in receptors	Memory and cognitive impairment
Reduced dendrites and dendritic spines	Metabolic (energy) disturbances	Electroencephalograph and sleep alterations
Synaptic or mitochondrial vulnerability	Reduced amounts of growth factors and increased amounts of inhibitory factors	Increased neurological and psychiatric pathology
Vascular lesions	Intra- or intercellular degeneration [neurofibrillary tangles, neuritic (amyloid) plaques]	Impaired homeostasis

inhibition of normal protein synthesis and assorted re-programming of cellular metabolism, including a major rearrangement of the cytoskeleton and nucleolar changes (Maresca & Lindquist, 1991). Likewise, aluminium is involved in many processes, including alterations in the metabolism of neurofilament and microtubule proteins. ATP-dependent, ubiquitin-dependent proteolysis is a major system responsible for preventing the accumulation of insoluble aggregates of denatured and abnormal proteins. The accumulation of ubiquitinated proteins associated with lesions in Alzheimer's disease may have important implications in the pathogenesis of this disease because accumulations of abnormal proteins are known to activate heat shock or cellular stress – possibly serving as a sink for free ubiquitin, which is itself a heat-shock protein (Cole & Timiras, 1987a, b). Ubiquitin is present in neuroblastoma LAN-5 cells where it interacts with tau protein (Mesco & Timiras, 1991). Increased immunoreactivity to tau in LAN-5 cells exposed to aluminium suggests a direct role for this cation in the generation of paired helical filaments, and supports epidemiological findings relating chronic exposure to slightly increased amounts of aluminium to neuropathology of Alzheimer's disease (Martyn et al., 1989; Mesco et al., 1991).

Our results of the inhibitory action of T_3 on proliferation of LAN-5 (Fig. 2) suggest, indirectly, that this hormone promotes neuronal maturation in vitro and in vivo both before and after differentiation (Draves et al., 1986). T_3 is necessary for normal brain development and maturation during ontogenesis and for maintenance of thermogenesis and some types of behaviour in the adult (Nunez, 1984; Timiras, 1988b). After exposure to stress, T_3 in 'physiological' doses has a protective action on cell proliferation, whereas high doses of T_3 are as effective in reducing cell proliferation in 'stressed' cells as they are in reducing it in non-stressed controls (Fig. 6). In the elderly, disturbances of thyroid function are frequent, and hypothyroidism has been implicated in the etiology of Alzheimer's disease (Mortimer & Hutton, 1985). Even though T_3 does not affect oxidative processes in the brain once maturation has been completed, it is possible that administration of thyroid hormones to hypothyroid elderly individuals with declining brain mitochondrial energy may improve oxidative metabolism or prevent its decline.

Loss of neuronal plasticity in the adult brain may be due to a lack of appropriate amounts of growth promoters or inhibitors rather than to an intrinsic inability of neurones to divide or regenerate. Indeed, reconstruction of an early ontogenetic environment by the administration of NGF or other growth factors has proven effective in restoring neuronal plasticity in the ageing brain (Confort et al., 1991; Ebendal et al., 1991; Reynolds & Weiss, 1992). T_3 regulates NGF synthesis and actions in primary cultures of cerebellar neuroblasts (Charasse et al., in press). Thus, NGF and T_3 would provide complementary support of neuronal growth and, eventually, regeneration: T_3 having a long-term, permissive role and NGF having a local, short-term action (Clos & Legrand, 1990; Legrand & Clos, 1991).

The human neuroblastoma cells, such as those used in these investigations, provide a possible model to study some aspects of the neurobiology of ageing and the effects of intrinsic and extrinsic factors involved in this process. They may also serve as a rapid and inexpensive means for screening for agents potentially effective in delaying ageing and preventing associated degenerative diseases.

The authors would like to thank C. V. Ramakrishnan for his scientific advice in the planning and performance of the experiments. This work was supported in part by the F. M. Kirby Foundation and the Biomedical Research Support Grant, University of California, Berkeley. M. Isaeff was the recipient of a University of California (Berkeley) Undergraduate Research Fellowship.

References

Angelucci, L., Alema, S., Ferraris, O., Imperato, A., Ramacci, M.T., Scrocco, M.G. & Vertechy, M. (1991) Ordered disorder in the aged brain. In *Plasticity and Regeneration of the Nervous System*, pp. 277–290. Eds P. S. Timiras, A. Privat, E. Giacobini, J. Lauder & A. Vernadakis. Plenum Press, New York.

Argasinski, A., Sternberg, H., Fingado, B. & Huynh, P. (1989) Doxorubicin affects tau protein metabolism in human neuroblastoma cells. *Neurochemical Research* **14**, 927–931.

Blass, J.P. & Gibson, G.E. (1991) The role of oxidative abnormalities in the pathophysiology of Alzheimer's disease. *Revue Neurologique (Paris)* **147**, 513–525.

Brizzee, K.R., Sherwood, N. & Timiras, P.S. (1968) A comparison of cell populations at various depth levels in cerebral cortex of young adults and aged Long-Evans rats. *Journal of Gerontology* **23**, 289–298.

Charasse, S., Jehan, F., Confort, C., Brachet, P. & Clos, J. Thyroid hormone promotes transient nerve growth factor synthesis in rat cerebellar neuroblasts. *Developmental Neuroscience* (in press).

Clos, J. & Legrand, C. (1990) An interaction between thyroid hormone and nerve growth factor promotes the development of the hippocampus, olfactory bulbs and cerebellum: a comparative biochemical study of normal and hypothyroid rats. *Growth Factors* **3**, 205–220.

Confort, C., Charrasse, S. & Clos, J. (1991) Nerve growth factor enhances DNA synthesis in cultured cerebellar neuroblasts. *NeuroReport* **2**, 566–568.

Cole, G.M., Timiras, P.S. & Wu, K. (1985) A culture model for age related human neurofibrillary pathology. *International Journal of Developmental Neuroscience* **3**, 23–32.

Cole, G.M. & Timiras, P.S. (1987a) Ubiquitin–protein conjugates in Alzheimer's lesions. *Neuroscience Letters* **79**, 207–212.

Cole, G.M. & Timiras, P.S. (1987b) Aging-related pathology in human neuroblastoma and teratocarcinoma cell lines. In *Model Systems of Development and Aging of the Nervous System*, pp. 453–473. Eds A. Vernadakis, A. Privat, J. Lauder, P. S. Timiras & E. Giacobini. Martinus Nijhoff Publishing, Boston.

Cole, G.M. & Timiras, P.S. (1989) Lipid peroxidation and Alzheimer amyloid precursor processing *in vitro*. In *Phospholipid Research and the Nervous System (Fidia Research Series, Vol. 17)*, pp. 115–119. Eds N. G. Bazan, L. A. Horrocks & G. Toffano. Liviana Press, Padova.

Draves, D.J. & Timiras, P.S. (1980) Thyroid hormone effects in neural (tumor) cell culture: differential effects on triiodothyronine nuclear receptors, Na^+-K^+-ATPase activity and intracellular electrolyte levels in tissue culture. In *Neurobiology*, pp. 291–301. Eds E. Giacobini, A. Vernadakis & A Shahar. Raven Press, New York.

Draves, D.J., Manley, N.B. & Timiras, P.S. (1986) Glial hormone receptors: thyroid hormones and microtubules in gliomas and neuroblastomas. In *Astrocytes, Cell Biology and Pathology of Astrocytes* (Vol. 3), pp. 183–310. Eds S. Fedoroff & A. Vernadakis. Academic Press, Orlando, Florida.

Ebendal, T., Soderstrom, S., Hallbook, F., Ernfors, P., Ibanez, C.F., Persson, H., Wetmore, C., Stromberg, I. & Olson, L. (1991) Human nerve growth factor: biological and immunological activities, and clinical possibilities in neurodegenerative disease. In *Plasticity and Regeneration of the Nervous System*, pp. 207–225. Eds P. S. Timiras, A. Privat, E. Giacobini, J. Lauder & A. Vernadakis. Plenum Press, New York.

Firestone, G.L., John, N.J. & Yamamoto, K.R. (1986) Glucocorticoid regulated glycoprotein maturation in wild type and mutant rat cell lines. *Journal of Cell Biology* **103**, 119–123.

Goya, L. & Timiras, P.S. (1991) Characterization of nuclear T_3 receptors in human neuroblastoma cells SH-SY5Y: effect of differentiation with sodium butyrate and nerve growth factor. *Neurochemical Research* **16**, 113–116.

Hardy, J.A. & Higgins, G.A. (1992) Alzheimer's disease: the amyloid cascade hypothesis. *Science* **256**, 184–185.

Hinegardner, R.T. (1971) An improved fluorometric assay for DNA. *Analytical Biochemistry* **39**, 197–201.

Hoyer, S. (1992) The biology of the aging brain. Oxidative and related metabolism. *European Journal of Gerontology* **1**, 157–165.

Ino, M., Cole, G.M. & Timiras, P.S. (1986) Tyrosine hydroxylase and monoamine oxidase-A activity increases in differentiating human neuroblastoma after elimination of dividing cells. *Developmental Brain Research* **30**, 120–123.

John, N.J., Lew, G.M., Goya, L. & Timiras, P.S. (1991) Effects of serotonin on tyrosine hydroxylase and tau protein in a human neuroblastoma cell line. *Plasticity and Regeneration of the Nervous System*, pp. 69–80. Eds P. S. Timiras, A. Privat, E. Giacobini, J. Lauder & A. Vernadakis. Plenum Press, New York.

Laemmli, U.K. (1970) Cleavage of structural proteins during the assembly of bacteriophage T4. *Nature* **227**, 680–685.

Legrand, C. & Clos, J. (1991) Biochemical, immunocytochemical and morphological evidence for an interaction between thyroid hormone and nerve growth factor in the developing cerebellum of normal and hypothyroid rats. *Development Neuroscience* **13**, 382–396.

Lew, G.M., Mesco, E.R., Quay, W.B. & Timiras, P.S. (1990) Molecular action of melatonin on microtubules: changes of tau protein in human neuroblastoma cells. In *Neurendocrinology: New Frontiers*, pp. 296–305. Eds D. Gupta, H. Wollmann & M. B. Ranke. Brain Research Promotion, Tubingen.

Maresca, B. & Lindquist, S. (1991) *Heat Shock*. Springer-Verlag, New York.

Margarity, M., Matsokis, N. & Valcana, T. (1983) Characterization of nuclear triiodothyronine (T_3) and tetraiodothyronine (T_4) binding in developing brain tissue. *Molecular and Cell Endocrinology* **31**, 333.

Martyn, C.N., Baker, D.J., Osmond, C., Harris, E.C., Edwardson, J.A. & Lacey, R.F. (1989) Geographical relation between Alzheimer's disease and aluminum in the drinking water. *Lancet* **1**, 59–62.

Meites, J. (1983) *Neuroendocrinology of Aging*. Plenum Press, New York.

Mesco, E.R., Kachen, C. & Timiras, P.S. (1991) Effects of aluminum on tau proteins in human neuroblastoma cells. *Molecular and Chemical Neuropathology* **14**, 199–212.

Mesco, E.R. & Timiras, P.S. (1991) Tau–ubiquitin protein conjugates in a human cell line. *Mechanisms of Ageing and Development* **61**, 1–9.

Mortimer, J.A. & Hutton, J.T. (1985) Epidemiology and etiology of Alzheimer's disease. In *Senile Dementia of the Alzheimer's Type*, pp. 177–196. Eds J. T. Hutton & H. O. Kenny. Alan R. Liss, New York.

Naidoo, S., Valcana, T. & Timiras, P.S. (1978) Thyroid hormone receptors on the developing rat brain. *American Zoologist* **18**, 522–545.

Nunez, J. (1984) Thyroid hormones. In *Handbook of Neurochemistry*, pp. 1–16. Ed. A. Lajtha. Plenum Press, New York.

Nunez, J., Fellous, A., Francon, J. & Lennon, A.M. (1979) Competitive inhibition of colchicine-binding to tubulin by microtubule-associated proteins. *Proceedings of the National Academy of Sciences USA* **76**, 86–90.

Ooka, H., Fujita, S. & Yoshimoto, E. (1983) Pituitary–thyroid activity and longevity in neonatally thyroxine-treated rats. *Mechanisms of Ageing and Development* **22**, 113–120.

Ooka, H. & Shinkai, T. (1986) Effects of chronic hyperthyroidism on the lifespan of the rat. *Mechanisms of Ageing and Development* **33**, 275–282.

Pavelic, K. & Spaventi, S. (1987) Nerve growth factor (NGF) induced differentiation of human neuroblastoma cells. *International Journal of Biochemistry* **19**, 1237–1240.

Pennypacker, K.R., Kuhn, D.M. & Billingsley, M.L. (1989) Changes in expression of tyrosine hydroxylase immunoreactivity in human SMS-KCNR neuroblastoma following retinoic acid or phorbol ester-induced differentiation. *Molecular Brain Research* **5**, 251–258.

Pettegrew, J.W., Panchalingam, K., Withers, G., McKeag, D. & Strychor, S. (1991) Changes in brain energy and phospholipid metabolism during development and aging of the Fischer 344 rat. *Journal of Neuropathology and Experimental Neurology* **49**, 237–249.

Prasad, K.N. (1980) Butyric acid; a small fatty acid with diverse biological functions. *Life Sciences* **27**, 1351–1358.

Reynolds, B.A. & Weiss, S. (1992) Generation of neurons and astrocytes from isolated cells of the adult mammalian central nervous system. *Science* **255**, 1707–1710.

Reynolds, C.P. & Perez-Polo, J.R. (1989) Nerve growth factor induces neurite outgrowth in a clone derived from an NGF-insensitive human neuroblastoma cell line. *International Journal of Developmental Neuroscience* **17**, 125–132.

Safaei, R. & Timiras, P.S. (1985) Thyroid hormone binding and regulation of adrenergic enzymes in two neuroblastoma cell line. *Journal of Neurochemistry* **45**, 1405–1410.

Sapolsky, R.M., Krey, L.C. & McEwen, B.S. (1986) The neuroendocrinology of stress and aging: The glucocorticoid cascade hypothesis. *Endocrinological Review* **7**, 284–301.

Sidell, N. & Horn, R. (1985) Properties of human neuroblastoma cells following induction by retinoic acid. In *Advances in Neuroblastoma Research (Progress in Clinical and Biological Research*, Vol. 175), pp. 39–53. Eds A. E. Evans, G. J. D'Angio & R. C. Seeger. Alan Liss, New York.

Timiras, P.S. (1988a) Thyroid hormones and the developing brain. In *Handbook of Human Growth and Developmental Biology* (Vol. I, Part C), pp. 59–82. Eds E. Meisami and P. S. Timiras, CRC Press, Florida.

Timiras, P.S. (1988b) *Physiological Basis of Aging and Geriatrics*. Macmillan, New York.

Timiras, P.S. (1991) Physiology of aging: Aspects of neuroendocrine regulation. In *Principles and Practice of Geriatric Medicine* (2nd edn), pp. 31–54. Ed. M. S. J. Pathy. John Wiley & Sons, New York.

Towbin, H., Stehelin, T. & Gordon, J. (1979) Electrophoretic transfer of protein from polyacrylamide gels to nitrocellulose sheets: procedure and some applications. *Proceedings of the National Academy of Sciences USA* **76**, 4354–4356.

Valcana, T. & Timiras, P.S. (1978) Nuclear triiodothyronine receptors in the brain. *Molecular and Cellular Endocrinology* **11**, 31–41.

Walker, R.F. & Timiras, P.S. (1982) Pacemaker insufficiency and the onset of aging. In *Cellular Pacemakers* (Vol. 2), pp. 345–365. Ed. D. Carpenter. Wiley Interscience, New York.

Wallace, D.C. (1992) Mitochondrial genetics: a paradigm for aging and degenerative diseases? *Science* **256**, 628–632.

Waymire, J.C., Bjur, R. & Weiner, N. (1971) Assay of tyrosine hydroxylase by coupled decarboxylation of DOPA formed from [1-^{14}C]-L-tyrosine. *Analytical Biochemistry* **43**, 588–600.

Neuroendocrine ageing: its impact on the reproductive system of the female rat

P. M. Wise

Department of Physiology, University of Maryland, School of Medicine, Baltimore, MD 21201, USA

Summary. Numerous changes occur with age at all levels of the reproductive axis. Clearly, changing ovarian function plays a critical role in the cessation of reproductive cycles. Likewise, many changes in the function of neurotransmitters, gonadotrophin-releasing hormone and gonadotrophin itself appear to contribute to the ageing of the reproductive axis. It appears that the effects of ageing on neural time-keeping mechanisms may be important in the cascade of events that lead to reproductive dysfunction. The use of modern neurobiological and molecular methods to assess neural function within small regions of the brain should deepen our understanding of the complex interactions between neuroendocrine systems that underlie female reproductive cycles and cause them to change with age.

Keywords: reproduction; ageing; neural pacemaker; hypothalamus; rat

Introduction

This article focuses on the neuroendocrine factors that regulate the age-related transition to infertility. An increasing body of evidence demonstrates that these changes play a major role in the cascade of events that lead to age-related infertility and acyclicity. In some species, changes in the pattern of release of neurotransmitters and of gonadotrophin-releasing hormone (GnRH) occur during the early stages of reproductive ageing, suggesting that these neuroendocrine alterations may have an impact on the normal pattern of follicular development and steroid secretion during middle age.

The ageing reproductive system of the female rat is an excellent model in which to evaluate the processes that regulate ageing of the brain. Since female reproductive function declines early during the life span of many species, investigators can examine ageing of this system in the absence of age-related changes in other endocrine and other physiological systems. In addition, it should be possible to examine factors that regulate ageing relatively unencumbered by age-related diseases that are frequently confounding factors in studies on ageing.

Some of the earliest support for the concept that the hypothalamus plays a role in reproductive ageing came from classic studies using two experimental methods. First, when ovaries of old rats were transplanted to the kidney capsule of young regularly cycling female rats that had previously been ovariectomized, the senescent ovary exhibited follicular development and ovulation (Krohn, 1955, 1962, 1966; Peng & Huang, 1972; Aschheim, 1983). This suggested that the depletion of ovarian oocytes is not the cause of the acyclic state. In addition, grafts of fetal hypothalamus placed into the third ventricle of old hosts restored ovarian weight, and follicles and corpora lutea reappeared at various stages of development (Matsumoto *et al.*, 1984; Huang, 1988). Second, administration of drugs that reinstate the level or activity of monoamines (Clemens *et al.*, 1969; Quadri *et al.*, 1973; Huang *et al.*, 1976; Clemens & Bennett, 1977; Cooper, 1977; Cooper & Walker, 1979) or progesterone treatment that may act upon reproductive cyclicity through the central nervous system (Everett, 1940, 1980, 1984; Clemens *et al.*, 1969; Huang *et al.*, 1976; Everett & Tyrey, 1982) restored surges of luteinizing hormone (LH), oestrous cyclicity and ovulation. Electrochemical stimulation of the preoptic area of old constant-oestrus female rats stimulated LH release (Wuttke & Meites, 1973; Clemens & Bennett, 1977) and resulted in ovulation followed by a brief period of oestrous cyclicity (Clemens *et al.*, 1969). These results strongly suggested that deterioration in hypothalamic function is an important element in reproductive decline.

Age-related changes in pulsatile hormone secretion

More recently, our work and that of others indicates that changes in the pulsatile, circadian and cyclic aspects of hypothalamic function during ageing occur prior to changes in the average concentrations of neurotransmitters or hormones. Hypothalamic neurotransmitter activity plays a critical role in the maintenance of the ultradian, diurnal and cyclic patterns of secretion of GnRH, gonadotrophins and ovarian steroids that occur during normal reproductive cycles. These rhythmic properties of hypothalamic neuroendocrine activity, which are essential to cyclic reproductive function in young rodents, appear to be very vulnerable to the effects of age (Mosko *et al.*, 1980; Ingram *et al.*, 1982; Weitzman *et al.*, 1982; Lonning *et al.*, 1989; Liu *et al.*, 1990).

In sexually mature animals, the concentration of GnRH in hypophyseal portal plasma or in perfusates from push–pull cannulae placed in the medial basal hypothalamus (Carmel *et al.*, 1976; Levine *et al.*, 1985) exhibits an ultradian rhythm. The amplitude and frequency of this rhythm of secretion regulate the pattern of pulsatile secretion of LH and follicle-stimulating hormone (FSH) (Dierschke *et al.*, 1970; Gay & Sheth, 1972; Yen *et al.*, 1972; Filicori *et al.*, 1986). In turn, the amplitude and frequency of gonadotrophin secretion partly determine the pattern of secretion of oestradiol and progesterone (Baird, 1978; Sodersten & Eneroth, 1981; Djahanbakhch *et al.*, 1984). The frequency of GnRH pulses is thought to reflect the status of the 'pulse generator' for hormonal secretion in the hypothalamus (Lincoln *et al.*, 1985; Rasmussen, 1986a). Thus, changes in the frequency of GnRH pulses and subsequently in the frequency of LH pulses during ageing may indicate changes in this neural pacemaker.

We analysed the pulsatile pattern of LH secretion in ageing ovariectomized rats to assess the status of the pulse generator, and found that several characteristics of the pulsatile pattern of LH release are evident. Young rats (2–3·5 months old) that had shown regular oestrous cycles of 4 or 5 days and middle-aged rats (9·5–12 months old) that exhibited either regular cycles, irregular cycles or persistent oestrus were bilaterally ovariectomized 4 weeks before the experiment. Rats were implanted with atrial cannulae and were bled 2 days later at 5 min intervals for 3 h. The mean inter-peak interval of pulses of LH increased in middle-aged irregularly cycling and persistent-oestrus rats (Fig. 1). The frequency distribution of inter-peak intervals was found to be significantly different in middle-aged regularly cycling rats compared with that in young regularly cycling rats (Fig. 2). Middle-aged rats displayed fewer short inter-peak intervals and a greater frequency of longer intervals between LH pulses. Duration of LH pulses increased gradually in parallel with increasing reproductive senescence (Fig. 3). These data are evidence of changing pulse generator function in middle-aged rats that had previously exhibited no change in the regularity of their oestrous cycles, and they also suggest that changes in the pulse generator may play a role in initiating the age-related transition to acyclicity.

Ageing and patterns of neurotransmitter activity

Monoamines play an important role in GnRH secretion in young animals. In young rats, preovulatory and steroid-induced LH surges are accompanied by a diurnal rhythm in noradrenaline and 5-HT activity in several hypothalamic nuclei (Rance *et al.*, 1981; Wise *et al.*,

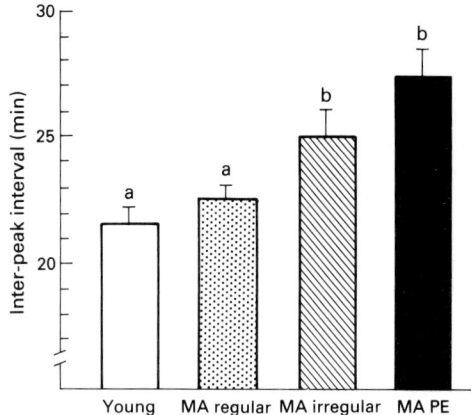

Fig. 1. Inter-peak intervals of luteinizing hormone pulses in young and middle-aged rats, as determined by the PULSAR program (Scarbrough & Wise, 1990). Bars represent the mean value ±SEM. Letters in common above the bars denote groups that are not significantly different from each other; $P < 0.05$. MA regular: middle-aged rats that had previously displayed regular oestrous cycles; MA irregular: middle-aged rats that had previously exhibited irregular oestrous cycles; MA PE: middle-aged rats that had exhibited persistent oestrus before ovariectomy.

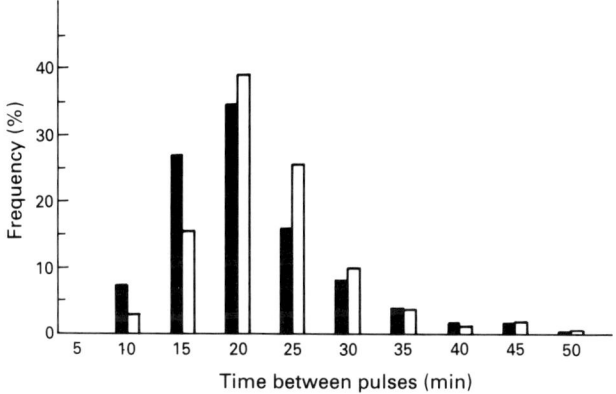

Fig. 2. Frequency distributions of inter-peak intervals of pulses of luteinizing hormone from young, previously regularly cycling rats (■) and middle-aged, previously regularly cycling rats (□) (Scarbrough & Wise, 1990). Chi-square analysis shows that the distribution of inter-peak intervals is different in the two groups.

1981). We examined whether changes in the diurnal rhythm of neurotransmitter activity occur during middle age. Noradrenaline activity was examined 2 and 4 days after oestradiol implantation in several specific hypothalamic nuclei at 10:00 h, when LH concentrations were basal, and at 15:00 h, when the LH surge occurs (Wise, 1984) (Fig. 4). In young rats (3–4 months old), there is a diurnal rhythm in noradrenaline turnover rates in all of the hypothalamic nuclei examined on days 2 and 4: the turnover was low in the morning and was high during the afternoon in the anterior hypothalamic nuclei (suprachiasmatic and medial preoptic) and in the medial basal hypothalamic area (median eminence). In middle-aged rats (9–12 months old), no significant increase was observed during the afternoon on either day in the two anterior hypothalamic areas, although the diurnal rhythm was maintained in the median eminence. The absence of a diurnal pattern of

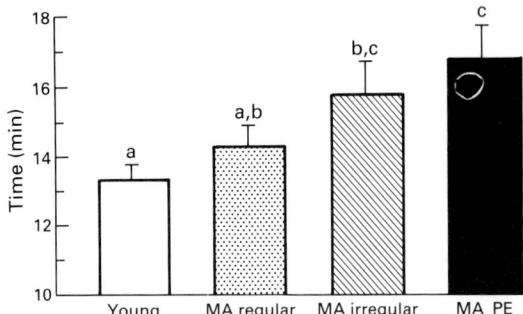

Fig. 3. Duration of pulses of luteinizing hormone exhibited by young and middle-aged rats (Scarbrough & Wise, 1990). Bars represent the mean value ±SEM. Letters in common above the bars denote groups that are not significantly different from each other; $P < 0.05$. MA regular: middle-aged rats that had previously displayed regular oestrous cycles; MA irregular: middle-aged rats that had previously exhibited irregular oestrous cycles; MA PE: middle-aged rats that had exhibited persistent oestrus before ovariectomy.

turnover rates in middle-aged rats is not simply because turnover rates or concentrations are uniformly lower in these rats; rather, it would seem that in middle-aged rats oestradiol cannot depress turnover rates during the morning. Thus, there is a relatively steady turnover rate during the entire day with no significant increase during the time of the expected LH surge. The data demonstrate that age-related alterations in noradrenaline turnover are initially limited specifically to the suprachiasmatic–preoptic area of the hypothalamus. The suprachiasmatic nucleus is known as a 'biological clock' because it is a critical endogenous neural pacemaker area of the brain that entrains and regulates the timing of many circadian rhythms (for reviews see Inouye & Kawamura, 1979; Schwartz et al., 1980; Inouye & Kawamura, 1982; Moore, 1983). Thus, the data point to the possibility that ageing involves initial changes in the function of this critical pacemaker area, which then have multiple important repercussions as animals continue to age.

It was important to consider whether other neurotransmitters involved in reproductive cyclicity and diurnal rhythms are also affected during ageing, and whether oestrogen influences these alterations. A second neurotransmitter that modulates cyclic LH release is 5-HT (Kordon et al., 1981; Walker, 1980, 1983; Walker & Wilson, 1983), and this neurotransmitter has been implicated as one that relays circadian information (Kordon et al., 1981). We determined whether turnover of 5-HT exhibits a diurnal rhythm in ovariectomized and oestradiol-treated rats and whether ageing influences this rhythm (Cohen & Wise, 1988). The same oestradiol-treated young and middle-aged animal model that tested noradrenaline activity was used. Turnover of 5-HT was determined at 08:00, 12:00, 18:00 and 24:00 h in several specific hypothalamic nuclei including the suprachiasmatic nucleus. In young (3–4 months old) ovariectomized rats, the turnover rates exhibited a distinct diurnal rhythm: turnover rates were higher during the light than during the dark (Fig. 5). Treatment with oestradiol reversed this rhythm. No diurnal rhythm was detected in either ovariectomized or oestradiol-treated middle-aged (8–10 months old) rats. Thus, ageing influenced the diurnal rhythm and the ability of oestradiol to alter the diurnal rhythm of this important neurotransmitter in this critical neural pacemaker area of the brain.

The ability of a neurotransmitter to influence GnRH secretion depends not only upon the activity of the neurotransmitter but on the presence of receptors to mediate the action of the neurotransmitter. Several studies demonstrate that receptor densities change in ageing animals. We were particularly interested in determining whether the density of α_1-adrenergic receptors exhibits a diurnal rhythm and whether this rhythm or the average density of receptors changes in older animals, since this receptor mediates the stimulatory effects of noradrenaline on GnRH release. To analyse age-related changes in the density of these receptors, young (2–4 months old) and middle-aged (9–11 months old) rats were ovariectomized after exhibiting at least three

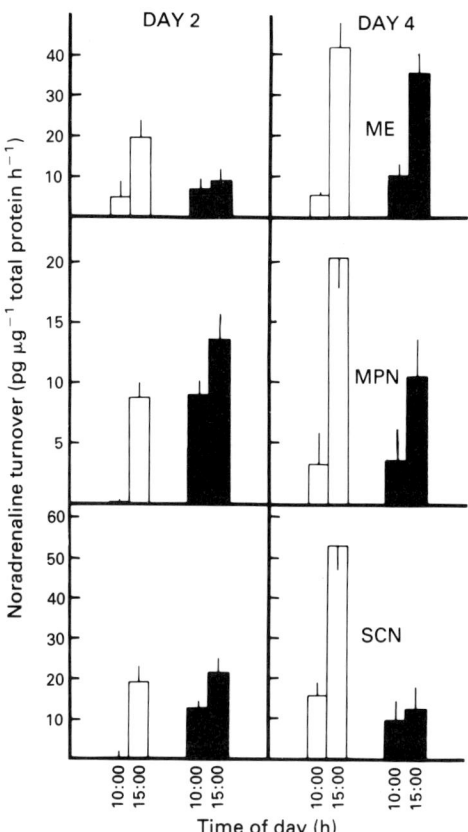

Fig. 4. Noradrenaline turnover rates in the median eminence (ME), medial preoptic nucleus (MPN) and suprachiasmatic nucleus (SCN of young (□) and middle-aged (■) ovariectomized rats treated with oestradiol for 2 days (day 2) or 4 days (day 4) (Wise, 1984). In young rats the noradrenaline turnover increased during the afternoon in all brain regions examined on both days 2 and 4. In middle-aged rats, turnover rates in the median eminence increased on day 4. In all other brain regions no diurnal rhythm was detected.

oestrous cycles 4–6 days in length (Weiland & Wise, 1990). Old animals (16–19 months old) were ovariectomized after exhibiting at least two consecutive periods of leukocytic smear patterns, each lasting 20–22 days. Rats were killed at seven different times of day over 24 h, and brain regions were assayed for α_1-adrenergic receptor concentrations using autoradiographic methods. In the medial preoptic nucleus of young rats, the density of α_1 receptors exhibited a diurnal rhythm. This rhythm was lost in middle-aged rats, although the mean concentration of receptors did not change. By the time animals were old, the diurnal rhythm was absent and the mean concentration of receptors had declined (Fig. 6). Similar age-related changes were observed in the suprachiasmatic nucleus, but not in other hypothalamic nuclei.

These data demonstrate that progressive alterations in the concentration of α_1 receptors occur in the ageing rat. Although a decrease in the concentration of α_1 receptors occurs, this is confined to particular brain regions (data not shown). In addition, alterations in the diurnal pattern and changes in the average density of receptors do not necessarily occur at the same stage of ageing. Age-related changes in diurnal rhythmicity of receptor densities may have different effects on the ageing reproductive system than do decreases in the average receptor densities. The loss of the diurnal rhythm in the density of α_1 receptors in critical pacemaker areas such as the suprachiasmatic and medial preoptic nuclei of middle-aged rats may contribute to the increased

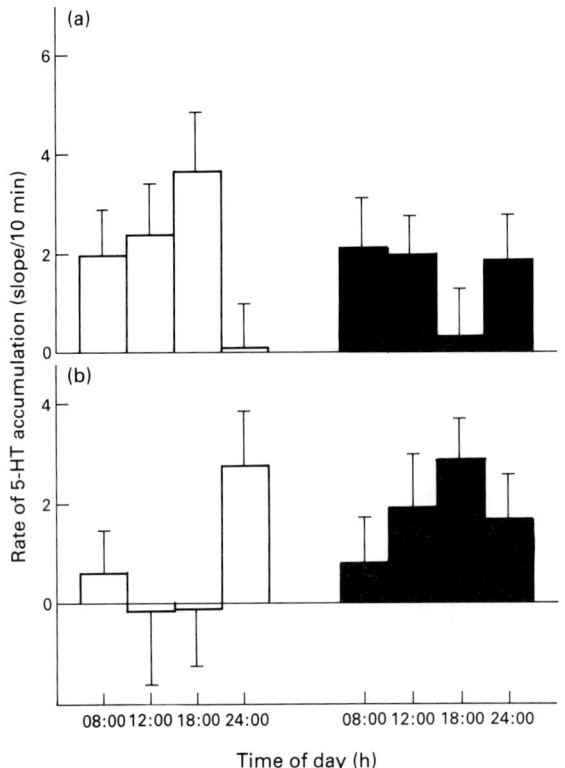

Fig. 5. Rate of accumulation of 5-HT after treatment with pargyline (75 mg kg^{-1} body weight, i.p.) in the suprachiasmatic nucleus of young (□) or middle-aged (■) female rats (Cohen & Wise, 1988). Pargyline, a monoamine oxidase inhibitor, blocks the metabolism of 5-HT; thus, the rate of accumulation of 5-HT (in the presence of pargyline) reflects the rate of turnover of 5-HT. Rats used in this experiment had been (a) ovariectomized 9 days beforehand, or (b) ovariectomized and after 7 days treated with oestradiol for 2 days. Animals that were killed at 24:00 h were decapitated under dim red light illumination. There is a significant difference between 5-HT accumulation during the light and during the dark in young animals; $P < 0.05$. No rhythm of 5-HT accumulation or effect of oestradiol treatment was observed in middle-aged rats.

frequency of irregular oestrous cyclicity or to deficits in cyclic LH surges, since the integrity of these two hypothalamic areas is essential to cyclic physiological functions. As mentioned above, the suprachiasmatic nucleus is the putative centre for the biological clock regulating entrainment to the photoperiod of many rhythmic functions. The medial preoptic nucleus is also involved in the maintenance of diurnal and cyclic physiological functions. It contains cell bodies for neurones that contain luteinizing-hormone-releasing hormone, the axons of which course posteriorly and terminate in the median eminence. Destruction of this brain region interferes with body temperature regulation and reproductive cycles.

Opiates inhibit the plasma LH concentration and modulate the frequency of LH pulses in young rats (reviewed in Meites *et al.*, 1983; Kalra, 1986; Rasmussen, 1986b). The concentration of opiate peptides in the hypothalamus, the number of immunocytochemically localized β-endorphinergic neurones, the amount of proopiomelanocortin mRNA, the responsiveness to opiate agonists and antagonists, and the density of opiate receptors all decrease in ageing rats and mice. However, it is unclear whether changes in opiate tone in animals regulate age-related changes in LH secretion or the age-related progression to acyclicity. Equivalent decreases in

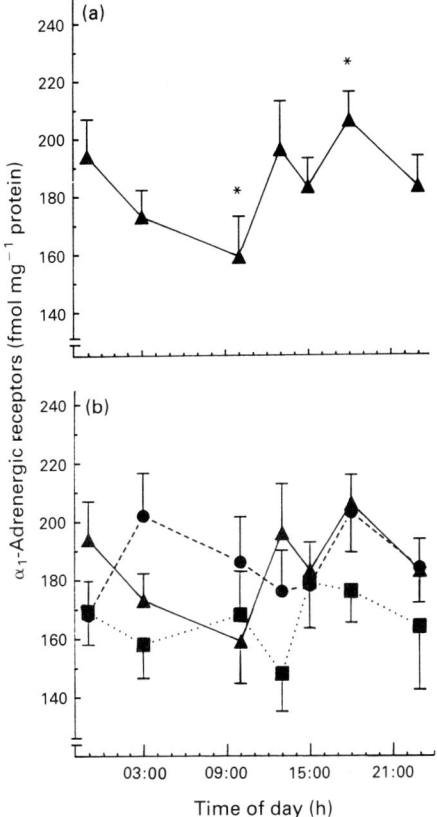

Fig. 6. The density of α_1-adrenergic receptors in the medial preoptic nucleus of (a) young rats and of (b) young (▲), middle-aged (●) and old rats (■) (Weiland & Wise, 1990). In young rats, the density of receptors exhibited a diurnal rhythm. No rhythm was detected in middle-aged or old rats. The mean concentration of receptors was equivalent in young and middle-aged rats but was decreased in old rats. *Values are significantly different; $P < 0.05$.

proopiomelanocortin mRNA levels in the periarcuate region of the hypothalamus were observed in groups of middle-aged (10–12 months old) and old (17–19 months old) rats that exhibited varying degrees of reproductive senescence (Lloyd et al., 1991). Furthermore, no further deterioration in the amount of proopiomelanocortin mRNA was observed in old animals in which more advanced stages of reproductive senescence were evident. In a more recent study, we examined the effects of age and steroid treatment on proopiomelanocortin gene expression in the hypothalamus to determine whether changes in diurnal rhythmicity extend to the level of gene expression (Weiland et al., 1992). It was thought that changes in the amount of proopiomelanocortin mRNA, the ability of this gene to respond to steroid treatment, or alterations in the diurnal rhythm of proopiomelanocortin gene expression may influence multiple neuroendocrine and endocrine changes in ageing animals.

Three groups of rats were ovariectomized: (1) young (2–4 months old) rats that had displayed two consecutive oestrous cycles lasting 4 or 5 days; (2) middle-aged (9–11 months old) rats that had had two consecutive oestrous cycles lasting 4 or 5 days; and (3) old (16–19 months old) rats that had exhibited at least two pseudopregnancies lasting 20–22 days prior to ovariectomy. One week after ovariectomy, half of the animals received oestradiol for 2 days. Groups of rats were killed at 23:00 h on day 8 and at 03:00, 10:00, 13:00, 15:00, 18:00, and 23:00 h on day 9 after ovariectomy. The brains were removed, frozen and sectioned. Brain sections were thaw-mounted on gelatin-coated slides and stored at $-70°C$ until *in situ* hybridization histochemistry was performed according to the methods of Wise *et al.* (1990). The concentration of mRNA on films was measured by placing a fixed circular window over the region of the arcuate nucleus and measuring the relative optical density using an image analysis system.

In young ovariectomized animals, two days of treatment with oestradiol facilitated the expression of a rhythm in the amount of proopiomelanocortin mRNA in the periarcuate region of the hypothalamus (Fig. 7) that was very similar to the rhythm exhibited by intact rats on proestrus (Wise *et al.*, 1990). The amount of proopiomelanocortin mRNA reached peak values early in the morning and declined to basal values at 23:00 h. In addition, oestradiol caused an overall suppression of the mean amount of this mRNA. No diurnal rhythm in the mRNA was detected in ovariectomized rats. The amount of proopiomelanocortin mRNA declined in middle-aged and old ovariectomized rats compared with that in young rats. Treatment with oestradiol failed to induce a rhythm and no longer suppressed the mean amount of proopiomelanocortin mRNA in either middle-aged or old rats.

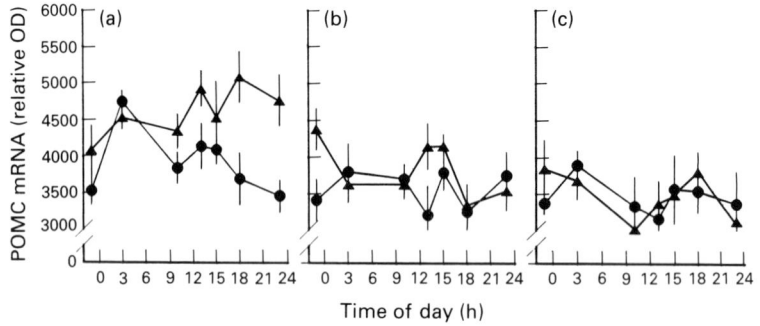

Fig. 7. The amount of proopiomelanocortin (POMC) mRNA expressed as specific optical density (OD) in ovariectomized (▲) and ovariectomized, oestradiol-treated (●) (a) young, (b) middle-aged and (c) old rats (Weiland *et al.*, 1992). Treatment with oestradiol induced a rhythm and caused an overall suppression in mean amounts of proopiomelanocortin mRNA in young rats. The amount of mRNA declined in middle-aged and old ovariectomized rats compared with that in young rats. Treatment with oestradiol failed to induce a rhythm or suppress the mean values of proopiomelanocortin mRNA in middle-aged or old rats.

The biological clock and ageing

A common thread that interweaves through all of these studies is the role of changing rhythmic neurotransmitter and neuroendocrine function in age-related reproductive dysfunction. It appeared possible that changes in the integrity of the biological clock or in its ability to entrain neurochemical events may explain the diverse changes in the diurnal patterns of multiple neurochemical events. We therefore measured the local cerebral glucose utilization, since this parameter is an index of local brain function. Particular attention was paid to the dorsal and ventral suprachiasmatic nucleus, since this is a critical pacemaker area of the brain. Young and middle-aged rats were examined to determine whether the overall pattern of neural function in this critical neural pacemaker changes during the early stages of reproductive ageing (Wise *et al.*, 1988). Young (3–4 months old) and middle-aged (12–14 months old) rats were ovariectomized one week beforehand and treated with oestradiol for two days. The external jugular vein was cannulated to the level of the right atrium, and the local cerebral glucose utilization was measured at various times of day by the autoradiographic 2-deoxy-D-[1–14C]glucose method of Sokoloff (Sokoloff *et al.*, 1977).

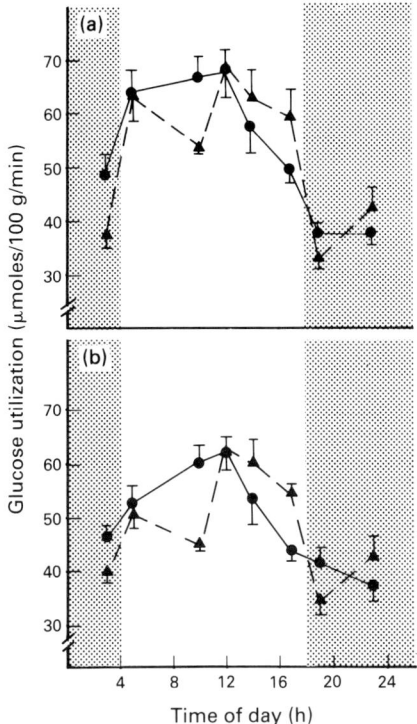

Fig. 8. Glucose utilization in (a) the ventral and (b) dorsal aspects of the suprachiasmatic nucleus of young (▲) and middle-aged (●) ovariectomized, oestradiol-treated rats (Wise *et al.*, 1988). In young rats, local cerebral glucose utilization increased when lights went on at 04.00 h, and again just before the initiation of the surge of luteinizing hormone, between 10:00 and 12:00 h. The glucose utilization decreased when lights went off at 18:00 h. In middle-aged rats glucose utilization increased between 24:00 and 03:00 h and decreased between 14:00 and 19:00 h. ▨ Lights off.

A circadian rhythm in the local cerebral glucose utilization in the suprachiasmatic nucleus of young rats was detected: it rose within 1 h of the lights being turned on, increased further just prior to the initiation of the LH surge and decreased within 1 h of lights being turned off. In contrast, the response to light–dark cycles in middle-aged rats was dampened, and the local cerebral glucose utilization appeared to increase in advance of lights on and decrease earlier in anticipation of lights off compared with the response in young rats. Thus, the circadian rhythm of the local cerebral glucose utilization appears to be phase advanced in middle-aged rats (Fig. 8). Together, the data demonstrate that multiple aspects of circadian function change during the initial stages of reproductive ageing and lead to the speculation that the integrity of the time-keeping system breaks down with age.

Conclusion

The decay of temporal organization and the altered phase relationships or desynchronization among neurotransmitter systems during ageing may account for increasing duration and decreased amplitude and frequency of pulsatile LH release, the delay and increased variability of diurnal hormone release, and the transition to oestrous cycles of irregular and unpredictable length. Many other biological rhythms dampen with age. It seems possible that temporal desynchronization of neural signals has deleterious effects on a wide variety of physiological functions and may even influence life span (see Brock, 1991).

This report was supported by NIH AG02224 and HD15955. P. M. Wise is an NIH MERIT Awardee.

References

Aschheim, P. (1983) Relation of neuroendocrine system to reproductive decline in female rats. In *Neuroendocrinology of Aging*, pp. 73–101. Ed J. Meites. Plenum Press, New York.

Baird, D.T. (1978) Pulsatile secretion of LH and ovarian oestradiol during the follicular phase of the sheep estrous cycle. *Biology of Reproduction* **18**, 359–364.

Brock, M.A. (1991) Chronobiology and aging. *Journal of the American Geriatrics Society* **39**, 74–91.

Carmel, P.W., Araki, S. & Ferin, M. (1976) Pituitary stalk portal blood collection in rhesus monkeys: evidence for pulsatile release of gonadotropin-releasing hormone (GnRH). *Endocrinology* **99**, 243–248.

Clemens, J.A. & Bennett, D.R. (1977) Do aging changes in the preoptic area contribute to loss of cyclic endocrine function? *Journal of Gerontology* **32**, 19–24.

Clemens, J.A., Amenomori, Y., Jenkins, T. & Meites, J. (1969) Effects of hypothalamic stimulation, hormones, and drugs on ovarian function in old female rats. *Proceedings of the Society for Experimental Biology and Medicine* **132**, 561–563.

Cohen, I.R. & Wise, P.M. (1988) Age-related changes in the diurnal rhythm of serotonin turnover in microdissected brain areas of estradiol-treated ovariectomized rats. *Endocrinology* **122**, 2626–2633.

Cooper, R.L. (1977) Reinstatement of ovarian cycles in aged female rats fed L-tyrosine supplemented diets. *Gerontologist* **17**, 49.

Cooper, R.L. & Walker, R.F. (1979) Potential therapeutic consequences of age-dependent changes in brain physiology. *Interdisciplinary Topics in Gerontology* **15**, 54–76.

Dierschke, D.J., Bhattacharya, A.N., Atkinson, L.E. & Knobil, E. (1970) Circhoral oscillations of plasma LH levels in the ovariectomized rhesus monkey. *Endocrinology* **87**, 850–853.

Djahanbakhch, O., Warner, P., McNeilly, A.S. & Baird, D.T. (1984) Pulsatile release of LH and oestradiol during the periovulatory period in women. *Clinical Endocrinology* **20**, 579–589.

Everett, J.W. (1940) The restoration of ovulatory cycles and corpus luteum formation in persistent estrous rats by progesterone. *Endocrinology* **27**, 681–686.

Everett, J.W. (1980) Reinstatement of estrous cycles in middle-aged spontaneously persistent estrous rats: importance of circulating prolactin and the resulting facilitative action of progesterone. *Endocrinology* **106**, 1691–1696.

Everett, J.W. (1984) Further study of oestrous cycles that follow interruption of spontaneous persistent oestrus in middle-aged rats. *Journal of Endocrinology* **102**, 271–276.

Everett, J.W. & Tyrey, L. (1982) Comparison of luteinizing hormone surge responses to ovarian steroids in cyclic and spontaneously persistent estrous rats of middle age. *Biology of Reproduction* **26**, 663–672.

Filicori, M., Santoro, N., Merriam, G.R. & Crowley, W.F., Jr (1986) Characterization of the physiological pattern of episodic gonadotropin secretion throughout the human menstrual cycle. *Journal of Clinical Endocrinology and Metabolism* **62**, 1136–1144.

Gay, V.L. & Sheth, N.A. (1972) Evidence for a periodic release of LH in castrated male and female rats. *Endocrinology* **90**, 158–162.

Huang, H.H. (1988) Rejuvenation of the aging hypothalamic-pituitary axis with fetal hypothalamic graft. *Interdisciplinary Topics in Gerontology* **24**, 141–149.

Huang, H.H., Marshall, S. & Meites, J. (1976) Induction of estrous cycles in old non-cyclic rats by progesterone, ACTH, ether stress or L-dopa. *Neuroendocrinology* **20**, 21–34.

Ingram, D.K., London, E.D. & Reynolds, M.A. (1982) Circadian rhythmicity and sleep: effects of aging in laboratory animals. *Neurobiology of Aging* **3**, 287–297.

Inouye, S.T. & Kawamura, H. (1979) Persistence of circadian rhythmicity in a mammalian hypothalamic 'island' containing the suprachiasmatic nucleus. *Proceedings of the National Academy of Sciences USA* **76**, 5962–5966.

Inouye, S.T. & Kawamura, H. (1982) Characteristics of a circadian pacemaker in the suprachiasmatic nucleus. *Journal of Comparative Physiology* **146**, 153–160.

Kalra, S.P. (1986) Neural circuitry involved in the control of LHRH secretion: a model for preovulatory LH release. In *Frontiers in Neuroendocrinology (Vol. 9)*, pp. 31–75. Eds W. F. Ganong and L. Martini. Raven Press, New York.

Kordon, C., Hery, M., Szafarczyk, A., Ixart, G. & Assenmacher, I. (1981) Serotonin and the regulation of pituitary hormone secretion and of neuroendocrine rhythms. *Journal of Physiology (Paris)* **77**, 489–496.

Krohn, P.L. (1955) Tissue transplantation techniques applied to the problem of the ageing of the organs of reproduction. In *Ciba Foundation Colloquia on Ageing*, pp. 141–161. Eds G. E. W. Wolstenholme and M. P. Cameron. J. A. Churchill, London.

Krohn, P.L. (1962) Review lectures on senescence II. Heterochronic transplantation in the study of aging. *Proceedings of the Royal Society of London, Series B* **157**, 128–147.

Krohn, P.L. (1966) Transplantation and aging. In *Topics in the Biology of Ageing*, pp. 125–148. Ed. P. L. Krohn. Wiley, New York.

Levine, J.E., Norman, R.L., Gliessman, P.M., Oyama, T.T., Bangsberg, D.R. & Spies, H.G. (1985) In vivo gonadotropin-releasing hormone release and serum luteinizing hormone measurements in ovariectomized, estrogen-treated rhesus macaques. *Endocrinology* **117**, 711–721.

Lincoln, D.W., Fraser, H.M., Lincoln, G.A., Martin, G.B. & McNeilly, A.S. (1985) Hypothalamic pulse generators. *Recent Progress in Hormone Research* **41**, 369–419.

Liu, C.H., Laughlin, G.A., Fischer, U.G. & Yen, S.S.C. (1990) Marked attenuation of ultradian and circadian rhythms of dehydroepiandrosterone in postmenopausal women: evidence for a reduced 17,20-desmolase enzymatic activity. *Journal of Clinical Endocrinology and Metabolism* **71**, 900–906.

Lloyd, J.M., Scarbrough, K., Weiland, N.G. & Wise, P.M. (1991) Age-related changes in proopiomelanocortin (POMC) gene expression in the periarcuate region of ovariectomized rats. *Endocrinology* **129**, 1896–1902.

Lonning, P.E., Dowsett, M., Jacobs, S., Schem, B., Hardy, J. & Powles, T.J. (1989) Lack of diurnal variation in plasma levels of androstenedione, testosterone, estrone and estradiol in postmenopausal women. *Journal of Steroid Biochemistry* **34**, 551–553.

Matsumoto, A., Kobayashi, S., Murakami, S. & Arai, Y. (1984) Recovery of declined ovarian function in aged female rats by transplantation of newborn hypothalamic tissue. *Proceedings of the Japanese Academy, Series B* **60**, 73–76.

Meites, J., Van Vugt, D.A., Forman, L.J., Sylvester, P.W., Jr, Ieiri, T. & Sonntag, W. (1983) Evidence that endogenous opiates are involved in control of gonadotropin secretion. In *The Anterior Pituitary Gland*, pp. 327–340. Ed. A. S. Bhatnagar. Raven Press, New York.

Moore, R.Y. (1983) Organization and function of a central nervous system circadian oscillator: the suprachiasmatic hypothalamic nucleus. *Federation Proceedings* **42**, 2783–2789.

Mosko, S.S., Erickson, G.F. & Moore, R.Y. (1980) Dampened circadian rhythms in reproductively senescent female rats. *Behavioural Neural Biology* **28**, 1–14.

Peng, M-T. & Huang, H-H. (1972) Aging of hypothalamic–pituitary–ovarian function in the rat. *Fertility and Sterility* **23**, 535–542.

Quadri, S.K., Kledzik, G.S. & Meites, J. (1973) Reinitiation of estrous cycles in old constant-estrous rats by central-acting drugs. *Neuroendocrinology* **11**, 248–255.

Rance, N., Wise, P.M., Selmanoff, M.K. & Barraclough, C.A. (1981) Catecholamine turnover rates in discrete hypothalamic areas and associated changes in median eminence luteinizing hormone-releasing hormone and serum gonadotropins on proestrus and diestrous day 1. *Endocrinology* **108**, 1795–1802.

Rasmussen, D.D. (1986a) Physiological interactions of the basic rest–activity cycle of the brain: pulsatile luteinizing hormone secretion as model. *Psychoneuroendocrinology* **11**, 389–405.

Rasmussen, D.D. (1986b) New concepts in the regulation of hypothalamic gonadotropin releasing hormone (GnRH) secretion. *Journal of Endocrinological Investigation* **9**, 427–437.

Scarbrough, K. & Wise, P.M. (1990) Age-related changes in the pulsatile pattern of LH release precede the transition to estrous acyclicity and depend upon estrous cycle history. *Endocrinology* **126**, 884–890.

Schwartz, W.J., Davidsen, L.C. & Smith, C.B. (1980) In vivo metabolic activity of a putative circadian oscillator, the rat suprachiasmatic nucleus. *Journal of Comparative Neurology* **189**, 157–167.

Sodersten, P. & Eneroth, P. (1981) Serum levels of oestradiol-17β and progesterone in relation to sexual receptivity in intact and ovariectomized rats. *Journal of Endocrinology* **89**, 45–54.

Sokoloff, L., Reivich, M., Kennedy, C., Des Rosiers, M.H., Patlak, C.S., Pettigrew, K.D., Sakurada, O. & Shinohara, M. (1977) The [14C]deoxyglucose method for the measurement of local cerebral glucose utilization: theory, procedure, and normal values in the conscious and anesthetized albino rat. *Journal of Neurochemistry* **28**, 897–916.

Walker, R.F. (1980) Serotonin neuroleptics change patterns of preovulatory secretion of luteinizing hormone in rats. *Life Sciences* **27**, 1063–1068.

Walker, R.F. (1983) Quantitative and temporal aspects of serotonin's facilitatory action on phasic secretion of luteinizing hormone in female rats. *Neuroendocrinology* **36**, 468–474.

Walker, R.F. & Wilson, C.A. (1983) Changes in hypothalamic serotonin associated with amplification of LH surges by progesterone in rats. *Neuroendocrinology* **37**, 200–205.

Weiland, N.G. & Wise, P.M. (1990) Aging progressively alters the diurnal rhythms and decreases the densities of alpha-1-adrenergic receptors in selected hypothalamic regions. *Endocrinology* **126**, 2392–2397.

Weiland, N.G., Scarbrough, K. & Wise, P.M. (1992) Aging abolishes the estradiol-induced suppression and diurnal rhythm of POMC gene expression in the arcuate nucleus. *Endocrinology* **131**, 2959–2964.

Weitzman, E.D., Moline, M.L., Czeisler, C.A. & Zimmerman, J.C. (1982) Chronobiology of aging: temperature, sleep-wake rhythms and entrainment. *Neurobiology of Aging* **3**, 299–309.

Wise, P.M. (1984) Estradiol-induced daily luteinizing hormone and prolactin surges in young and middle-aged rats: correlations with age-related changes in pituitary responsiveness and catecholamine turnover rates in microdissected brain areas. *Endocrinology* **115**, 801–809.

Wise, P.M., Rance, N. & Barraclough, C.A. (1981) Effects of estradiol and progesterone on catecholamine turnover rates in discrete hypothalamic regions in ovariectomized rats. *Endocrinology* **108**, 2186–2193.

Wise, P.M., Cohen, I.R., Weiland, N.G. & London, E.D. (1988) Aging alters the circadian rhythm of glucose utilization in the suprachiasmatic nucleus. *Proceedings of the National Academy of Sciences USA* **85**, 5305–5309.

Wise, P.M., Scarbrough, K., Weiland, N.G. & Larson, G.H. (1990) Diurnal pattern of proopiomelanocortin gene expression in the arcuate nucleus of proestrous, ovariectomized and steroid-treated rats: a possible role in cyclic luteinizing hormone secretion. *Molecular Endocrinology* **4,** 886–892.

Wuttke, W. & Meites, J. (1973) Effects of electrochemical stimulation of medial preoptic area on prolactin and luteinizing hormone release in old female rats. *Pflügers Archives* **341,** 1–6.

Yen, S.S.C., Tsai, C.C., Naftolin, F., Vandenberg, G. & Ajabor, L. (1972) Pulsatile patterns of gonadotropin release in subjects with and without ovarian function. *Journal of Clinical Endocrinology* **34,** 671–675.

Ageing of the neuroendocrine system in the brain of male rats: receptor mechanisms and steroid metabolism

F. Piva, F. Celotti, D. Dondi, P. Limonta, R. Maggi, E. Messi, P. Negri-Cesi, M. Zanisi, M. Motta and L. Martini

Department of Endocrinology, University of Milan, Via Balzaretti 9, 20133 Milan, Italy

Summary. The work described in this article gives information on the effects of ageing on the hypothalamo–pituitary–testicular axis in rats. The hypothalami of young and old male rats contain similar amounts of luteinizing-hormone-releasing hormone (LHRH); when perifused *in vitro* they release comparable amounts of LHRH under basal conditions and in response to K^+. The addition of an LHRH analogue to the perifusion medium blocks the release of LHRH induced by K^+ from the hypothalami of young and old male rats, indicating that the ultrashort feedback mechanism controlling LHRH release functions normally in aged male rats. Ageing also exerts important effects on the density of μ- and κ-opioid receptors in the brain. The number of hypothalamic μ-opioid receptors was significantly decreased in aged animals; a replacement treatment with testosterone does not reverse this decrease, indicating that the decline of hypothalamic μ receptors and of serum titres of testosterone in old rats are independent phenomena. The number of κ-opioid receptors in the brain increases in the amygdala and in the thalamus with ageing. Apparently ageing does not influence the number of δ receptors in any of the brain areas investigated. The number of pituitary LHRH receptors decreases in old animals, which might explain the low serum concentration of gonadotrophins in aged rats caused by an inadequate response of the pituitary to hypothalamic LHRH. The impaired secretion of testosterone in aged male rats is accompanied by an increase in the number of testicular LHRH receptors, indicating that the intratesticular mechanisms controlling testosterone release also undergo significant alterations during ageing. The rate of conversion of testosterone to dihydrotestosterone (DHT) and 5α-androstane-3α,17β-diol (3α-diol) is the same in the hypothalami of young and old rats. However, the yields of DHT obtained from the pituitaries of aged male rats are significantly lower than those recorded in the pituitaries of young animals. These results show that the enzymes necessary for metabolizing testosterone via the 5α-reductase pathway are maintained both in the hypothalamus and in the anterior pituitary of aged male rats. However, the 5α-reductase activity of the anterior pituitary of senescent animals appears to be lower than that in the younger controls.

Keywords: LHRH; hypothalamus; pituitary; testosterone; opioid receptors; rat

Introduction

Age has been reported to exert profound influences on the hypothalamic–pituitary–gonadal axis of the rat. In particular, it has been observed that in comparison with young rats old male rats exhibit a decrease in the amount of serum testosterone (Riegle *et al.*, 1977; Bethea & Walker, 1979; Miller & Riegle, 1982; Kinoshita *et al.*, 1985), luteinizing hormone (LH), and follicle-stimulating hormone (FSH) (Meites, 1982; Karpas *et al.*, 1983). Moreover, the pulsatile secretion of LH is altered in old male rats (Karpas *et al.*, 1983; Steiner *et al.*, 1984). These alterations have been attributed either to a degeneration of the neurones synthesizing and releasing luteinizing-hormone-releasing hormone (LHRH), or to age-linked modifications of the synthesis, metabolism and release of brain neurotransmitters that control LHRH secretion (such as 5-HT, catecholamines and opioids) (Simpkins *et al.*, 1977; Meites, 1982). Alterations in the feedback mechanisms controlling gonadotrophin and prolactin release have also been reported to occur in old animals (Shaar *et al.*, 1975; Pirke *et al.*, 1978; Karpas *et al.*, 1983; Sarkar *et al.*, 1983). This article summarizes the evidence obtained in our laboratory on the effects of ageing on: (1) the capability of the hypothalamus of male rats to release LHRH; (2) the ultrashort feedback mechanism controlling LHRH release; (3) the binding characteristics of brain opioid receptors involved in the control of gonadotrophin secretion; (4) the binding characteristics of LHRH receptors in the anterior pituitary and in the testis; and (5) the metabolism of testosterone in the hypothalamus and in the anterior pituitary.

Effect of ageing on the ability of the hypothalamus of male rats to release LHRH

Experiments were designed to determine whether the hypothalamus of old male rats can release LHRH *in vitro* in a manner similar to that of the hypothalamus of young animals. The medial basal hypothalami of 18-month-old male rats of the Sprague-Dawley strain were perifused *in vitro*, and the release of LHRH was measured in the effluent in basal conditions and after exposure to a depolarizing stimulus induced by K^+ (110 mmol l^{-1}). The medial basal hypothalami of young adult (6-month-old) male rats of the same strain served as controls.

The mean spontaneous output of LHRH (before any K^+ stimulus was applied) from the perifused hypothalami was $6·58 \pm 0·7$ pg ml^{-1} in young rats and $6·93 \pm 1·3$ pg ml^{-1} in the old rats. These two values were not significantly different. It is obvious from Fig. 1a that the K^+ stimulus induced quantitatively similar LHRH responses each time it was applied to the hypothalamus of young animals. The response of the hypothalami of old animals to the K^+ stimulus is similar to that obtained in young animals, even though the amount of LHRH released appears to be somewhat smaller (Fig. 1b).

The increase in LHRH secretion induced by K^+ in the hypothalamus of young and old animals is illustrated in Fig. 2. In young animals, all K^+ pulses were followed by an increase in LHRH release; this increase was significantly less upon the third stimulation compared with the first response when a two-way analysis of variance was applied. After an interruption of 1 h between the third and fourth application of K^+, the amount of LHRH released was similar to that obtained in the first part of the experiment. The hypothalami of old animals also released LHRH in response to each K^+ pulse (Fig. 2); once again, a decrease in the response was observed upon the third stimulus and this decrease was statistically significant compared with the first response when a two-way analysis of variance was applied. Responses identical to those obtained at the beginning of the experiment also occurred after an interruption of 1 h between the third and fourth application of K^+. The increase in LHRH secretion obtained from the medial basal hypothalamus of young and old animals in response to K^+ was not significantly different from each other when analysed by two-way analysis of variance for repeated measures (Zanisi *et al.*, 1987a).

The amount of LHRH in the nonperifused medial basal hypothalamus of young rats ($n = 5$) was $5259·7 \pm 660$ pg and $5017·5 \pm 1701$ pg in old animals ($n = 4$). The difference was not statistically significant, possibly because of the small number of animals tested. At the end of the experiment, the amount of LHRH in the perifused hypothalamus was $5212·9 \pm 696$ pg in young animals and $2721·9 \pm 705$ pg in old animals. These two values were not significantly different from each other, or from those of the hypothalami of nonperifused animals.

These results show first of all that the basal secretion of LHRH from the perifused hypothalami of young and old male rats is quantitatively similar. Moreover, the hypothalami of young and old animals can respond over a prolonged period to the administration of K^+ stimuli with repeated bursts of LHRH hypersecretion. It is interesting to note that, from a quantitative point of view,

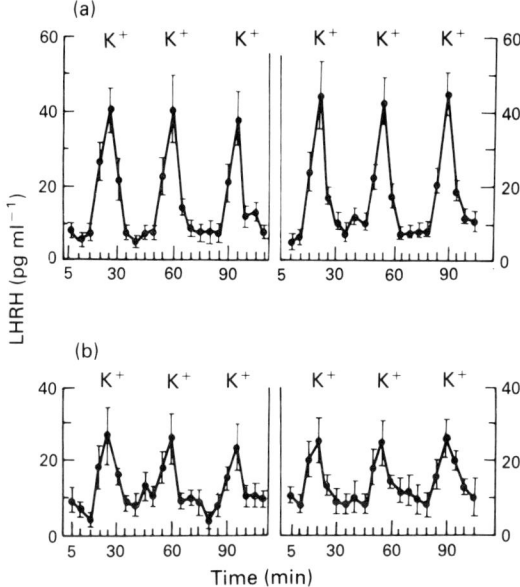

Fig. 1. Release of luteinizing-hormone-releasing hormone (LHRH) from the mediobasal region of hypothalami derived from (a) young ($n = 8$) and (b) old ($n = 6$) male rats that had been perifused with a standard Krebs–Ringer medium (basal conditions) and then stimulated by the addition of K^+ (110 mmol l^{-1}) to the medium in pulses lasting 5 min. Between the end of the third K^+ pulse and the start of the fourth K^+ pulse, there was an interruption of 1 h. Values are the means ± SEM.

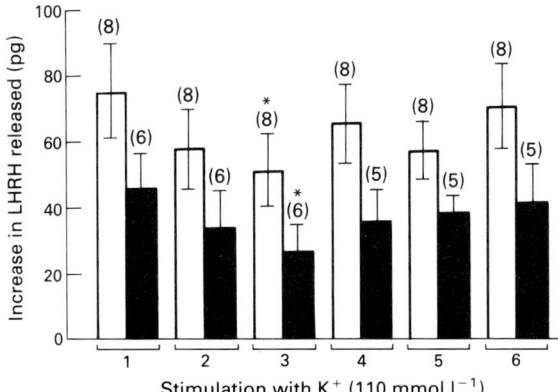

Fig. 2. Effect of perifusion with a medium enriched with K^+ (110 mmol l^{-1}) on luteinizing-hormone-releasing hormone (LHRH) release from the medial basal hypothalami of young (□) and old (■) male rats *in vitro*. Values represent the means ± SEM of differences between values before and after addition of K^+. Numbers in parentheses indicate the number of experiments. Asterisks indicate a significantly ($P < 0.05$) lower increase in the release of LHRH in response to K^+ compared with the increase in response to K^+ observed when it was first applied.

young and old rats respond similarly to the K^+ stimulus; although the responses to K^+ of the hypothalami of old animals appear to be somewhat lower than those of the hypothalami of young animals, the differences are not statistically significant (Zanisi *et al.*, 1987a). It also emerges from the data that the amount of LHRH in the medial basal hypothalamus is similar in young and old animals, both before and after the perifusion period. Since it is known that castration usually induces a decrease in intrahypothalamic LHRH stores (Shin & Howitt, 1975; Kalra & Kalra, 1980), and that old male rats have decreased concentrations of circulating testosterone (Riegle *et al.*, 1977; Bethea & Walker, 1979; Miller & Riegle, 1982; Kinoshita *et al.*, 1985), it appears that the age-linked decline of serum testosterone does not induce the same effect as that produced by castration in young animals.

In conclusion, the results described here suggest that the hypothalamic LHRH-releasing machinery is not substantially different in old and young animals (Zanisi *et al.*, 1987a). It may be suggested that alterations in the function of the hypothalamic–pituitary complex observed in aged male rats are not due to an intrinsic age-related defect of the LHRH-synthesizing neurones. Therefore, it could be that the ageing of the 'central' reproductive system is brought about by age-linked alterations in the neurotransmitter systems controlling LHRH release *in vivo* (Simpkins *et al.*, 1977; Meites, 1982; Piva *et al.*, 1987).

Effect of ageing on the ultrashort feedback mechanism controlling LHRH release

Of the various types of feedback system regulating the hypothalamic–pituitary–gonadal axis (Piva *et al.*, 1979), the long feedback loops are altered in old male rats, since serum concentrations of LH and testosterone become simultaneously low (Riegle *et al.*, 1977; Bethea & Walker, 1979). Moreover, castration leads to a significantly smaller rise in the serum gonadotrophin concentration in aged male rats than in younger animals (Pirke *et al.*, 1978; Karpas *et al.*, 1983). Finally, lower doses of testosterone are needed to depress the amount of serum LH in old than in young animals (Shaar *et al.*, 1975; Pirke *et al.*, 1978). Little evidence is available as to whether short loop feedback systems are also altered in old rats, except for a reduced inhibitory effect of prolactin on serum prolactin concentration and pulsatility in 24–26-month-old ovariectomized rats (Sarkar *et al.*, 1983).

Recently, studies *in vivo* and *in vitro* have suggested that there is a negative feedback effect exerted by LHRH on its own secretion (i.e. an ultrashort loop feedback mechanism). In particular, Zanisi *et al.* (1987b) have shown that perifusion of the medial basal hypothalamus of normal adult male rats with an LHRH analogue decreases both the basal and the K^+-stimulated LHRH release *in vitro*. The existence of other ultrashort feedback systems that control the release of somatostatin and growth-hormone-releasing hormone (GHRH) has been proposed by other authors (Lumpkin *et al.*, 1985; Katakami *et al.*, 1986).

A series of experiments was designed to evaluate whether the ultrashort feedback mechanism controlling LHRH release in the hypothalamus is altered with ageing. An agonist of LHRH (buserelin: D-Ser-(TBu)^6-Des-Gly^{10} LHRH-ethylamide), which does not cross-react in the radioimmunoassay used to measure endogenous amounts of LHRH, was added to the medium superfusing the medial basal hypothalami of old animals. LHRH release was evaluated both in basal conditions and following K^+ stimulation. Figure 3 summarizes the results obtained when the hypothalami of old male rats were perifused throughout the experiment either with a control medium (Krebs-Ringer solution) or with medium enriched with the LHRH analogue buserelin. The hypothalamic fragments were stimulated three times with K^+ (110 mmol l^{-1}). After a resting period of 1 h (during which the effluent was not collected), three additional K^+ pulses were applied. It is clear from the figure that when the hypothalami are perifused with Krebs–Ringer solution, they maintain their ability to respond to K^+ stimulations with quantitatively comparable bursts of LHRH for a period of over 5 h. It was also observed that before K^+ was added the basal release of LHRH (1·46 ± 0·8 pg ml^{-1}) from the hypothalami perifused with medium containing the LHRH analogue was significantly lower ($P < 0.001$) than that observed for the hypothalami perifused with Krebs–Ringer alone (11·97 ± 1·3 pg ml^{-1}) (data not shown). Moreover, the presence of the LHRH analogue in the perifusion medium strongly reduces or completely abolishes the K^+-induced release of LHRH (Messi *et al.*, 1990).

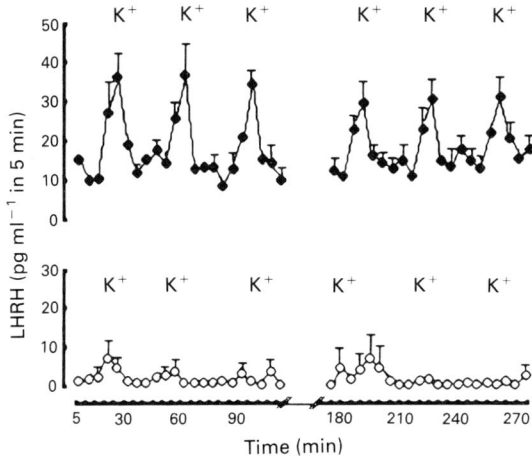

Fig. 3. Effect of continuous perifusion with an analogue of luteinizing-hormone-releasing hormone (LHRH) (buserelin; 5 μmol l^{-1}) (◇) compared with continuous perifusion with Krebs–Ringer solution (◆) on the release of LHRH induced by K$^+$ (110 mmol l^{-1}) from the medial basal hypothalami of old male rats. Between the third and fourth K$^+$ pulse, there was an interruption of 1 h. Values are means of three experiments ±SEM. Krebs–Ringer medium (in mmol l^{-1}): Nacl, 119; KCl, 4·6; CaCl$_2$, 1·89; NaHCO$_3$, 25; Na$_2$PO$_4$, 1·14; MgCl$_2$, 6·6; glucose, 10·5. Bacitracin (0·11 mmol l^{-1}) was added to prevent peptide degradation.

These experiments show that perifusion with an LHRH analogue inhibits the basal as well as the K$^+$-induced release of endogenous LHRH from the hypothalami of old rats, in a fashion similar to that previously reported for the hypothalami of young animals (Zanisi et al., 1987b). The ultrashort feedback mechanism through which LHRH is able to affect its own secretion does not therefore appear to be altered in old male rats.

Effect of ageing on μ-, κ- and δ-opioid receptors in the brain

It is known that the effects of the naturally occurring opioids (such as Met-enkephalin, Leu-enkephalin, β-endorphin and dynorphin) are exerted through interactions with specific binding sites. Different classes of opioid receptor (μ, κ and δ) have been described (Paterson et al., 1983). Endogenous brain opioids are involved in the control of the secretion of several anterior pituitary hormones (Gabriel et al., 1983; Piva et al., 1985) as well as of important neuroendocrine phenomena such as puberty and the ovulatory cycle (Sirinathsinghji et al., 1985). Particularly relevant in this respect are the interactions of brain opioids with the μ receptors (Pfeiffer et al., 1983).

Very little information is available on how age affects the number and binding characteristics of brain opioid receptors. The experiments described here were designed to determine whether the binding capability of brain μ, κ and δ receptors is modified by age in the male rat.

In one experiment, the concentration of μ receptors was studied in the hypothalami of male rats, at 2 or 22 months of age. In this experiment it was also investigated whether the administration of exogenous testosterone might modify the number of μ binding sites in the hypothalamus of old animals. Dihydromorphine was used as a specific ligand for the μ receptors. Serum concentrations of testosterone, prolactin, LH and FSH were also evaluated in the young and old animals. Table 1 shows that serum testosterone concentrations are significantly decreased in old rats; this phenomenon can be reversed by the implantation of Silastic capsules filled with testosterone. Table 1 also shows that age induces a small decrease in the amount of serum LH and FSH and an increase in serum prolactin. The implantation of Silastic capsules containing testosterone brings about a significant decrease in the amount of serum LH and FSH, while the serum prolactin concentration remains unchanged (Piva et al., 1987).

It is apparent from Fig. 4 that the concentration of opioid receptors binding dihydromorphine in the hypothalamus decreases significantly between 2 and 22 months of age. The data also indicate that although the administration of testosterone is able to bring the amount of serum testosterone back up towards normal and to inhibit gonadotrophin secretion (see Table 1), it cannot restore the number of opioid receptors in the hypothalami of 22-month-old animals. The decrease in the number of μ receptors with ageing was not accompanied by a change in the affinity constant K_a.

These results agree, in general, with those reported in the only other study in which dihydromorphine binding has been evaluated in the brains of old male rats. Messing et al. (1981) have found that fewer sites bind this ligand in the frontal poles, anterior cortex and striatum of 26-month-old rats than in the same structures in young male rats. The hypothalamus was not studied by these authors. The age-linked decrease in the number of hypothalamic μ-opioid receptors reported here does not seem to be linked to a lack of testosterone, since the administration of exogenous testosterone does not restore the number of μ-opioid receptors to normal (i.e. to that found in young rats) in the hypothalamus.

In a second experiment, the binding characteristics of κ-receptors were evaluated in selected areas of the brain of male rats aged either 2 or 19 months. The areas examined were the hypothalamus, the amygdala, the hippocampus, the thalamus, the corpus striatum, the mesencephalon, the frontal poles, and the anterior and posterior cerebral cortex. The ligand selected was bremazocine, which was used after having protected μ and δ receptors with dihydromorphine and D-Ala-D-Leu-enkephalin, respectively. The results obtained are recorded in Table 2. It appears that the number of κ receptors in the different areas investigated is extremely variable in young animals. High concentrations of κ receptors have been found in the hypothalamus, in the striatum, in the mesencephalon and in the amygdala. The number of κ receptors in the thalamus, frontal poles, hippocampus, anterior and posterior cerebral cortex was found to be much lower; in these structures, the density of κ receptors is very similar. Age does not seem to influence the number of κ-binding sites in most of the areas examined, except in the amygdala and in the thalamus where the number significantly increased in aged animals: such an increase was not accompanied by a change in the affinity constant (Maggi et al., 1989).

To our knowledge, no data are available in the literature on this issue. On the basis of the fact that the amygdala has been repeatedly shown to be involved in the control of gonadotrophin secretion (for review see Piva et al., 1980), it is possible that the change in the number of κ-opioid receptors occurring in this structure might be important in the modification of gonadotrophin secretion that is observed in old animals. However, there has been no indication so far that the thalamus might be involved in the control of gonadotrophin secretion. It is, therefore, possible that the reported increase in thalamic κ-opioid receptors in aged animals is correlated with changes in behavioural phenomena (e.g. pain) occurring in old animals.

In a third experiment, the binding characteristics of δ-opioid receptors were evaluated in the hypothalamus, amygdala, hippocampus, thalamus, corpus striatum, mesencephalon, frontal poles, and anterior and posterior cerebral cortex of male rats of either 3 or 24 months of age (Table 3). This study was performed using the highly selective δ-opioid receptor ligand (D-Pen^2-D-Pen^5)enkephalin.

It is evident from Table 3 that, in 3-month-old male rats, the concentration of δ-opioid receptors in these areas of the brain is extremely variable. It is high in the anterior and posterior cortex, and lower in the frontal poles, corpus striatum, hippocampus, amygdala, thalamus, hypothalamus and in the mesencephalon (Dondi et al., 1992). Table 3 also shows that in the brain of 24-month-old male rats the distribution of δ-opioid receptors is similar to that observed in young animals. Apparently, there are no significant differences in the concentrations of this type of receptor in any of the structures considered between young adult and old male rats (Dondi et al., 1992). The

Table 1. Effect of ageing and of testosterone administration on serum concentrations of luteinizing hormone (LH), follicle-stimulating hormone (FSH), prolactin and testosterone (T) in male rats

Age (months)	LH (ng ml^{-1}) NIH S-20	FSH (ng ml^{-1}) NIADDK-RP-2	Prolactin (ng ml^{-1}) NIADDK-RP-3	Testosterone (ng ml^{-1})
2	1·38 ± 0·16 (10)	7·83 ± 0·39 (10)	5·07 ± 0·74 (9)	2·59 ± 0·83 (9)
22	0·98 ± 0·17 (11)	6·43 ± 0·61 (11)	11·78 ± 2·47 (10)	0·87 ± 0·30* (9)
22 + T	0·58 ± 0·09* (10)	3·63 ± 0·35*† (10)	9·46 ± 2·50 (10)	1·53 ± 0·37 (9)

Values are means ± SEM. The number of animals tested is shown in parentheses.
*($P < 0·05$) indicates a significant difference compared with 2-month-old rats.
†($P < 0·05$) indicates a significant difference compared with 22-month-old rats.

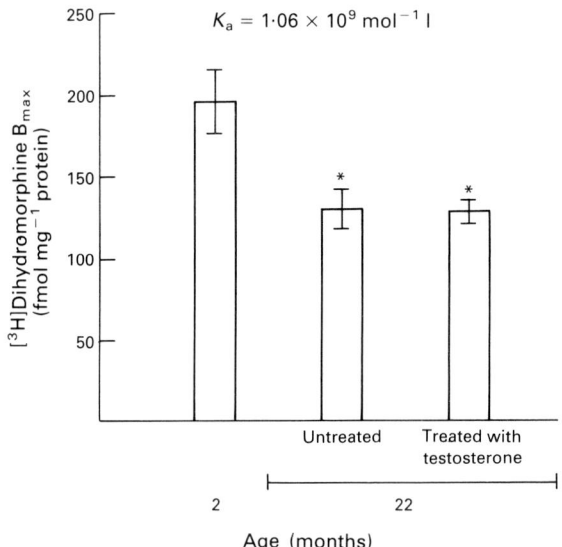

Fig. 4. Effect of ageing and testosterone replacement on the number of hypothalamic μ-opioid receptors in male rats. Asterisks indicate a significant ($P < 0·05$) difference between 22-month-old rats and 2-month-old rats. The affinity constant K_a was unchanged with ageing. Values are means derived from eight hypothalami ± SEM.

distribution of δ-opioid receptors observed in this study in the various brain areas of young (3-month-old) male rats is, in general, in agreement with previous data (Gulya et al., 1986; Mansour et al., 1987; Sharif & Hughes, 1989). These workers suggest that δ-binding sites are mainly localized in the forebrain with particularly high concentrations occurring in the different layers of the cortex, in the olfactory bulb and in the caudate–putamen region. Lower concentrations of δ-opioid sites have been reported to be present in the hypothalamus, the mesencephalon and the thalamus (Gulya et al., 1986; Mansour et al., 1987; Sharif & Hughes, 1989).

Our data show the absence of age-related variations in the number of δ-opioid receptors, and underline the fact that age may affect the different types of brain opioid receptors in different ways. Apparently, ageing induces a selective decrease in the number of μ receptors in some brain regions (Piva et al., 1987), increases the concentration of κ receptors in other areas (Maggi et al., 1989), and has no effect on the concentration of δ receptors (Dondi et al., 1992) in the brain regions of male rats so far studied.

Table 2. Effect of ageing on the concentration of κ-opioid receptors in discrete brain regions of male rats

Brain region	Young (2-month-old rats)	Old (19-month-old rats)
Hypothalamus	117·58 ± 11·05	116·11 ± 5·72
Striatum	111·56 ± 6·33	92·27 ± 7·66
Amygdala	75·67 ± 4·22	101·82 ± 8·60*
Mesencephalon	71·85 ± 8·63	70·61 ± 5·93
Thalamus	35·81 ± 2·21	70·06 ± 13·10*
Frontal poles	29·33 ± 5·89	27·56 ± 3·08
Anterior cortex	22·58 ± 2·08	28·35 ± 1·63
Posterior cortex	19·37 ± 1·42	19·63 ± 3·64
Hippocampus	18·25 ± 3·66	17·09 ± 3·30

Groups of eight animals were used.
Values (mean ± SEM) are expressed as B_{max} of [^{3}H]bremazocine (fmol mg^{-1} protein).
*$P < 0.05$ indicates a significant difference compared with 2-month-old animals.
$K_a = 0.8\text{--}2.1 \times 10^9$ mol^{-1} l.

Table 3. Effect of ageing on the concentration of δ-opioid receptors in discrete brain regions of male rats

Brain region	Young (3-month-old rats)	Old (24-month-old rats)
Anterior cortex	51·76 ± 4·65	49·15 ± 3·19
Posterior cortex	45·58 ± 2·78	43·20 ± 5·10
Frontal poles	34·10 ± 2·01	32·23 ± 2·62
Corpus striatum	30·09 ± 4·60	33·50 ± 3·37
Hippocampus	19·45 ± 2·24	20·89 ± 2·07
Amygdala	18·42 ± 2·79	20·96 ± 2·87
Thalamus	13·59 ± 3·14	14·39 ± 2·17
Hypothalamus	11·80 ± 1·21	8·75 ± 1·32
Mesencephalon	11·45 ± 1·67	10·33 ± 1·97
K_d values; nmol l^{-1}	1·63 (22%)	2·11 (33%)

Groups of eight animals were used.
Values of B_{max} of (D-Pen^2-D-Pen^5)enkephalin (fmol mg^{-1} protein) are presented as mean ± SEM.
Values of K_d (nmol l^{-1}) are presented as mean with percentage coefficient of variation (in parentheses), obtained from simultaneous fitting of the curves by the program LIGAND.

Effect of ageing on the binding characteristics of LHRH receptors in the anterior pituitary and in the testis

Among the other endocrine abnormalities brought about by ageing, it has been shown that the pituitary of old male rats is less responsive than that of young animals to the administration of exogenous LHRH (Miller & Riegle, 1982). It is possible that a change in the concentration or affinity of pituitary receptors for LHRH is responsible for the reduced response of LH to LHRH in aged animals.

LHRH receptors are also present on the membranes of Leydig cells in the rat (Clayton & Catt, 1981) and it has been shown that an 'LHRH-like' peptide is present in the testis; this factor is probably produced by the Sertoli cells, and may influence testosterone secretion from the Leydig cells in a paracrine fashion (Sharpe, 1984). This peptide specifically binds to the testicular LHRH receptors (Sharpe, 1986), which appear to be positively regulated by it (Bourne et al., 1982; Bourne & Marshall, 1984).

To verify whether the process of ageing changes the number or the affinity of LHRH receptors in the pituitary and testis the affinity and concentration of pituitary and testicular LHRH receptors were evaluated in male rats of 3 and 19 months of age, using the LHRH analogue buserelin as a selective ligand. A significant decrease in the number of LHRH receptors occurs in the anterior pituitary of aged male rats (Fig. 5). This provides a likely explanation for the decreased response of LH to the exogenous application of LHRH to the pituitaries of old male rats (Miller & Riegle, 1982), and suggests that the age-linked impairment of LH secretion observed in male rats may be due, at least in part, to a decrease in the number of pituitary LHRH binding sites.

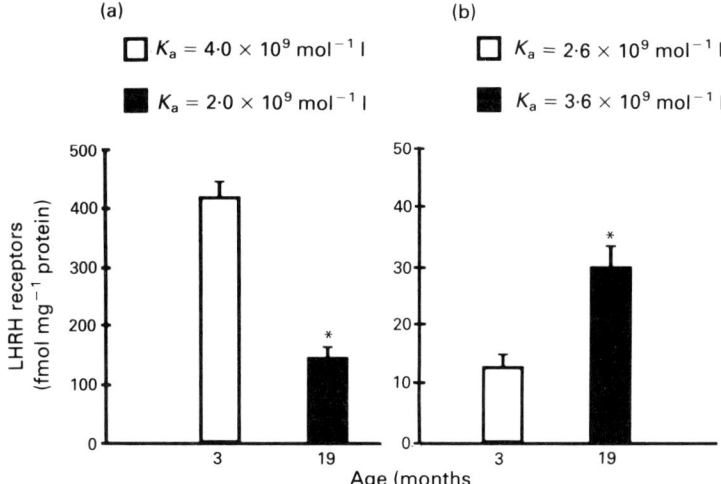

Fig. 5. Effect of ageing on the number of luteinizing-hormone-releasing hormone (LHRH) receptors in (a) the anterior pituitary and (b) the testis of male rats of 3 and 19 months old. Asterisks indicate a significant ($P < 0.05$) difference between 19-month-old rats and 3-month-old rats. Values are means derived from eight tissues from each age group ±SEM.

These data have also shown that the age-induced alteration in testicular function is accompanied by a significant increase in the number of LHRH receptors on the Leydig cells. Because of this, it is possible that the activity of the 'LHRH-like' material present in the testis might be more effective in inhibiting testosterone secretion in old animals. The age-related increase in the concentration of testicular LHRH binding sites reported here might be due either to a primary alteration in the testis, or to events occurring outside the testis. Data from the literature appear to support the latter possibility. Bourne & Marshall (1984) have shown that hypophysectomy induces a significant increase in the number of LHRH receptors on the rat Leydig cells. This increase is completely reversed by subcutaneous injections of LH (Bourne & Marshall, 1984), indicating that the concentration of serum LH may control the number of testicular LHRH receptors, possibly by regulating the synthesis of the 'LHRH-like' peptide originating from the Sertoli cells (Perrin et al., 1980; Bourne & Marshall, 1984). On the basis of these observations, it is possible that in old male rats, the reduction in the amount of LH in the serum leads to an increase in the synthesis of the 'LHRH-like' peptide and, in turn, in the number of LHRH receptors of the Leydig cells. Studies are in progress to test this hypothesis further.

Effect of ageing on the metabolism of testosterone in the hypothalamus and in the anterior pituitary

It is known that, in young animals, a decline in the concentration of testosterone in the serum is usually accompanied by an increase in the amount of serum LH and FSH (Piva et al., 1979). As previously mentioned, castration of old male rats leads to a significantly smaller rise in serum gonadotrophin concentration than that observed in younger animals (Shaar et al., 1975; Pirke et al., 1978; Karpas et al., 1983; Sarkar et al., 1983). However, old male rats exhibit a simultaneous decline in serum LH and testosterone concentrations (Riegle et al., 1977; Bethea & Walker, 1979; Meites, 1982; Miller & Riegle, 1982; Karpas et al., 1983; Kinoshita et al., 1985). On the basis of these findings it has been hypothesized that the feedback mechanisms controlling gonadotrophin secretion are altered in rats with ageing (Shaar et al., 1975; Pirke et al., 1978; Karpas et al., 1983; Sarkar et al., 1983). A recent theory suggests that the feedback effect of testosterone on gonadotrophin secretion is mediated by 5α-androstane-17β-ol-3-one [dihydrotestosterone (DHT)] and by 5α-androstane-3α,17β-diol (3α-diol) – two 5α-reduced metabolites of testosterone that are formed in the anterior pituitary and in the hypothalamus through the action of 5α-reductase and 3α-hydroxysteroid dehydrogenase, respectively (Martini, 1982).

Thus, it was interesting to study the capability of the hypothalamus and of the anterior pituitary of old animals to metabolize testosterone into its 5α-reduced metabolites. The experiments described here were performed *in vitro* using tissues collected from young (3-month-old), old (>20 months old) and old, testosterone-treated animals (testosterone was administered via subcutaneous Silastic capsules). Labelled testosterone was used as the substrate. The hypothalamus of both young and old animals can convert testosterone into DHT and 3α-diol (Fig. 6), DHT being the major metabolite of testosterone at both ages. Treatment of old rats with testosterone does not seem to exert any effect on the metabolism of testosterone in the hypothalamus.

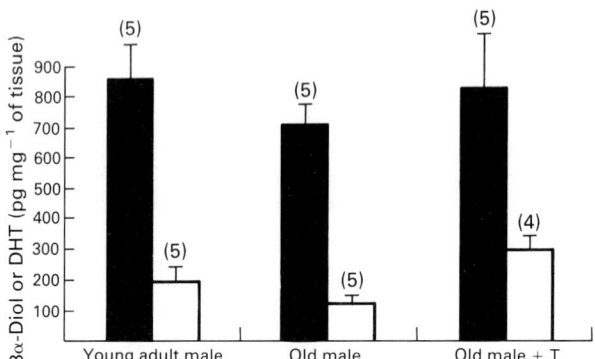

Fig. 6. Effect of ageing on testosterone metabolism in the hypothalamus of male rats. The numbers in parentheses represent the number of experiments performed. Values are the means ± SEM. 3α-Diol: 5α-androstane-3α,17β-diol (□); DHT: dihydrotestosterone (■); T: testosterone.

Figure 7 summarizes the data on metabolism of testosterone in the anterior pituitary of young, old, and old, testosterone-treated animals. It is clear that the pituitary of young animals can convert testosterone into DHT and 3α-diol with considerable yields. In the old animals, the gland retains its capability of metabolizing testosterone into DHT and 3α-diol; however, the yields of DHT are significantly lower than those found in the pituitary of young animals. Treatment of the pituitary with testosterone induces a decrease in the amount of DHT and 3α-diol formed; however, only the decline of DHT was statistically significant. These results show that the enzymes necessary

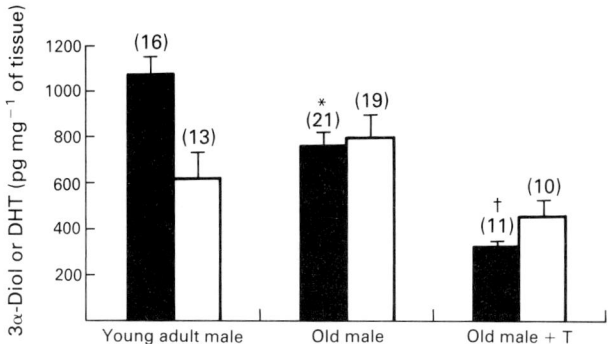

Fig. 7. Effect of ageing on testosterone metabolism in the anterior pituitary of male rats. The numbers in parentheses represent the number of experiments performed. Values are the means ± SEM. *($P < 0.05$) indicates a significant difference between the amount of DHT (dihydrotestosterone) (■) produced in old rats compared with that formed in young rats. †($P < 0.05$) indicates a significant difference compared with old rats. The amounts of 3α-diol (5α-androstane-3α,17β-diol) formed at different ages are indicated (□). T: testosterone.

for metabolizing testosterone via the 5α-reductase pathway are maintained both in the hypothalamus and in the anterior pituitary of aged male rats. However, the 5α-reductase activity of the anterior pituitary of senescent animals appears to be lower than that present in the younger controls.

In agreement with these observations, Marrone & Karavolas (1982) have shown that the anterior pituitary, but not the hypothalamus, of old female rats (18–20 months old) in constant oestrus forms less 5α-dihydroprogesterone when incubated in the presence of labelled progesterone. In further agreement with the results presented here, these authors found that the amounts of 5α-pregnane-3α-ol-20-one (the equivalent of 3α-diol among the 5α-reduced metabolites derived from progesterone) formed by both the pituitary and the hypothalamus do not diminish with advancing age in female animals (Marrone & Karavolas, 1982).

Our data also show that testosterone therapy in old animals does not influence the 5α-reductase activity in the hypothalamus, but decreases the activity of this enzyme in the anterior pituitary – a fact that is consistent with previous findings in young animals (see Martini, 1982 for references).

In the anterior pituitary at least, age induces a clear-cut alteration in a metabolic step that is believed to be crucial for testosterone to exert its feedback activity on gonadotrophin secretion. This finding, while explaining why the feedback mechanisms controlling gonadotrophin release are altered in old animals (Shaar et al., 1975; Pirke et al., 1978; Karpas et al., 1983; Sarkar et al., 1983), does not explain why old male rats should have simultaneously low serum concentrations of testosterone and gonadotrophins (Riegle et al., 1977; Bethea & Walker, 1979; Meites, 1982; Miller & Riegle, 1982; Karpas et al., 1983; Sarkar et al., 1983). If it is accepted that DHT and 3α-diol are the androgenic modulators of gonadotrophin secretion, an increased secretion of LH and FSH should be observed when the formation of these metabolites is decreased – as has been shown to occur in aged animals.

Conclusion

The data presented indicate that the ageing of the male neuroendocrine system is a multifactorial process, which involves the brain (where changes in the number of opioid μ and κ receptors occur), the pituitary (where a decrease in the number of LHRH receptors and a decrease in 5α-reductase activity occur) and the testis (where an increase in the number of LHRH receptors occurs). Surprisingly, in aged animals, the hypothalamus still contains normal amounts of LHRH and can respond almost normally to appropriate stimuli (such as depolarization by K^+); moreover, the ultrashort feedback mechanisms controlling LHRH secretion (which provides a sophisticated and fine-tuning system for controlling the secretion of this hypothalamic hormone) is still operational in old male rats.

The studies reported here have been supported by Consiglio Nazionale delle Ricerche through the Target Projects 'Ageing' (No. 92.00356 PF 40) 'Factors of Disease' (No. 92.00142 PF 41) and through contract No. 92.02684 CT 04, and by funds from the Ministry for the University. Thanks are also due to P. Assi for her skilful technical assistance.

References

Bethea, C.L. & Walker, R.F. (1979) Age-related changes in reproductive hormones and Leydig cell responsivity in the male Fischer 344 rat. *Journal of Gerontology* **34**, 21–27.

Bourne, G.A. & Marshall, J.C. (1984) Anterior pituitary hormonal regulation of testicular gonadotropin-releasing hormone receptors. *Endocrinology* **115**, 723–727.

Bourne, G.A., Dockrill, M.R., Regiani, S., Marshall, J.C. & Payne, A.H. (1982) Induction of testicular gonadotropin-releasing hormone (GnRH) receptors by GnRH: effects of pituitary hormones and relationship to inhibition of testosterone production. *Endocrinology* **110**, 727–733.

Clayton, R.N. & Catt, K.J. (1981) Gonadotropin-releasing hormone receptors: characterization, physiological regulation and relationship to reproductive function. *Endocrine Reviews* **2**, 186–209.

Dondi, D., Maggi, R., Limonta, P., Martini, L. & Piva, F. (1992) Binding characteristics of delta opioid receptors in different regions of the brain of young and old male rats as studied with the highly selective ligand (D-Pen^2-D-Pen^5) enkephalin. *Aging* **4**, 89–95.

Gabriel, S.M., Simpkins, J.W. & Kalra, S.P. (1983) Modulation of endogenous opioid influence on luteinizing hormone secretion by progesterone and estrogen. *Endocrinology* **113**, 1806–1811.

Gulya, K., Gehlert, D.R., Wamsley, J.K., Mosberg, H., Hruby, V.J. & Yamamura, N.I. (1986) Light microscopic autoradiographic localization of delta opioid receptors in the rat brain using a highly selective bis-penicillamine enkephalin analog. *Journal of Pharmacology and Experimental Therapeutics* **238**, 720–726.

Kalra, P.S. & Kalra, S.P. (1980) Modulation of hypothalamic LHRH levels by intracranial and subcutaneous implants of gonadal steroids in castrated rats: effect of androgen and estrogen antagonists. *Endocrinology* **106**, 390–397.

Karpas, A.E., Bremner, W.J., Clifton, D.K., Steiner, R.A. & Dorsa, D.M. (1983) Diminished luteinizing hormone pulse frequency and amplitude with aging in the male rat. *Endocrinology* **112**, 788–792.

Katakami, H., Arimura, A. & Frohman, L.A. (1986) Growth hormone (GH)-releasing factor stimulates hypothalamic somatostatin release: an inhibitory feedback effect on GH secretion. *Endocrinology* **118**, 1872–1877.

Kinoshita, Y., Hiashi, Y., Winters, S.J., Oshima, H. & Troen, P. (1985) An analysis of the age-related decline in testicular steroidogenesis in the rat. *Biology of Reproduction* **32**, 309–314.

Lumpkin, M.D., Samson, W.K. & McCann, S.M. (1985) Effects of intraventricular growth hormone-releasing factor on growth hormone release: further evidence for ultrashort-loop feedback. *Endocrinology* **116**, 2070–2074.

Maggi, R., Limonta, P., Dondi, D., Martini, L. & Piva, F. (1989) Distribution of κ opioid receptors in the brain of young and old male rats. *Life Sciences* **45**, 2085–2092.

Mansour, A., Khachaturian, H., Lewis, M.E., Akil, H. & Watson, S.J. (1987) Autoradiographic differentiation of μ, δ and κ opioid receptors in the rat forebrain and midbrain. *Journal of Neurosciences* **7**, 2445–2464.

Marrone, B.L. & Karavolas, H.Y. (1982) Progesterone metabolism by the hypothalamus, pituitary, and uterus of the aged rat. *Endocrinology* **111**, 162–167.

Martini, L. (1982) The 5α-reduction of testosterone in the neuroendocrine structures. Biochemical and physiological implications. *Endocrine Reviews* **3**, 1–25.

Meites, J. (1982) Changes in neuroendocrine control of anterior pituitary function during aging. *Neuroendocrinology* **34**, 151–156.

Messi, E., Zanisi, M. & Martini, L. (1990) Ageing does not influence the ultrashort feedback control of GnRH secretion *in vitro*. *Acta Endocrinologica* **122**, 329–335.

Messing, R.B., Vasquez, B., Samaniego, B., Jensen, R.A., Martinez, J.L., Jr & McCaugh, J.L. (1981) Alterations of dihydromorphine binding in cerebral hemispheres of aged male rats. *Journal of Neurochemistry* **36**, 784–787.

Miller, A.E. & Riegle, G.D. (1982) Temporal patterns of serum luteinizing hormone and testosterone and endocrine response to luteinizing hormone releasing hormone in aging male rats. *Journal of Gerontology* **37**, 522–528.

Paterson, S.J., Robertson, L.E. & Kosterlitz, H.V. (1983) Classification of opioid receptors. *British Medical Bulletin* **39**, 31–36.

Perrin, M.H., Vaughan, J.M., Rivier, J.E. & Vale, W.W. (1980) High affinity GnRH binding to testicular membrane homogenates. *Life Sciences* **26**, 2251–2255.

Pfeiffer, D.G., Pfeiffer, A., Shimohigashi, Y., Merriam, G.R. & Loriaux, D.L. (1983) Predominant involvement of μ- rather than δ- or κ- opiate receptors in LH secretion. *Peptides* **4**, 647–649.

Pirke, K.M., Geiss, M. & Sintermann, R. (1978) A quantitative study on feedback control of LH by testosterone in young adult and old male rats. *Acta Endocrinologica* **89**, 789–795.

Piva, F., Motta, M. & Martini, L. (1979) Regulation of hypothalamic and pituitary function: long, short and ultrashort feedback loops. In *Endocrinology* (Vol. 1), pp. 21–33. Ed. L. J. De Groot. Grune and Stratton, New York.

Piva, F., Borrell, J., Limonta, P., Gavazzi, G. & Martini, L. (1980) Cholinergic inputs to the amygdala and the control of gonadotrophin release. *Acta Endocrinologica* **93**, 1–6.

Piva, F., Maggi, R., Limonta, P., Motta, M. & Martini, L. (1985) Effect of naloxone on luteinizing hormone, follicle stimulating hormone and prolactin secretion in the different phases of the estrous cycle. *Endocrinology* **117**, 766–772.

Piva, F., Maggi, R., Limonta, P., Dondi, D. & Martini, L. (1987) Decrease of μ opioid receptors in the brain and in the hypothalamus of the aged male rat. *Life Sciences* **40**, 391–398.

Riegle, G.D., Meites, J., Miller, A.E. & Wood, S.M. (1977) Effect of aging on hypothalamic LH-releasing and prolactin inhibiting activities and pituitary responsiveness to LHRH in the male laboratory rat. *Journal of Gerontology* **32**, 13–18.

Sarkar, D.K., Miki, N. & Meites, J. (1983) Failure of prolactin short loop feedback mechanism to operate in old as compared to young female rats. *Endocrinology* **113**, 1452–1458.

Shaar, J., Euker, J.S., Riegle, G.D. & Meites, J. (1975) Effects of castration and gonadal steroids on serum luteinizing hormone and prolactin in old and young rats. *Journal of Endocrinology* **66**, 45–51.

Sharif, N.A. & Hughes, J. (1989) Discrete mapping of brain μ and δ opioid receptors using selective peptides: quantitative autoradiography, species differences and comparison with κ receptors. *Peptides* **10**, 499–522.

Sharpe, R.M. (1984) Intratesticular factors controlling testicular function. *Biology of Reproduction* **30**, 29–49.

Sharpe, R.M. (1986) Paracrine control of the testis. *Clinical Endocrinology and Metabolism* **15**, 185–207.

Shin, S.G. & Howitt, C.J. (1975) Effect of castration on LH and LHRH in the male rat. *Journal of Endocrinology* **65**, 447–450.

Simpkins, J.W., Mueller, G.P., Huang, H.H. & Meites, J. (1977) Evidence for a depressed catecholamine and enhanced serotonin metabolism in aging male rats: possible relation to gonadotropin secretion. *Endocrinology* **100**, 1672–1678.

Sirinathsinghji, D.J.S., Motta, M. & Martini, L. (1985) Induction of precocious puberty in the female rat after chronic naloxone administered during the neonatal period: the opiate 'brake' on prepubertal gonadotrophin secretion. *Journal of Endocrinology* **104**, 299–307.

Steiner, R.A., Bremner, W.J., Clifton, D.K. & Dorsa, D.M. (1984) Reduced pulsatile luteinizing hormone and testosterone secretion with aging in the male rat. *Biology of Reproduction* **31**, 251–258.

Zanisi, M., Messi, E. & Martini, L. (1987a) In vitro release of luteinizing hormone-releasing hormone from the hypothalamus of old male rats. *Endocrinology* **120**, 49–54.

Zanisi, M., Messi, E. & Martini, L. (1987b) Ultrashort feedback control of luteinizing hormone-releasing hormone secretion *in vitro*. *Endocrinology* **121**, 2199–2204.

Premature ageing in transgenic mice expressing different growth hormone genes

R. W. Steger, A. Bartke and M. Cecim

Department of Physiology, Southern Illinois University School of Medicine, Carbondale, IL 62901, USA

Summary. Transgenic mice expressing various growth hormone genes have markedly reduced life spans, with few animals surviving beyond 12 months in some of the lines. Except for an increased incidence of mammary tumours in female mice expressing human growth hormones, pathological findings in debilitated or moribund transgenic mice resemble the well-documented degenerative changes that occur at a much greater chronological age in normal rodents. This study demonstrates that 10-month-old male transgenic mice expressing bovine growth hormone (known as 25-copy PEPCK . bGH transgenic mice) also show age-related changes in hypothalamic and striatal neurotransmitter metabolism that are not seen in normal litter mate controls until at least 24 months of age. Female mice and male mice with a lower circulating concentration of bGH (known as 5-copy PEPCK . bGH transgenic mice) live longer and fail to show the same magnitude of change in neurotransmitter synthesis and release. Although more work needs to be done to determine the physiological significance of these changes and to determine their relationship to the general effects of ageing on the CNS, transgenic mice expressing various growth hormone genes may provide an interesting and valuable model with which to study the ageing process.

Keywords: ageing; growth hormone; hypothalamus; dopamine; transgenic mice

Introduction

Rodents are popular animal models for studies of ageing because of their short life span. However, even these relatively short-living mammals generally live 2–3 years, which translates into enormous cost and logistic problems in their procurement, maintenance and experimentation. During studies of neuroendocrine and reproductive functions in transgenic mice expressing various growth hormone (GH) genes, it has been noted that the life span of these animals is greatly reduced, with only a few surviving beyond 12 months of age in some of the lines. This seemed to suggest that transgenic animals with a chronic excess of GH might provide a novel and convenient model for the study of some aspects of ageing.

In the case of females expressing human GH (hGH) or hGH variant (hGH . var) genes, early mortality is largely due to development of mammary tumours and this represents a phenomenon that may be specific to mice, or even to mice of this particular genetic background (C57BL/6J × C3H/J, with the C3H strain being susceptible to mammary tumours). However, in males from the same lines and in animals from different lines (in which the life span is even shorter), no abnormalities that might be unique to rodents chronically exposed to an excess of GH were observed. Indeed, pathological findings in debilitated or moribund transgenic mice suggested that glomerulonephritis is the most common cause of death (Cecim, M. and Bartke, A., unpublished), and this resembles the well-documented degenerative changes that occur at a much later stage in normal rodents.

In ongoing studies of reproductive function in these animals, it has been noted that young (2–3 months old) transgenic females exhibit regular ovarian cycles, but females in most of the lines begin to lose cyclicity and apparently become anovulatory as early as 2 months later. Two-month-old males are generally fertile, except for approximately 50% of the males of genotype MT . hGH . var, which express the hGH . var genes driven by the mouse metallothionein-1 (MT-1) promoter and which do not breed. However, starting at 4 months of age, an increasing proportion of males become sterile. This is almost certainly due to deficits in sexual behaviour and erectile mechanisms (Bartke et al., 1991; Keller, P., Mayerhofer, A. and Bartke, A., unpublished).

The above observations, although preliminary in nature, are quite striking. Decline in reproduction function and behaviour in the mouse usually develops much later, namely in the second year of life (Nelson et al., 1982; Felicio et al., 1984; Finch et al., 1984; Parkening, 1989), while normal animals between 4 and 6 months old are at the prime age for breeding. Moreover, age-related reproductive deficits in the normal male are due primarily, if not exclusively, to increased incidence of disease and to the general decline in body functions (Craigen & Bronson, 1982), while in transgenic animals they develop during the period when the animals are young, actively growing, and apparently thriving in every other respect.

The evidence for dependence of virtually every aspect of reproductive function on the CNS will not be reviewed here. Although the possible involvement of peripheral (e.g. pituitary, ovarian and penile) mechanisms in the observed premature reproductive ageing in transgenic mice from these lines has to be considered, these changes almost certainly represent consequences of abnormal function of specific neuronal groups in the brain – most likely, the hypothalamus. Major abnormalities of both noradrenergic and dopaminergic transmission have consistently been found in the hypothalamus of transgenic mice (Bartke et al., 1988, 1990; Steger et al., 1990, 1991). These findings are intriguing because decline of catecholamine function is an established correlate of CNS ageing in rodents (Morgan et al., 1987; Meites, 1990). Moreover, Flood & Morley (1990) recently reported that the noradrenergic system appears to play a role in the age-related decline of memory in mice. The objective of our studies was therefore to elucidate age-related alterations in hypothalamic neurotransmitter metabolism that might be responsible for the premature loss of reproductive function in mice expressing various GH transgenes.

Materials and Methods

Transgenic mice used in this study were derived from transgenic males generously provided by Dr Thomas Wagner and June Yun of the Edison Biotechnology Centre, Athens, OH, USA. To produce the founder animals of the various lines a mouse metallothionein-1 (MT-1) promoter–regulatory region of approximately 700 bp (KPn1–Bgl11 fragment), or a region of the phosphoenolpyruvate carboxykinase (PEPCK) promoter either 460 or 2000 bp long was ligated to entire hGH, bGH or hGH . var structural genes at the Bam H1 site, and multiple copies of the resulting DNA constructs were then injected into male pronuclei of recently fertilized ova of F1 hybrid mice (Wagner et al., 1981; McGrane et al., 1988; Selden et al., 1988, 1989). As expected from the known properties of these promoters, the transgenes were expressed in multiple organs with most of the foreign GH in the peripheral circulation being derived presumably from hepatic and renal synthesis and, in the case of the MT-1 promoter, also from intestinal and dermal synthesis. Each of the lines used in these studies was derived from a single founder animal. The lines were propagated by mating transgenic males with C57BL/6J × C3H/J F1 hybrid females purchased from the Jackson Laboratory, Bar Harbor, ME. Animals used in this study were housed four or five per cage after they were weaned in a temperature-controlled (22 ± 2°C) room on a 12 h:12 h light:dark cycle (lights on at 07:00 h). Food (TekLad, Harlan Sprague-Dawley, Madison, WI, USA) and tap water were provided ad libitum. Some characteristics of transgenic animals from the various lines, including average life span, are summarized in Table 1.

For the studies described here, young (3–4 month old) and old (8–11 month old) transgenic mice and their normal (non-transgenic) siblings were used. An additional group of very old (>24 month) normal male mice was also used. To avoid fluctuations related to the oestrous cycle in the analysis of hypothalamic–pituitary function, the females were bilaterally ovariectomized 8 days before sample collection. Ovariectomies were carried out under ether anaesthesia through bilateral flank incisions. Some of the data for young transgenic mice have been published (Steger et al., 1991; Bartke et al., 1992) and are provided for comparative purposes.

Table 1. Some characteristics of the various lines of transgenic mice currently maintained in our breeding colony

Mouse promoter used	Structural gene inserted	No. of copies	Heterologous GH (ng ml^{-1})	Life span (months) Males	Life span (months) Females
mMT-1	hGH	1	~10	13–17	9–14
PEPCK	hGH	1	~450	7–10	5–9
mMT-1	hGH.var	1	nd	13–17	9–14
mMT-1	bGH	1	~90	24+	18+
PEPCK	bGH	1	>2000	8–10	7–10
PEPCK	bGH	5	>2000	10–12	7–10
PEPCK	bGH	25	>2000	8–10	7–10
Normal	n/a	n/a	0	25–35	20–30

Although in some of the lines, the life span data are based on a limited number of observations, this characteristic is consistent within a line.

bGH: bovine growth hormone; hGH: human growth hormone; hGH.var: human growth hormone variant genes; mMT-1: mouse metallothionein-1; n/a: not applicable; nd: not determined (since radioimmunoassay is not available for hGH.var); PEPCK: phosphoenolpyruvate carboxykinase.

Sixty minutes before they were killed, half of the mice in some experiments were injected with the tyrosine hydroxylase inhibitor α-methyl-*p*-tyrosine (αMPT; 250 mg kg^{-1} body weight, i.p.) for determination of catecholamine turnover rates in defined brain regions. The turnover rate provides an estimate of neurotransmitter release (Steger *et al.*, 1983). In other experiments, mice were injected with the aromatic amino acid decarboxylase inhibitor 3-hydroxybenzylhydrazine (NSD-1015, 100 mg kg^{-1}, i.p.) 40 min before they were killed to determine L-dihydroxyphenylalanine (DOPA) and 5-hydroxytryptophan (5-HTP) accumulation. Measurements of DOPA and 5-HTP accumulation provide an estimate of catecholamine and 5-HT synthetic rates that under steady-state conditions should be proportional to transmitter release. Immediately before the mice were killed by decapitation, they were anaesthetized with ether, and blood was collected by cardiac puncture. EDTA was used as an anticoagulant and plasma was harvested and stored frozen until assayed for luteinizing hormone and, in some cases, for heterologous GH. All mice were killed between 08:00 and 10:00 h. At the time of autopsy, the brain was quickly removed and the median eminence was dissected free and frozen. The remaining brain was rapidly frozen on dry ice for subsequent dissection and preparation for amine analysis.

Before the assay, the brains were partially thawed, and the medial basal hypothalamus and anterior hypothalamus were dissected free as previously described (Steger *et al.*, 1983; Steger *et al.*, 1990). The striatum was also removed in some experiments. The medial basal hypothalamus, anterior hypothalamus and striatum were weighed and then sonicated in HClO$_4$ (0·1 mol l^{-1}), which contained the internal standards for the catecholamine assay (dihydroxybenzylamine) and the 5-HT assay (methyl 5-HT), and sodium bisulfite (1 mmol l^{-1}). The median eminence was sonicated in the same solution but without the methyl 5-HT. Median eminence, medial basal hypothalamus, anterior hypothalamus and striatum supernatants were subjected to alumina extraction and high-performance liquid chromatography. Noradrenaline and dopamine were measured by electrochemical detection as previously described (Steger *et al.*, 1983). Concentrations of 5-HT and 5-hydroxyindole acetic acid (5-HIAA) were determined in unextracted tissue homogenates using high-performance liquid chromatography with electrochemical detection according to previously described procedures (Steger *et al.*, 1983). Catecholamine turnover rates were estimated using the formula $K = k[CA]_0$, where $[CA]_0$ equals the mean catecholamine concentration at zero time (non-injected controls), and the rate constant k represents the $-$log of the slope of the line describing the decline of noradrenaline or dopamine concentration during the 1 h after the blockade of tyrosine hydroxylase with αMPT (Brodie, 1966; Steger *et al.*, 1983). Tissues from animals treated with NSD-1015 were also sonicated in HClO$_4$ (0·1 mol l^{-1}) containing dihydroxybenzylamine. Noradrenaline, DOPA, dopamine, 5-HTP, 5-HT and 5-HIAA were separated by high-performance liquid chromatography and quantitated with an electrochemical detector. Since the enzyme for the decarboxylation of 5-HTP to form 5-HT (or DOPA to form dopamine) has a low Michaelis-Menten constant (K_m) and high velocity relative to the hydroxylation of tryptophan to form 5-HTP (or tyrosine to form DOPA), the rate of 5-HT (or DOPA) synthesis may be considered to be equal to the amount of 5-HTP (or DOPA) formed per unit time after decarboxylase inhibition with NSD-1015 (King *et al.*, 1985).

Plasma amounts of luteinizing hormone were measured by radioimmunoassay using reagents provided by the National Institute of Digestive Diabetic and Kidney Disorders (NIDDK) as described previously (Bartke *et al.*, 1987). Plasma levels of bGH were measured using an antiserum to ovine GH, and ovine GH was used both for iodination and for the standard. Reagents for this assay were also provided by the NIDDK and Dr A. Parlow (UCLA Harvard Medical School, Torrance, CA, USA).

The effects of age and transgene expression on hormone concentrations and neurotransmitter content and turnover were evaluated using analysis of variance or Student's *t* test. Differences between the mean values for the various groups were considered significant when $P < 0.05$.

Results

Male mice

Normal control males. In the normal (non-transgenic) control mice, body mass increased significantly between 3 and 12 months of age but no further increase was seen between 12 and 24 months (Table 2). However, it was not determined if this lack of difference reflected lack of weight gain during this time or a weight gain followed by a weight loss as the mice approached the end of their life span. The masses of the seminal vesicles, adrenals, liver, kidneys and spleen increased with advancing age whereas the anterior pituitary and the testes remained at a constant mass (Table 2).

Indices of neurotransmitter metabolism, including content and turnover or intermediate metabolite accumulation after decarboxylase inhibition, did not differ between young (3–4 month) and old (10–12 month) animals in any of the brain areas examined. However, in normal male mice over 24 months of age, dopamine turnover in the median eminence and striatum and noradrenaline turnover in the median eminence were significantly depressed in comparison to the controls, which were 3 and 12 months old. Data for the normal control animals are presented below along with the results for the various lines of transgenic male mice.

25-copy PEPCK . bGH males. Intact 25-copy PEPCK . bGH mice showed a significant increase in body mass between 3 and 10 months of age (Table 2). The masses of the seminal vesicles and spleen increased significantly during this time. The masses of the pituitary, adrenals, liver and kidneys also increased numerically but not significantly during this time. The testes showed no increase in mass.

The plasma concentration of bGH in the transgenic mice did not change with age (3051 ± 311 ng ml^{-1} compared with 2913 ± 529 ng ml^{-1}). Bovine GH was undetectable in the plasma of control mice. The concentration of luteinizing hormone in the plasma was slightly reduced in young 25-copy PEPCK . bGH mice compared with young controls (Fig. 1). Plasma amounts of luteinizing hormone increased slightly but not significantly between 3 and 11 months of age in the transgenic mice.

Dopamine content was unchanged with age in either the median eminence or striatum in either control or transgenic mice (Fig. 2). DOPA accumulation after decarboxylase inhibition shows an age-related reduction in the median eminence and the striatum of the 25-copy PEPCK . bGH mice. Dopamine turnover in these two areas was also reduced with age in the transgenic mice and although striatal dopamine turnover was not measured in young transgenic mice, striatal dopamine turnover was four times lower in the 10-month-old transgenic mice than in normal animals of the same age. Dopamine content, DOPA accumulation and dopamine turnover in the medial basal hypothalamus of the 25-copy PEPCK . bGH mice were not affected by age (data not shown).

The amount of noradrenaline in the median eminence remained constant during the age interval examined, but the transgenic animals exhibited a significant decline in noradrenaline turnover (Fig. 3). Neither noradrenaline content nor turnover in the medial basal hypothalamus were affected by age.

Synthesis of 5-HT, as reflected by 5-HTP accumulation, decreased significantly with age in the median eminence of 25-copy PEPCK . bGH mice (Fig. 4). This change was reflected in a slight but nonsignificant drop in 5-HT content. The level of synthesis and content of 5-HT tended to rise with age in the medial basal hypothalamus of transgenic mice, but neither of these apparent increases proved significant.

5-copy PEPCK . bGH males. Intact 5-copy PEPCK . bGH mice also increased in body mass between 4 and 10–12 months of age (Table 2), as did animals with 25 copies of the same hybrid gene. The amount of luteinizing hormone in the plasma tended to decrease with age in these mice but the difference did not prove to be significant (0.81 ± 0.12 ng ml^{-1} versus 0.55 ± 0.16 ng ml^{-1}; $P < 0.10$). In contrast with age-related changes in the accumulation of DOPA in the median

Table 2. Effects of advancing age on body and selected organ masses of male mice expressing various GH transgenes

Mouse promoter used	Structural gene inserted	No. of copies	Body mass (g)	Anterior pituitary (mg)	Testes (g)	Seminal vesicles (g)	Adrenal (mg)	Liver (g)	Kidney (g)	Spleen (g)
mMT-1	hGH	1								
Young (14)[a]			56·5 ± 2·3	0·72 ± 0·16	0·33 ± 0·01	0·62 ± 0·09	nd	3·08 ± 0·27	0·74 ± 0·06	0·15 ± 0·01
Old (10)			59·9 ± 2·7	1·56 ± 0·20	0·29 ± 0·02	2·12 ± 0·52*	7·31 ± 1·09	3·97 ± 0·34	0·93 ± 0·07	0·28 ± 0·04
mMT-1	hGH . var	1								
Young (12)[a]			58·0 ± 2·0	0·99 ± 0·08	0·25 ± 0·02	0·59 ± 0·047	nd	4·05 ± 0·30	0·99 ± 0·06	0·27 ± 0·04
Old (6)			58·0 ± 2·4	1·41 ± 0·13	0·26 ± 0·02	1·90 ± 0·56*	18·74 ± 3·43	4·56 ± 0·36	0·99 ± 0·02	0·26 ± 0·02
mMT-1	bGH	1								
Young (7)[a]			53·2 ± 2·0	0·75 ± 0·07	0·28 ± 0·01	0·53 ± 0·05	nd	3·56 ± 0·27	0·76 ± 0·04	0·16 ± 0·02
Old (3)			53·0 ± 4·7	1·63 ± 0·25	0·23 ± 0·04	0·73 ± 0·02*	12·6 ± 2·59	3·26 ± 0·55	0·77 ± 0·14	0·21 ± 0·04
PEPCK	bGH	1								
Young (17)			50·1 ± 0·8	1·15 ± 0·07	0·36 ± 0·09	0·25 ± 0·02	7·21 ± 0·59	3·98 ± 0·11	0·86 ± 0·03	0·23 ± 0·01
Old (15)			60·5 ± 1·2*	1·37 ± 0·18	0·26 ± 0·03	0·35 ± 0·04*	7·98 ± 0·53	4·69 ± 0·21*	1·08 ± 0·06*	0·28 ± 0·03
PEPCK	bGH	5								
Young (6)			51·2 ± 3·0	1·54 ± 0·09	0·23 ± 0·02	0·31 ± 0·02	8·47 ± 0·64	nd	nd	nd
Old (17)			58·9 ± 1·20*	1·20 ± 0·08*	0·24 ± 0·01	0·38 ± 0·04	9·24 ± 0·57	4·43 ± 0·25	1·10 ± 0·06	0·31 ± 0·02
PEPCK	bGH	25								
Young (10)			52·5 ± 1·2	1·32 ± 0·09	0·24 ± 0·01	0·32 ± 0·02	6·41 ± 0·90	4·16 ± 0·22	0·89 ± 0·05	0·22 ± 0·02
Old (16)			62·7 ± 1·9*	1·58 ± 0·12	0·24 ± 0·01	0·41 ± 0·02*	7·97 ± 0·69	5·04 ± 0·29	1·03 ± 0·06	0·35 ± 0·05*
Normal	n/a	n/a								
Young (21)			30·1 ± 0·6	1·41 ± 0·04	0·21 ± 0·01	0·22 ± 0·08	5·38 ± 0·51	1·44 ± 0·07	0·47 ± 0·02	0·08 ± 0·00
Old (63)			41·1 ± 0·9*	1·54 ± 0·04	0·22 ± 0·01	0·31 ± 0·01*	5·43 ± 0·27	1·95 ± 0·08*	0·64 ± 0·06*	0·12 ± 0·01*
>24 months (15)			43·4 ± 1·4	1·41 ± 0·09	0·20 ± 0·01	0·56 ± 0·06*	7·90 ± 1·19*	2·35 ± 0·31	0·99 ± 0·13	nd

Values are reported as mean ± SEM. The number of mice in each group is reported in the first column. Young mice are 3–4 months old, old mice are 8–11 months old, and very old mice are >24 months old.
Asterisks denote statistical difference between young and old mice ($P < 0.05$).
[a] Some data previously published in Steger et al., 1991 or in Bartke et al., 1992.
bGH: bovine growth hormone; hGH: human growth hormone; hGH . var: human growth hormone variant genes; mMT-1: mouse metallothionein-1; n/a: not applicable; nd: not determined; PEPCK: phosphoenolpyruvate carboxykinase.

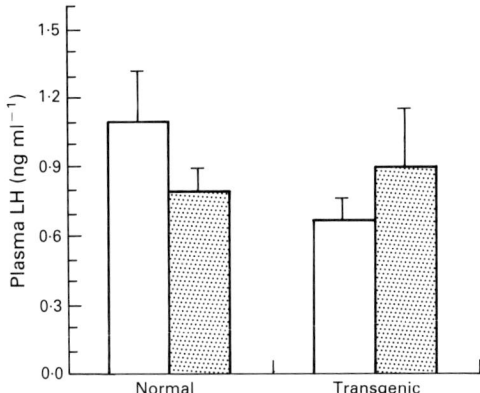

Fig. 1. The effects of advancing age on the plasma concentration of luteinizing hormone (LH) in intact male 25-copy PEPCK.bGH mice (transgenic) and their non-transgenic litter mates (normal). Animals were 3 months (young) (□) or 10 months (old) (▨) of age. Values represent the mean ± SEM of 5–6 mice per group. bGH: bovine growth hormone; PEPCK: phosphoenolpyruvate carboxykinase.

eminence and striatum as seen in the intact 25-copy PEPCK.bGH mice, no significant changes in DOPA accumulation were observed in the 5-copy PEPCK.bGH males (Fig. 5). Similarly, dopamine turnover in the median eminence and striatum did not vary significantly between the young and old transgenic mice (data not shown). The 5-copy PEPCK.bGH mice also did not show the decrement in 5-HTP accumulation in the median eminence that was seen in the 25-copy PEPCK.bGH mice.

MT.hGH males. Dopamine turnover in the median eminence was markedly reduced in 10-month-old MT.hGH male mice compared with 3-month-old mice (Fig. 6). Despite this decrease in dopamine turnover, noradrenaline turnover in the median eminence did not decline with age. As noted previously (Bartke *et al.*, 1991, 1992) there was a very prominent age-related increase in seminal vesicle mass in these mice (Table 2).

Female mice

Normal ovariectomized control females. In the normal (non-transgenic) control mice, body mass increased significantly between 3 and 12 months of age (Table 3). Increases in uterine (8 days after ovariectomy), adrenal and kidney masses were also observed (Table 3). Indices of neurotransmitter metabolism including content and turnover or intermediate metabolite accumulation after decarboxylase inhibition did not differ between young (3–4 month) and old (10–12 month) non-transgenic controls in any of the brain areas examined (Tables 4, 5).

25-copy PEPCK.bGH ovariectomized females. Body mass was significantly greater in the old than in the young transgenic mice from this line (Table 3). There appeared to be no age-related atrophy of the uterus, adrenal, liver, kidney or spleen based on organ mass. However, the tissues from these animals have not been subject to examination under the microscope.

Plasma concentration of bGH in the transgenic mice did not change with age (2472 ± 236 ng ml^{-1} versus 1996 ± 723 ng ml^{-1}). Bovine GH was undetectable in the plasma of control mice. Plasma concentrations of luteinizing hormone in control and transgenic females appeared to decline with age but these apparent differences were not significant (data not shown). There were no age-related differences in catecholamine content or DOPA accumulation in the median eminence, medial basal hypothalamus or striatum (Table 4). Advancing age in the female mice was also without effect on median eminence or medial basal hypothalamic 5-HT content or 5-HTP accumulation (Table 5).

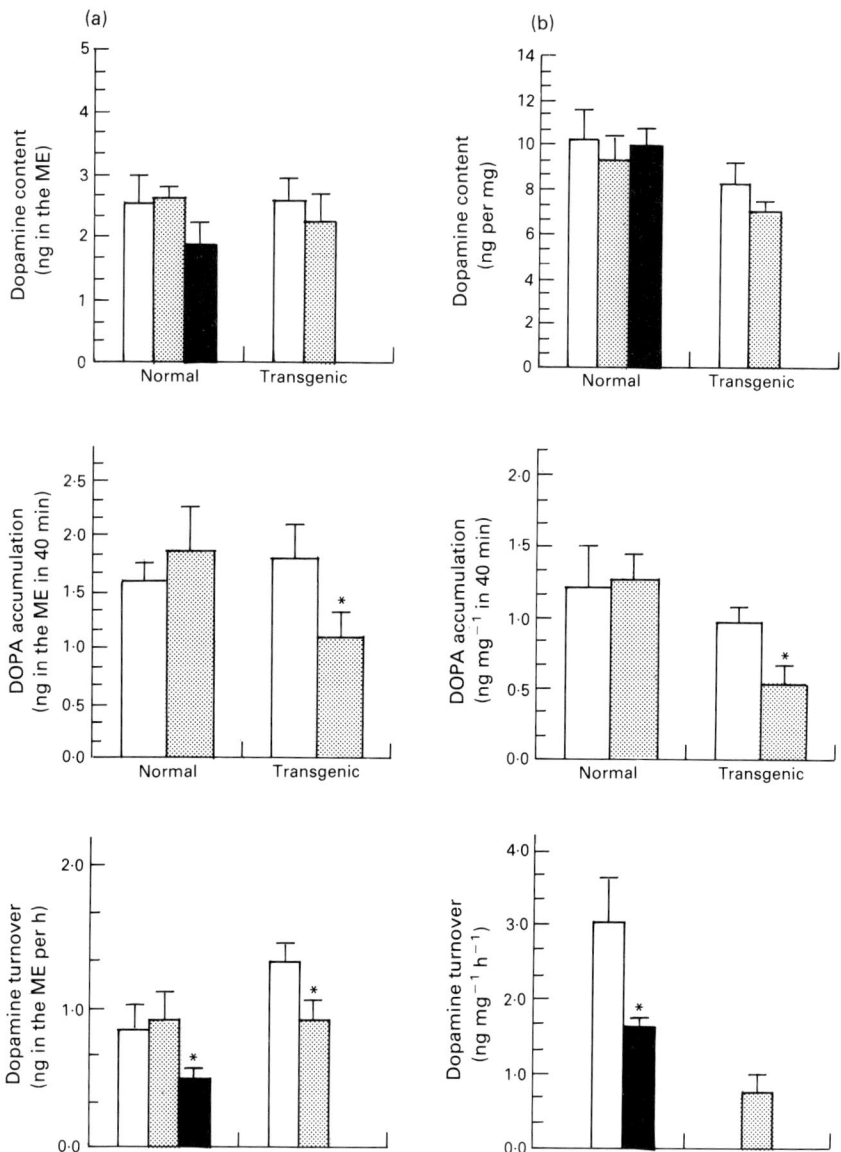

Fig. 2. The effects of age on several indices of dopaminergic neurone function in (a) the median eminence (ME) and (b) the striatum of intact male 25-copy PEPCK . bGH mice (transgenic) and their non-transgenic litter mates (normal). Animals were 3 months (young) (□), 10 months (old) (▩) or >24 months (very old) (■) of age. The accumulation of L-dihydroxyphenylalanine (DOPA), an index of dopamine synthesis, was measured during the 40 min after inhibition of aromatic amino acid decarboxylase with 3-hydroxybenzylhydrazine (NSD-1015). Dopamine turnover, an index of dopamine release, was calculated from the decline in dopamine content after inhibition of dopamine synthesis with α-methyl-p-tyrosine. Dopamine turnover and DOPA accumulation were measured in separate groups of animals. Values represent the mean ± SEM of 5–10 mice per group. Asterisks denote statistical difference from values for young mice ($P < 0.05$). bGH: bovine growth hormone; PEPCK: phosphoenolpyruvate carboxykinase.

Other lines of ovariectomized transgenic females. Body mass also increased with age in the MT . hGH . var and in the PEPCK . hGH female mice (Table 3). Uterine, adrenal, liver, kidney and

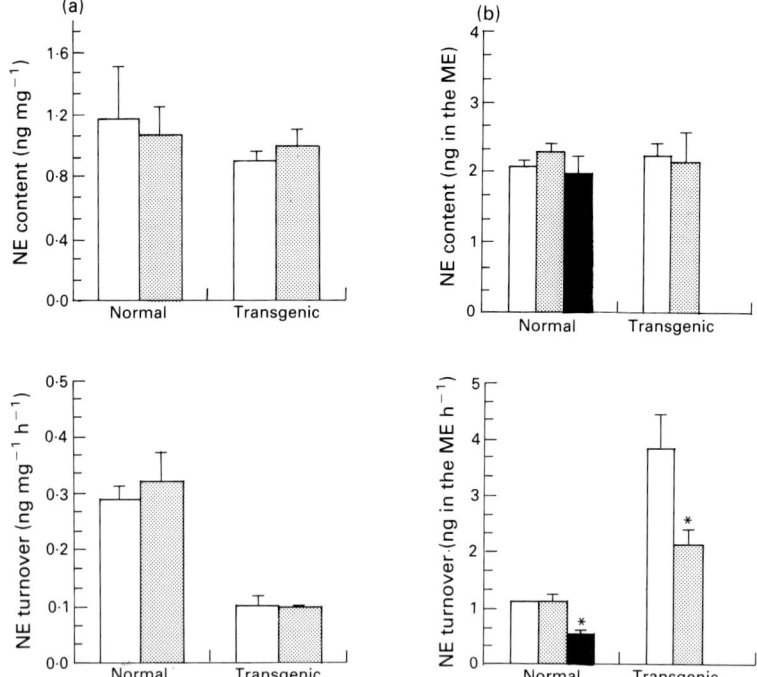

Fig. 3. (a) Medial basal hypothalamic and (b) median eminence (ME) noradrenaline content and turnover in male 25-copy PEPCK . bGH mice (transgenic) and their non-transgenic litter mates (normal). Animals were 3 months old (young) (□), 10 months old (old) (▨) or >24 months old (very old) (■). These animals had already been tested for dopaminergic neurone function (see Fig. 2). Noradrenaline (NE) turnover, an index of noradrenaline release, was calculated from the decline in noradrenaline content after inhibition of noradrenaline synthesis with α-methyl-*p*-tyrosine. Values represent the mean ± SEM of 5–10 mice per group. Asterisks denote statistical difference from values for young mice ($P < 0.05$). bGH: bovine growth hormone; PEPCK: phosphoenolpyruvate carboxykinase.

spleen mass all tended to increase with age in both of these lines. Body and organ mass for young ovariectomized mice of the other lines were not recorded but the masses of the old animals are provided to compare size differences between the lines.

Discussion

The results of this study demonstrate that transgenic mice expressing the bGH transgene show age-related changes in CNS neurotransmitter metabolism that are not seen in age-matched, non-transgenic controls. However, they resemble the changes that occur in normal mice at a much later age. Furthermore, the magnitude of these changes is affected by the promoter used to express the foreign gene, the number of foreign gene copies incorporated, the concentration of GH in the plasma and the sex of the animal.

Because of the early loss of fertility in various lines of bGH transgenic mice, it was expected that the concentration of luteinizing hormone in the plasma might be reduced and that such changes might be secondary to changes in hypothalamic catecholamine metabolism, as has been demonstrated in the rat (Simpkins *et al.*, 1977; Wise *et al.*, 1985; Steger *et al.*, 1987a). Measurements of luteinizing hormone in the plasma made during this study and preliminary data from other transgenic mouse lines do not support this hypothesis. However, unlike the female rat, transition to

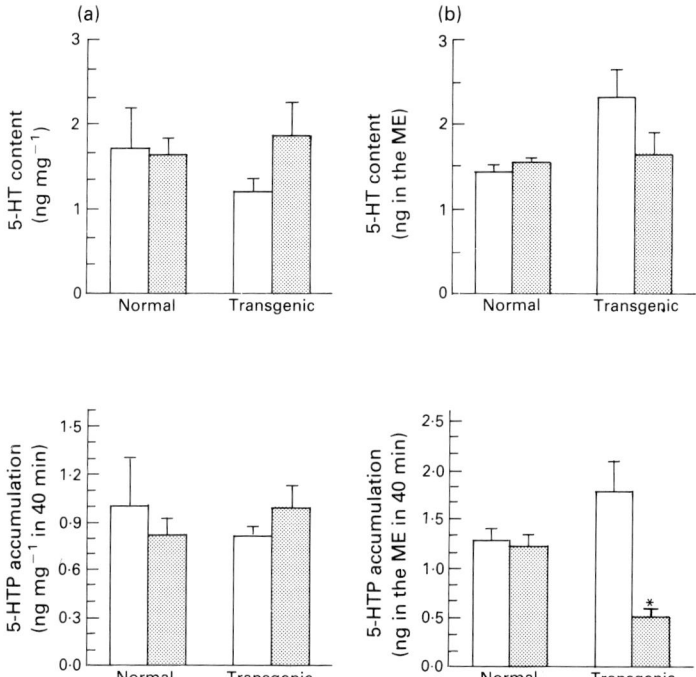

Fig. 4. (a) Medial basal hypothalamic and (b) median eminence (ME) 5-HT content and 5-hydroxytryptophan (5-HTP) accumulation in male 25-copy PEPCK . bGH mice (transgenic) and their non-transgenic litter mates (normal). Animals were 3 months old (young) (□) or 10 months old (old) (▨). These animals had already been tested for dopaminergic and noradrenergic neurone function (see Figs 2 and 3). The accumulation of 5-HTP, an index of 5-HT synthesis, was measured during the 40 min after inhibition of aromatic amino acid decarboxylase with 3-hydroxybenzylhydrazine (NSD-1015). 5-HT content was measured in mice that had not been injected with α-methyl-p-tyrosine. Values represent the mean ± SEM of 5–10 mice per group. Asterisk denotes statistical difference from value for young mice ($P < 0.05$). bGH: bovine growth hormone; PEPCK: phosphoenolpyruvate carboxykinase.

acyclicity in ageing C57BL/6J mice is primarily due to oocyte exhaustion (Gosden *et al.*, 1983). The testosterone concentration decreases in ageing C57BL/6NNia mice but it is not known whether this is due to hypothalamic, pituitary or testicular factors (Parkening, 1989). Ageing CBF1 mice have peak luteinizing hormone amounts at 12 months of age, which have declined significantly by 18 months (Bronson & Desjardins, 1977).

Noradrenaline is a primary stimulus for luteinizing-hormone-releasing hormone and consequently for release of luteinizing hormone. Numerous studies have demonstrated that deficits in hypothalamic noradrenaline metabolism can result in reduced secretion of luteinizing hormone (Steger *et al.*, 1982; Kalra & Kalra, 1983; Steger *et al.*, 1987b; Terasawa *et al.*, 1988). Noradrenaline turnover in the median eminence did decline with age in the 25-copy PEPCK . bGH mice, but turnover rates remained higher than those seen in the young or old controls and normal amounts of luteinizing hormone in the plasma were maintained, presumably via other regulatory mechanisms.

There were marked age-related changes in dopamine activity in the median eminence of male 25-copy PEPCK . bGH mice that were not seen in the non-transgenic controls. Dopamine content was not affected but dopamine synthesis was significantly depressed, as indicated by the reduced rate of DOPA accumulation after inhibition of aromatic amino acid decarboxylase with NSD-1015. The maintenance of dopamine content despite reduced dopamine synthesis, and the coupling of dopamine synthesis and release provide strong evidence for reductions in dopamine release. This

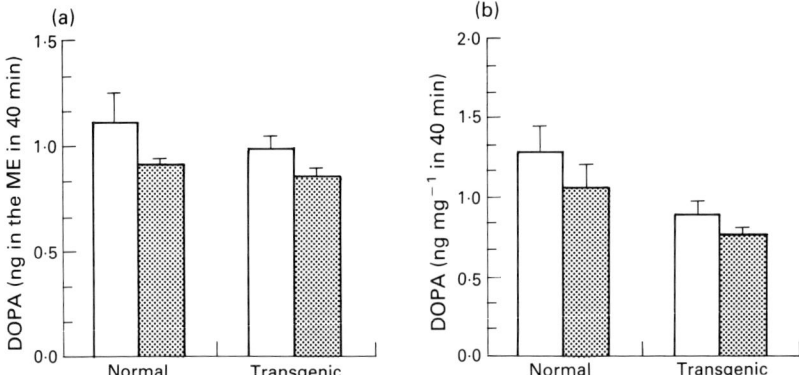

Fig. 5. The effects of age on dopamine synthesis in (a) the median eminence (ME) and (b) striatum of intact male 5-copy PEPCK . bGH mice (transgenic) and their non-transgenic litter mates (normal). Animals were 3 months (young) (□) or 10 months (old) (▨) of age. The accumulation of dihydroxyphenylalanine (DOPA), an index of dopamine synthesis, was measured during the 40 min after inhibition of aromatic amino acid decarboxylase with 3-hydroxybenzylhydrazine (NSD-1015). Dopamine turnover, an index of dopamine release, was calculated from the decline in dopamine content after inhibition of dopamine synthesis with α-methyl-p-tyrosine. Dopamine turnover and DOPA accumulation were measured in several groups of animals. Values represent the mean ± SEM of 5–10 mice per group. bGH: bovine growth hormone; PEPCK: phosphoenolpyruvate carboxykinase.

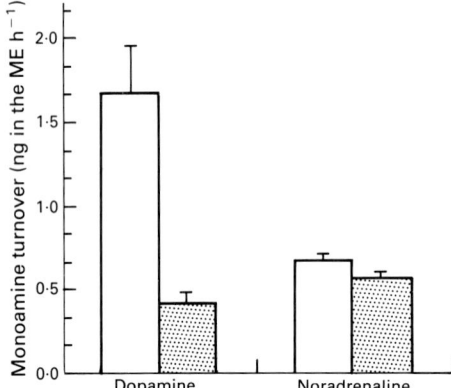

Fig. 6. The effects of age on dopamine and noradrenaline turnover in the median eminence (ME) of intact male MT . hGH mice (transgenic) and their non-transgenic litter mates (normal). Values represent the mean ± SEM of 4–8 mice per group. Animals were 3 months old (young) (□) or 10 months old (old) (▨). hGH: human growth hormone; MT: metallothionein.

hypothesis is supported by the dopamine turnover measurements that demonstrated a reduction in the decline of dopamine content in the median eminence after dopamine synthesis was blocked with the tyrosine hydroxylase inhibitor αMPT. These changes specifically affected the terminals of the tuberoinfundibular dominergic neurones (the TIDA system), as dopamine metabolism in the medial basal hypothalamus was unaffected by age in these mice. The median eminence contains the principal terminal field for tuberoinfundibular dopaminergic neurones. These neurones are involved in inhibitory control of prolactin release and studies are now underway to determine the effects of age on pituitary hormone release in 25-copy PEPCK . bGH mice. There are considerable data from the rat demonstrating an age-related increase in prolactin release associated with changes in TIDA function (Demarest et al., 1980; Gudelsky et al., 1981; Gregerson & Selmanoff, 1990).

Table 3. *Effects of advancing age on the masses of the body and selected organs of female mice expressing various GH transgenes*

Mouse promoter used	Structural gene	No. of copies	Body mass (g)	Uterus (g)	Adrenal (mg)	Liver (g)	Kidney (g)	Spleen (g)
mMT-1	hGH.var	1						
Young (7)			39·6 ± 1·3	34·3 ± 4·0	7·43 ± 0·45	3·14 ± 0·18	0·58 ± 0·03	0·24 ± 0·02
Old (6)			48·2 ± 2·4*	46·8 ± 6·0	11·27 ± 1·82*	5·19 ± 0·66*	0·77 ± 0·07*	0·42 ± 0·08*
PEPCK	bGH	1						
Young								
Old (6)			51·3 ± 1·01	50·0 ± 11·1	15·54 ± 2·65	5·05 ± 0·36	0·81 ± 0·05	0·39 ± 0·05
PEPCK	bGH	5						
Young								
Old (9)			44·2 ± 1·6	72·3 ± 8·6	23·0 ± 2·9	3·26 ± 0·24	0·65 ± 0·05	0·34 ± 0·03
PEPCK	bGH	25						
Young (5)			36·8 ± 1·0	34·6 ± 4·6	8·35 ± 0·52	3·07 ± 0·14	0·58 ± 0·04	0·27 ± 0·02
Old (4)			52·3 ± 3·7*	57·4 ± 9·2	11·83 ± 1·88	4·66 ± 0·43*	0·82 ± 0·16	0·53 ± 0·21
PEPCK	hGH	1						
Young (7)			46·0 ± 1·0	31·9 ± 6·0	4·29 ± 0·99	4·11 ± 0·09	0·66 ± 0·03	0·28 ± 0·02
Old (28)			54·7 ± 1·1*	47·5 ± 2·4*	9·30 ± 0·55*	4·73 ± 0·14	0·86 ± 0·04*	0·44 ± 0·04*
Normal	n/a	n/a						
Young (27)			24·0 ± 0·8	41·4 ± 5·8	6·60 ± 0·46	1·40 ± 0·07	0·35 ± 0·01	0·14 ± 0·01
Old (63)			29·0 ± 0·7*	55·6 ± 3·9*	9·55 ± 0·67*	1·52 ± 0·06	0·43 ± 0·01*	0·17 ± 0·01

Values are reported as mean ± SEM. The number of mice in each group is reported in the first column. Young mice are 3–4 months old and old mice are 8–11 months old. Asterisks denote statistical difference between young and old mice ($P < 0.05$).
bGH: bovine growth hormone; hGH: human growth hormone; hGH.var: human growth hormone variant genes; mMT-1: mouse metallothionein-1; n/a: not applicable; PEPCK: phosphoenolpyruvate carboxykinase.

Table 4. The effects of advancing age on catecholamine content and DOPA accumulation in select brain regions of ovariectomized, non-transgenic (normal) and 25-copy PEPCK. bGH (transgenic) mice

Brain region analysed	Normal		Transgenic	
	Young (3–4 months)	Old (9–10 months)	Young (3–4 months)	Old (9–10 months)
Median eminence				
DA content (ng in the ME)	2·54 ± 0·41	2·34 ± 0·34	1·55 ± 0·49	1·73 ± 0·51
NA content (ng in the ME)	2·25 ± 0·29	2·89 ± 0·16	2·34 ± 0·17	2·17 ± 0·16
DOPA (ng in the ME in 40 min)	1·15 ± 0·33	0·90 ± 0·32	1·24 ± 0·17	0·61 ± 0·32
Medial basal hypothalamus				
DA content (ng mg^{-1})	nd	nd	nd	nd
NA content (ng mg^{-1})	1·32 ± 0·16	1·26 ± 0·14	1·09 ± 0·14	1·20 ± 0·17
DOPA (ng mg^{-1} in 40 min)	0·78 ± 0·11	0·52 ± 0·12	0·68 ± 0·09	0·57 ± 0·11
Striatum				
DA content (ng mg^{-1})	8·55 ± 1·49	11·54 ± 0·46	7·19 ± 1·84	11·06 ± 1·17
DOPA (ng mg^{-1} in 40 min)	1·06 ± 0·17	1·14 ± 0·04	1·15 ± 0·35	1·02 ± 0·10

Accumulation of L-dihydroxyphenylalanine (DOPA) was measured 40 min after decarboxylase inhibition with 3-hydroxybenzylhydrazine (NSD-1015). Values are mean ± SEM. The number of mice in each group varies between four and nine.
DA: dopamine; ME: median eminence; NA: noradrenaline.

Table 5. The effects of advancing age on 5-HT content and 5-HTP accumulation in select brain regions of ovariectomized, non-transgenic (normal) and 25-copy PEPCK. bGH (transgenic) mice

Brain region analysed	Normal		Transgenic	
	Young (3–4 months)	Old (9–10 months)	Young (3–4 months)	Old (9–10 months)
Median eminence				
5-HT content (ng in the ME)	1·71 ± 0·32	1·74 ± 0·20	1·38 ± 0·04	1·35 ± 0·20
5-HTP (ng in the ME in 40 min)	1·87 ± 0·37	1·21 ± 0·13	1·05 ± 0·21	1·85 ± 0·72
Medial basal hypothalamus				
5-HT content (ng mg^{-1})	2·03 ± 0·27	1·92 ± 0·21	1·51 ± 0·33	1·92 ± 0·30
5-HTP (ng mg^{-1} in 40 min)	1·08 ± 0·18	1·42 ± 0·22	1·28 ± 0·09	1·18 ± 0·15

Accumulation of 5-hydroxytryptophan (5-HTP) was measured 40 min after decarboxylase inhibition with 3-hydroxybenzylhydrazine (NSD-1015). Values are mean ± SEM. The number of mice in each group varies between four and nine.
ME: median eminence.

Dopamine synthesis in the median eminence of male 5-copy PEPCK . bGH mice did not decline with age but there was a marked decline in dopamine turnover in the median eminence of male MT . hGH mice. Dopamine turnover in this part of the brain has previously been shown to be high in MT . hGH mice compared with non-transgenic litter mates (Bartke *et al.*, 1987; Steger *et al.*, 1990). This is most likely due to the lactogenic activity that hGH has in rodents (Forsyth *et al.*, 1965; Hartree *et al.*, 1965). On the basis of findings in the rat, it has been suggested that age-related reductions in TIDA activity and neurone number is due to the deleterious effects of long-term exposure to high prolactin levels (Sarkar *et al.*, 1982). Although it has been argued that chronic oestrogen treatment used to induce hyperprolactinaemia in these experiments results in the suppression of TIDA neurones and that TIDA neurones are not lost (Bartke *et al.*, 1984; Kohama *et al.*, 1992), 'neurotoxic' effects of prolonged exposure to severe hyperprolactinaemia remain a possibility. Results of the studies described here suggest that ligands that bind to prolactin receptors may have an adverse effect on these neurones also in the mouse. Certainly, additional studies of TIDA structure and function in ageing MT . hGH mice are warranted.

There was a suggestion that dopamine synthesis in the median eminence also declines with age in the ovariectomized female 25-copy PEPCK . bGH mice, but variations in DOPA accumulation between animals are very large and the apparent differences are not significant. Additional studies will be of interest since it has been shown that prolactin concentration is high in ovariectomized MT . bGH and PEPCK . bGH mice compared with ovariectomized normal mice (Steger et al., 1991; Steger, R. W. and Bartke, A., unpublished). Previous studies in female C57BL/6J mice showed no loss of TIDA neurones up to 13 months of age (Kohama et al., 1992), but at older ages a loss of 30% of arcuate neurones (the location of TIDA cell bodies) has been reported (Miller et al., 1989).

Declines in various 'psychomotor' types of behaviour are characteristic of ageing in humans and numerous other species. There is abundant evidence to suggest that alterations in the striatal dopamine system are a primary cause of these changes (Joseph et al., 1986; Morgan et al., 1987). Two indices of striatal dopamine function, namely dopamine turnover and DOPA accumulation, indicated that dopamine metabolism was significantly depressed as early as 10 months of age in the 25-copy male PEPCK . bGH mice. Studies still need to be completed to describe the functional significance of these changes. Interestingly, striatal dopamine function was not impaired in the ageing female 25-copy PEPCK . bGH mice. It has been demonstrated that the nigrostriatal dopamine system is sexually dimorphic and that oestrogen can act directly on striatal neurones to affect dopamine release (Becker, 1990), and it is possible that such factors could account for differential ageing of male and female dopaminergic neurones. Although male 5-copy PEPCK . bGH mice tended to have lower levels of striatal dopamine synthesis than normal males, there was no further age-related decline.

Data from these studies also indicate that male 25-copy PEPCK . bGH mice exhibit some evidence of age-related changes in 5-HT metabolism. The amount of 5-HT did not change in the median eminence or medial basal hypothalamus but 5-HT synthesis, as estimated by measuring 5-HTP accumulation after aromatic amino acid decarboxylase inhibition with NSD–1015, declined in the median eminence. No significant changes in these parameters were seen in the ovariectomized female 25-copy PEPCK . bGH mice. 5-HT terminals in the median eminence are involved in the regulation of pituitary hormone release, and studies are now underway in ageing transgenic mice to determine the role that these changes in serotonergic transmission may have in the control of endocrine function.

In addition to the effects of various transgenes on neurotransmitter metabolism, the dramatic effects on life span should also be noted (Table 1). Shortening the life span appears to be related to abnormal levels of heterologous GH in the circulation: the PEPCK . hGH or PEPCK . bGH mice have shorter life spans and higher circulating levels of heterologous GH than do the MT . hGH or MT . bGH lines. Differences in life span between the MT and PEPCK lines may also relate to developmental effects of heterologous GH, since the MT promoter is activated as early as day 13 of pregnancy while the PEPCK promoter is activated after birth (Yun, J., pers. commun.). It is unlikely that insertional mutagenesis is responsible for the effects of these transgenes since neurotransmitter data for young 1- and 25-copy PEPCK . bGH males are very similar; overall, phenotypic effects of 1-, 5- and 25-copy lines are very close and similar effects of the transgenes have been described in several independently derived lines of MT . hGH lines (Hammer et al., 1985; Steger et al., 1990, 1991; Steger, R. W. and Bartke, A., unpublished). Finally, adrenal hormones may be partially responsible for accelerated ageing in mice expressing either bGH or hGH since corticosterone levels are high in these mouse lines (Cecim et al., 1991) and the actions of glucocorticoids in the CNS have been proposed to be an important mechanism of ageing (Landfield, 1978; Sapolsky, 1987). However, corticosterone concentrations in different lines do not correlate with life span.

In summary, high concentrations of heterologous GH expression that occur in transgenic mice expressing either hGH or bGH are associated with accelerated ageing and markedly shortened life spans. Age-related changes include alterations in central neurotransmitter metabolism. Importantly, some of these changes closely resemble those occurring in normal mice at much later chronological ages. More work needs to be done to describe the physiological significance of these changes and to determine their relationship to the general effects of ageing on the CNS.

We wish to thank G. Gow, R. Cerven, and C. Fadden for their excellent technical assistance. The authors also thank the Hormone Distribution Branch, NIDDK, NIH, and Dr A. Parlow for supplying the materials used in the pituitary hormone RIAs. Portions of this work were supported by NIH grants DK42137 and HD 20001 as well as by pilot project funds from the Alzheimer's Disease Center Core Grant (NIA, AG08014).

References

Bartke, A., Doherty, P.C., Steger, R.W., Morgan, W.W., Amador, A.G., Siler-Khodr, T.M., Smith, M.S., Klemcke, H.G. & Hymer, W.C. (1984) Effects of estrogen-induced hyperprolactinemia on endocrine and sexual functions in adult male rats. *Neuroendocrinology* 39, 126–135.

Bartke, A., Morgan, W.W., Clayton, R.N., Banerji, T.K., Brodie, A.M., Parkening, T.A. & Collins, T.J. (1987) Neuroendocrine studies in hyperprolactinaemic male mice. *Journal of Endocrinology* 112, 215–220.

Bartke, A., Steger, R.W., Hodges, S.L., Parkening, T.A., Collins, T.J., Yun, J.S. & Wagner, T.E. (1988) Infertility in transgenic female mice with human growth hormone expression: Evidence for luteal failure. *Journal of Experimental Zoology* 248, 121–124.

Bartke, A., Steger, R.W., Parkening, T.A., Collins, T.J., Yun, J.S. & Wagner, T.E. (1990) Influence of human and bovine growth hormones on the regulation of prolactin release of transgenic mice. In *Neuroendocrinology: New Frontiers*, pp. 39–48. Eds D. Gupta, H. A. Wollmann and M. B. Ranke. Brain Research Promotion, London.

Bartke, A., Shire, J.G.M., Chandrashekar V., Steger R.W., Mayerhofer A., Amador, A.G., Bain, P., Tang, K., Yun, J.S. & Wagner, T.E. (1991) Effects of human growth hormone on reproductive and neuroendocrine functions in transgenic mice. In *Transgenic Animals*, pp. 237–248. Eds N. First and F. Haseltine. Butterworth-Heinemann, Boston.

Bartke A.E.M., Naar E.M., Johnson L., May M.R., Cecim M., Yun J.S. & Wagner T. (1992) Effects of expression of human or bovine growth hormone genes on sperm production and male reproductive performance in four lines of transgenic mice. *Journal of Reproduction and Fertility* 95, 109–118.

Becker, J.B. (1990) Direct effect of 17β-estradiol on striatum: Sex differences in dopamine release. *Synapse* 5, 157–164.

Brodie, B.B., Costa, E., Dlabar, A. & Smooker, H.H. (1966) Application of steady state kinetics to the estimation of synthesis rate and turnover time of tissue catecholamines. *Journal of Pharmacological and Experimental Therapeutics* 154, 493–499.

Bronson, F.H. & Desjardins, C. (1977) Reproductive failure in aged CBF1 male mice: Interrelationships between pituitary gonadotrophic hormones, testicular function and mating success. *Endocrinology* 101, 939–945.

Cecim, M., Ghosh, P.K., Esquifino, A.I., Began, T., Wagner, T.E., Yun, J.S. & Bartke, A. (1991) Elevated corticosterone levels in transgenic mice expressing human or bovine growth hormone genes. *Neuroendocrinology* 53, 313–316.

Craigen, W. & Bronson, F.H. (1982) Deterioration of the capacity for sexual arousal in aged male mice. *Biology of Reproduction* 26, 869–874.

Demarest, K.T., Riegle, G.D. & Moore, K.E. (1980) Characteristics of dopaminergic neurons in the aged male rat. *Neuroendocrinology* 31, 222–227.

Felicio, L.S., Nelson, J.F. & Finch, C.E. (1984) Longitudinal studies of estrous cyclicity in aging C57BL/6J mice: II. Cessation of cyclicity and the duration of persistent vaginal cornification. *Biology of Reproduction* 31, 327–339.

Finch, C.E., Felicio, L.S., Mobbs, C.V. & Nelson, J.F. (1984) Ovarian and steroidal influences on neuroendocrine aging processes in female rodents. *Endocrinological Reviews* 5, 467–497.

Flood, J.F. & Morley, T.E. (1990) Pharmacological enhancement of long-term memory retention in old mice. *Journal of Gerontology* 45, B101–B104.

Forsyth, I.A., Folley, S.J. & Chadwick, A. (1965) Lactogenic and pigeon crop-stimulating activities of human pituitary growth hormone preparations. *Journal of Endocrinology* 31, 115–126.

Gosden, R.G., Laing, S.C., Felicio, L.S., Nelson, J.F. & Finch, C.E. (1983) Imminent oocyte exhaustion and reduced follicular recruitment mark the transition to acyclicity in aging C57BL/6J mice. *Biology of Reproduction* 28, 255–260.

Gregerson, K.A. & Selmanoff, M. (1990) Changes in the kinetics of [^{3}H]dopamine release from median eminence and striatal synaptosomes during aging. *Endocrinology* 126, 228–234.

Gudelsky, G.A., Nansel, D.D. & Porter, J.C. (1981) Dopaminergic control of prolactin secretion in the aging rat. *Brain Research* 204, 446–452.

Hammer, R.E., Brinster, R.L. & Palmiter, R.D. (1985) Use of gene transfer to increase animal growth. *Cold Spring Harbor Symposium on Quantitative Biology* 501, 379.

Hartree, A.S., Kovacic, N. & Thomas, M. (1965) Growth-promoting and luteotrophic activities of human growth hormone. *Journal of Endocrinology* 33, 249–258.

Joseph, J.A., Roth, G.S. & Lippa, A.S. (1986) Reduction of motor behavioral deficits in senescent animals via chronic prolactin administration. *Neurobiology of Aging* 7, 31–35.

Kalra, S.P. & Kalra, P.S. (1983) Neural regulation of luteinizing hormone secretion in the rat. *Endocrine Reviews* 4, 311–351.

King, T.S., Steger, R.W. & Morgan, W.W. (1985) Effect of hypophysectomy and subsequent prolactin administration on hypothalamic 5-hydroxytryptamine synthesis in ovariectomized rats. *Endocrinology* **116**, 485–491.

Kohama, S.G., Brown, S.A., Finch, C.E. & McNeill, T.H. (1992) Chronic estradiol administration did not cause loss of hypothalamic LHRH or TIDA neurons in young or middle-aged C57BL/6J mice. *Brain Research* **574**, 341–344.

Landfield, P.W. (1978) An endocrine hypothesis of brain aging and studies on brain-endocrine correlations and monosynaptic neurophysiology during aging. *Advances in Experimental Medicine and Biology* **113**, 179–199.

McGrane, M.M., de Vente, J., Yun, J., Bloom, J., Park, E., Wynshaw, A., Wagner, T., Rottman, E.M. & Hanson, R.W. (1988) Tissue specific expression and dietary regulation of a chimeric phosphoenolpyruvate carboxykinase/bovine growth hormone gene in transgenic mice. *Journal of Biological Chemistry* **263**, 11 443–11 451.

Meites, J. (1990) Aging: hypothalamic catecholamines, neuroendocrine-immune interactions, and dietary restriction. *Proceedings of the Society for Experimental Biology and Medicine* **195**, 304–311.

Miller, M.M., Gould, B.E. & Nelson, J.F. (1989) Aging and long-term ovariectomy alter the cytoarchitecture of the hypothalamic-preoptic area of the C57BL/6J mouse. *Neurobiology of Aging* **10**, 683–690.

Morgan, D.G., May, P.C. & Finch, C.E. (1987) Dopamine and serotonin systems in human and rodent brain: effects of age and neurodegenerative disease. *Journal of the American Geriatrics Society*. **35**, 334–345.

Nelson, J.F., Felicio, L.S., Randall, P.K., Sims, C. & Finch, C.E. (1982) A longitudinal study of estrous cyclicity in aging C57BL/6J mice: I. Cycle frequency, length and vaginal cytology. *Biology of Reproduction* **27**, 327–339.

Parkening, T. (1989) Fertilizing ability of spermatozoa from aged C57BL/6NNia mice. *Journal of Reproduction and Fertility* **87**, 727–733.

Sapolsky, R.M. (1987) Second generation questions about senescent neuron loss. *Neurobiology of Aging* **8**, 547–548.

Sarkar, D.K., Gottschall, P.E. & Meites, J. (1982) Damage to hypothalamic dopaminergic neurons is associated with development of prolactin-secreting pituitary tumors. *Science* **218**, 684–686.

Selden, R.F., Wagner, T.E., Blethan, S., Tun, J.S., Rowe, M.E. & Goodman, H.M. (1988) Expression of the human growth hormone variant in cultured fibroblasts and transgenic mice. *Proceedings of the National Academy of Sciences USA* **85**, 8241–8245.

Selden, R.F., Yun, J.S., Moore, D.D., Rowe, M.E., Malia, M.A., Wagner, T.E. & Goodman H.M. (1989) Glucocorticoid regulation of human growth hormone expression in transgenic mice and transiently transfected cells. *Journal of Endocrinology* **122**, 49–60.

Simpkins, J.W., Mueller, G.P., Huang, H.H. & Meites, J. (1977) Evidence for depressed catecholamine and enhanced serotonin metabolism in aging male rats: Possible relation to gonadotrophin secretion. *Endocrinology* **100**, 1672–1678.

Steger, R.W., Bartke, A. & Goldman, B.D. (1982) Alterations in neuroendocrine function during photoperiod induced testicular atrophy and recrudescence in the golden hamster. *Biology of Reproduction* **26**, 437–444.

Steger, R.W., DePaolo, L.V., Asch, R.H. & Silverman, A.Y. (1983) Interactions of delta 9-tetrahydrocannabinol (THC) with hypothalamic neurotransmitters controlling luteinizing hormone and prolactin release. *Neuroendocrinology* **37**, 361–370.

Steger, R.W. (1987a) The effects of age on the neuroendocrine system. In *Handbook of Endocrinology, Vol. II*, pp. 23–42. Eds G. Gass and H. Kaplan. CRC Press, Boca Raton, Florida.

Steger, R.W., Bartke, A., Bain, P.A. & Chandrashekar, V. (1987b) Hyperprolactinemia disrupts neuroendocrine responses of male rats to female conspecifics. *Neuroendocrinology* **46**, 499–503.

Steger, R.W., Bartke, A., Parkening, T.A., Collins, T., Yun, J.S. & Wagner, T.E. (1990) Neuroendocrine function in transgenic male mice with human growth hormone expression. *Neuroendocrinology* **52**, 106–111.

Steger, R.W., Bartke, A., Parkening, T.A., Collins, T., Buonomo, F., Tang, K., Wagner, T.E. & Yun, J.S. (1991) Effects of heterologous growth hormones on hypothalamic and pituitary function in transgenic mice. *Neuroendocrinology* **53**, 365–372.

Terasawa, E., Krook, C., Hei, D.L., Gearing, M., Schultz, N.J. & Davis, G.A. (1988) Norepinephrine is a possible neurotransmitter stimulating pulsatile release of luteinizing hormone-releasing hormone in the rhesus monkey. *Endocrinology* **123**, 1808–1816.

Wagner, T.E., Hoppe, P.C., Jollick, J.D., Scholl, D.R., Hodinka, R.L. & Gault, J.B. (1981) Microinjection of a rabbit β-globin gene into zygotes and its subsequent expression in adult mice and their offspring. *Proceedings of the National Academy of Sciences* **78**, 6376–6380.

Wise, P.M. (1985) Changes in hypothalamic catecholamines associated with aging and reproductive functions. In *Catecholamines as Hormone Regulators*, pp. 51–64. Eds N. Ben-Jonathan, J. Bahr and R. Weiner. Raven Press, New York.

Sexually differentiated expression of genes encoding the P4502C cytochromes in rat liver – a model system for studying the action of growth hormone

A. Mode

Department of Medical Nutrition, Karolinska Institute, Huddinge University Hospital F60, Novum S-141 86 Huddinge, Sweden

Summary. Growth hormone (GH) is an important regulator of the expression of several members of the cytochrome P4502C subfamily in rat liver. The sexually differentiated pattern of secretion of GH in the adult rat leads to a sex-dependent expression of the GH-regulated P450 genes. The continuous presence of GH in serum is characteristic of the female rat and maintains a high expression of *P4502C12* while it represses P4502C11 expression. By contrast, the P4502C11 form is induced by the intermittent, male characteristic, GH pattern. A direct effect of GH on the hepatocyte is evident from studies using primary adult rat hepatocytes in culture and, furthermore, the regulation has been shown to occur at the level of transcription.

How the hepatocyte can distinguish between different patterns of GH exposure is as yet unresolved and neither are the signalling pathway(s) that are involved in the mediation of the GH effects known. However, a cascade of phosphorylations starting at the receptor are triggered. Our data indicate that protein kinase C activity is necessary for the GH effect on *P4502C12* and that some other kinase, sensitive to staurosporine, is a determining transducer. The dual regulation by GH of the genes encoding P4502C11 and P4502C12 and the GH responsiveness of primary hepatocytes offer versatile tools for studies aimed at understanding the cellular and molecular mechanisms of GH action.

Keywords: rat; liver; cytochrome P450; growth hormone; gene regulation

Introduction

The role of growth hormone (GH) in maintaining postnatal growth and its major influence on intermediary metabolism are well known. GH deficiency in early life leads to changes in metabolism that can be corrected with GH therapy. Similar changes in metabolic rate and body composition seen in GH-deficient children have also been found to be associated with ageing. The decline or even absence of GH secretion in the elderly has thus indicated the potential use of GH supplementation to prevent or delay some of the manifestations of ageing. The broadening implications for GH therapy and also the abuse of GH among young athletes emphasize the importance of understanding the mechanisms involved in GH action.

Although the existence of GH was discovered at the beginning of this century, the mechanism(s) of GH action are still unclear. However, cloning of the genes encoding GH, the GH receptor and specific target genes, together with the development of systems in which to study GH action *in vitro*, are now powerful tools for investigating GH, making it the subject of active research. A longstanding interest in hormonal regulation of the sexual dimorphism in rat liver steroid metabolism has developed into studies of the molecular mechanism(s) of GH regulation of cytochrome P450 gene expression.

Cytochrome P450 enzymes

Cytochrome P450 enzymes are ubiquitous, membrane-bound heme proteins that are involved in a vast array of oxidation reactions on numerous drugs, carcinogens and environmental pollutants as well as on naturally occurring substances like steroids, fatty acids and prostaglandins (Black & Coon, 1986). A cytochrome P450 enzyme can be classified as constitutive or inducible: constitutive forms are found in normal untreated animals, while inducible P450 forms increase in concentration, often from undetectable levels, following exposure to certain xenobiotic compounds. The great number of different P450 enzymes are expressed by genes belonging to the supergene family *CYP*. On the basis of sequence similarities, the *CYP* genes have been classified in families and subfamilies (Nebert *et al.*, 1991). To date, at least 38 genes encoding different P450 forms have been identified in the rat alone.

GH regulation of *P4502C11* and *P4502C12* expression

In the liver of adult rats there is a pronounced sexual dimorphism in oxidative metabolism due to a sexually differentiated expression of *CYP* genes. The predominant P450 forms responsible for the sexually differentiated hepatic metabolism of steroids are members of the *CYP2C* gene subfamily in which the *CYP2C11* and *CYP2C12* genes have attracted most interest because of their marked sexual differences in expression. The *CYP2C11* gene encodes a specific testosterone 16α-hydroxylase predominantly expressed in the liver of male rats, whereas the *CYP2C12* gene encodes a steroid sulfate 15β-hydroxylase characteristic of the liver of female rats (Morgan *et al.*, 1985; MacGeoch *et al.*, 1984). The expression of the *CYP2C11* and *CYP2C12* genes is developmentally regulated and is manifested in adult animals. The development of the sex-specific P450 phenotype coincides with the maturation of the pattern of GH release and, indeed, GH has been shown to be the major regulator of *P4502C11* and *P4502C12* expression (Gustafsson *et al.*, 1983; Mode *et al.*, 1988). GH has profound effects on many genes in the liver other than *CYP* genes and also on specific genes in other tissues. Some proteins encoded by target genes for GH action are listed in Table 1.

Table 1. Examples of proteins encoded by genes that are regulated by growth hormone (GH) in the rat

Protein regulated by GH	Tissue	Refs
Insulin-like growth factor I	Liver and others	Mathews *et al.*, 1986; Doglio *et al.*, 1989; Nilsson *et al.*, 1989
CYP proteins	Liver	Legraverend *et al.*, 1992a
Prolactin receptors	Liver	Norstedt, 1982
Epidermal growth factor receptor	Liver	Johansson, S. *et al.*, 1989
Growth hormone receptors	Liver and others	Mathews *et al.*, 1989; Vikman *et al.*, 1991; Nilsson *et al.*, 1990
Low density lipoprotein receptors	Liver	Rudling *et al.*, 1992
Albumin	Liver	Keller & Taylor, 1979
Serine protease inhibitor	Liver	Le Cam *et al.*, 1987; Yoon *et al.*, 1990
c-Myc product	Liver	Murphy *et al.*, 1987
Somatostatin	Hypothalamus	Rogers *et al.*, 1988
GH releasing factor	Hypothalamus	DeGennaro *et al.*, 1988
Myosin heavy chain	Muscle	Fong *et al.*, 1989
c-Fos product	Fat	Doglio *et al.*, 1989; Slootweg *et al.*, 1990

In all species GH secretion is pulsatile and the degree of pulsatility of GH release has effects on the magnitude of the biological response. The reason for the sexually differentiating effect of GH on P450 expression resides in the sex-dependent mode of GH secretion in rats (Edén, 1979; Müller *et al.* on pp. 99–114 of this volume for control of GH secretion). The male pattern of GH secretion is characterized by regular peaks every 3–4 h with low, often undetectable, levels in between. In female rats, GH secretion is more irregular with lower peak amplitudes but higher basal levels than in males. In hypophysectomized rats, devoid of GH, there is no sex difference in *P4502C11* or *P4502C12* expression. By treating the hypophysectomized animals with GH continuously, mimicking the female pattern of GH release, the *P4502C12* expression is increased and the low basal expression of *P4502C11* is virtually abolished. In contrast, when GH is administered intermittently, to mimic the male pattern, *P4502C11* is induced (Mode et al., 1988). The importance of the pulsatile pattern rather than the absolute amount of GH is evident from the observation that dwarf rats, having less than 5% of normal pituitary GH content, exhibit the sex-characteristic profile of GH release and express normal amounts of *P4502C11* and *P4502C12* (Legraverend et al., 1992a). Furthermore, the critical feature of GH pulsatility has been ascribed to the interpeak trough times of no detectable GH in plasma in male animals (Waxman et al., 1991).

A direct effect of GH on the hepatocyte is evident from the primary rat hepatocyte cultures in which GH stimulates induction of *P4502C12* and repression of *P4502C11* (Guzelian et al., 1988; Tollet et al., 1990; Liddle et al., 1992). Preliminary data indicate that *P4502C11* can be induced by intermittent GH administration into primary hepatocytes, although consistent results have not yet been obtained.

Insulin-like growth factor 1 (IGF-1) is believed to be an important mediator of GH effects on body growth. Early investigations led to the hypothesis that the GH effects were mediated by IGF-1 produced in the liver. However, studies showing direct effects of GH on bone and other tissues have provided evidence that it is in fact local production of IGF-1 that mediates the growth response (Green et al., 1985; Isaksson et al., 1987). There is no evidence that IGF-1 is a mediator of metabolic responses to GH in the liver, which is in agreement with the observation that it does not mimic the effects of GH on hepatic P450 enzymes (Noshiro & Negishi, 1986; Guzelian et al., 1988; Tollet et al., 1990). Although the major regulator of *P4502C11* and *P4502C12* expression is GH, other hormones such as glucocorticoids, thyroid hormone and insulin also contribute to their overall regulation (Yamazoe et al., 1989; Ram & Waxman, 1990; Liddle et al., 1992).

Cloning of the cDNAs encoding P4502C11 and P4502C12 has permitted the assessment of the regulation of the expression of these genes by GH at a pre-translational level, and recent data have provided firm evidence that it is tightly controlled at the level of transcription (Legraverend et al., 1992b; Sundseth et al., 1992). Transcriptional regulation by GH of several genes such as the serine protease inhibitor gene (*Spi* 2.1) and the gene encoding IGF-1 has been described (Yoon et al., 1990; Mathews et al., 1986). A putative GH-responsive consensus sequence has been inferred but this sequence has not yet been identified within the available genomic clones of either *CYP2C11* or *CYP2C12*. In addition, the induction of *Spi* 2.1 by GH does not require on-going protein synthesis whereas that of *P4502C12* does (Tollet et al., 1990). Transcription analysis *in vitro* of *CYP2C11* and *CYP2C12* 5'-flanking DNA to define GH-responsive elements has so far been unsuccessful (Legraverend et al., 1992b; Sundseth et al., 1992). DNAase I footprinting analysis has revealed several footprints in the upstream region of each gene without indicating any significant differences between male and female liver nuclear extracts. However, observed differences in DNAase I cleavage patterns could be indicative of potential sites for GH-mediated regulation (Sundseth et al., 1992; Ström, A. & Mode, A., unpublished).

The GH receptor

It is a most intriguing question how a cell can distinguish between a continuous (female) and an intermittent (male) pattern of GH exposure. The cellular effects of GH, including expression of, for example, *CYP* genes, transport of metabolites into the cell, and cell proliferation and differentiation, vary depending on the target cell but they are all believed to be initiated through binding of GH to its cognate membrane-associated receptor. Hence, the number or the affinity of receptors, different types of receptor or the fate of the receptor in response to GH pulsatility could constitute the discriminating locus.

The recent purification and cloning of the GH receptor from several species including the rat have provided information on its structure and expression (Leung et al., 1987; Mathews et al., 1989). The cloned receptor expresses a mature protein of between 614 and 624 amino acids, showing a 70–80% sequence identity between species, and it is predicted to be a single membrane-spanning receptor. It is closely related to the prolactin receptor and shows sequence similarity to some cytokine receptors (Boutin et al., 1988; Bazan, 1990). In addition to the membrane-bound GH receptor, a soluble GH-binding protein has been identified. This GH-binding protein appears to be identical to the extracellular domain of the membrane-bound receptor. In rodents the GH-binding protein and the GH receptor are thought to originate from alternative splicing of the same primary transcript, whereas in humans and rabbits the GH-binding protein has been proposed to be produced by proteolytic cleavage of the extracellular domain of the receptor (Leung et al., 1987; Sadeghi et al., 1990). Additional subpopulations of the receptor may occur as suggested from epitope mapping studies, the presence of several mRNA species and the possibility of interactions between the receptor and membrane-associated proteins (Barnard et al., 1985; Smith et al., 1989; Stred et al., 1990).

Whether or not a sex difference exists in GH receptor content in rat liver is a controversial issue, though it seems clear that the expression is developmentally regulated and that sustained high levels of GH increase the GH receptor expression (Maes et al., 1983; Husman et al., 1985; Mathews et al., 1989; Orian et al., 1991). The ratio of GH receptor to GH-binding protein differs between tissues in the rat, shows sex differences and appears to be dependent on GH itself (Carlsson et al., 1990; Tiong & Herington, 1991). It is therefore possible that the soluble GH-binding protein could have an important role in the modulation of GH-dependent sex differences in the liver. Recent studies performed *in vitro* have shown that one molecule of GH can bind two molecules of the soluble GH-binding protein, and the proposition was made that hormone-induced receptor dimerization could be relevant to the GH signal transduction mechanism (Cunningham et al., 1991). Such a dimerization phenomenon has been shown for other polypeptide hormone receptors (Ullrich & Schlessinger, 1990). In the case of the epidermal growth factor receptor, it has been demonstrated that the membrane receptor dimerizes with the soluble receptor in the presence of the ligand (Basum et al., 1989). With respect to the interleukin 6 receptor, a transmembrane protein can interact with the soluble receptor without involvement of the membrane receptor, and transduce signalling (Taga et al., 1989; Hibi et al., 1990). Thus, it is possible that discrimination between a male and a female secretory pattern of GH within the cell relates to different amounts of receptor present, different subpopulations of receptors at the cell surface or even to different types of interaction at the plasma membrane.

After ligand binding, the GH receptor has been shown to be internalized (Roupas & Herington, 1987). Not all internalized receptors are targeted to lysosomal degradation, and GH receptors with the estimated size of the binding protein have been shown to occur in the cytosol and in the nucleus (Roupas & Herington, 1987; Herington et al., 1989; Lobie et al., 1992). This suggests that the soluble receptor may interact with the transcription machinery directly.

GH signalling

The establishment of systems *in vitro* is crucial for studies on the intracellular mechanisms of GH action. Owing to a lack of any response to GH in most established cell lines such studies have proved to be more difficult than anticipated; in particular, hepatoma cells appear to be unresponsive. Cloning of the receptor has helped to overcome this problem by using DNA transfections to express cloned receptors in tissue culture cells (Billestrup et al., 1990; Emtner et al., 1990; Francis, S. M. & Norstedt, G., unpublished). Transfections of an insulin-producing rat islet tumour cell line with the full-length GH receptor cDNA or with various truncated constructs have shown that domains within the carboxy-terminal half of the cytoplasmic part of the receptor are required for the transduction signal necessary to trigger GH-stimulated insulin synthesis, whereas cytoplasmic domains proximal to the transmembrane region are involved in receptor-mediated GH internalization (Moldrup et al., 1991). Several GH receptor transfected hepatoma cell lines have been analysed for GH induction of endogenous or co-transfected *CYP2C12* reporter gene constructs without success (Mode, A. and Ström, A., unpublished). However, most P450 genes appear to require a high degree of cell differentaition for their expression, and essential factors associated with such differentiation might be absent in the tested cell lines.

The need for well-maintained cellular differentiation to study P450 gene expression *in vitro* is well recognized. Great efforts have therefore been directed towards using monolayers of primary non-proliferating adult rat hepatocytes for studying these genes (Schuetz et al., 1988). Primary adult rat hepatocytes cultured on matrigel, a reconstituted basement membrane prepared by salt extraction of the Engelbreth-Holm-Swarm sarcoma, in a medium free from serum and hormones, have been found to maintain the expression of many differentiated liver-specific genes. This system has proved to be very useful for studies *in vitro* on both xenobiotic induction of inducible P450 enzymes and hormonal regulation of constitutive P450 enzymes (e.g. by GH) (Guzelian et al., 1988; Schuetz et al., 1990). This system is currently being used to explore the various aspects of GH regulation of P4502C enzymes (Tollet et al., 1990, 1991; Legraverend et al., 1992a).

Analysis of the GH receptor sequence has not revealed any similarities to receptors of known signal transduction mechanisms. Despite the lack of a consensus sequence for tyrosine kinases, a primary event after GH receptor occupancy seems to be an increased phosphorylation of tyrosyl residues on the receptor (Foster et al., 1988). A tight association of GH receptors with tyrosine kinase activity has been demonstrated in various cell types from different species, including rat hepatocytes (Stred et al., 1990). A recent study has demonstrated that GH stimulates microtubule-associated protein (MAP) kinase activity in 3T3-F442A fibroblasts (Campbell et al., 1992). MAP kinase, a serine–threonine–tyrosine kinase, is thought to be a common element in response cascades initiated by tyrosine kinase.

Several investigations suggest that phospholipid hydrolysis is important in the GH signalling process. In tissues and cells studied so far, GH treatment leads to increased diacylglycerol formation (Rogers & Hammerman, 1989; Catalioto et al., 1990; Johnson et al., 1990). A five-fold increase in diacylglycerol production 30 s after GH addition to primary hepatocytes has been observed, and phosphatidylcholine has been shown to be the source of diacylglycerol (Tollet et al., 1991; Mode, A. and Tollet, P., unpublished). Hydrolysis of phosphatidylcholine in response to GH has also been found in adipocytes (Catalioto et al., 1990).

The accumulating evidence for GH-induced production of diacylglycerol indicates that protein kinase C (PKC) could be a mediator of GH effects. Indeed, the effects of GH on both lipogenesis and lipolysis in rat adipose tissue have been shown to be blocked by inhibitors of PKC (Smal & De Meyts, 1989; Gorin et al., 1990). It has also been reported that the GH-induced expression of the proto-oncogene c-*fos* is attenuated after inhibition of PKC in Ob 1771 and 3T3-F442A pre-adipocytes (Doglio et al., 1989; Gurland et al., 1990). These findings prompted an investigation into the possible involvement of PKC in the GH-mediated induction of P4502C12 and IGF-1 in primary hepatocytes in culture (Tollet et al., 1991). Stimulation of PKC by phorbol ester treatment in the presence or absence of a Ca^{2+} ionophore was not sufficient to induce P4502C12 or IGF-1. However, inhibition of PKC activity, obtained by prolonged pretreatment of the cells with the phorbol ester, interfered with the induction of both mRNAs by GH. Furthermore, when the cells were treated with GH in combination with the potent but less specific kinase inhibitor staurosporin, the effect of GH was blocked. It seems that PKC activity is necessary for the effect of GH and that some other kinase(s) is a determining transducer. In this respect, it is of interest that in the study of Campbell et al. (1992) referred to above, it was found that staurosporin inhibits GH-stimulated MAP kinase activity.

Complex interactions and a cascade of events in GH mechanisms of action are inferred from the above and much further work is needed before the nature of second messengers, *cis*-acting elements and *trans*-acting factors involved in the regulation of gene expression by GH are resolved in detail.

Ageing

Growth hormone secretion decreases as a function of age, and the overall appearance of the GH secretion profile in the senescent male rat appears to be like that of the female (Sonntag *et al.*, 1980; Cocchi *et al.*, 1986). Cytochrome P450 expression has also been studied in livers of old rats, and the amount of total P450 shows a slight decrease with age. However, immunoquantitative analysis of individual forms have shown that the amounts of P4502C11 and P4502C12 change in different ways that result in a general 'feminization' of P450 expression, i.e. *P4502C11* expression falls and *P4502C12* expression increases (Imaoka *et al.*, 1991). An age-dependent decrease in the amount of P4502C12 in female rats has also been demonstrated, although no evidence for increased expression of male-characteristic P450 forms was found.

The amount of *P4502C11* and *P4502C12* mRNA in livers of male rats of various ages has been analysed, and the way in which the response to continuous GH treatment varies with age has been investigated (Fig. 1). As shown, the amount of *P4502C11* mRNA decreases with age. In contrast to the results of Imaoka *et al.* (1991) no increase in the amount of *P4502C12* mRNA with ageing in normal rats was found. This may be explained by the difference in the ages of the rats used in the two studies [rats up to 18 months of age were used in our study, while Imaoka *et al.* (1991) used rats up to 24 months of age]. Continuous GH treatment 'feminized' the livers at all ages, i.e. decreased the *P4502C11* and increased the *P4502C12* mRNA expression, although the responsiveness to GH appeared to be lower at 72 weeks than at younger ages. It can be concluded that the expression of the sex-specific P4502C11 enzyme in rat liver changes with ageing and that the age dependency may be due to changes in the GH secretory profile and possibly also to a reduced sensitivity to GH.

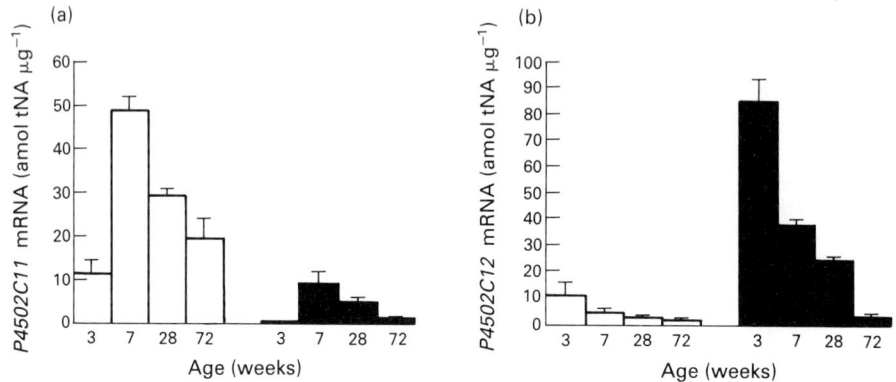

Fig. 1. (a) Cytochrome *P4502C11* and (b) *P4502C12* mRNA content in livers of normal male rats and male rats treated with growth hormone (GH) at various ages. GH at 600 μg kg^{-1} day^{-1} was administered continuously for 1 week via osmotic minipumps. Samples of total nucleic acids (tNA) from the liver were prepared and analysed for the amounts of *P4502C11* and *P4502C12* mRNA in solution hybridization assays (Mode *et al.*, 1989). Values are means ± SEM, n = 4 or 5; (□) controls; and (■) GH-treated animals.

Extrapolating data derived in rodents to humans

There appear to be only subtle sex differences in patterns of GH secretion in humans but a diminished secretion with age seems to be evident (Stolar & Baumann, 1986; Ho *et al.*, 1987; Zadik *et al.*, 1985). In a recent investigation by Schmucker *et al.* (1991), no evidence for a correlation between specific human liver P450 enzymes and either gender or age could be demonstrated, indicating that these human liver *CYP* genes may not be targets for GH action. However, treatment of GH-deficient children with GH has been shown to alter hepatic drug metabolism (Redmond *et al.*, 1980), and it may be speculated that GH could affect inducible P450s in humans. Direct extrapolation of data derived from rodents on the regulation of oxidative liver metabolism by GH to humans is obviously not valid. However, results regarding intracellular mechanisms of GH-dependent gene regulation should be of general significance and the mechanisms will almost certainly be conserved between species.

The work presented here reflects the efforts of a large number of investigators and I would like to mention in particular J.-Å. Gustafsson, C. Legraverend, P. Tollet, A. Ström, G. Norstedt and I.C.A.F. Robinson. I would also like to thank J. Lund for his critical advice. The work was supported by a grant from the Swedish Medical Research Council (no. D3X-06807) and the Magn. Bergvall fund.

References

Barnard, R., Bundesen, P.G., Rylatt, D.B. & Waters, M.J. (1985) Evidence from the use of monoclonal antibody probes for structural heterogeneity of the growth hormone receptor. *Biochemical Journal* **231**, 459–468.

Basum, A., Raghunath, M., Bishayee, S. & Das, M. (1989) Inhibition of tyrosine kinase activity of the epidermal growth factor receptor (EGF) by a truncated receptor form that binds to EGF: role of the interreceptor interaction in kinase regulation. *Molecular and Cellular Biology* **9**, 671–677.

Bazan, J.F. (1990) Structural design and molecular evolution of a cytokine receptor superfamily. *Proceedings of the National Academy of Science, USA* **87**, 6934–6938.

Billestrup, N., Moldrup, A., Serup, P., Mathews, L.S., Norstedt, G. & Nielsen, J.H. (1990) Introduction of exogenous growth hormone receptors augments growth hormone-responsive insulin biosynthesis in rat insulinoma cells. *Proceedings of the National Academy of Sciences, USA* **87**, 7210–7214.

Black, S. & Coon, M.J. (1986) Comparative structures of P-450 cytochromes. In *Cytochrome P-450 Structure, Mechanism and Biochemistry*, pp. 161–216. Eds. P. R. Ortiz de Montellano. Plenum Press, New York.

Boutin, J-M., Jolicoeur, C., Okamura, H., Gagnon, J., Edery, M., Shirota, M., Banville, D., Dusanter-Fourt, I., Djiane, J. & Kelly, P.A. (1988) Cloning and expression of the rat prolactin receptor, a member of the growth hormone–prolactin receptor gene family. *Cell* **53**, 69–77.

Campbell, G.S., Pang, L., Miyasaka, T., Saltiel, A.R. & Carter-Su, C. (1992) Stimulation by growth hormone of MAP kinase activity in 3T3-F442A fibroblasts. *Journal of Biological Chemistry* **267**, 6074–6080.

Carlsson, B., Billig, H., Rymo, L. & Isaksson, O.G.P. (1990) Expression of growth hormone-binding protein messenger RNA in the liver and extrahepatic tissues in the rat: coexpression with the growth hormone receptor. *Molecular and Cellular Endocrinology* **73**, R1–R6.

Catalioto, R. M., Ailhaud, G. & Negrel, R. (1990) Diacylglycerol production induced by growth hormone in Ob 1771 preadipocytes arises from phosphatidylcholine breakdown. *Biochemical Biophysical Research Communication* **173**, 840–848.

Cocchi, D., Calderini, G., Ganzetti, I. & Müller, E. E. (1986) Aspects of the control of prolactin and growth hormone secretion in aging. In *Neuroendocrine Perspectives*. Eds E. E. Müller & R. M. MacLeod. Elsevier, Amsterdam.

Cunningham, B.C., Ultsch, M., de Vos, A.M., Mulkerrin, M.G., Clauser, K.R. & Wells, J.A. (1991) Dimerization of the extracellular domain of the growth hormone receptor by a single hormone molecule. *Science* **254**, 821–825.

DeGennaro, C.V., Colonna, V., Cattaneo, E., Cocchi, D., Müller, E.E. & Maggi, A. (1988) Growth hormone regulation of growth hormone-releasing hormone gene expression. *Peptides* **9**, 985–988.

Doglio, A., Dani, C., Grimaldi, P. & Ailhaud, G. (1989) Growth hormone stimulates c-*fos* gene expression by means of protein kinase C without increasing inositol lipid turnover. *Proceedings of the National Academy of Sciences, USA* **86**, 1148–1152.

Edén, S. (1979) Age- and sex-related differences in episodic growth hormone secretion in the rat. *Endocrinology* **105**, 555–560.

Emtner, M., Mathews, L.S. & Norstedt, G. (1990) Growth hormone (GH) stimulates protein synthesis in cells transfected with GH receptor complementary cDNA. *Molecular Endocrinology* **4**, 2014–2020.

Fong, Y., Rosenbaum, M., Tracey, K.J., Raman, G., Hesse, D.G., Matthews, D.E., Leibel, R.L., Gertner, J.M., Fischman, D.A. & Lowry, S.F. (1989) Recombinant growth hormone enhances muscle myosin heavy-chain mRNA accumulation and amino acid accrual in humans. *Proceedings of the National Academy of Sciences, USA* **86**, 3371–3374.

Foster, C.M., Shafer, J.A., Rozsa, F.W., Wang, X.Y., Lewis, S.D., Renken, D.A., Natale, J.E., Schwartz, J. & Carter-Su, C. (1988) Growth hormone-promoted tyrosyl phosphorylation of growth hormone receptors in murine 3T3-F442A fibroblasts and adipocytes. *Biochemistry* **27**, 324–334.

Gorin, E., Tai, L.R., Honeyman, T.W. & Goodman, H.M. (1990) Evidence for a role of protein kinase C in the stimulation of lipolysis by growth hormone and isoproterenol. *Endocrinology* **126**, 2973–2982.

Green, H., Morikawa, M. & Nixon, T. (1985) A dual effector theory of growth hormone action. *Differentiation* **29**, 195–198.

Gurland, G., Ashcom, G., Cochran, B.H. & Schwartz, J. (1990) Rapid events in growth hormone action. Induction of c-*fos* and c-*jun* transcription in 3T3-F442A preadipocytes. *Endocrinology* **99**, 1033–1045.

Gustafsson, J.-Å., Mode, A., Norstedt, G., Eneroth, P. & Hökfelt, T. (1983) Growth hormone: a regulator of the sexually differentiated steroid metabolism in rat liver. In *Developmental Pharmacology*, pp. 37–59. Eds S. M. MacLeod, A. B. Okey & S. P. Spielberg. A. Liss, New York.

Guzelian, P. S., Li, D., Schuetz, E. G., Thomas, P., Levin, W., Mode, A. & Gustafsson, J.-Å. (1988) Sex changes in cytochrome P450 phenotype by growth hormone treatment of adult rat hepatocytes maintained in a new culture system on matrigel. *Proceedings of the National Academy of Sciences, USA* **85**, 9783–9787.

Herington, A.C., Ymer, S., Roupas, P. & Stevenson, J. (1986) Growth hormone-binding proteins in high speed cytosols of multiple tissues of the rat. *Biochimica et Biophysica Acta* **881**, 236–240.

Hibi, M., Murakami, M., Saito, M., Hirano, T., Taga, T. & Kishimoto, T. (1990) Molecular cloning and expression of an IL-6 transducer, gp130. *Cell* **63**, 1149–1157.

Ho, K.Y., Evans, W.S., Blizzard, R.M., Veldhuis, J.D., Merriam, G.R., Samojlik, E., Furlanetto, R., Rogol, A.D., Kaiser, D.L. & Thorner, M.O. (1987) Effects of age and sex on the 24-hour profile of growth hormone secretion in man: importance of endogenous estradiol concentrations. *Journal of Clinical Endocrinology and Metabolism* **64**, 51–57.

Husman, B., Andersson, G., Norstedt, G. & Gustafsson, J.-Å. (1985) Characterization and subcellular distribution of the somatogenic receptor in rat liver. *Endocrinology* **116**, 2605–2611.

Imaoka, S., Fujita, S. & Funae, Y. (1991) Age-dependent expression of cytochrome P450s in rat liver. *Biochimica et Biophysica Acta* **1097**, 187–192.

Isaksson, O.G.P., Lindahl, A., Nilsson, A. & Isgaard, J. (1987) Mechanism of the stimulatory effect of growth hormone on longitudinal bone growth. *Endocrine Reviews* **8**, 426–438.

Johansson, S., Husman, B., Norstedt, G. & Andersson, G. (1989) Growth hormone regulates the rodent hepatic epidermal growth factor receptor at a pretranslational level. *Journal of Molecular Endocrinology* **3**, 113–120.

Johnson, R.M., Napier, M.A., Cronin, M.J. & King, K.L. (1990) Growth hormone stimulates the formation of sn-1,2-diacylglycerol in rat hepatocytes. *Endocrinology* **127**, 2099–2103.

Keller, G.H. & Taylor, J.M. (1979) Effect of hypophysectomy and growth hormone treatment on albumin mRNA levels in the rat liver. *Journal of Biological Chemistry* **254**, 276–278.

Le Cam, A., Pagès, G., Auberger, P., Le Cam, G., Leopold, P., Benarous, R. & Glaichenhaus, N. (1987) Study of growth hormone regulated protein secreted by rat hepatocytes, cDNA cloning, anti-protease activity and regulation of its synthesis by various hormones. *EMBO Journal* **6**, 1225–1232.

Legraverend, C., Mode, A., Wells, T., Robinson, I. & Gustafsson, J.-Å. (1992a) Hepatic steroid hydroxylating enzymes are controlled by the sexually dimorphic pattern of GH secretion in normal and dwarf rats. *FASEB Journal* **6**, 711–718.

Legraverend, C., Mode, A., Westin, S., Ström, A., Eguchi, H., Zaphiropoulos, P.G. & Gustafsson, J.-Å. (1992b) Transcriptional regulation of rat P450 2C gene subfamily members by the sexually dimorphic pattern of growth hormone secretion. *Molecular Endocrinology* **6**, 259–266.

Leung, D.W., Spencer, S.A., Cachianes, G., Hammonds, R.G., Collins, C., Henzel, W.J., Barnard, R., Waters, M.J. & Wood, W.I. (1987) Growth hormone receptor and serum binding protein: purification, cloning and expression. *Nature* **330**, 537–543.

Liddle, C., Mode, A. & Gustafsson, J.-Å. (1992) Constitutive expression and hormonal regulation of male sexually differentiated cytochromes P450 in primary cultured rat hepatocytes. *Archives of Biochemistry & Biophysics* **298**, 159–166.

Lobie, P.E., García-Aragón, J., Wang, B.S., Baumbach, W.R. & Waters, M.J. (1992) Cellular localization of the growth hormone binding protein (GHBP) in the rat. *Endocrinology* **130**, 3057–3065.

MacGeoch, C., Morgan, E.T. & Gustafsson, J.-Å. (1984) Hypothalamo-pituitary regulation of cytochrome P450 apoprotein levels in rat liver. *Endocrinology* **117**, 2085–2092.

Maes, M., De Hetog, R., Watrin-Granger, P. & Kestlegers, J.M. (1983) Ontogeny of liver somatotropic and lactogenic binding sites in male and female rats. *Endocrinology* **113**, 1325–1332.

Mathews, L.S., Norstedt, G. & Palmiter, R.D. (1986) Regulation of insulin-like growth factor I by growth hormone. *Proceedings of the National Academy of Sciences, USA* **83**, 9443–9447.

Mathews, L.S., Enberg, B. & Norstedt, G. (1989) Regulation of rat growth hormone receptor gene expression. *Journal of Biological Chemistry* **264**, 9905–9910.

Mode, A., Wiersma-Larsson, E., Ström, A., Zaphiropoulos, P.G. & Gustafsson, J.-Å. (1988) A dual role of growth hormone as a feminizing and masculinizing factor in the control of sex-specific cytochrome P-450 isozymes in rat liver. *Journal of Endocrinology* **120**, 311–317.

Mode, A., Wiersma-Larsson, E. & Gustafsson, J.-Å. (1989) Transcriptional and posttranscriptional regulation of sexually differentiated rat liver cytochrome P-450 by growth hormone. *Molecular Endocrinology* **3**, 1142–1147.

Moldrup, A., Allevato, G., Dyrberg, T., Nielsen, J.H. & Billestrup, N. (1991) Growth hormone action in rat insulinoma cells expressing truncated growth hormone receptors. *The Journal of Biological Chemistry* **266**, 17441–17445.

Morgan, E.T., MacGeoch, C. & Gustafsson, J.-Å. (1985) Hormonal and developmental regulation of expression of the hepatic microsomal steroid 16α-hydroxylase cytochrome P-450 apoprotein in the rat. *Journal of Biological Chemistry* **260**, 11895–11898.

Murphy, L.J., Bell, G.I. & Friesen, H.G. (1987) Tissue distribution of insulin-like growth factor I and II messenger ribonucleic acid in the adult rat. *Endocrinology* **120**, 1806–1812.

Nebert, D.W., Nelson, D.R., Coon, M.J., Estabrook, R.W., Feyereisen, R., Fuij-Kuriyama, Y., Gonzalez, F.J., Guengerich, F.P., Gunsalus, I.C., Johnson, E.F., Loper, J.C., Sato, R., Waterman, M.R. & Waxman, D.J. (1991) The P450 superfamily: update on new sequences, gene mapping, and recommended nomenclature. *DNA and Cell Biology* **10**, 1–14.

Nilsson, A., Carlsson, B., Isgaard, J., Isaksson, O. & Rymo, L. (1989) Regulation by GH of insulin-like growth-factor-I mRNA in rat epiphyseal growth plate as studied with *in situ* hybridization. *Journal of Endocrinology* **123**, 69–77.

Nilsson, A., Carlsson, B., Mathews, L. & Isaksson, O.G.P. (1990) Growth hormone regulation of the growth hormone receptor mRNA in cultured rat epiphyseal chondrocytes. *Molecular and Cellular Endocrinology* **70**, 237–246.

Norstedt, G. (1982) A comparison between the effects of growth hormone on prolactin receptors and estrogen receptors in rat liver. *Endocrinology* **110**, 2101–2112.

Noshiro, M. & Negishi, M. (1986) Pretranslational regulation of sex-dependent testosterone hydroxylase by growth hormone in mouse liver. *Journal of Biological Biochemistry* **261**, 15923–15927.

Orian, J.M., Snibson, K., Stevenson, J.L., Brandon, M.R. & Herington, A.C. (1991) Elevation of growth hormone (GH) and prolactin receptors in transgenic mice expressing ovine GH. *Endocrinology* **128**, 1238–1246.

Ram, P.A. & Waxman, D.J. (1990) Pretranslational control by thyroid hormone of rat liver steroid 5α-reductase and comparison to the thyroid dependence of two growth hormone regulated CYP2C mRNAs. *Journal of Biological Chemistry* **265**, 19223–19229.

Redmond, G.P., Bell, J.J., Nichola, P.S. & Perel, J.M. (1980) Effects of growth hormone on human drug metabolism: timecourse and substrate specificity. *Pediatric Pharmacology* **1**, 63–70.

Rogers, K.V., Vician, L., Steiner, R.A. & Clifton, D.K. (1988) The effect of hypophysectomy and growth hormone administration on pre-prosomatostatin messenger ribonucleic acid in the periventricular nucleus of the rat hypothalamus. *Endocrinology* **122**, 586–591.

Rogers, S.A. & Hammerman, M.R. (1989) Growth hormone activates phospholipase C in proximal tubular basolateral membranes from canine kidney. *Proceedings of the National Academy of Sciences, USA* **86**, 6363–6366.

Roupas, P. & Herington, A.C. (1989) Cellular mechanisms in the processing of growth hormone and its receptor. *Molecular and Cellular Endocrinology* **61**, 1–12.

Rudling, M., Norstedt, G., Olivecrona, H., Reihnér, E., Gustafsson, J-Å. & Angelin, B. (1992) Importance of growth hormone for the induction of hepatic low density lipoprotein receptors. *Proceedings of the National Academy of Sciences, USA* **89** 6983–6987.

Sadeghi, H., Wang, B.S., Lumanglas, A.L., Logan, J.S. & Baumbach, W.R. (1990) Identification of the origin of the growth hormone-binding protein in rat serum. *Molecular Endocrinology* **4**, 1799–1805.

Schmucker, D.L., Woodhouse, K.W., Wang, R.K., Wynne, H., James, O.F., McManus, M. & Kremers, P. (1991) Effects of age and gender on *in vitro* properties of human liver microsomal monooxygenase. *Clinical Pharmacology & Therapeutics* **48**, 365–374.

Schuetz E.G., Li, D., Omiecinski, C.J., Muller-Eberhard, U., Kleinman, H.K., Elswick, B. & Guzelian, P.S. (1988) Regulation of gene expression in adult rat hepatocytes cultured on a basement membrane matrix. *Journal of Cellular Physiology* **134**, 309–323.

Schuetz, E.G., Schuetz, J.D., May, B. & Guzelian, P.S. (1990) Regulation of cytochrome P-450b/e and P-450p gene expression by growth hormone in adult rat hepatocytes cultured on a reconstituted basement membrane. *Journal of Biological Chemistry* **265**, 1188–1192.

Slootweg, M.C., van Genesen, S.T., Otte, A.P., Duursma, S.A. & Kruijer, W. (1990) Activation of mouse osteoblast growth hormone receptor: c-*fos* oncogene expression independent of phosphoinositide breakdown and cyclic AMP. *Journal of Molecular Endocrinology* **4**, 265–274.

Smal, J. & De Meyts, P. (1989) Sphingosine, an inhibitor of protein kinase C, suppresses the insulin-like effects of growth hormone in rat adipocytes. *Proceedings of the National Academy of Sciences, USA* **86**, 4705–4709.

Smith, W.C., Kuniyoshi, J. & Talamantes, F. (1989) Mouse serum growth hormone (GH) binding proteins has GH receptor extracellular and substituted transmembrane domains. *Molecular Endocrinology* **3**, 984–990.

Sonntag, E.W., Steger, W.R., Forman, J.L. & Meites, J. (1980) Decreased pulsatile release of growth hormone in old male rats. *Endocrinology* **107**, 1875–1879.

Stolar, M.W. & Bauman, G. (1986) Secretory patterns of growth hormone during basal periods in man. *Metabolism* **35**, 883–888.

Stred, S.E., Stubbart, J.R., Argetsinger, L.S., Shafer, J.A. & Carter-Su, C. (1990) Demonstration of growth hormone (GH) receptor-associated tyrosine kinase activity in multiple GH-responsive cell types. *Endocrinology* **127**, 2506–2516.

Sundseth, S.S., Alberta, J.A. & Waxman, D.J. (1992) Sex-specific, growth hormone regulated transcription of the cytochrome P450 2C11 and 2C12 genes. *Journal of Biological Chemistry* **267**, 3907–3914.

Taga, T., Hibi, M., Hirata, Y., Yamasaki, K., Yasukawa, K., Matsuda, T., Hirano, T. & Kishimoto, T. (1989) Interleukin-6 triggers the association of its receptor with a possible signal transducer, gp130. *Cell* **58**, 573–581.

Tiong, T.S. & Herington, A.C. (1991) Tissue distribution, characterization, and regulation of messenger ribonucleic acid for growth hormone receptor and serum binding protein. *Endocrinology* **129**, 1628–1634.

Tollet, P., Enberg, B. & Mode, A. (1990) Growth hormone regulation of cytochrome P450IIC12, insulin-like growth factor I and growth hormone receptor mRNA expression in primary hepatocytes: a hormonal interplay with insulin, IGF-1 and thyroid hormone. *Molecular Endocrinology* **4**, 1934–1942.

Tollet, P., Legraverend, C., Gustafsson, J-Å. & Mode, A. (1991) A role for protein kinases in the growth hormone regulation of cytochrome P4502C12 and insulin like growth factor-I messenger RNA expression in primary adult rat hepatocytes. *Molecular Endocrinology* **5**, 1351–1358.

Ullrich, A. & Schlessinger, J. (1990) Signal transduction by receptors with tyrosine kinase activity. *Cell* **61**, 203–212.

Vikman, K., Carlsson, B., Billig, H. & Edén, S. (1991) Expression and regulation of the growth hormone receptor mRNA in rat adipose tissue, adipocytes and adipocyte precursor cells: GH regulation of GH receptor mRNA. *Endocrinology* **129**, 1155–1161.

Waxman, D.J., Pampori, N.A., Ram, P.A., Agrawal, A.K. & Shapiro, B.H. (1991) Interpulse interval in circulating growth hormone patterns regulates sexual dimorphism of hepatic P450. *Proceedings of the National Academy of Sciences, USA* **88**, 6868–6872.

Yamazoe, Y., Murayam, N., Shimada, M., Yamauchi, K. & Kato, R. (1989) Cytochrome P450 in livers of diabetic rats: Regulation by growth hormone and insulin. *Archives of Biochemistry and Biophysics* **268**, 567–575.

Yoon, J.B., Berry, S.A., Seelig, S. & Towle, H.C. (1990) An inducible factor binds to a growth hormone-regulated gene. *The Journal of Biological Chemistry* **265**, 19947–19954.

Zadik, Z., Chalew, S.A., McCarter, M.J., Meistat, M. & Kowarski, A.A. (1985) The influence of age on the 24-hour integrated concentration of growth hormone in normal individuals. *Journal of Clinical Endocrinology and Metabolism* **60**, 513–516.

The regulation and mechanisms of action of growth hormone and insulin-like growth factor 1 during normal ageing

A. P. D'Costa, R. L. Ingram, J. E. Lenham and W. E. Sonntag

Department of Physiology and Pharmacology, Bowman Gray School of Medicine, Wake Forest University, Medical Center Blvd, Winston-Salem, NC 27157-1083, USA

Summary. The decrease in tissue function that is observed in ageing animals has been linked to the decline in rates of protein synthesis. These changes may be caused, in part, by reduced secretion of growth hormone (GH) and insulin-like growth factor 1 (IGF-1). It is well established that growth hormone-releasing hormone (GHRH) and somatostatin have an important role in the regulation of GH secretion and results from several studies suggest that an age-related increase in release of somatostatin has an important role in altering the secretion of GH. When the amounts of somatostatin mRNA were examined, there was a decrease in the aged rats but the amount of somatostatin mRNA bound to polysomes increased in these animals. This suggests that translational regulatory mechanisms are compromised in ageing animals. Moderate dietary restriction, which has been shown to increase life span, increases the amplitude of GH pulses and the capacity of tissues to synthesize protein. We have used the caloric restriction model to investigate the regulation and roles of GH and IGF-1 during ageing. Our results suggest that neuroendocrine regulation of GH secretion plays an important role in the process of biological ageing and that part of the beneficial effects of moderate dietary restriction may be mediated by altering the GH, IGF-1 axis.

Keywords: growth hormone; IGF-1; ageing; dietary restriction; protein synthesis

Introduction

It is widely accepted that during the ageing process a number of alterations occur at both the cellular and tissue level, ranging from a reduction in metabolic processes to structural and morphological changes in several tissues. There is abundant empirical and scientific evidence to support the hypothesis that ageing processes are closely related to a decline in protein synthesis (Richardson, 1981), but the mechanisms responsible for these deficiencies remain elusive. As early as the late 1800s, it was proposed that alterations in humoral secretions contribute to the decline in tissue function with age, but the early attempts at establishing the endocrine basis for ageing were quickly disputed. However, more recent and carefully designed studies have unequivocally established that a decline in several anabolic hormones occurs in ageing animals, and that hormone replacement therapy increases both tissue protein synthesis and function. These hormones include growth hormone (GH), which is secreted by the anterior pituitary gland, and insulin-like growth factor 1 (IGF-1), which is primarily secreted by the liver but has recently been identified in many other tissues. The purpose of this article is to review recent studies on the regulation and mechanisms of action of GH and IGF-1 in ageing animals and to discuss their potential use in reversing the decline in tissue function with age.

History

Since the early part of this century, it has been known that a substance present in blood promotes growth, but it was only after Li et al. (1945) isolated pure bovine GH from the pituitary gland in 1945 that the biological effects of GH became evident. It was subsequently shown to stimulate amino acid uptake into tissues, DNA, RNA and protein synthesis, and have a role in cell division and hypertrophy. Soon after the discovery of GH, highly purified pituitary extracts were used to stimulate growth in GH-deficient children. An assay for determining circulating concentrations of GH was developed by Utiger et al. (1962), and the amino acid sequence was determined by Li et al. (1969) and revised by Niall et al. (1971). Analysis of plasma concentrations of GH showed that they exhibited marked variability, but in the late 1970s it was recognized that this was because GH is secreted in discrete pulses that increase after the onset of sleep (Finkelstein et al., 1972). Although the precise function of this ultradian pattern remains unknown, the pulsatile release of GH has been confirmed in every species examined to date and is closely related to the biological actions of the hormone.

During this period, another set of investigators were studying the involvement of serum factors that appeared to mediate the actions of GH. In 1957, Salmon & Daughaday discovered a factor that was regulated by GH and promoted the incorporation of sulfate into cartilaginous tissue. This led to the purification of the somatomedin family (Van Wyk et al., 1974), which are peptides of small molecular mass (about 7·5 kDa) that circulate in the blood at high concentrations. These peptide hormones have been shown to induce mitogenic activity in cultured fibroblasts and fetal cell lines, stimulate anabolic activity in many cell and tissue types, and induce DNA and protein synthesis (Shermer et al., 1987). Somatomedin C, which is also termed insulin-like growth factor 1 (IGF-1), has been shown to be structurally related to insulin (Rinderknecht & Humbel, 1978) and exhibits similar, though less potent, effects on glucose regulation compared with insulin. IGF-1 binds with high affinity to the type-1 IGF receptor through which it exerts its actions (Rechler & Nissley, 1985), and these receptors are found in tissues throughout the body. It has been demonstrated that the type-1 IGF receptor shares 50% amino acid sequence similarity with insulin, and competitive binding and affinity cross-linking studies have demonstrated that IGF-1 binds to the insulin receptor with 100 times lower affinity than to the IGF-1 receptor (Rechler & Nissley, 1985). IGF-1 is synthesized mainly in the liver under regulation of GH but is also synthesized in smaller quantities in almost all tissues (Daughaday & Rotwein, 1989). Although the regulation of the paracrine activity of IGF-1 is poorly understood, alterations in the activity of this hormone or its receptors at the tissue level have a significant effect on many intracellular processes.

IGF-1 circulates in the blood either free (with a half-life of 15–20 min) or bound to specific binding proteins that prolong the half-life of the peptide. At present, six binding proteins have been identified (Binoux et al., 1986) and constitute an intricate transport system for the IGFs that regulates their availability to specific tissues. It is now clear that the binding proteins are important regulators of IGF-1 activity and may also prevent hypoglycaemic conditions, which can be induced by IGF-1.

Over the past decade, there has been increasing interest in determining whether GH acts directly on tissues or whether the effects are mediated through IGF-1. Although investigators initially proposed that all of the actions of GH were mediated through the secretion of IGF-1, other studies provided relatively convincing data that GH could have direct anabolic effects on specific tissues (Beach & Kostyo, 1968; Goldspink & Goldberg, 1975). However, subsequent studies have demonstrated that IGF-1 is present in most tissues of the body and that the 'local' actions of GH, observed by others, were actually mediated via paracrine secretion of IGF-1. These studies have led to the concept that GH stimulates IGF-1 secretion from hepatic tissue, thereby increasing the concentration of IGF-1 in the plasma, and that GH may also regulate the secretion of IGF-1 from local tissues, thereby influencing the paracrine or local activities of IGF-1.

Regulation of GH release

Although release of GH in humans is characterized by relatively low-amplitude pulses throughout the day and a large pulse after the onset of sleep, release in rats is characterized by an ultradian rhythm with high-amplitude secretory pulses every 3·5 h; between pulses, GH concentrations decrease to almost undetectable values (Tannenbaum & Martin, 1976). It was later discovered that the regulation of this pattern involved two different hormones released by the hypothalamus: GH-releasing hormone (GHRH) (Rivier *et al.*, 1982; Ling *et al.*, 1984), which increases GH release, and somatostatin (Brazeau *et al.*, 1973), which inhibits its release. The results of several studies suggested that both hormones are secreted in a phasic manner, with GHRH contributing to high-amplitude GH pulses and somatostatin being secreted during trough periods (Tannenbaum & Ling, 1984). The dynamic interrelationship between these hypothalamic hormones is responsible for pulsatile GH secretion. A number of factors contribute to the regulation of GH release – either by acting directly on the pituitary gland, or by regulating hypothalamic somatostatin or GHRH secretion. Both GH and IGF-1 inhibit further GH release (Berelowitz *et al.*, 1981) in a typical feedback relationship; GH increases somatostatin release from the hypothalamus and IGF-1 inhibits GH release from pituitary somatotrophs (i.e. the responsive cells).

Various neurotransmitters as well as opioid and other neuroactive peptides also influence the release of somatostatin and GHRH and subsequently release of GH from the pituitary. The specific actions of these compounds have been previously reviewed (Sonntag & Meites, 1988). More recently, there has been an increased interest in small peptides (growth-hormone-releasing peptides, GHRPs) that stimulate the release of GH. One of the peptides, GHRP-6 (His-D-Trp-Ala-Trp-D-Phe-Lys-NH_2) stimulates GH release and although it does not appear to interact with the GHRH receptor, it has been shown to act synergistically with GHRH (Bowers *et al.*, 1990). Although the exact mechanism of action of this peptide is still unclear, this type of peptide is particularly important because, as it is small, it may offer resistance to proteolysis so that its activity after oral administration is unaffected.

GH and IGF-1 have an important role in the ageing process

Research over the past decade has clearly established that alterations in the neuroendocrine axis and specifically in the regulation of GH have an important role in the physiological and biochemical changes normally associated with ageing. Early studies in humans indicated that the amplitude of GH pulses and the rise in the concentration of GH were blunted after insulin-induced hypoglycaemia (Laron *et al.*, 1970). Subsequent studies by Sonntag *et al.* (1980) demonstrated a prominent decrease in the amplitude of GH pulses in old rats and a reduction in GH content in the pituitary gland. The amplitude of most GH pulses in the old animals averaged about half of that observed in young animals. There appeared to be no changes in basal concentrations of GH or in the ultradian rhythm. Other investigators reported a progressive reduction in the plasma concentration of IGF-1 in rats when measured with radioimmunoassay (Florini & Roberts, 1979; Florini *et al.*, 1981); these results were confirmed in humans (Johanson & Blizzard, 1981; Rudman *et al.*, 1981). Later studies in various strains of rats and mice (Sonntag *et al.*, 1980; Florini *et al.*, 1981; Breese *et al.*, 1991), non-human primates (Kahler *et al.*, 1986), and humans (Carlson *et al.*, 1972; Prinz *et al.*, 1983) consistently confirmed the decline in GH and IGF-1 concentrations with age and suggested that these declines are a robust marker of biological ageing in mammalian species.

Subsequent to the identification of a decline in GH pulse amplitude, a number of investigators recognized the potential clinical significance of decreases in GH, and instituted replacement therapy. Earlier investigations had shown that purified GH preparations appeared to have beneficial effects in old animals and humans but the measures were unrelated to specific deficiencies that normally appear with age (Asling *et al.*, 1952; Emerson, 1955; Everitt, 1959; Beck *et al.*, 1960;

Root & Oski, 1969). Studies by Sonntag et al. (1984) related a specific deficiency occurring with age, the decline in protein synthetic capacity, to the age-related reduction in the plasma concentration GH. Protein synthetic capacity was observed to decrease by approximately 40% in diaphragm muscle of Sprague-Dawley rats, and administration of GH over 8 days significantly increased protein synthesis in old animals to values greater than those in young animals. Although this study did not address the question of whether response to GH diminished with age, it clearly indicated that (1) tissue from aged animals can show an increase in protein synthesis and (2) the decrease in plasma GH concentrations may be a causative factor in the decrease in protein synthesis with age.

Other reports were published demonstrating that GH or IGF-1 administration could partially reverse the decline in immune function (Kelley et al., 1986) and increase the expression of aortic elastin (Foster et al., 1990), and that administration of GH alone could increase lean body mass, skin thickness and vertebral bone density in elderly men (Rudman et al., 1990). These studies support the idea that the decrease in the concentration of GH has clinical significance and may be responsible for some of the tissue changes that accompany normal ageing.

Pituitary sensitivity to hypothalamic hormones

As previously described, GH release from the anterior pituitary is regulated by both somatostatin and GHRH release from hypothalamic neurones. If young rats are passively immunized with GHRH antibody the pulsatile secretion of GH is completely inhibited (Wehrenberg et al., 1982), whereas if somatostatin antiserum is administered, the amount of basal GH is increased, although pulsatile secretion remains evident. This has led to the concept that a phase shift in the secretory profiles of the two regulatory hormones occurs, with high concentrations of somatostatin coinciding with low concentrations of GHRH – resulting in high-amplitude secretion of GH (Tannenbaum & Ling, 1984).

Alterations in the secretory pattern of either hormone or changes in the responsiveness of the somatotrophs could contribute to the decline in GH release in aged animals. However, studies designed to assess pituitary sensitivity to GHRH have been inconclusive. Studies *in vivo*, for example, have found either no change (Wehrenberg & Ling, 1983) or a decrease (Sonntag et al., 1983; Ceda et al., 1986; Sonntag & Gough, 1988) in GHRH-induced release of GH with age. Differences between these results are partly due to the use of different strains of animals or methodological differences, including the dose of anaesthetic used to inhibit endogenous GH pulses.

In an effort to resolve this controversy, Sonntag & Gough (1988) compared GHRH-induced release of GH after administration of two agents that inhibit GH pulses (diethyldithiocarbamate or pentobarbital or both together), before and after elimination of endogenous somatostatin by passive immunization with antiserum. The results demonstrated that (1) the methods used to inhibit endogenous GH pulses influence the response to GHRH (by modifying endogenous somatostatin release), and (2) after neutralization of endogenous somatostatin, no differences in pituitary sensitivity to GHRH are observed with age using either drug. These studies have led to the concept that increased release of endogenous somatostatin may be part of the mechanism responsible for diminished GH secretion with age. However, these experiments did not eliminate the possibility that the coordination of somatostatin and GHRH release may be disrupted or that the capacity for GHRH release may be decreased with age. Studies in humans have only added to the confusion over GHRH-induced release of GH. Early studies demonstrated a decline with age but later experiments have failed to confirm this decrease. Further studies of endogenous somatostatin and GHRH release in young and old animals are needed to understand how decreased pituitary sensitivity to GHRH affects GH release.

Additional studies designed to eliminate the influence of endogenous hypothalamic hormones using procedures *in vitro* have also produced inconsistent results. Ceda et al. (1986) have reported an age-related decrease in the pituitary response to GHRH in primary cultures of cells from young and old animals. However, superinfusion of pituitary slices with GHRH induced a decrease in both basal and GHRH-induced release of GH from older animals, but no significant differences in these values were observed when data were expressed as a percentage increase of baseline values (Sonntag & Gough, 1988). In subsequent studies, it was also observed that enzymes used for dispersal of pituitary cells in animals from different age groups can damage cells (possibly by damaging membrane proteins), and that either the extent of the injury or the duration of the recovery period in cells from ageing animals differs from that in young animals (Spik et al., 1991). It became apparent that specific criteria related to normal cellular function would have to be developed before validating the primary cell culture model and carrying out comparisons between age groups.

Somatostatin secretion and ageing

To date, there have been numerous studies supporting the conclusion that somatostatin secretion increases with age. Studies of the pituitary response of GHRH *in vivo* with or without passive immunization against somatostatin provide some of the best indirect evidence suggesting increased somatostatinergic tone with ageing. In addition, a decline in somatostatin receptors in pituitaries from older animals has been reported (Spik & Sonntag, 1989) suggesting a down-regulation in response to increased somatostatin secretion. In addition, analysis of somatostatin concentrations in the pituitary gland have revealed a 40% increase in 22-month-old compared with 6–8-month-old animals. Studies *in vitro* also indicate that either K^+ depolarization (Sonntag et al., 1986) or glucopenia increase somatostatin release to a greater extent in old compared with young animals. In addition, analysis of the somatostatin released into the superfusate revealed greater concentrations of somatostatin 28 than somatostatin 14 in old animals. These results clearly suggest that somatostatin secretion increases with age and that there may be alterations in post-translational processing of the molecule leading to high concentrations of somatostatin 28, which has previously been shown to be more potent than somatostatin 14 in blocking release of GH (Tannenbaum et al., 1982). Although increased secretion of somatostatin has an important role in the decline of high-amplitude GH pulses in ageing animals, this inhibitory hormone is only one factor involved in this decline.

Because of the varied responses to anaesthetics with age and the impact of these compounds on the secretion of neuropeptides into hypophyseal portal blood, a comparison of the secretion of these hormones between young and old animals has not been attempted. Since there is abundant indirect evidence to support the conclusion that the somatostatin concentration in the plasma increases with age, studies were designed to assess the molecular mechanisms responsible for these changes, assuming a direct relationship between the amount of somatostatin mRNA and expressed peptide. In the initial study, changes in total somatostatin mRNA in hypothalamic neurones were measured and an unexpected decrease was found with ageing (Sonntag et al., 1990). Because this finding appeared to conflict with the increase in the amount of somatostatin peptide with ageing previously reported, the amount of somatostatin mRNA in hypothalamic neurones of young and old animals was compared using *in situ* hybridization. The results demonstrated abundant hybridization of the somatostatin antisense probe to periventricular neuronal cell bodies in young animals and, confirming the other results, a substantial decrease in hybridization with age.

In subsequent studies this experiment was repeated using the Brown-Norway rat strain and both total somatostatin mRNA and somatostatin mRNA bound on polysomes were compared in young and old rats. The hypothesis was that possible alterations in the rates of degradation of somatostatin mRNA or recruitment onto polysomes would be observed in aged animals. A comparison of total somatostatin mRNA in young, middle-aged and old rats again revealed a decrease with age, but when somatostatin mRNA bound to polysomes was expressed as a ratio to total somatostatin mRNA, ageing rats exhibited a two-fold increase compared with young or middle-aged animals.

Although these measurements do not assess the activity of the polysome, they provide insight into possible differences in the distribution of somatostatin mRNA within the cell that could lead to increases in production of the somatostatin peptide. Since recent evidence suggests that cells contain translational regulatory proteins that bind to mRNA thereby preventing translation into protein, it is possible that this type of regulatory control is compromised in ageing animals. Plasma GH and IGF-1 concentrations decrease with age, which (owing to the absence of negative feedback) should suppress somatostatin mRNA synthesis. The observed decline in somatostatin mRNA in ageing animals suggest that regulation of mRNA synthesis remains intact. By contrast, a higher proportion of somatostatin mRNA bound onto polysomes in the older animal indicates a specific deficiency in translational regulation. We are currently investigating the regulation of somatostatin translational control by neuropeptides and neurotransmitters, and its modification in ageing animals.

Regulation and importance of GH and IGF-1 in moderate dietary restriction

In recent years, there has been a growing interest in the biological effects of moderate dietary restriction, since it has been shown to increase life span and prevent the onset of disease. Early studies (McCay, 1943; Yu et al., 1982; Weindruch & Walford, 1988; Iwasaki et al., 1988) all reported that caloric restriction to 60% of that given to freely fed animals increases the life span of rodents. More recent studies have demonstrated that this paradigm prevents age-related pathologies (Bronson & Lipman, 1991). Studies have also reported that caloric restriction increases the capacity for total protein synthesis in the kidney and liver *in vitro* (Birchenall-Sparks et al., 1985; Ricketts et al., 1985). These findings were recently confirmed (Sonntag et al., 1992) using measures of protein synthesis *in vivo*, and it was noted that dietary restriction either increases the capacity for total protein synthesis or prevents the age-related decline in protein synthesis in the heart, liver, skeletal muscle and brain. These findings have been consistently found in C57/BL6 mice and in Brown-Norway rats.

Since protein synthesis is regulated at least in part by circulating hormones such as IGF-1, it was logical to test the hypothesis that dietary restriction may act by altering GH or IGF-1 concentrations in plasma. Early in the development of our hypotheses on the mechanisms of action of dietary restriction, we attempted to reconcile the known action of caloric restriction to lower the concentration of IGF-1 in the plasma with the increase in protein synthesis that was characteristic of this feeding regimen. It was at first suggested that dietary restriction initially lowers the plasma IGF-1 concentration but prevents an age-related decline in this hormone by eventually leading to elevated plasma concentrations in older animals. However, in all subsequent studies, it was found that the amount of IGF-1 is diminished in aged animals in response to dietary restriction, and the clear up-regulation of this peptide that had been predicted was not observed. In some cases, plasma IGF-1 concentrations were equivalent between old freely fed and dietary-restricted animals (Breese et al., 1991). These results clearly indicate that the increases in protein synthesis in dietary-restricted animals are not dependent on the amount of plasma IGF-1 alone and that other hypotheses should be developed and tested.

One alternative hypothesis tested the effects of ageing and dietary restriction on the plasma IGF-1-binding proteins that are known to regulate IGF-1 activity. Although there appeared to be a decline in the amount of several of the binding proteins with age in freely fed animals, these changes generally followed alterations in the amount of plasma IGF-1. Dietary restriction did not produce any marked changes in IGF-1-binding proteins that could account for the increase in protein synthesis (Breese et al., 1991).

Another hypothesis examined type-1 IGF receptors. No changes in the concentration of these receptors in freely fed animals were observed with age but 1·5–2·5 times as many receptors in the liver, heart and skeletal muscle from dietary-restricted animals were found compared to the density of these receptors in freely fed rats (Fig. 1). It was therefore suggested that part of the mechanism for increased protein synthesis is related to an enhanced tissue response to IGF-1. This appears to be the first evidence linking dietary restriction to an enhanced response to hormones known to regulate protein synthesis. Thus, the decline in protein synthesis in freely fed animals is at least partly the result of a decline in plasma IGF-1 concentrations; dietary restriction increases protein synthesis by increasing the tissue response to IGF-1 (i.e. by increasing the number of type-1 IGF-1 receptors) and by possibly attenuating the age-related decline in the plasma IGF-1 concentration.

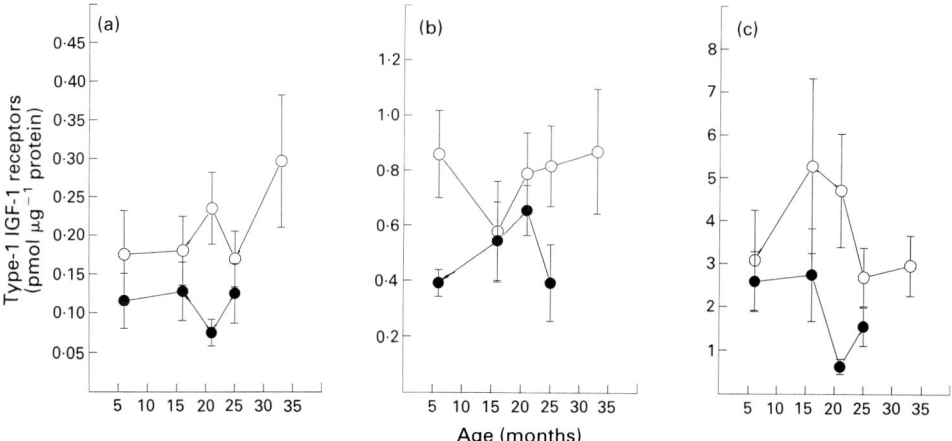

Fig. 1. Type-1 insulin-like growth factor 1 (IGF-1) receptor densities in (a) liver, (b) heart and (c) diaphragm of young and old freely fed (●) or dietary-restricted (○) Brown-Norway rats. Data represent means ± SEM. Receptors appear to undergo variable changes in freely fed animals but in almost all cases dietary restriction increases receptor number.

In addition to the presence of IGF-1 in plasma, it is well-known that tissues express both IGF-1 mRNA and IGF-1 peptide (Murphy et al., 1978; D'Ercole et al., 1984; Noguchi et al., 1987; Wether et al., 1990; Delafontaine et al., 1991). Although the regulation of IGF-1 paracrine activity in tissues is poorly understood, alterations in the activity of this hormone at the tissue level could have a significant impact on protein synthesis. The results of studies to date are suggestive of hierarchical levels of control of tissue protein synthesis. For example, intrinsic factors within the cell are the initial level of control followed by the action of local (paracrine) factors such as tissue-derived IGF-1, which binds to type-1 IGF receptors. Finally, endocrine control of tissue protein synthesis is manifested by the action of circulating plasma IGF-1 or GH. A complete understanding of the mechanisms responsible for the decline in protein synthesis with age and its reversal by dietary restriction requires assessment of the cellular, paracrine and endocrine factors that regulate protein synthesis.

It has been demonstrated that at least part of the reduction in IGF-1 and protein synthesis with age results from a reduction in the amount of GH secreted from the anterior pituitary gland (Sonntag et al., 1980; Sonntag et al., 1984; Sonntag, 1987). Because of the decreases in IGF-1 in response to dietary restriction observed in previous studies and the close association of IGF-1 with GH concentrations (Florini et al., 1985), the secretory dynamics of GH itself had not been analysed in dietary-restricted animals. However, our results demonstrating an increase in protein synthesis in dietary-restricted animals coupled with increases in the number of type-1 IGF receptors led us to search for hormonal factors that could mediate these changes. It was initially proposed that alterations in GH secretion may be responsible for the rise in the density of type-1 IGF receptors. Confirming previous studies, it was found that the amplitude of GH secretory pulse decreases with age and, as expected, dietary restriction diminishes the amplitude of GH pulses in young animals.

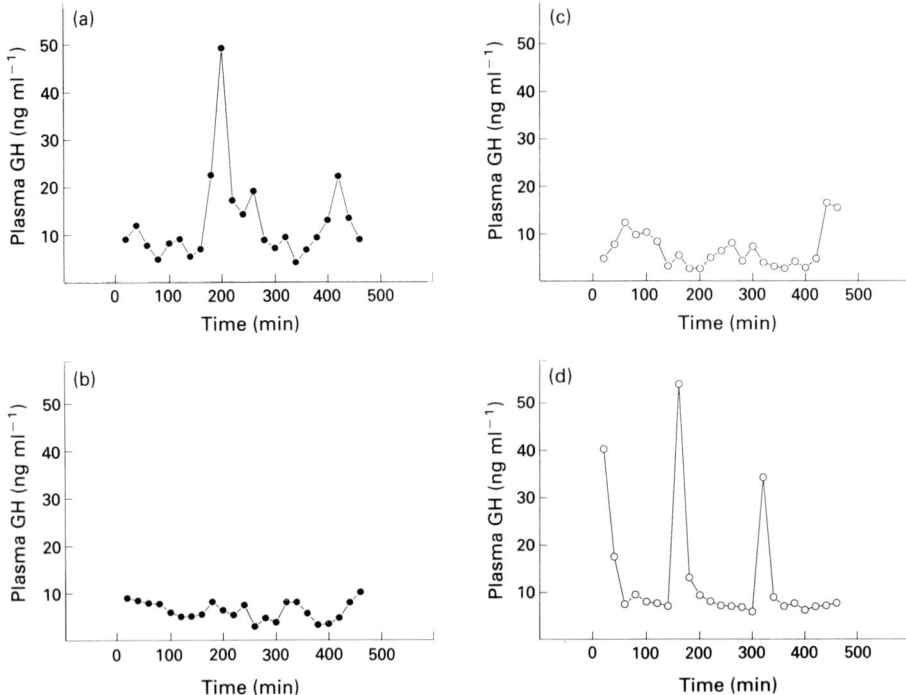

Fig. 2. Profiles of growth hormone (GH) secretory dynamics in (a) young freely fed, (b) old freely fed, (c) young dietary-restricted and (d) old dietary-restricted Brown-Norway rats. Data are representative of animals in each group ($n = 10$), and show that the amplitude of growth hormone pulses decreases with age in freely fed animals. Long-term dietary restriction increases the amplitude of growth hormone pulses as well as the mean amount of growth hormone (data not shown).

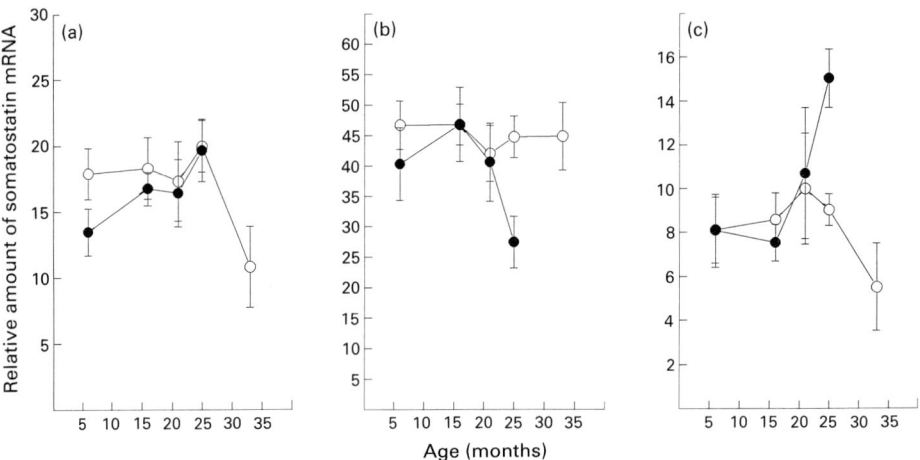

Fig. 3. (a) Polysomal-bound somatostatin mRNA, (b) total somatostatin mRNA and (c) the ratio of polysomal to total mRNA in the hypothalami from ageing freely fed (●) and dietary-restricted Brown-Norway rats (○). Data represent mean ± SEM. These studies demonstrate an increased association of somatostatin mRNA with polysomes in ageing rats; this may result from a decline in translational regulatory factors with age, which is prevented by dietary restriction.

However, in older dietary-restricted animals, GH pulses are similar to that in young, freely fed animals (Fig. 2). This increase in the amount of GH in old dietary-restricted animals was unexpected but both the number of GH pulses detected and the mean GH concentration increased. It seems that after some initial period of adaptation, dietary-restricted animals exhibit increases in high-amplitude GH secretion, which are maintained into old age. Since the plasma concentration of IGF-1 was diminished in the presence of increased tissue protein synthesis in these animals, the studies also suggest the possibility that an increased amount of GH may act directly at the tissue level to drive either paracrine IGF-1 activity or IGF-1 receptor activity. In either case, the studies demonstrate that GH secretory dynamics are associated with age (longevity) and may be part of the mechanism for increases in protein synthesis in response to dietary restriction.

Alterations in somatostatin secretion in dietary-restricted animals

The results showing that dietary restriction increases GH pulse amplitude led us to compare amounts of total and polysomal-bound somatostatin mRNA in freely fed and dietary-restricted animals. The strategy was to determine whether dietary restriction could act by modifying the recruitment of somatostatin mRNA onto polysomes and whether any modification that occurred was associated with the increase in GH pulses observed in these animals. It was found that caloric restriction prevented both the age-related decline in total somatostatin mRNA and the recruitment of mRNA onto the polysome (Fig. 3). Although additional experiments will be necessary, these data suggest that dietary restriction decreases the synthesis and release of somatostatin 14 and somatostatin 28, which then leads to an increase in the amplitude of GH pulses.

The dietary restriction model may also provide further insight into both the normal mechanisms for regulation of GH pulses and how this system changes with age. Additional studies to assess the importance of translational regulation of somatostatin mRNA are currently in progress. However, it is clear that the decrease in the total amount of somatostatin mRNA with age is most likely a physiological response to the decrease in the concentration of GH in the plasma. The feedback signal from circulating GH is intact in aged animals, and hypothalamic neurones respond appropriately by decreasing transcription of somatostatin mRNA. The deficiency in somatostatin secretion most likely results from an inability of cellular regulatory factors to suppress the translation of somatostatin mRNA into protein – resulting in increased somatostatin synthesis and a reduction in the amplitude of GH pulses.

Conclusion

Our studies over the past several years have given new insights into the biological mechanisms of ageing. First, it appears that alterations within the endocrine axis result in a cascade of events that culminate in a decrease in the amplitude of GH pulses, decreases in the amount of IGF-1 secreted and subsequently a decline in the capacity of tissues to synthesize protein. Although research is warranted, the broad range of actions of GH and ubiquitous distribution of IGF-1 suggest that we are only starting to understand which phenomena of ageing result from decreases in the concentration of GH. Second, dietary restriction influences type-1 IGF receptor densities in tissues and possibly the tissue response to IGF-1. The increase in GH secretion in response to this regimen with age and its contribution to IGF-1 paracrine activity and subsequently protein synthesis remain to be determined. Finally, the influence of translation regulation and its contribution to increased somatostatin release may provide additional insights into biological mechanisms by ageing and the regulation of hormone secretion in general. The fact that diminished GH secretion contributes to some of the phenomena that are considered to be part of normal ageing requires us to reassess our basic concepts of biological ageing.

This work was supported, in part, by NIH grant AG07752.

References

Asling, C.W., Moon, H.D., Bennet, L.L. & Evans, H.M. (1952) Relation of the anterior hypophysis to problems of aging. *Journal of Gerontology* **9**, 292–299.

Beach, R.K. & Kostyo, J.L. (1968) Effect of growth hormone on DNA content of muscles of young hypophysectomized rats. *Endocrinology* **82**, 882–884.

Beck, J.C., McGarry, E.E., Dyrenfurth, I., Morgen, R.O., Bird, E.D. & Venning, E.H. (1960) Primate growth hormone studies in man. *Metabolism* **9**, 699–716.

Berelowitz, M., Szabo, M., Frohman, L.A., Firoslone, S., Cha, L. & Hintz, R.L. (1981) Somatomedin-C mediates growth hormone negative feedback by effects on both the hypothalamus and the pituitary. *Science* **212**, 1279–1281.

Binoux, M., Hossenloop, L., Hardouin, S., Seurin, D., Lassarre, C. & Gourmelen, M. (1986) Somatomedin (insulin-like growth factors)-binding proteins: molecular forms and regulation. *Hormone Research* **24**, 141–151.

Birchenall-Sparks, M.C., Roberts, M.S., Staecker, J., Hardwick, J.P. & Richardson, A. (1985) Effect of dietary restriction on liver protein synthesis in rats. *Journal of Nutrition* **115**, 944–950.

Bowers, C.Y., Reynolds, G.A., Durham, D., Barrera, C.M., Pezzoli, S.S. & Thorner, M.O. (1990) Growth hormone releasing peptide stimulates growth hormone release in normal men and acts synergistically with growth hormone-releasing hormone. *Journal of Clinical Endocrinology and Metabolism* **70**, 975–982.

Brazeau, P., Vale, W., Burgus, R., Ling, N., Butcher, M., Rivier, J. & Guillemin, R. (1973) Hypothalamic polypeptide that inhibits the secretion of immunoreactive pituitary growth hormone. *Science* **179**, 77–79.

Breese, C.R., Ingram, R.L. & Sonntag, W.E. (1991) Influence of age and long-term dietary restriction on plasma insulin-like growth factor-1 (IGF-1), IGF-1 gene expression, and IGF-1 binding proteins. *Journal of Gerontology* **46**, B180–B187.

Bronson, R.T. & Lipman, R.D. (1991) Reduction in rate of occurrence of age-related lesions in dietary restricted laboratory mice. *Growth, Development and Aging* **55**, 169–184.

Carlson, H., Gillin, J., Gorden, P. & Snyder, F. (1972) Absence of sleep-related growth hormone peaks in aged normal subjects and in acromegaly. *Journal of Clinical Endocrinology & Metabolism* **34**, 1102–1107.

Ceda, G.P., Valenti, G., Butturini, U. & Hoffman, A. (1986) Diminished pituitary response to growth hormone releasing factor in aging male rats. *Endocrinology* **118**, 2109–2114.

Daughaday, W.H. & Rotwein, P. (1989) Insulin-like growth factors I and II. Peptide, messenger ribonucleic acid and gene structures, serum and tissue concentrations. *Endocrine Reviews* **10**, 68–91.

Delafontaine, P., Bernstein, K.E. & Alexander, R.W. (1991) Insulin-like growth factor-1 gene expression in vascular cells. *Hypertension* **17**, 639–699.

D'Ercole, A.J., Stiles, A.D. & Underwood, L.E. (1984) Tissue concentrations of somatomedin-C: further evidence for multiple sites of synthesis and paracrine or autocrine mechanisms of action. *Proceedings of the National Academy of Sciences, USA* **81**, 935–939.

Emerson, J.D. (1955) Development of resistance to growth hormone action of anterior pituitary hormone. *American Journal of Physiology* **181**, 390–402.

Everitt, A.V. (1959) The effect of pituitary growth hormone on aging male rats. *Journal of Gerontology* **14**, 415–421.

Finkelstein, J., Roffwarg, H., Boyar, R., Kream, J. & Hellman, L. (1972) Age-related changes in the twenty-four hour spontaneous secretion of growth hormone. *Journal of Clinical Endocrinology and Metabolism* **35**, 665–670.

Florini, J.R. & Roberts, S.B. (1979) Effect of age on blood levels of somatomedin-like growth factor. *Journal of Gerontology* **35**, 23–30.

Florini, J., Harned, J., Richman, R. & Weiss, J. (1981) Effect of rat age on serum levels of growth hormone and somatomedins. *Mechanisms of Age and Development* **15**, 165–176.

Florini, J.R., Prinz, P.N., Vitiello, M.V. & Hintz, R.L. (1985) Somatomedin-C levels in healthy young and old men: Relationship to peak and 24-hour integrated levels of GH. *Journal of Gerontology* **40**, 2–7.

Foster, J.A., Rich, C.B., Miller, M., Benedict, M.R., Richman, R.A. & Florini, J.R. (1990) Effect of age and IGF-1 administration on elastin gene expression in rat aorta. *Journal of Gerontology* **45**, B113–B118.

Goldspink, D.F. & Goldberg, A.L. (1975) Influence of pituitary growth hormone on DNA synthesis in rat tissues. *American Journal of Physiology* **228**, 302–309.

Iwasaki, K., Gleiser, C.A., Masoro, E.J., McMahan, C.A., Seo, E.J. & Yu, B.P. (1988) Influence of the restriction of individual dietary components on longevity and age-related disease of fischer rats: the fats component and the mineral component. *Journal of Gerontology & Biological Sciences* **43**, B13–B21.

Johanson, A. & Blizzard, R. (1981) Low somatomedin-C levels in older men rise in response to growth hormone administration. *John Hopkins Medical Journal* **149**, 115–117.

Kahler, L.W., Gleissman, P., Craven, J., Hill, J. & Critchlow, V. (1986) Loss of enhanced nocturnal growth hormone secretion in aging rhesus monkeys. *Endocrinology* **119**, 1281–1284.

Kelley, K., Brief, S., Westly, H., Novakofski, J., Bechtel, P., Simon, J. & Walker, E. (1986) GH pituitary adenoma cells can reverse thymic aging in rats. *Proceedings of the National Academy of Sciences* **83**, 5663–5667.

Laron, A., Doron, M. & Arnikan, B. (1970) Plasma growth hormone in men and women over 70 years of age. *Medical Sports and Physical Activity in Aging* **4**, 126–129.

Li, C.H., Evans, H.M. & Simpson, M.E. (1945) Isolation and properties of the anterior hypophysial growth hormone. *Journal of Biological Chemistry* **159**, 353–356.

Li, C.H., Dixon, J.S. & Liu, W.K. (1969) Human pituitary growth hormone, XIX. The primary structure of the hormone. *Archives in Biochemistry and Biophysics* **133**, 70–91.

Ling, N., Esch, F., Bohlen, P., Brazeau, P., Wehrenberg, W.B. & Guillemin, R. (1984) Isolation, primary structure, and synthesis of human hypothalamic somatocrinin: growth hormone-releasing factor. *Proceedings of the National Academy of Sciences USA* **81**, 4302–4306.

McCay, C.M., Sperling, G. & Barnes, L.L. (1943) Growth, aging, chronic diseases and life-span in rats. *Archives in Biochemistry & Biophysics* **2**, 469–479.

Murphy, L.J., Bell, G.I., Freisen, H.G. (1978) Tissue distribution of insulin-like growth factor I and II messenger ribonucleic acid in the adult rat. *Endocrinology* **120**, 1279–1282.

Niall, H.D. (1971) A revised primary structure for human growth hormone. *Nature New Biology* **230**, 90–91.

Noguchi, T., Kurata, L.M. & Sugisaki, T. (1987) Presence of a somatomedin-C immunoreactive substance in the central nervous system: immunohistochemical mapping studies. *Neuroendocrinology* **46**, 277–282.

Prinz, P.N., Weitzman, E.D., Cunningham, G.R. & Karacan, I. (1983) Plasma growth hormone during sleep in young and aged men. *Journal of Gerontology* **38**, 519–524.

Rechler, M.M. & Nissley, P.S. (1985) The nature and regulation of the receptors for insulin-like growth factors. *Annual Review of Physiology* **47**, 425–442.

Richardson, A. (1981) The relationship between aging and protein synthesis. In *Handbook of Biochemistry in Aging*, pp. 70–105. Ed. J. Florini. CRC Press, Boca Raton, Florida.

Ricketts, W.G., Birchenall-Sparks, M.C., Hardwick, J.P. & Richardson, A. (1985) Effect of age and dietary restriction of protein synthesis by isolated kidney cells. *Journal of Cell Physiology* **125**, 492–498.

Rinderknecht, E. & Humbel, R.E. (1978) The amino acid sequence of human insulin like growth factor-1 and its structure homology with proinsulin. *Journal of Biological Chemistry* **253**, 2769–2776.

Rivier, J., Spiess, J., Thorner, M. & Vale, W. (1982) Characterization of a growth hormone-releasing factor from a human pancreatic islet tumor. *Nature* **300**, 276–278.

Root, A.W. & Oski, F.A. (1969) Effects of human growth hormone in elderly males. *Journal of Gerontology* **24**, 97–103.

Rudman, D., Kutner, M.H., Rogers, C.M., Lubin, M.F., Fleming, G.A. & Bain, R.P. (1981) Impaired growth hormone secretion in the adult population. *Journal of Clinical Investigation* **67**, 1361–1369.

Rudman, D., Axel, G.F., Nagraj, H.S., Gergans, G.A., Lalitha, P.Y., Goldberg, A.F., Schlenker, R.A., Cohn, L., Rudman, I.W. & Mattson, D.E. (1990) Effects of growth hormone in men over 60 years old. *New England Journal of Medicine* **323**, 1–6.

Salmon, W.D. & Daughaday, W.H. (1957) A hormonally controlled serum factor which stimulates sulfate incorporation by cartilage *in vitro*. *Journal of Laboratory and Clinical Medicine* **49**, 825–831.

Shermer, J., Raizada, M.K., Masters, B.A., Ota, A. & LeRoith, D. (1987) Insulin-like growth factor I receptors in neural and glial cells. Characterization and biological effects in primary culture. *Journal of Biological Chemistry* **262**, 7693–7697.

Sonntag, W.E. (1987) Hormone secretion and action in aging animals and man. *Review of Biological Research in Aging* **3**, 279–315.

Sonntag, W.E. & Gough, M.A. (1988) Growth hormone releasing hormone induced release of growth hormone in aging rats: Dependence of pharmacological manipulation and endogenous somatostatin. *Neuroendocrinology* **47**, 482–488.

Sonntag, W.E. & Meites, J. (1988) Decline in growth hormone secretion in aging animals and man. *Interdisciplinary Topics in Gerontology* **24**, 111–124.

Sonntag, W.E., Steger, R.W., Forman, L.J. & Meites, J. (1980) Decreased pulsatile release of growth hormone in old male rats. *Endocrinology* **107**, 1875–1879.

Sonntag, W.E., Hylka, V.W. & Meites, J. (1983) Impaired ability of old male rats to secrete growth hormone *in vivo* but not *in vitro* in response to hpGRF (1-44). *Endocrinology* **113**, 2305–2307.

Sonntag, W.E., Hylka, V.W. & Meites, J. (1984) Growth hormone restores protein synthesis in skeletal muscle of old male rats. *Endocrinology* **107**, 1875–1879.

Sonntag, W.E., Gotschall, P.E. & Meites, J. (1986) Increased secretion of somatostatin-28 from hypothalamic neurons of aged rats *in vitro*. *Brain Research* **380**, 229–234.

Sonntag, W.E., Boyd, R.L. & Booze, R.M. (1990) Somatostatin gene expression in hypothalamus and cortex of aging male rats. *Neurobiology of Aging* **11**, 409–416.

Sonntag, W.E., Lenham, J.E. & Ingram, R.L. (1992) Effects of aging and dietary restriction on tissue protein synthesis: relationship to plasma insulin-like growth factor-1. *Journal of Gerontology* **47**, B159–B163.

Spik, K.W. & Sonntag, W.E. (1989) Increased pituitary response to somatostatin in aging male rats: relationship to somatostatin receptor number and affinity. *Neuroendocrinology* **50**, 489–494.

Spik, K.W., Boyd, R.L. & Sonntag, W.E. (1991) Effect of aging on growth hormone releasing factor-induced growth hormone from anterior pituitary cells in primary culture. *Journal of Gerontology* **46**, B72–B77.

Tannenbaum, G.S. & Ling, N. (1984) The interrelationships of growth hormone releasing factor and somatostatin in generation of the ultradian rhythm of growth hormone secretion. *Endocrinology* **115**, 1952–1957.

Tannenbaum, G.S. & Martin, J. (1976) Evidence for an endogenous ultradian rhythm governing growth hormone secretion in the rat. *Endocrinology* **98**, 562–568.

Tannenbaum, G.S., Ling, N. & Brazeau, P. (1982) Somatostatin-28 is longer acting and more selective than somatostatin-14 on pituitary and pancreatic hormone release. *Endocrinology* **111**, 101–108.

Utiger, R.D., Parker, M.L. & Daughaday, W. (1962) Studies on human growth hormone, I. A radioimmunoassay for human growth hormone. *Journal of Clinical Investigation* **41**, 254–261.

Van Wyk, J.J., Underwood, L.E., Hintz, R.L., Clemmones, D.R., Voina, S.J. & Weaver, R.P. (1974) The somatomedins: family of insulin-like hormones under growth hormone control. *Recent Progress in Hormone Research* **22**, 259–318.

Wehrenberg, W.B. & Ling, N. (1983) The absence of an age-related change in the pituitary response to growth hormone-releasing factor in rats. *Neuroendocrinology* **37**, 463–466.

Wehrenberg, W.B., Brazeau, P., Luben, R., Bohlen, P. & Guillimin, R. (1982) Inhibition of the pulsatile secretion of GH by monoclonal antibodies to the hypothalamic growth hormone releasing factor (GRF). *Endocrinology* **111**, 2147–2148.

Weindruch, R. & Walford, R.L. (1988) *The retardation of aging and disease by dietary restriction.* Charles C. Thomas, Springfield, Illinois.

Wether, G.A., Abate, M., Hogg, A., Cheesman, H., Oldfield, B., Hards, D., Hudson, P., Power, B., Freed, K. & Herington, A.C. (1990) Localization of insulin-like growth factor I mRNA in rat brain by *in-situ* hybridization – relationship to IGF-1 receptors. *Molecular Endocrinology* **4**, 773–778.

Yu, B.P., Masoro, E.J., Murata, I., Bertrand, H.A. & Lynd, F.T. (1982) Life-span study of SPF Fischer 344 males fed ad libitum or restricted diets: longevity, growth, lean body mass and disease. *Journal of Gerontology* **37**, 130–141.

Aspects of the neuroendocrine control of growth hormone secretion in ageing mammals

E. E. Müller[1], S. G. Cella[1], V. De Gennaro Colonna[1], M. Parenti[1], D. Cocchi[2] and V. Locatelli[1]

[1]*Department of Pharmacology, School of Medicine, University of Milan, Milan, Italy; and* [2]*Department of Biology and Pharmacology, School of Pharmacy, University of Bari, Italy*

Summary. In aged animals and humans the pulsatile secretion of growth hormone (GH), the mean amounts of GH released over 24 h, and the response of GH to the administration of GH-releasing hormone (GHRH) are lower than in young adults. Pituitary somatotrophic cells in old male and female rats show an impaired responsiveness to GHRH, and the reduced secretion of GH *in vitro* is linked with a diminished stimulation of adenylate cyclase by GHRH. Pretreatment with GHRH *in vivo* decreases the high basal adenylate cyclase activity in old male rats. This pretreatment does not affect the rise of adenylate cyclase concentration in these rats that is subsequently induced by GHRH administration *in vitro*. However, it does induce a small rise in adenylate cyclase concentration in old female rats. In young rats of either sex the same GHRH schedule does not alter adenylate cyclase activity, but it does reduce the effectiveness of subsequent acute exposure to GHRH to stimulate enzymatic activity. Short-term administration of GHRH in some aged subjects increases the response of GH to a subsequent acute challenge with GHRH. However, primary or secondary alterations in somatotrophic cells are also present in aged mammals, such as a reduction in the number of GH-immunoreactive structures or post-receptor alterations. In aged rats, major alterations in brain neurotransmitters and neuropeptides are present in hypothalamic and extrahypothalamic structures, especially in catecholaminergic and acetylcholinergic neurones. These alterations are probably due to defects in neurosecretory GHRH and somatostatin neurones. GHRH synthesis is impaired in the hypothalamus of senescent male rats, as shown by a reduction in GHRH mRNA levels and GHRH-like immunoreactivity. Although the expression of somatostatin seems to decrease with age in the rat hypothalamus, secretion and activity of this hormone is increased, resulting in an altered relationship between GHRH and somatostatin gene expression and secretion. Catecholamines induce GH release in most animal species by stimulating GHRH neurones and inhibiting somatostatin-releasing neurones. Acetylcholine stimulates GH release via muscarinic receptors, and thus inhibits the effect of somatostatin neurones. In male rats of various ages, except very young rats, systemic administration of pilocarpine, an agonist of muscarinic receptors, potentiates the GH response to GHRH during the entire lifespan. Although pilocarpine does not restore the response of GH to GHRH in aged rats to the level present in rats aged between 3 and 8 months, it does restore it in 18–19-month-old rats to that observed in 15-month-old rats. These data, which are consistent with similar findings obtained in humans, suggest that in aged mammals the reduced GH response to GHRH is only partly due to an intrinsic defect in the somatotrophic cells, and that suprapituitary influences under cholinergic control are involved. In old beagle dogs, clonidine (an α_2-adrenergic agonist) increases the pulsatile pattern of GH secretion, so that it is indistinguishable from that of young dogs. In old dogs, simultaneous administration of clonidine and GHRH potentiates GHRH-induced GH release, and clonidine and GHRH administered together for 10 days significantly augment the frequency of GH release, the mean GH peak amplitude, and the total amount of GH released.

Keywords: growth hormone; neural control; ageing; somatotrophs; neurotransmitters; mammals

Introduction

The availability of unlimited amounts of growth hormone (GH) by cDNA technology has considerably expanded the potential therapeutic uses of this peptide to previously not considered pathologies, e.g. Turner's syndrome, chronic renal failure, ovary resistant syndrome, GH-deficient and catabolic adults (Underwood, 1991). Supporting this trend has also been the awareness that GH is necessary not only for normal infant and childhood growth but also in the regulation of normal body composition in adulthood – as suggested by the findings of increased lean body and muscle mass, and reduced fat mass following treatment of adults with GH deficiency with recombinant human GH (see *The Seville hGH Symposium*, 1990).

Potential candidates for receiving GH replacement therapy are also elderly subjects. It has been known for some years that there are some similarities between the alterations in structure and function occurring with advancing age and those occurring in GH-deficient patients. Both conditions are characterized by reduction of lean body mass, expansion of adipose mass, and diminution in renal function and in the rate of cell division. Moreover, both types of subject exhibit a reduction in bone mass and density, dental deficits and a decrease in Ca^{2+} absorption. Consistent with these observations, about a third of a large group of old subjects (50–80 years old) exhibited very low concentrations of somatomedin C or insulin-like growth factor 1 (IGF-1) (Rudman, 1985), the GH-related peptide responsible for most of the biological effects of GH (Underwood & Van Wyk, 1985).

Since defective GH secretion may be one of the pacemakers of ageing (Rudman *et al.*, 1981), and administration of human GH to elderly subjects has been shown to reverse some indices of protein catabolism (Marcus *et al.*, 1990; Rudman *et al.*, 1990), it is important to discover the mechanism(s) underlying the reduced GH secretion in aged humans and animals. A pharmacological approach can then be made to attempt to counteract the age-related phenomena.

Basal and stimulated GH secretion in senescent mammals

The secretion of GH is physiologically regulated by the opposite actions of two specific neurohormones, i.e. GH-releasing hormone (GHRH) and somatostatin (Müller, 1987). GHRH and somatostatin interact functionally at both hypothalamic and pituitary levels, and these interactions are responsible for the episodic pattern of GH release in mammals (Müller, 1987). In young mature male rats GH release is pulsatile in nature with a periodicity of approximately 3·3 h (Tannenbaum & Martin, 1976). The amplitude of the GH pulses is significantly reduced in ageing male and female rats, and in male rats this results in a diminished mean secretion of GH to about a third of that in young rats (Sonntag *et al.*, 1980; Takahashi *et al.*, 1987). In both female and male old rats, the frequency of GH pulses does not change with age.

Similarly, in humans, the mean concentration of GH over a 24 h period after the fourth decade of life is similar to that found in hypopituitary children, and is about a quarter of that found in prepubertal subjects (Zadik *et al.*, 1985). Although young women secrete more GH than young men, there is no sex-related difference in GH secretion between old women and old men (Ho *et al.*, 1987).

It is noteworthy that GHRH administered to aged rats induces a markedly lower GH release than in young controls, irrespective of whether GHRH is administered according to body weight or as a fixed dose per rat (Cocchi et al., 1986). A similar pattern is present in dogs in which the regulation of GH is similar to that of humans (Cocola et al., 1976). In six male and female beagle dogs aged between 10 and 14 years, administration of GHRH induced a rise in the plasma GH concentration that was significantly lower than that evoked in young dogs (3–4 years old) (Müller et al., 1988). A blunted GH response to GHRH also occurs in aged human subjects (Shibasaki et al., 1984), although other authors have related this effect to the amount of body fat and not to ageing itself (Pavlov et al., 1986).

Parallel to the findings *in vivo*, an impaired responsiveness to GHRH is evident in pituitary somatotrophic hormones in old male and female rats (Cocchi et al., 1986; Ceda et al., 1986; Takahara et al., 1984), although there is one conflicting report (Sonntag et al., 1983). GHRH specifically elicits release of GH and activation of adenylate cyclase, thus promoting the accumulation of intracellular cAMP in a manner dependent on the concentration of adenylate cyclase (Lewin et al., 1983).

Studies *in vitro* of young (2 months) and aged (14 months) male and female Sprague-Dawley rats showed that the reduced secretion of GH after GHRH administration is linked with a diminished GHRH-induced stimulation of adenylate cyclase in pituitary membranes from aged male and female rats (Fig. 1). In addition, the basal adenylate cyclase activity in pituitary membranes of aged rats is significantly higher in old male, but not old female rats, than in young rats. Pretreatment with GHRH *in vivo* (5 μg per rat, daily for 3 days) decreases the high basal adenylate cyclase activity in aged rats, but does not affect the subsequent GHRH-stimulated rise in adenylate cyclase concentration in old male rats *in vitro*. This pretreatment induces a small but unequivocal rise in adenylate cyclase activity in old female rats. Interestingly, treatment of young male and female rats with the same GHRH schedule does not change basal adenylate cyclase activity in the pituitary, but markedly reduces the effectiveness of subsequent acute exposure to GHRH to induce enzymatic activity (Parenti et al., 1987). These findings suggest that short-term GHRH treatment has a sensitizing effect on pituitary GHRH receptors in old rats, whereas it induces desensitization of the same receptors in young rats.

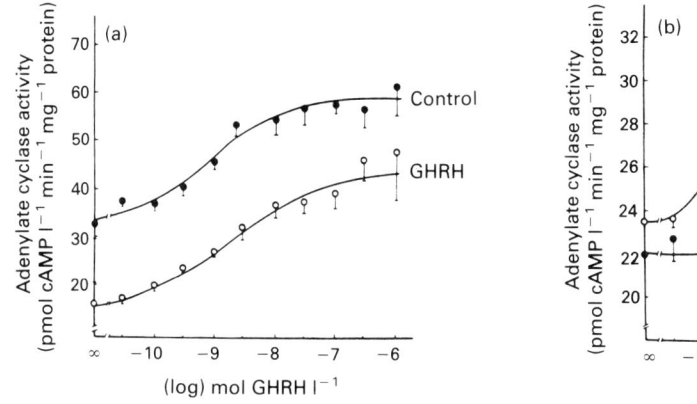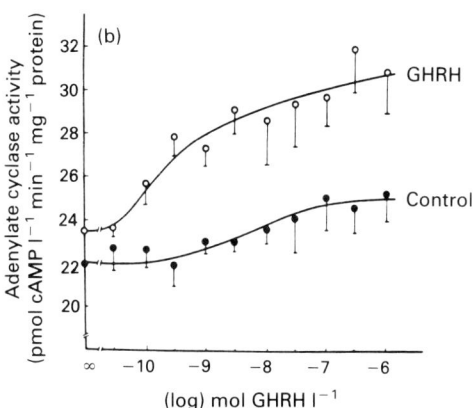

Fig. 1. Effect of rat growth hormone-releasing hormone (rGHRH) on adenylate cyclase activity in anterior pituitary membranes from old (14 months) male (a) and female (b) rats, pretreated or not with rGHRH *in vivo* [curves marked 'GHRH' or 'control' (i.e. pretreated with saline only), respectively]. Rat GHRH was administered i.v. for 3 days at the daily dose of 5 μg per rat, the daily dose being subdivided into three equal injections. The figure shows the mean value (±SEM) of at least three distinct experiments run in duplicate. (Reproduced with permission from Parenti et al., 1987.)

The results obtained by measuring adenylate cyclase activity are supported by data on GH secretion from cultured pituitary cells. The amount of GH secreted from pituitary cells of aged and young female rats is similar, when expressed as a ratio between the amount detected in the medium and the intracellular content. Addition of GHRH induces a significantly lower release of GH into the medium of cells from old as compared with young rats. Pretreatment with GHRH *in vivo* (5 μg per rat, daily for 3 days) reduces both the basal GH secretion and the acute responsiveness to GHRH in cells from young rats, but does not affect these indices in aged rats (Parenti *et al.*, 1987).

GHRH induces not only GH release, but also synthesis of this hormone (Gick *et al.*, 1984); it also sensitizes somatotrophic cells, at least in some circumstances (Borges *et al.*, 1984; Jansson *et al.*, 1985). Overall, the findings are consistent with the view that the diminished pituitary GH content and the reduced response to GHRH in aged rats are due to a defective hypothalamic secretion of the neurohormone (see below). The results obtained from old rats reflect the ability of injected GHRH to increase responsiveness to GH in mammals that are deficient in GHRH or GH – as shown in hypophysectomized rats with an ectopic pituitary (Jansson *et al.*, 1985) – or in GH-deficient humans (Borges *et al.*, 1984).

Attempts have also been made to stimulate the sluggish somatotrophic function in elderly humans using GHRH. In aged normal male and female subjects administration of GHRH i.v. (80 μg twice daily for 10 days) had a sensitizing effect on the release of GH, which was induced by this acute administration of GHRH and increased plasma concentration of IGF-1 (Müller *et al.*, 1988). Similar results were obtained when 100 μg GHRH were administered i.v. every 2 days for 12 days (Iovino *et al.*, 1989). In post-menopausal women, there is a negative correlation between both age and duration of menopause and response of GH to acute administration of GHRH. Repeated GHRH injections (80 μg GHRH once a day for 8 days, i.v.) induces a significant increase in the concentration of IGF-1 and GH between days 4 and 8. No phosphate or Ca^{2+} parameters were modified, but plasma osteocalcin rose between days 2 and 8 (Franchimont *et al.*, 1989). More recently, the effects of continuous subcutaneous infusion of GHRH (1 or 2 mg in 24 h) have been examined in old men, with blood samples taken every 20 min. Both treatment doses evoked significant increases in the mean amount of GH measured over 24 h, the basal amount of GH, the number of peaks of GH activity, but not in the area under peak, peak amplitude or peak duration of GH release (Corpas *et al.*, 1992).

The aged pituitary: morphology and function of somatotrophic cells

Although data described so far indicate a primary impairment in hypothalamic control of GH release in ageing, it seems pertinent to discuss some aspects of the control that are more closely related to the pituitary.

In the human pituitary gland there is an age-related reduction in the number and size of GH-immunoreactive cells (Sun *et al.*, 1984). This observation is consistent with the results of immunocytochemical studies performed on the pituitaries of senescent male and female rats (Rossi *et al.*, 1991). Using the light microscope, the number of pituitary somatotrophs and the number of GH-immunoreactive structures appeared to be higher in male than female rats. These findings agree with the higher content and synthesis rate of GH found in male than in female rats, and with the observation that GH secretion is greater from cultured male than from female pituitary cells (see Batson *et al.*, 1989).

The number of GH-immunoreactive structures was considerably reduced in old rats of both sexes, which could indicate that with increasing age somatotrophs become either reduced in number or grouped in clusters. However, compared with young adult rats of the same sex, the total GH immunoreactivity and area of immunoreactive material per unit surface area of pituitary tissue was increased in old male and decreased in old female rats (Table 1). Thus, the reduced number of GH-immunoreactive structures associated with increased total immunoreactivity and increased area of GH-labelled cytoplasm in old male somatotrophs may be explained by a moderately increased cell size, which leads to the formation of cell clusters. By contrast, in old female rats the total immunoreactivity and area of GH-labelled cytoplasm, as well as the number of GH-immunoreactive structures, were reduced. This could indicate that ageing generally diminishes the somatotrophic function of female rats.

Table 1. Densitometric measurement of growth hormone in pituitary glands from young and old male and female rats

Group	Total immuno-reactivity per μm² of tissue (A)	No. of structures per mm² of tissue	Area of immuno-reactive material per mm² of tissue (μm² × 10^{-3}) (B)	(A/B) × 10^3
Male				
Young adult	4·10 ± 0·311	4432 ± 181·1[b]	134·2 ± 9·60	30·5 ± 0·24
Old	5·78 ± 0·649[b,c]	2813 ± 268·5[b,d]	176·7 ± 19·56[b]	32·7 ± 0·55[a,d]
Female				
Young adult	3·84 ± 0·540	2564 ± 164·4	121·9 ± 16·60	31·4 ± 0·43
Old	2·35 ± 0·370[c]	1692 ± 208·2[d]	68·8 ± 10·71[d]	34·2 ± 0·14[d]

Values are mean ± SEM. There were seven rats per group.
[a]($P < 0·05$) and [b]($P < 0·01$) denote a significant difference between males and females. [c]($P < 0·05$) and [d]($P < 0·01$) denote a significant difference between young and old adult rats.
Taken from Rossi et al., 1991.

Somatotrophic responsiveness to GHRH gradually decreases with ageing, although this is not a unanimous observation (Sonntag et al., 1983; Spik & Sonntag, 1989). Conversely, pituitary responsiveness to somatostatinergic input gradually increases with age (Rieutort, 1981). To explain the changes in somatotrophic responsiveness to GHRH and somatostatin during the lifespan of the rat, it might be postulated that stimulatory and inhibitory GTP-binding regulatory proteins (G proteins), which are coupled to adenylate cyclase, mature and age at different times.

Experiments were performed in which the effect of different concentrations of GHRH and somatostatin on adenylate cyclase activity were evaluated in pituitary membranes from rats of different ages. In addition, the amounts of stimulatory and inhibitory G proteins (G_s and G_i) were measured by evaluating the stimulatory and inhibitory effects of different concentrations of GTP on adenylate cyclase (Parenti et al., 1991). Briefly, GHRH induced less adenylate cyclase activity in membranes from infant and old rats than from adult rats, while somatostatin inhibited the stimulation of adenylate cyclase by forskolin less effectively in membranes from infant and old rats than from adult rats (Fig. 2).

However, it must be noted that despite a reduced hormonal sensitivity to GHRH, the absolute synthesis of cAMP was higher in the pituitaries of the old rats. This might suggest that during ageing a functional uncoupling between GHRH receptors and the adenylate cyclase effectors develops, i.e. adenylate cyclase partially loses the ability to be regulated by the hormone. The observation that activation of adenylate cyclase by GTP is about 2·5 times higher in the aged than in neonatal and adult pituitaries might indicate that an increase in the activity or number of G_s molecules could account for the increased basal adenylate cyclase activity, and suggests that the uncoupling event takes place between the GHRH receptor and the G protein. The reduced ability of somatostatin to inhibit the adenylate cyclase that has been stimulated in aged pituitaries, taken together with the fact that these membranes are more sensitive to adenylate cyclase inhibition when GTP concentration is high, indicates that somatostatin receptors are diminished or uncoupled from the enzyme. The first hypothesis is consonant with the reported reduction in the number of somatotrophs (see Sun et al., 1984; Rossi et al., 1991) in aged pituitaries.

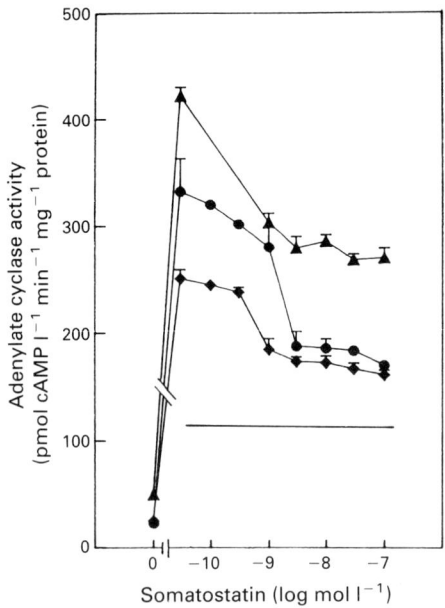

Fig. 2. Effect of somatostatin on forskolin-stimulated adenylate cyclase activity in the anterior pituitary of 8-day-old (♦), 3-month-old (●) and 21–23-month-old (▲) rats. All the experimental points above the bar were measured in the presence of 30 μmol forskolin l^{-1}. Values are means ± SEM of three experiments each performed in duplicate. (Reproduced with permission from Parenti et al., 1991.)

Taken together, these data indicate that in the rat different mechanisms underlie the age-related changes in the somatotrophic responsiveness to GHRH and somatostatin. In aged rats the presence of an increased activity of the GTP stimulatory protein (G_s) under basal conditions may be the reason for the inability of GHRH to stimulate pituitary adenylate cyclase activity further and, hence, to affect GH release. Interestingly, the observed alteration in basal adenylate cyclase activity is similar to that found by Vallar et al. (1987) in a sub-group of human GH-secreting adenomas, which, in contrast to pituitaries of aged rats, secrete GH at a high level. Pituitary membranes of aged rats display a higher G_i protein activity than adult animals; thus, the impaired ability of somatostatin to inhibit adenylate cyclase activity probably results from the reduction in the number of somatotrophic cells and, hence, receptors.

Neural regulation of GH secretion in senescent mammals

Although the existence of an age-related pituitary impairment can be envisaged from the evidence reported here and from other studies (Abribat et al., 1991), there is now accumulating evidence to suggest that major alterations in ageing may be located at the hypothalamic or suprahypothalamic level.

It is now unequivocally established that neurosecretory neurones that manufacture hypothalamic regulatory hormones for the control of pituitary function are in turn regulated by a host of neurotransmitters and neuropeptides (Müller & Nisticò, 1989). Hypothalamic neurones that manufacture GHRH and somatostatin are regulated largely by catecholamines and acetylcholine (ACh) (Müller et al., 1991).

The use of double labelling with dopamine-β-hydroxylase (DBH) and phenylethanolamine-N-methyltransferase (PNMT) for tracing the catecholaminergic system has revealed that the distribution of catecholaminergic fibres is similar to that of GHRH-immunoreactive neurones in the arcuate nucleus (Liposits et al., 1989), where the vast majority of GHRH-synthesizing neurones are located (Bloch et al., 1984). The simultaneous detection of immunoreactivity to PNMT and GHRH using the electron microscope has demonstrated axodendritic and axosomatic synaptic specialization between these systems. These observations provide strong morphological support for the notion that functional activation of the catecholaminergic system stimulates GH secretion in the rat via release of GHRH (Miki et al., 1984; Kabayama et al., 1986). Conversely, inhibition of noradrenaline (Edèn et al., 1981) or adrenaline (Terry et al., 1982) synthesis results in the suppression of pulsatile GH secretion.

There is also neuroanatomical evidence that somatostatin-synthesizing structures in the anterior periventricular nucleus of the hypothalamus are innervated by PNMT-immunoreactive axons (Liposits et al., 1990). Functional studies have demonstrated significant increases in the concentrations of somatostatin in the portal blood of urethane-anaesthetized rats after injection of noradrenaline (Chihara et al., 1979), which could be ascribed to the catecholaminergic component directly innervating somatostatin-synthesizing neurones. The arcuate nucleus is also the principal source in the hypothalamus of dopaminergic neurones and nerve terminals, which provide about a third of the whole innervation of the median eminence (Hökfelt et al., 1978). Interestingly, cell bodies in the ventrolateral part of the arcuate nucleus contain tyrosine hydroxylase (the key enzyme for catecholamine biosynthesis), γ-aminobutyric acid (GABA), ACh, neurotensin and galanin, as well as GHRH (Meister et al., 1987).

Topographical localization of cholinergic pathways in relation to neurones synthesizing GHRH and somatostatin is not so precise as that of catecholaminergic pathways. However, the presence of cholinergic neurones in the arcuate nucleus, based on choline acetyltransferase (ChAT) biochemistry and acetylcholinesterase (AChE) staining (Carson et al., 1977), has been suggested, and it has been more recently confirmed in immunohistochemical experiments using antibodies to ChAT (Rao et al., 1988; Tago et al., 1988).

The neurones immunoreactive to ChAT are seen primarily in the ventrolateral part of the arcuate nucleus, and the majority of these cells have immunoreactivity like that of tyrosine hydroxylase (Tinner et al., 1989). The position of these neurones and the co-existence of ChAT with tyrosine hydroxylase in virtually all ventrolateral arcuate neurones suggest that they also contain GABA, neurotensin, galanin and GHRH (see above) (Fig. 3). The lateral preoptic area, a major area of somatostatin biosynthesis in the CNS, is particularly rich in AChE-containing cells, and somatostatinergic and cholinergic terminals are distributed in a similar manner in the lateral region of the external layer of the median eminence (Hökfelt et al., 1978; Seybold & Wilcox, 1987).

It is beyond the scope of this article to review in detail the main age-related alterations in brain neurotransmitters and neuropeptides. It will suffice to say that age-related changes in noradrenaline metabolism, concentration and receptor function in the brain, and particularly in the mediobasal hypothalamus (Simpkins et al., 1977), and decreased dopamine concentration in the median eminence (Demarest et al., 1980) and also in the hypophyseal portal blood (Porter et al., 1985) have been detected in rodents. In addition, reduced concentrations of ACh in subcortical structures of aged rodents and humans, including the hippocampus and the hypothalamus, have been reported (Perry, 1987).

Changes that occur with ageing in the neurotransmission of catecholamines, ACh and other transmitters and peptide co-transmitters, and deficits that occur in receptor sites, receptor turnover, receptor–receptor interactions and transduction mechanisms (see Füxe et al., 1989) are probably instrumental in incurring changes in the functional activity of GHRH and somatostatin-synthesizing neurones.

In studies examining the distribution and staining intensities of GHRH and somatostatin in the hypothalamus of young and old rats by an immunocytochemical procedure, Morimoto et al. (1988) showed that the intensity of GHRH immunoreactivity in the median eminence of old rats is markedly reduced, compared with that of young rats. No remarkable difference could be detected

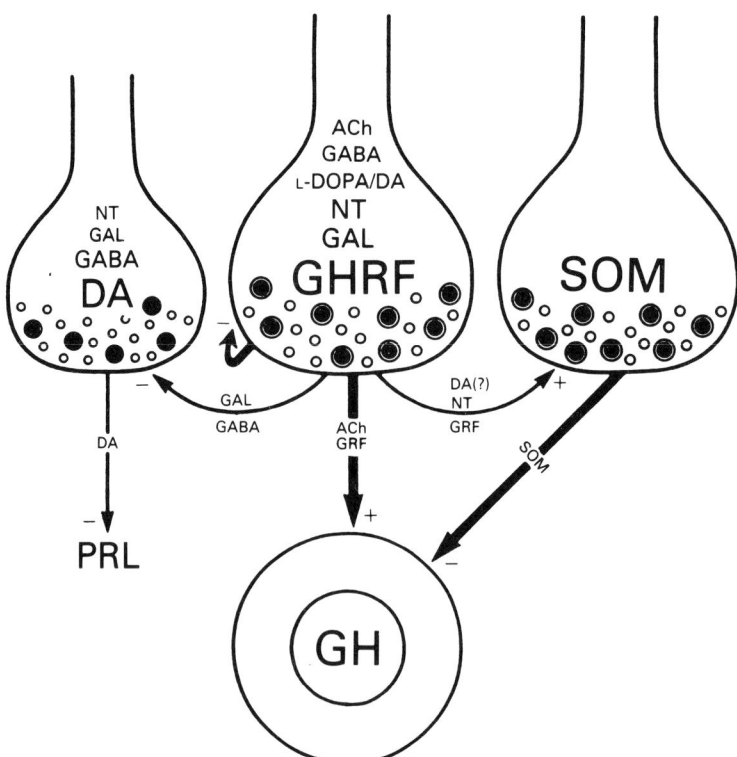

Fig. 3. Illustration of the effects of various compounds released from nerve terminals in the median eminence, and their possible interactions in the control of growth hormone (GH) secretion. Curved arrows coming from the nerve terminal in the centre show the effect exerted via galanin (GAL), γ-aminobutyric acid (GABA), dopamine (DA), neurotensin (NT), and GH-releasing factor (GHRF). Ach: acetylcholine; L-DOPA: L-dihydroxyphenylalanine; PRL: prolactin; SOM: somatostatin. (Reproduced with permission from Meister & Hökfelt, 1988.)

between the immunoreactivities to somatostatin in the young and old animals. Interestingly, in old colchicine-treated rats, GHRH and somatostatin-containing neuronal perikarya showed no change in distribution or immunoreactive intensities compared with young colchicine-treated rats. Moreover, no significant differences were found in the total number of immunoreactive neuronal perikarya of both types of peptidergic neurone between young and old colchicine-treated rats. Overall, these observations indicate that in the old animals GHRH and somatostatin-containing neurones, which are the origin of afferent projections to the median eminence, remain alive as the animal ages, and still have the capacity to synthesize the respective peptides.

What was altered in old male rats was the synthesis or release of the neurohormones, particularly in GHRH-containing neurones. A direct demonstration that GHRH synthesis was impaired was provided by De Gennaro Colonna *et al.* (1989), who reported a clear-cut reduction in GHRH mRNA levels (slot blot hybridization) and GHRH-like immunoreactivity (semiquantitative immunocytochemistry) in the hypothalamus of old male Sprague-Dawley rats.

Besides unaltered immunoreactivity to somatostatin in the hypothalamus and median eminence in old versus young rats (see above), an augmented secretion in cultures of hypothalamic neurones (Sonntag *et al.*, 1986) or from the hypothalamus under high K^+ stimulation (40 mmol l^{-1} (Sonntag *et al.*, 1986; Ferrara *et al.*, 1991) has been reported in aged rats. These findings and other observations, for example, that passive immunization with somatostatin antiserum increases GH concentrations equally in young and old animals (Sonntag *et al.*, 1981) and restores the pituitary response to GHRH in old rats (Locatelli et al., 1984), indicates that somatostatin has a significant role in the age-related decline in GH secretion (see also below). However, expression of somatostatin in the rat hypothalamus decreases consistently with age and in old rats it has been found to be approximately half of that observed in young animals (Sonntag et al., 1990). Similar results were obtained in middle-aged and ageing rats of both sexes by Martinoli et al. (1991).

The disparate findings of decreased somatostatin gene expression and reportedly increased somatostatin secretion are difficult to reconcile but are not mutually exclusive. Post-transcriptional regulatory mechanisms, e.g. an increase in the efficiency of somatostatin translation, could allow a small amount of somatostatin mRNA to synthesize the same or greater amounts of the peptide in older rats (see Sonntag et al., 1990, for review). Overall, it would appear that if the relationships between GHRH and somatostatin gene expression and peptide secretion are altered in aged rats this may play a key role in disrupting the GH secretory pattern.

Catecholaminergic and cholinergic neurotransmission: functional studies

The notion that functional activation of catecholaminergic and cholinergic pathways in the hypothalamus plays a major role in the control of GH secretion in many animal species, and that the underlying mechanism is via modulation of GHRH and somatostatin neurones (Müller et al., 1991), may be exploited to investigate somatotrophic function in GH-deficient states, e.g. in ageing.

Briefly, α-adrenergic mechanisms regulate GH secretion in both subprimate and primate species (Müller & Nisticò, 1989). Clonidine, an $α_2$-adrenoceptor agonist, stimulates GH release in most animal species, including humans – an effect that is counteracted by the $α_2$-adrenoceptor antagonist yohimbine (Camanni et al., 1989). Apparently, $α_2$-adrenergic agonists act by stimulating GHRH release (see above), a proposition supported by the detection of specific $α_2$-adrenergic nerve terminals in the arcuate nucleus (see above). However, the possibility has to be considered that clonidine may also act by inhibiting somatostatin release (Dieguez et al., 1989) (see below). Stimulation of $α_1$-adrenergic receptors, which inhibits GH release in rats (Krulich et al., 1982) and dogs (Cella et al., 1984), probably occurs via an increase in the release of hypothalamic somatostatin (Cella et al., 1987). β-Adrenergic pathways also inhibit GH release, and inferential evidence indicates that β-receptors regulate GH secretion via somatostatin (Müller, 1987).

Studies in rats and dogs have shown that central or peripheral administration of cholinergic muscarinic agonists or antagonists stimulates or suppresses, respectively, GH release (Müller, 1987). In humans, muscarinic agonists stimulate basal GH release, whereas muscarinic antagonists – regardless of whether or not they cross the blood–brain barrier – abolish the rise in plasma GH induced by a host of GH secretagogues, except insulin hypoglycaemia (Müller et al., 1991). Cholinergic modulation appears to affect GH release via stimulation or inhibition of hypothalamic somatostatin release (Locatelli et al., 1986). Depletion of hypothalamic somatostatin stores by cysteamine or impairment of somatostatin inputs by deafferentation of the hypothalamus are in fact capable of abolishing the modulatory effect of cholinergic drugs on GHRH-induced GH secretion (Locatelli et al., 1986). It is probably via this mechanism that atropine and pirenzepine, two muscarinic receptor antagonists, when administered to humans completely abolish the GHRH-induced GH rise, and the means by which pyridostigmine, an AChE inhibitor, greatly potentiates this response (Massara et al., 1986). In addition, studies in rats (Torsello et al., 1988) and humans (Ross et al., 1987) have suggested that cholinergic mechanisms are also involved in the autofeedback regulation of GH secretion.

It seems that muscarinic cholinergic agonists could be used to investigate the hypothalamic somatostatin system in different physiological or pathological conditions. To test this theory, the ability of pilocarpine, an agonist at muscarinic cholinergic receptors, to modulate the GH response to GHRH in rats aged between 10 days and 29 months has been evaluated. It is evident from Table 2 that after administration of GHRH alone there is an age-related decline in responsiveness of GH, after the age of 8 months. Administration of pilocarpine potentiated the GH response to GHRH during the entire life span of the rats – the only exception being 10-day-old rats, in which the drug was without effect (data not shown). Pilocarpine, although effective in potentiating the GH response to GHRH, did not restore GH stimulation in senescent rats to the concentration of that present in young (3-month-old) or adult (8-month-old) rats. However, the drug was effective in rejuvenating the response of GH to GHRH of the older rats (18 and 29 months old) to the concentration of that found in 15-month-old rats. Results obtained in humans are in keeping with these findings. In a group of elderly normal subjects, pretreatment with pyridostigmine potentiated the response of GH to GHRH; however, the response of GH to a combined administration of GHRH and pyridostigmine was significantly lower in elderly than in young subjects (Ghigo et al., 1990a).

Table 2. Peak plasma levels of growth hormone (GH) and GH-integrated areas following the administration of growth hormone-releasing hormone (GHRH) at $2\,\mu g\,kg^{-1}$ body weight, i.v.), either administered alone or preceded 15 min beforehand by pilocarpine ($3\,mg\,kg^{-1}$ body weight, i.v.) in male rats of different ages

Treatment	Age (months)				
	3	8	15	18	29
	Peak plasma GH (ng ml^{-1})				
GHRH	174 ± 11^b (8)	222 ± 16^c (8)	78 ± 16^d (11)	19 ± 6^d (7)	15 ± 7^d (5)
Pilocarpine + GHRH	416 ± 42^c (8)	325 ± 43^c (8)	140 ± 28^d (10)	91 ± 7^d (6)	134 ± 24^d (5)
	$P^e < 0.01$	0.05	ns	0.01	0.01
	GH integrated areas (ng ml^{-1} in 30 min)				
GHRH	2691 ± 228^c (8)	2348 ± 171^c (8)	$770 \pm 92^{b,d}$ (11)	422 ± 75^d (7)	148 ± 67^d (5)
Pilocarpine + GHRH	5860 ± 702^c (8)	$3898 \pm 471^{c,d}$ (8)	1457 ± 197^d (10)	1199 ± 73^d (6)	1295 ± 233^d (5)
	$P^e < 0.01$	0.01	0.01	0.01	0.01

Values are mean ± SE. Number of rats is given in parentheses.
[b] ($P < 0.05$) denotes a significant difference between that value and the corresponding value in the 29-month-old group (analysis of variance and Dunnett's t test).
[c] ($P < 0.01$) denotes a significant difference between that value and the corresponding value in the 29-month-old group (analysis of variance and Dunnett's t test).
[d] ($P < 0.01$) denotes a significant difference between that value and the corresponding value in the 3-month-old group (analysis of variance and Dunnett's t test).
[e] The probability value shown denotes a significant difference between GHRH treatment and GHRH plus pilocarpine treatment in the same age group.
ns: not significant.
Taken from Panzeri et al., 1990.

All in all, these findings support the idea that in aged mammals the reduced response of GH to GHRH is only partly due to an intrinsic defect of the somatotrophs, and that hypothalamic or extrahypothalamic inhibitory influences under cholinergic control are also involved. It is noteworthy in this context that cholinergic agonists induce a blunted GH response in aged humans (Raskind et al., 1990).

More direct evidence for the preservation of a pool of releasable GH in the human pituitary gland even during ageing has been obtained using arginine, an amino acid that purportedly acts by inhibiting hypothalamic somatostatin release (Alba-Roth et al., 1988). Pretreatment with arginine (30 g infused over 30 min) potentiates the response of GH to GHRH both in young and elderly subjects. However, the potentiating effect of arginine on the GHRH-induced GH response is greater in elderly than in young subjects; thus, the increase in GH induced by combined administration of arginine and GHRH was similar in both old and young subjects (Ghigo et al., 1990b).

The involvement of a more extensive neurotransmitter dysfunction in ageing is suggested by the results obtained with clonidine. In a group of old beagle dogs administration of clonidine (75 µg orally, twice a day for 14 days) increased the frequency and amplitude of spontaneous GH bursts and the mean peak area under the curve of GH release, which were evaluated for 6 h, 14 h after the last clonidine administration. After the administration of this peptide the secretory pattern of GH in these aged animals was quantitatively and qualitatively indistinguishable from that of young dogs under baseline conditions (Cella et al., 1989). These data indicate that an age-related dysfunction of α_2-adrenoceptors is present in the hypothalamus of old dogs (Füxe et al., 1989), and that this alteration subsides after administration of clonidine. It is noteworthy that in these studies administration of clonidine increased not only the pulse amplitude of GH release but also the pulse frequency – a secretory index that has been related to somatostatin function (Kraicer et al., 1986).

More cogent proof for an action of clonidine in promoting GH release by inhibition of somatostatin release (see above) has been provided both in humans (Arce et al., 1990a) and dogs (Arce et al., 1990b). Simultaneous administration of clonidine and GHRH induced an additive effect on GH release in young dogs, but potentiated GHRH-induced GH release in old dogs. Moreover, in two old dogs that had been repeatedly unresponsive to GHRH alone or after a 10-day GHRH pretreatment, administration of clonidine and GHRH together unmasked a sizeable GH response (Arce et al., 1990b). This finding also favours the view that the mechanism subserving the effect of clonidine is not exclusively the release of hypothalamic GHRH.

Overall, the data from humans, dogs and rats that have been discussed here suggests that a decreased GHRH or increased somatostatinergic activity are the main events underlying the age-related decline of GH secretion. To investigate this problem further, the effect was studied in old dogs of short-term administration of GHRH alone or GHRH given with clonidine on the GH secretory pattern and responsiveness of GH to an acute GHRH challenge or an acute challenge of GHRH and clonidine together. Briefly, GHRH given alone twice a day for 10 days to a group of old male and female dogs primed the pituitary, so that acute administration of GHRH or GHRH and clonidine together elicited mean peak GH responses that were higher than those observed before treatment. In dogs that were given GHRH and clonidine together twice a day, acute administration of GHRH elicited a mean GH peak response higher than that observed before treatment. However, acute administration of GHRH and clonidine together induced a mean GH peak response not different from that elicited by GHRH and clonidine before treatment, or by GHRH alone after treatment. In dogs that were given GHRH and clonidine together, but with clonidine given only once a day, acute administration of GHRH alone or GHRH and clonidine together elicited a mean GH peak response which was higher than those elicited by the same drugs before treatment (data not shown). Evaluation of the GH secretory pattern from blood samples taken at 10 min intervals for 6 h (cluster analysis), both before and at the end of the different treatments, showed that administration of GHRH alone did not modify any of the secretory indices that were evaluated, except for the increase in mean GH peak amplitude. However, administration of GHRH and clonidine together twice a day significantly augmented the frequency of spontaneous bursts of GH secretion, the mean GH peak amplitude and the total peak area. When clonidine was administered only once a day, all these indices increased even more than when GHRH and clonidine were administered together twice a day (Cella et al., 1992). Figure 4 shows the GH secretory pattern in two representative dogs undergoing the different treatments.

It seems paradoxical that administration of clonidine twice a day was less effective than when the drug was given only once a day, but it may be because the α_2-adrenergic agonist can downregulate its own receptors at the arcuate nucleus (Cella et al., 1990).

Conclusions

Evaluation of the mechanism(s) underlying the age-related decline of GH secretion in mammals has revealed the existence of a pituitary component that is probably manifested in a diminished

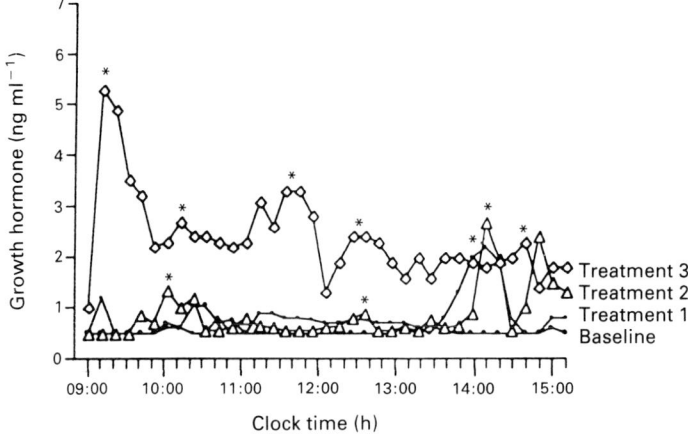
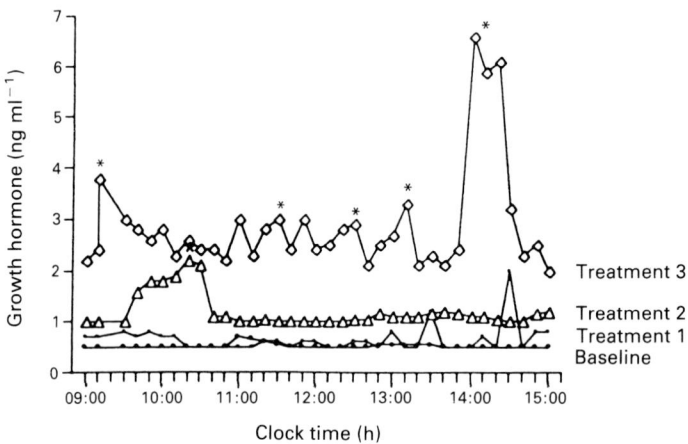

Fig. 4. Spontaneous growth hormone secretory pattern in two representative dogs before (baseline) or after a 10-day treatment with growth hormone-releasing hormone (GHRH) administered twice a day (treatment 1), GHRH and clonidine both given twice a day (treatment 2), or GHRH and clonidine, clonidine administered once a day (treatment 3). Blood samples were taken every 10 min for 6 h. Asterisks indicate the growth hormone peaks detected by cluster analysis.

number of somatotrophic cells and GHRH receptors, without ruling out the existence of post-receptor impairments (Parenti *et al.*, 1991). However, from the evidence reviewed it would seem that a defective function of the somatotroph does not play a major role, and that the maximal GH secretory capacity is preserved in the aged pituitary when specific hypothalamic influences are restored (by GHRH) or toned down (by somatostatin), respectively. The main cause of age-related decline in GH secretion therefore appears to be increasingly defective hypothalamic GHRH function coupled to a relative predominance in the effect of somatostatin.

Knowing about GH hyposecretion and that it may act as a pacemaker of ageing (Rudman, 1981, 1985) has led to preliminary attempts to substitute for the declining somatotrophic function in the elderly by administering GH. It is too early to know whether this replacement therapy will be beneficial on a long-term basis or whether reduced GH secretion would be a more desirable event. If replacement therapy turns out to be more effective, based on the ability of the aged pituitary to respond normally to pharmacological or dietary manoeuvres acting at the hypothalamus or the pituitary, it may be envisaged that stimulation of endogenous GH secretion – hopefully in a physiological, pulsatile manner – may help to counter structural and functional alterations related to somatotroph deficiency in the elderly.

This work was supported by the special C.N.R. project 'Progetto Finalizzato Invecchiamento', No. 921218.

References

Abribat, T., Deslauriers, N., Brazeau, P. & Gaudreau, P. (1991) Alterations of pituitary growth hormone-releasing factor binding sites in aging rats. *Endocrinology* **128**, 633–635.

Alba-Roth, J., Müller, O.A., Schopohl, J. & Von Werder, K. (1988) Arginine stimulates growth hormone secretion by suppressing endogenous somatostatin secretion. *Journal of Clinical Endocrinology and Metabolism* **67**, 1186–1189.

Arce, V., Lima, L., Tresguerres, N. & Devesa, J.A.F. (1990a) Clonidine inhibits hypothalamic somatostatin release in humans. *Neuroendocrinology* **52** (Suppl. 1), 119–124.

Arce, V., Cella, S.G., Loche, S., Ghigo, E., Devesa, J. & Müller, E.E. (1990b) Synergistic effect of growth hormone-releasing hormone (GHRH) and clonidine in stimulating GH release in young and old dogs. *Brain Research* **537**, 359–362.

Batson, J.M., Krieg, R.J., Jr, Martha, P.M. & Evans, W.S. (1989) Growth hormone (GH) response to GH-releasing hormone by perifused pituitary cells from male, female and testicular feminized rats. *Endocrinology* **124**, 444–448.

Bloch, B., Ling, N., Benoit, R., Wehrenberg, W.B. & Guillemin, R. (1984) Specific depletion of immunoreactive growth hormone releasing factor by monosodium glutamate in rat median eminence. *Nature* **307**, 272–273.

Borges, J.C.L., Blizzard, R.M., Evans, W.S., Furlanetto, R., Rogol, A.D., Kaiser, D.I., Rivier, J., Vale, W.C. & Thorner, M.O. (1984) Stimulation of growth hormone (GH) and somatomedin-C in idiopathic GH-deficient subjects by intermittent pulsatile administration of synthetic human pancreatic tumor GH-releasing factor. *Journal of Clinical Endocrinology and Metabolism* **59**, 1–6.

Camanni, F., Ghigo, E., Mazza, E., Imperiale, E., Goffi, S., Martina, V., De Gennaro Colonna, V., Cella, S.G., Cocchi, D., Locatelli, V. & Müller, E.E. (1989) Aspects of neurotransmitter control of GH secretion: basic and clinical studies. In *Advances in Growth Hormone and Growth Factor Research*, pp. 263–281. Eds E. E. Müller, D. Cocchi & V. Locatelli. Pythagora Press, Springer-Verlag, Berlin.

Carson, K.A., Nemeroff, C.B., Rone, M.S., Youngblood, W.W., Prange, A.J., Hanker, J.S. & Kizer, J.S. (1977) Biochemical and histochemical evidence for the existence of a tuberoinfundibular cholinergic pathway in the rat. *Brain Research* **129**, 169–173.

Ceda, G.P., Valenti, G., Butturini, U. & Hoffman, A.R. (1986) Diminished pituitary response to growth hormone releasing factor in aging male rats. *Endocrinology* **118**, 2109–2114.

Cella, S.G., Morgese, M., Mantegazza, P. & Müller, E.E. (1984) Inhibitory action of the α_1-adrenergic receptor on growth hormone secretion in the dog. *Endocrinology* **114**, 2406–2408.

Cella, S.G., Locatelli, V., De Gennaro, V., Wehrenberg, W.B. & Müller, E.E. (1987) Pharmacological manipulations of α-adrenoceptors in the infant rat and effects on growth hormone secretion: study of the underlying mechanisms of action. *Endocrinology* **120**, 1639–1643.

Cella, S.G., Moiraghi, V., Minuto, F., Barreca, A., Cocchi, D., De Gennaro Colonna, V., Reina, G. & Müller, E.E. (1989) Prolonged fasting or clonidine can restore the defective growth hormone secretion in old dogs. *Acta Endocrinologica (Copenhagen)* **121**, 177–184.

Cella, S.G., Mennini, T., Miari, A., Cavanus, S., Arce, V. & Müller, E.E. (1990) Down regulation of α_2-adrenoceptors involved in growth hormone control in the hypothalamus of infant rats receiving short-term clonidine administration. *Developmental Brain Research* **53**, 151–155.

Cella, S.G., Arce, V.M., Pieretti, F., Locatelli, V., Settembrini, B.P. & Müller, E.E. (1992) Combined administration of GHRH and clonidine restores the defective GH secretion in old dogs. *Neuroendocrinology*, in press.

Chihara, K., Arimura, A. & Schally, A.V. (1979) Effect of intraventricular injection of dopamine, norepinephrine, acetylcholine, and 5-hydroxytryptamine on immunoreactive somatostatin release into rat hypophyseal portal blood. *Endocrinology* **104**, 1656–1662.

Cocchi, D., Calderini, G., Ganzetti, I., Galbiati, E., Parenti, M. & Müller, E.E. (1986) Aspects of the control of prolactin and growth hormone secretion in aging. In *Neuroendocrine Perspectives* (Vol. 5), pp. 191–204. Eds E. E. Müller & R. M. MacLeod. Elsevier, Amsterdam.

Cocola, F., Udeschini, G., Panerai, A.E., Neri, F. & Müller, E.E. (1976) A rapid radioimmunoassay method for growth hormone in dog plasma. *Proceedings of the Society for Experimental Biology and Medicine* **151**, 140–145.

Corpas, E., Harman, S.M., Piñeiro, M., Roberson, R. & Blackman, M.R. (1992) Continuous subcutaneous infusion of GHRH 1–44 for 14 days increase GH and IGF-I levels in old men. In *Program & Abstracts 74th Annual Meeting Endocrine Society*, p. 320.

De Gennaro Colonna, V., Zoli, M., Cocchi, D., Maggi, A., Marrama, P., Agnati, L.F. & Müller, E.E. (1989) Reduced growth hormone releasing factor (GHRF)-like immunoreactivity and GHRF gene expression in the hypothalamus of aged rats. *Peptides* **10**, 705–708.

Demarest, K.T., Riegle, G.D. & Moore, K.E. (1980) Characteristics of dopaminergic neurons in the aged male rat. *Neuroendocrinology* **31**, 222–227.

Dieguez, C., Valcavi, R., Page, M.D., Zini, M., Casoli, P., Edwards, C.A., Portioli, I. & Scanlon, M.F. (1989) L-Dopa releases GH via a GRF-dependent mechanism in normal human subjects whereas arginine, clonidine and adrenaline plus propranolol do not. In *Neuroendocrine Perspectives* (Vol. 6), pp. 205–221. Eds E. E. Müller & R. M. MacLeod. Springer-Verlag, New York.

Edèn, S., Eriksson, E., Martin, J.B. & Modigh, K. (1981) Evidence for growth hormone releasing factor mediating alpha-adrenergic influence of growth hormone secretion in the rat. *Neuroendocrinology* **34**, 24–27.

Ferrara, C., Ceresoli, G., Marcozzi, C. & Cocchi, D. (1991) Hypothalamic–pituitary somatostatinergic system in middle-aged female rats. *Hormone Metabolic Research* **23**, 243–244.

Franchimont, P., Urbain-Choffray, D., Lambelin, P., Fontaine, M-A., Frangin, G. & Reginster, J-Y. (1989) Effects of repetitive administration of growth hormone releasing hormone on growth hormone secretion, insulin-like growth factor I, and bone metabolism in postmenopausal women. *Acta Endocrinologica (Copenhagen)* **120**, 121–128.

Füxe, K., Agnati, L.F., Zini, I., Merlo Pich, E., Cintra, A., Kitayama, I., Härfstrand, A., von Euler, G., Vale, W., Toffano, G. & Goldstein, M. (1989) Evidence for selective changes in peptide and monoamine synapses and their interactions in the aging rat brain. Possible loss of homeostatic responses and of trophic signals. In *New Trends in Aging Research*, pp. 3–20. Eds G. Pepeu, B. Tomlinson & C. M. Wischik. Liviana Press, Springer-Verlag, Berlin.

Ghigo, E., Goffi, S., Arvat, E., Nicolosi, M., Procopio, M., Bellone, J., Imperiale, E., Mazza, E., Baracchi, G. & Camanni, F. (1990a) Pyridostigmine partially restores the GH responsiveness to GHRH in normal aging. *Acta Endocrinologica (Copenhagen)* **123**, 169–174.

Ghigo, E., Goffi, S., Nicolosi, M., Arvat, E., Bellone, J., Procopio, M., Valente, F., Mazza, E., Ghico, M.C. & Camanni, F. (1990b) Growth hormone responsiveness to combined administration of arginine and GH-releasing hormone does not vary with age in man. *Journal of Clinical Endocrinology and Metabolism* **71**, 1481–1485.

Gick, G.C., Zeytin, F.N., Brazeau, P., Ling, N.C., Esch, F.S. & Bancroft, C. (1984) Growth hormone-releasing factor regulates growth hormone mRNA in primary cultures of rat pituitary cells. *Proceedings of the Society of the Academy of Sciences USA* **81**, 1553–1555.

Ho, K.Y., Evans, W.S., Blizzard, R.M., Veldhuis, J.D., Merriam, G.R., Samojlik, E., Furlanetto, R., Rogol, A.D., Kaiser, D.L. & Thorner, M.O. (1987) Effects of sex and age on the 24-hour profile of growth hormone secretion in man: importance of endogenous estradiol concentrations. *Journal of Clinical Endocrinology and Metabolism* **64**, 51–58.

Hökfelt, T., Elde, R., Fuxe, K., Johansson, O., Ljundahl, A., Goldstein, M., Luft, R., Efendic, S., Nillson, G., Terenius, L., Ganten, D., Jeffcoate, S.L., Rehfeld, J., Said, S., Perez de la Mora, M., Possani, L., Tapia, R., Teran, L. & Palacios, R. (1978) Aminergic and peptidergic pathways in the nervous system with special reference to the hypothalamus. In *The Hypothalamus*, pp. 69–135. Eds S. Reichlin, R. J. Baldessarini & J. B. Martin. Raven Press, New York.

Iovino, M., Monteleone, P. & Steardo, L. (1989) Repetitive growth hormone-releasing hormone administration restores the attenuated growth hormone (GH) response to GH-releasing hormone testing in normal aging. *Journal of Clinical Endocrinology and Metabolism* **69**, 910–913.

Jansson, J.O., Carlsson, L. & Isaksson, O.G.P. (1985) Growth hormone (GH)-releasing factor (GRF) pretreatment enhances the GRF-induced GH secretion in rats with the pituitary autotransplanted to the kidney capsule. *Endocrinology* **116**, 95–98.

Kabayama, Y., Kato, Y., Murakami, Y., Tanaka, H. & Imura, H. (1986) Stimulation by alpha-adrenergic mechanisms of the secretion of growth hormone-releasing factor mediating alpha-adrenergic influence on growth hormone secretion in the rat. *Endocrinology* **119**, 432–434.

Kraicer, J., Cowan, J.S., Sheppard, M.S., Lussier, B. & Moor, B.C. (1986) Effect of somatostatin withdrawal and growth hormone (GH)-releasing factor on GH release *in vitro*: amount available for release after disinhibition. *Endocrinology* **119**, 2047–2051.

Krulich, L., Mayfield, A., Steele, M.K., MacMillen, B.A. & McCann, S.M. (1982) Differential effects of pharmacological manipulations of central α_1- and α_2-adrenergic receptors on the secretion of thyrotropin and growth hormone in male rats. *Endocrinology* **110**, 196–204.

Lewin, M.J., Reyl-Desmars, F. & Ling, N. (1983) Somatocrinin receptor coupled with cAMP-dependent protein kinase on anterior pituitary granules. *Proceedings of the National Academy of Sciences USA* **80**, 6538–6542.

Liposits, Z., Hrabovszky, E. & Paull, W.K. (1989) Catecholaminergic afferents to growth hormone-releasing hormone (GHRH)-synthesizing neurons of the arcuate nucleus in the rat. *Biomedical Research* **40** (Suppl. 3), 1950–1952.

Liposits, Z., Kallò, I., Barkovics-Callò, M., Bohn, M. & Paull, W.K. (1990) Innervation of somatostatin synthesizing neurons by adrenergic, phenylethanolamine-N-methyltransferase (PNMT)-immunoreactive axons in the anterior periventricular nucleus of the rat hypothalamus. *Histochemistry* **94**, 13–20.

Locatelli, V., Arimura, A., Torsello, A., Cella, S.G. & Müller, E.E. (1984) Somatostatin antiserum antagonizes the impaired ability of hpGRF-40 to stimulate growth hormone release in old unanesthetized male rats. *Neuroendocrinology Letters* **6**, 261–265.

Locatelli, V., Torsello, A., Redaelli, M., Ghigo, E., Massara, F. & Müller, E.E. (1986) Cholinergic agonist and antagonist drugs modulate the growth hormone response to growth hormone-releasing hormone in the rat: evidence for mediation by somatostatin. *Journal of Endocrinology* **111**, 271–278.

Marcus, R., Butterfield, G., Holloway, L., Gilliland, L., Baylink, D.J., Hintz, R.L. & Sherman, B.M. (1990) Effects of short-term administration of recombinant human growth hormone to elderly people. *Journal of Clinical Endocrinology and Metabolism* **70**, 519–527.

Martinoli, M.G., Ouellet, J., Rhèaume, E. & Pelletier, G. (1991) Growth hormone and somatostatin gene expression as measured by quantitative *in situ* hybridization. *Neuroendocrinology* **54**, 607–615.

Massara, F., Ghigo, E., Demislis, K., Tangolo, D., Mazza, E., Locatelli, V., Müller, E.E., Molinatti, G.M. & Camanni, F. (1986) Cholinergic involvement in the growth hormone releasing hormone-induced growth hormone release: studies in normal and acromegalic subjects. *Neuroendocrinology* **43**, 670–675.

Meister, B. & Hökfelt, T. (1988) Peptide- and transmitter-containing neurons in the mediobasal hypothalamus and their relation to GABAergic systems: possible roles in control of prolactin and growth hormone secretion. *Synapse* **2**, 585–605.

Meister, B., Hökfelt, T., Johansson, O. & Hulting, A.-L. (1987) Distribution of growth hormone-releasing factor, somatostatin and coexisting messengers in the brain. In *Growth Hormone-Basic and Clinical Aspects*, pp. 29–52. Eds O. Isaksson, C. Binder, K. Hall & T. Hökfelt. Elsevier, Amsterdam.

Miki, N., Ono, M. & Shizume, K. (1984) Evidence that opiatergic and α-adrenergic mechanisms stimulate rat growth hormone release via growth hormone-releasing factor (GRF). *Endocrinology* **114**, 1950–1952.

Morimoto, N., Kawakami, F., Makino, S., Chihara, K., Hasegawa, M. & Ibata, Y. (1988) Age-related changes in growth hormone releasing factor and somatostatin in the rat hypothalamus. *Neuroendocrinology* **47**, 459–464.

Müller, E.E. (1987) Neural control of somatotropic function. *Physiological Reviews* **67**, 962–1053.

Müller, E.E. & Nisticò, G. (1989) *Brain Messengers and the Pituitary*. Academic Press, San Diego.

Müller, E.E., Coiro, V., Pioli, G., Nava, C., Cocchi, D. & Passeri, M. (1988) Short-term administration of GHRH in aged subjects: priming effect on the pituitary and increased plasma SM-C levels. In *Abstract Book of the 8th International Congress of Endocrinology*, p. 118, Kyoto, Japan.

Müller, E.E., Locatelli, V., Ghigo, E., Cella, S.G., Loche, S., Pintor, C. & Camanni, F. (1991) Involvement of brain catecholamines and acetylcholine in growth hormone deficiency states. Pathophysiological, diagnostic and therapeutic implications. *Drugs* **41** (2), 161–177.

Panzeri, G., Torsello, A., Cella, S.G., Müller, E.E. & Locatelli, V. (1990) Age-related modulatory activity by a cholinergic agonist on the growth hormone (GH) response to GH-releasing hormone in the rat. *Proceedings of the Society for Experimental Biology and Medicine* **193**, 301–305.

Parenti, M., Dall'Ara, A., Rusconi, L., Cocchi, D. & Müller, E.E. (1987) Different regulation of GHRH-sensitive adenylate cyclase in the anterior pituitary of young and old rats. *Endocrinology* **121**, 1649–1653.

Parenti, M., Cocchi, D., Ceresoli, G., Marcozzi, C. & Müller, E.E. (1991) Age-related changes of growth hormone secretory mechanisms in the rat pituitary gland. *Journal of Endocrinology* **131**, 251–257.

Pavlov, E.P., Harman, S.M., Merriam, G.M., Gelato, M.C. & Blackman, M.R. (1986) Responses of growth hormone (GH) and somatomedin-C to GH-releasing hormone in healthy aging men. *Journal of Clinical Endocrinology and Metabolism* **62**, 595–600.

Perry, E.K. (1987) Cortical neurotransmitter chemistry in Alzheimer's disease. In *Psychopharmacology: the Third Generation of Progress*, pp. 568–575. Ed. H. Meltzer. Raven Press, New York.

Porter, J.C., Reymond, M.J., Arita, J. & Sisson, J.F. (1985) Tuberoinfundibular dopaminergic neurons as hormone secreting cells and targets of drugs and hormones. In *Catecholamines as Hormone Regulators*, pp. 117–124. Eds N. Ben-Jonathan, J. M. Bahr & R. I. Weiner. Raven Press, New York.

Rao, Z.R., Yamano, M., Wanaka, A., Tatehata, T., Shiosaka, S. & Tohyama, M. (1987) Distribution of cholinergic neurons and fibers in the hypothalamus of the rat using choline acetyltransferase as a marker. *Neuroscience* **20**, 923–934.

Raskind, M.A., Peskind, E.R., Veith, R.C., Wilkinson, C.W., Federighi, D. & Dorsa, D. (1990) Differential effects of aging on neuroendocrine responses to physostigmine in normal men. *Journal of Clinical Endocrinology and Metabolism* **70**, 1420–1425.

Rieutort, M. (1981) Ontogenetic development of the inhibition of growth hormone release by somatostatin in the rat: *in vivo* and *in vitro* (perifusion) study. *Journal of Endocrinology* **89**, 355–363.

Ross, R.J.M., Borges, F., Grossman, A., Smith, R., Nhagafoong, L., Rees, L.H., Savage, M.O. & Besser, G.M. (1987) Growth hormone pretreatment in man blocks the response to growth hormone-releasing hormone: evidence for a direct effect of growth hormone. *Clinical Endocrinology* **26**, 117–123.

Rossi, G.L., Bestetti, G.E., Galbiati, E., Müller, E.E. & Cocchi, D. (1991) Sexually dimorphic effects of aging on rat somatotropes and lactotropes. *Journal of Gerontology: Biological Sciences* **46**, B152–158.

Rudman, D. (1985) Occasional hypothesis. *Journal of the American Geriatrics Society* **33**, 800–807.

Rudman, D., Kutner, M.H., Rogers, C.M., Lubin, M.F., Fleming, G.H. & Bain, R.P. (1981) Impaired growth hormone secretion in the adult population. *Journal of Clinical Investigation* **67**, 1361–1369.

Rudman, D., Feller, A.G., Nagraj, H.S., Gergans, G.A., Lalitha, P.Y., Goldberg, A.F., Schlenker, R.A., Cohn, L., Rudman, I. & Mattson, D.E. (1990) Effects of human growth hormone in men over 60 years old. *The New England Journal of Medicine* **323**, 1–6.

The Seville hGH Symposium (1990) Clinical aspects of growth hormone replacement therapy. *Hormone Research* **33** (Suppl. 4), 1–105.

Seybold, V.S. & Wilcox, B.J. (1987) Distribution of neurotransmitter binding sites in the cat median eminence. *Neuroendocrinology* **46**, 32–38.

Shibasaki, T., Shizume, K., Makahara, M., Masuda, A., Jibiki, K., Demura, H., Wakabayashi, I. & Ling, N. (1984) Age-related changes in plasma growth hormone response to growth hormone-releasing factor in man. *Journal of Clinical Endocrinology and Metabolism* **58**, 212–214.

Simpkins, J.W., Mueller, G.P., Huang, H.H. & Meites, J. (1977) Evidence for depressed catecholamine and enhanced serotonin metabolism in aging male rats: possible relation to gonadotropin secretion. *Endocrinology* **107**, 1672–1678.

Sonntag, W.E., Steger, R.W., Forman, L.J. & Meites, J. (1980) Decreased pulsatile release of growth hormone in old rats. *Endocrinology* **107**, 1875–1879.

Sonntag, W.E., Forman, L.J., Miki, N., Steger, R.W., Ramos, T., Arimura, A. & Meites, J. (1981) Effects of CNS acting drugs and somatostatin antiserum on growth hormone release in old male rats. *Neuroendocrinology* **33**, 73–78.

Sonntag, W.E., Hylka, V.W. & Meites, J. (1983) Impaired ability of old male rats to secrete growth hormone *in vivo* but not *in vitro* in response to hpGRF (1–44). *Endocrinology* **113**, 2305–2307.

Sonntag, W.E., Gottschall, P.E. & Meites, J. (1986) Increased secretion of somatostatin-28 from hypothalamic neurons of aged rats *in vitro*. *Brain Research* **380**, 229–234.

Sonntag, W.E., Boyd, R.L. & Booze, R.M. (1990) Somatostatin gene expression in hypothalamus and cortex of aging male rats. *Neurobiology of Aging* **11**, 409–416.

Spik, K. & Sonntag, W.E. (1989) Increased pituitary response to somatostatin in aging male rats: relationship to somatostatin receptor number and affinity. *Neuroendocrinology* **50**, 489–494.

Sun, Y.-K., Xi, Y.-P., Fenoglio, C.M., Pushparaj, N., O'Toole, K.M., Kledizik, G.S., Nette, E.G. & King, D.W. (1984) The effect of age on the number of pituitary cells immunoreactive to growth hormone and prolactin. *Human Pathology* **15**, 169–173.

Tago, H., McGeer, P.L., Bruce, G. & Hersch, L.B. (1987) Distribution of choline acetyltransferase-containing neurons of the hypothalamus. *Brain Research* **415**, 49–62.

Takahara, J., Niimi, M., Kawanishi, K. & Irino, S. (1984) Effects of age on GH responsiveness to human pancreatic GHRH in rats. In *Abstract Book of the 7th International Congress of Endocrinology*, p. 127. Excerpta Medica, Amsterdam.

Takahashi, S., Gottschall, P.E., Quigley, K.L., Goya, R.G. & Meites, J. (1987) Growth hormone secretory pattern in young, middle-aged and old female rats. *Neuroendocrinology* **46**, 137–142.

Tannenbaum, G.S. & Martin, J.B. (1976) The interrelationship of growth hormone (GH)-releasing factor and somatostatin in generation of the ultradian rhythm of GH secretion. *Endocrinology* **115**, 1952–1957.

Terry, C.K., Crowley, W.R., Lynch, C., Longserre, C. & Johnson, M.D. (1982) Role of central epinephrine in regulation of anterior pituitary hormone secretion. *Peptides* **3**, 311–318.

Tinner, B., Füxe, K., Köhler, C., Hersch, L., Andersson, K., Jansson, A., Goldstein, M. & Agnati, L.F. (1989) Evidence for the existence of a population of arcuate neurons costoring choline acetyltransferase and tyrosine hydroxylase immunoreactivities in the male rat. *Neuroscience Letters* **99**, 44–49.

Torsello, A., Panzeri, G., Cermenati, P., Caroleo, M.C., Ghigo, E., Camanni, F., Müller, E.E. & Locatelli, V. (1988) Involvement of somatostatin and cholinergic systems in the mechanism of growth hormone autofeedback regulation in the rat. *Journal of Endocrinology* **117**, 273–281.

Underwood, L.E. (1991) GH actions in non-GH-deficient states. In *Program and Abstract of the 73rd Annual Meeting of the Endocrine Society*, p. 8. Washington D.C.

Underwood, L.E. & Van Wyk, J.J. (1985) Normal and aberrant growth. In *Williams Textbook of Endocrinology*, pp. 155–205. Eds J. D. Wilson & D. W. Foster. W.B. Saunders, Philadelphia.

Vallar, L., Spada, A. & Giannattasio, G. (1987) Altered G_S and adenylate cyclase activity in human GH-secreting pituitary adenomas. *Nature* **330**, 566–568.

Zadik, Z., Chalew, S.A., McCarter, R. J., Meistas, M. & Kowarski, A.A. (1985) The influence of age on the twenty-four hour integrated concentration of growth hormone in normal individuals. *Journal of Clinical Endocrinology and Metabolism* **60**, 513–516.

Clinical uses of growth hormone in older people

R. Marcus, L. Holloway and G. Butterfield

Department of Medicine, Stanford University Aging Study Unit, VA Medical Center, Palo Alto, CA 94304, USA

Summary. Many of the age-related changes in body composition resemble those associated with growth hormone deficiency, and growth hormone secretion decreases with normal human ageing. With the availability of recombinant human growth hormone (rhGH), it is now possible to test the metabolic and structural effects of growth hormone administration to adults. Administration of rhGH to healthy elderly people acutely promotes nitrogen retention and activates bone remodelling. Chronic administration may increase lean mass in men, but appears to give less impressive results in women. Changes in bone remodelling are not accompanied by dramatic increases in bone mass. Thus, it is not likely that daily administration of rhGH as a single agent will prove to be an effective means for regaining deficits in bone, but it may be possible to incorporate rhGH into a multi-agent strategy. In healthy older humans growth hormone can be given without obvious adverse effects on cardiovascular risk factors.

Keywords: growth hormone; bone mineral density; bone remodelling; osteoporosis; body composition; older people

Introduction

Pituitary growth hormone (GH) is a classical endocrine hormone with profound effects on somatic growth and body composition. Circulating concentrations of GH decline with advancing age, as do GH secretion rates and pituitary GH responsiveness to a variety of provocative stimuli. These declines are accompanied by reduced concentrations of insulin-like growth factors (IGFs), the putative mediators of many of the actions of the hormone. Normal human ageing is associated with important alterations in body composition that are also characteristic of GH-deficient children. These include increased adiposity and reduced muscle mass and strength, and loss of bone mineral. Thus it seems reasonable to ask whether some age-related changes in body composition are brought about by a relative degree of GH deficiency and, whether GH therapy might have some clinical use in reversing these changes.

Recent evidence suggests an important role for IGF-1 as an osteotrophic agent, and an argument can be made that IGF-1 is a common mediator of skeletal response to multiple hormones. Like parathyroid hormone, GH activates cell surface receptors in cultured osteoblast-like cells to increase local IGF-1 production (Stracke *et al.*, 1984; Chenu *et al.*, 1990; Barnard *et al.*, 1991). Oestradiol promotes accumulation of IGF-1 and IGF-2 in cultured osteosarcoma cells. Both GH and oestradiol stimulate proliferation of osteoblast-like cells, an effect that can be obliterated by the presence of anti-IGF-1 immunoglobulin. In osteoblasts raised in serum-free medium, recombinant human GH(rhGH) stimulates proliferation and increases the relative amount of newly synthesized type-I collagen (Ernst & Froesch, 1988). *In vivo*, GH and IGF-1 both increase bone turnover. These various results invite the conclusion that GH or IGF-1 might specifically activate osteoblast proliferation and differentiated function to repair bone mineral deficits characteristic of osteoporosis. Until recently, GH treatment of other than GH-deficient children was limited by hormone supply. With the availability of rhGH, therapy of adults has become a practical, albeit expensive, strategy. The current status of GH therapy for older men and women is reviewed here.

Emphasis is placed on recent studies using rhGH rather than earlier studies with pituitary hormone.

Short-term administration of rhGH to healthy elderly humans

Our research group (Marcus *et al.*, 1990) reported the effects of rhGH administration over 7 days to 16 healthy older men and women (>60 years old). A brisk rise in circulating IGF-1 was produced, which was associated with striking changes in nitrogen retention, sodium excretion, and in the parathyroid–vitamin D axis. Urinary excretion of nitrogen and sodium over 24 h decreased by 38% and 50%, respectively, whereas urine excretion of calcium markedly increased. Thus, rhGH uncoupled the usually tight relationship between sodium and calcium excretion. Significant increases were observed in the circulating concentration of osteocalcin and in urinary hydroxyproline, suggesting that bone remodelling had been activated.

Sustained treatment of elderly men and women

The most widely publicized GH trial to date was reported by Rudman *et al.* (1990). These authors conducted a randomized, placebo-controlled intervention trial in 21 elderly men. The administration of rhGH (0·03 mg kg^{-1} body weight, three times per week) for 6 months was found to produce significant increases in lean mass by ^{40}K analysis (the measurement of the total amount of this isotope in the body). Bone density was assessed at nine different sites by dual photon absorptiometry, and a 1·6% increase in lumbar spine mineral density was reported. No significant change in skin-fold estimates of adiposity was observed. The authors state that '... the effects of 6 months of hGH on lean body mass and adipose-tissue mass were equivalent in magnitude to the changes incurred during 10 to 20 years of aging'. This statement has been transformed subsequently by news media to suggest that GH reverses the effect of ageing!

Although the results of this experiment were provocative and interesting, concerns about several aspects of their interpretation must be raised. The ^{40}K data provide convincing evidence of a true increase in lean mass. However, the stated changes in adiposity did not achieve statistical significance, and skin-fold thickness is an inadequate method with which to assess adiposity in the face of fluid retention. The changes in bone mass were marginally significant at best, and pose questions about the methods of analysis. The authors measured bone mass at nine different sites. Even if these measurements were truly independent of one another, it would not be surprising for one site to be significantly different at the level where $P < 0.05$. Clearly, bone mass at one site is not independent from that at other sites, so the confounding effect of multiple comparisons may be substantial. The statistical analysis made no adjustment for multiple comparisons, so it seems that the bone density changes are unconvincing.

We have recently completed a randomized placebo-controlled intervention trial of rhGH (0·025 mg kg^{-1} day^{-1}) in 22 healthy elderly women, aged between 65–81 years. Eight women received rhGH as a daily injection for one year. Compared with the placebo group, circulating levels of IGF-1 were significantly increased and maintained throughout the intervention. A persistent increase in bone turnover was clearly stimulated by rhGH. Sustained elevations were observed in circulating levels of osteocalcin, type-I procollagen peptide and bone alkaline phosphatase, as well as in urinary excretion of hydroxyproline in the group that was treated. These increases reverted to baseline values by 3 months after stopping treatment. On the other hand, no significant changes were observed in bone mineral density at either the lumbar spine or proximal femur. It is of interest that bone mineral density at the femoral trochanter and Ward's triangle decreased significantly in the placebo group but did not change in the hormone-treated subjects. Thus, although rhGH did not increase bone mass, there appears to have been a maintenance effect at the hip.

No significant changes in lean mass or adiposity were observed by hydrostatic weighing, although an increase in lean mass was suggested by skin-fold thickness. Basal metabolic rate was significantly raised at 6 months in the treatment group, but reverted to baseline levels by 12 months. In a limited number of subjects (4 who were treated, and 6 controls), no changes in nitrogen or calcium balance were observed at 6 or 12 months.

Similar to the results of our short-term trial, rhGH produced a sustained decrease in urinary sodium excretion that persisted throughout the 12-month trial. At the dose of hormone used this effect caused only mild symptoms of fluid retention in a few subjects. However, related changes in fluid balance may have produced alterations in total and extracellular water compartments that may confound the body composition measurements. For example, we observed the same changes in skin thickness that were reported by Rudman *et al.* (1990) within 7 days of starting rhGH injections. At this time interval such a result must reflect water changes rather than a true loss of fat mass. This issue has not been adequately addressed and must be resolved in future studies.

With respect to the safety of rhGH administration, results of this trial were fairly reassuring. A transient increase in resistance to insulin was observed several weeks after starting therapy, but this resolved by 6 weeks and remained at baseline levels for the duration of the trial. No significant changes were observed at any time in blood pressure, lipoprotein constituents, thyroid function status, or fibrinogen levels. Thus, with respect to a list of cardiovascular risk factors rhGH administration appears to have been a safe intervention. One woman from the hormone-treated group developed classical manifestations of temporal arthritis during the course of the study.

It is important to note that the margin of safety may not be very large for rhGH. An attempt to treat a different group of 22 older women (60–82 years of age) with rhGH (0.05 mg kg^{-1} day^{-1}) led to intolerable fluid retention in most subjects, and symptoms of carpal tunnel compression in two cases.

Role of GH in therapy of osteoporosis

The osteotrophic actions of GH in growing skeletons were described above and suggest a rationale for considering the ability of this hormone to increase bone mass in patients with osteopenia. Aloia *et al.* (1976) reported an experiment with GH in several osteoporotic patients, but the results did not support the clinical use of this agent. In a subsequent report from this same group (Aloia *et al.*, 1985), combined sequential therapy with GH and calcitonin produced a small but persistent increase in whole-body calcium content of osteoporotic patients. Unfortunately, neither the results of Rudman *et al.* (1990) nor of our own experiments (outlined above) permit any enthusiasm that rhGH, given as single daily monotherapy, will offer a way of achieving meaningful increases in bone mass. Although a maintenance effect may have occurred at the hip, a variety of antiresorptive agents currently offer similar protection, and it would be hard to justify the use of an expensive, injectable protein hormone to achieve this result. Since the doses used are close to maximally tolerated levels, it is unlikely that a simple adjustment of dose will rectify this situation.

The results do clearly establish that rhGH promptly induces a sustained increase in bone remodelling. Since bone remodelling is an inherently inefficient process, anything that activates remodelling should aggravate bone loss. Therefore, if there is a role for GH in osteoporosis it will likely involve a complex therapeutic strategy. A number of questions require clarification before such a role can be established. Should treatment be reserved for patients with low concentrations of IGF-1? What are the effects of rhGH on bone remodelling as defined by dynamic histomorphometry? Should GH be used cyclically in combination with an antiresorptive agent? Recombinant IGF-1 itself will probably soon be available for clinical studies. Some of the adverse metabolic effects of GH may be obviated with IGF-1, so the relative actions of this agent on skeletal turnover will be of great interest.

Finally, it should be remembered that GH, at least transiently, promotes nitrogen retention in adults. Since decreased muscle mass and strength contribute to the risk of falling, and therefore to the risk of incurring hip fracture, a therapeutic role for rhGH might be defined that is independent of bone mass *per se*. Although our own results do not confirm a persistent effect of rhGH on nitrogen balance, it is conceivable that the hormone could be applied in synergy with an exercise programme to improve muscle mass and strength.

Conclusion

The availability of rhGH theoretically makes replacement therapy an option for elderly men and women. In particular, this hormone produces a striking increase in bone turnover that might eventually be exploited to repair deficits in bone mass. At present, however, we do not have enough information regarding the effects of GH on body composition, on its long-term toxicity, or on the dose and treatment schedules that might maximize desired effects to warrant any conclusions regarding its ultimate place in therapeutics.

References

Aloia, J.F., Zanzi, I., Ellis, K. & Jowsey, J. (1976) Effects of growth hormone in osteoporosis. *Journal of Clinical Endocrinology and Metabolism* **43**, 992–999.

Aloia, J.F., Vaswani, A., Kapoor, A., Yeh, J.K. & Cohn, S.H. (1985) Treatment of osteoporosis with calcitonin, with and without growth hormone. *Metabolism* **34**, 124–129.

Barnard, R., Ng, K.W., Martin, T.J. & Waters, M.J. (1991) Growth hormone (GH) receptors in clonal osteoblast-like cells mediate a mitogenic response to GH. *Endocrinology* **128**, 1459–1464.

Chenu, C., Valentin-Opran, A., Chavassieux, P., Saez, S., Meunier, P.I. & Delmas, P.D. (1990) Insulin-like growth factor I hormonal regulation by growth hormone and by 1,25(OH)$_2$D$_3$ and activity on human osteoblast-like cells in short-term cultures. *Bone* **11**, 81–86.

Ernst, M. & Froesch, E.R. (1988) Growth hormone dependent stimulation of osteoblast-like cells in serum-free cultures via local synthesis of insulin-like growth factor I. *Biochemistry and Biophysics Research Communications* **151**, 142–147.

Marcus, R., Butterfield, G., Holloway L., Gilliland L., Baylink, D.J., Hintz, R.L. & Sherman, B.L. (1990) Effects of short term administration of recombinant human growth hormone to elderly people. *Journal of Clinical Endocrinology and Metabolism* **70**, 519–527.

Rudman, D., Feller, A.G., Nagraj, H.S., Gergans, G.A., Lalitha, P.Y., Goldberg, A.F., Schlenker, R.A., Cohn, L., Rudman, I.W. & Mattson, D.E. (1990) Effects of human growth hormone in men over 60 years old. *New England Journal of Medicine* **323**, 1–6.

Stracke, H., Schultz, A., Moeller, D., Rossol, S. & Schatz, H. (1984) Effect of growth hormone on osteoblasts and demonstration of somatomedin C/IGF-1 in bone organ culture. *Acta Endocrinology* **107**, 16–24.

Effects of genotype on age-related alterations in the concentrations of stress hormones in plasma and hypothalamic monoamines in rats

G. M. Gilad[1]*, R. Li[1], R. J. Wyatt[1] and Y. Tizabi[2]

[1] *Neuropsychiatry Branch, NIMH Neuroscience Research Center at St Elizabeth's Hospital, Washington, DC 20032, USA;* and [2] *Department of Pharmacology, College of Medicine, Howard University, Washington, DC 20059, USA*

Summary. The adaptive response of the neuroendocrine system to stress is known to be impaired during ageing, and this impairment may be genetically determined. To elucidate further the effect of genotype, inbred male rats of the Wistar-Kyoto (WKY) strain, characterized by their hyper-reactivity to stressors and shorter life span, were compared with Brown-Norway (BN) rats. In young BN rats, resting prolactin concentrations were lower than in WKY animals and were reduced with age, while in WKY rats they remained unchanged with age. In young rats of both strains prolactin concentrations were highest after subjecting them to stressful stimuli for 15 min. After 2 h of restraint stress (during which the animals were confined to a narrow space that restricted movement) prolactin concentrations in young rats returned to pre-stress values, while remaining high in aged rats of both strains. Concentrations of corticotrophin (or adrenocorticotrophic hormone, ACTH) were lower in BN than in WKY rats and did not change with age in either strain. After 2 h of stress, ACTH concentrations were still slightly higher than normal in both young and aged BN rats, but not in WKY rats. Corticosterone concentrations were similar in young WKY and BN rats and were reduced in aged rats of both strains. After 2 h of stress, corticosterone concentrations were still high in aged, but not in young rats of both strains. However, this stress-induced increase was larger (3·7 times as much) in the BN strain than in the WKY strain (in which the increase was 1·7 times as much). The concentrations of hypothalamic monoamines were similar in young rats of both strains, although stress resulted in reduced noradrenaline concentrations, as previously documented, and in minor increases in 3,4-dihydroxyphenylacetic acid in both strains. During ageing, basal noradrenaline concentrations were reduced only in WKY rats, while the amount of 5-HT increased selectively in BN rats. Concentrations of 5-hydroxyindoleacetic acid were increased after stress in aged WKY rats only. The results demonstrate that resting plasma concentrations of the stress hormones ACTH and corticosterone and of prolactin are lower in BN than in WKY rats. In ageing, however, the stress-induced increases in the concentrations of these hormones are relatively higher in the BN strain, which is characterized by a longer life span. Taken together with previous findings, this study indicates that higher basal activity and increased stress-induced activation of the neuronal and endocrine systems are directly associated with the behavioural hyper-reactivity to stressors. However, the study implies that a

---

*Present address: Department of Morphological Sciences, The Bruce Rappaport Faculty of Medicine, Technion-Israel Institute of Technology, PO Box 9649, 31096 Haifa, Israel.

robust neuroendocrine response to stressors during ageing may be directly correlated with longevity.

Keywords: ageing; restraint stress; rat; stress hormones; monoamines

Introduction

Ageing is associated with changes in the response of neuroendocrine systems to stressful stimuli (Selye, 1976; Elm, 1984; Dilman *et al.*, 1986; Meites *et al.*, 1987; Everitt & Walton, 1988). These changes may become maladaptive and result in the acceleration of ageing (Dilman *et al.*, 1986; Sapolsky *et al.*, 1986a, b; Meites *et al.*, 1987). Age-related maladaptive changes in the response to stressful stimuli have recently been reported to occur in components of the hypothalamo–pituitary–adrenocortical (HPA) system (Sapolsky *et al.*, 1986a, b) and in the hypothalamic dopamine–pituitary prolactin system (Meites, 1990a; Reymond, 1990; Goya *et al.*, 1991). Both of these neuroendocrine systems play important roles in the adaptive response to stressors. Thus, increased stress-induced secretion of adrenal glucocorticoids (Landfield *et al.*, 1978; Sapolsky *et al.*, 1986a, b) and prolactin (Sarkar *et al.*, 1984a) have been implicated in accelerated age-related degeneration of selective neurone populations in the hippocampus and the hypothalamus, respectively.

Large differences in longevity are known to exist among individuals in heterogeneous populations. It is possible that these differences may stem in part from underlying primary genetic differences (Masoro, 1991). Inbred strains of laboratory animals provide the opportunity to study the interactions of environmental stressors and genetic differences in ageing and longevity. It has previously been reported that inbred rats of the Wistar-Kyoto (WKY) strain are much more reactive to stressful stimuli than Brown-Norway (BN) rats, as characterized by behavioural, physiological and neurochemical parameters (McCarty & Kopin, 1978; Gilad, 1987; Gilad *et al.*, 1990). Additionally, hyper-reactive WKY rats have a much shorter life span (about 2 years average life expectancy under standard laboratory conditions) compared with BN rats (about 3 years) (Gilad & Gilad, 1987). Several of the responses following stress in young adult rats vary, depending upon the rat strain. (1) While in WKY rats the peripheral sympatho-adrenal catecholamine system is more active, no strain- or stress-induced differences are apparent in the central catecholamine systems of both BN and WKY strains (Gilad & McCarty, 1981). (2) In contrast, both the central and peripheral cholinergic systems are much more active in WKY rats (Gilad *et al.*, 1979; McCarty *et al.*, 1979; Gilad & McCarty, 1981). (3) Finally, no strain- or stress-induced differences have been found between the amounts of plasma corticosterone, the main adrenal glucocorticoid hormone, in WKY and BN strains (Gilad & Jimerson, 1981).

In ageing, strain-dependent deficits have been found in forebrain cholinergic (Gilad & Gilad, 1987; Gilad *et al.*, 1987) and striatal dopaminergic (Gilad & Gilad, 1987) systems. However, studies demonstrating these effects indicate that deficits in these neurotransmitter systems are related to the biological rather than chronological age of the animals. Thus, cholinergic deficits that occurred earlier in the shorter-lived WKY strain did eventually occur in the longer-lived BN strain, but at a later age (Gilad *et al.*, 1987). This suggests that the rate of neuronal degeneration may be genetically determined and coupled to the general rate of ageing in the animal. Alternatively, neuronal degeneration may occur secondarily in response to maladaptive changes in the regulation of such hormones as glucocorticoids (Landfield *et al.*, 1978; Sapolsky *et al.*, 1986a, b) and prolactin (Sarkar *et al.*, 1984a, b).

In the experiments described here, WKY and BN inbred strains were used as models to characterize the role of stress-responsive neuroendocrine systems in the ageing of animals with different genetic backgrounds. The specific goals were as follows: (1) to examine whether stress-induced changes in plasma corticotrophin (or adrenocorticotrophic hormone, ACTH), prolactin and corticosterone concentrations are dependent on strain or age; and (2) to determine if alterations in plasma ACTH or prolactin concentrations correlate with changes in the concentrations of hypothalamic monoamines.

Materials and Methods

Animals and treatments

Experiments were performed on young adult (3–4 month old) and aged (21-month-old) inbred WKY and BN male rats (Harlan Sprague-Dawley, Indianapolis, IN, USA). To obtain aged rats, animals were purchased at 6–8 months of age and were allowed to age in the vivarium at the National Institute of Mental Health Neuroscience Center. The animals were housed two to a cage, supplied freely with food and water, and maintained at 24°C with a 12 h light–dark cycle (lights on from 07:00 to 19:00 h).

To subject the rats to restraint stress, they were placed in Plexiglas restrainers (Harvard Apparatus, South Natick, MA, USA). Young animals were kept under these conditions for 15, 30 or 120 min, while aged rats, because of animal shortage, were stressed for 2 h only. Animals left undisturbed in their home cages served as unhandled controls.

Tissue collection

Rats were decapitated between 10:00 and 13:00 h, within 5 s of their removal from the restrainers or home cages. Trunk blood, approximately 5 ml, was collected for 20 s into tubes containing 5 mg EDTA and 500 kallikrein-inhibiting units (aprotinin). The tubes were centrifuged at 1000 g for 20 min at 4°C, and the plasma was collected and stored at -20°C for subsequent prolactin, ACTH and corticosterone assays.

The brain was excised immediately after decapitation, and the hypothalamus was rapidly dissected as described by Reis & Ross (1973), frozen on solid CO_2 and stored at -70°C for subsequent assays of monoamines.

Hormone assays

Plasma prolactin, ACTH and corticosterone concentrations were determined by standard radioimmunoassays at Hazelton Washington Laboratories, Vienna, VA, USA. The lower limits of assay sensitivity were as follows: 2.0 ± 0.2 ng prolactin ml^{-1}, 7.5 ± 0.5 pg ACTH ml^{-1}; and 0.5 ± 0.1 μg corticosterone dl^{-1}. The intra-assay coefficients of variation (SD calculated for ten assays) were 11.4%, 3.3% and 10.3%, respectively.

Monoamine assays

The hypothalamus was sonicated in 0.5 ml of a buffer solution, pH 4.0, containing sodium acetate (13.8 g l^{-1}), citric acid (14.0 g l^{-1}), 1-octanesulphonic acid (sodium salt) (0.1 g l^{-1}) and EDTA (0.05 g l^{-1}). The homogenate was centrifuged at 11 000 g for 30 min, and the resulting supernatant was filtered through an anisotropic, hydrophilic YMT ultrafiltration membrane (Amicon Division, W. R. Grace & Co., Beverly, MA, USA) by centrifugation at 1000 g for 20 min. Noradrenaline, dopamine, homovanillic acid, 3,4-dihydroxyphenylacetic acid (DOPAC), 5-hydroxytryptamine (5-HT) and 5-hydroxyindoleacetic acid (5-HIAA) in the filtered homogenate were measured by high-performance liquid chromatography with a dual-electrode coulometric electrochemical detection system, according to Hall et al. (1989). The minimum detectable amounts of monoamines and their metabolites were less than 100 pg in 1 mg protein (or less than 5 pg per injection). Measurements of noradrenaline and of 5-HT and its metabolites provided markers for noradrenergic and serotoninergic (5-HT) terminals in the whole hypothalamus, while dopamine and its metabolites were considered indices of mainly arcuate dopaminergic neurons.

Statistical analysis

A factorial ANOVA test (two- or three-way) followed by Tukey's post-hoc test was used for statistical analysis. Differences were considered significant when $P \leq 0.05$.

Results

Effects of stress and ageing on plasma prolactin

In young WKY rats, resting plasma prolactin concentrations were about twice as high as in BN rats (Fig. 1). After subjection to stress, prolactin concentrations in young rats of both strains were transiently increased, depending on the duration of stress. The peak increase occurred after 15 min of stress. Plasma prolactin concentrations diminished after 30 min of stress and were back at resting values after 120 min of stress (Fig. 1).

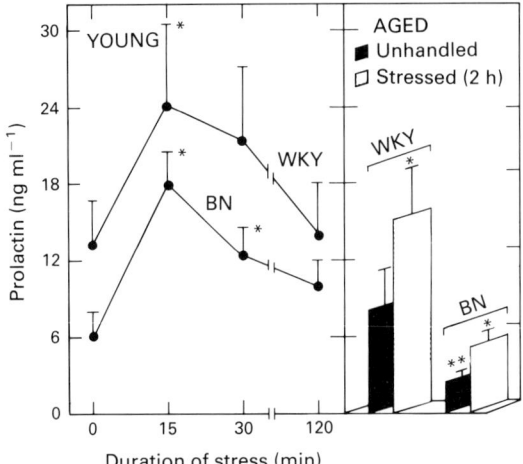

Fig. 1. Effects of restraint stress and age on plasma prolactin levels in Wistar-Kyoto (WKY) and Brown-Norway (BN) rats. Results are the mean ($\pm$ SEM) values of 6–12 animals. For young rats, the data were analysed by two-way ANOVA, weighing the effects of the strain used and of stress. Aged rats were compared to their young counterparts after a single 2 h interval of stress, and data were analysed by three-way ANOVA, weighing the effects of strain, age and stress. Note the interruption of the abscissa. *($P < 0.05$) denotes a significant difference in prolactin concentrations induced by stress within the same strain. **($P < 0.01$) denotes a significant difference in prolactin concentrations brought about by ageing within the same strain. Values in unhandled rats were significantly different ($P < 0.05$) between the strains.

In aged WKY rats, baseline prolactin concentrations did not differ from that in their young counterparts, but in aged BN rats, the baseline prolactin concentrations were drastically reduced (Fig. 1). In contrast to their young counterparts, prolactin concentrations in aged rats of both strains were still high after 2 h of sustained stress (Fig. 1). However, the increment in prolactin in stressed animals was larger for aged BN rats (2·167 times as much as in control aged animals) than for aged WKY rats (1·876 times as much as in control aged animals).

Hypothalamic monoamines in stress and ageing

Table 1 summarizes the analysis of the results obtained for the effects of age and stress on the concentrations of hypothalamic monoamines. In young rats, no strain differences were observed in the concentrations of any of the measured monoamines or in their metabolites.

In aged rats, two changes were noted: (1) a 34·6% decrease in noradrenaline concentration in aged compared with young WKY rats; and (2) an increase in 5-HT concentration in aged BN rats, to amounts that not only were higher than those of their own young counterparts (by 25·5%), but were also higher ($P < 0.01$) than those of both young (by 48·8%) and old (by 39·1%) WKY rats (Table 1).

After 2 h of restraint stress, three basic changes were noted: (1) a trend towards a statistically significant reduction in noradrenaline concentration in young WKY rats and aged BN rats; (2) a statistically significant increase in DOPAC concentration in aged WKY rats and in young and aged BN rats; and (3) a statistically significant increase in 5-HIAA concentration in aged WKY rats only (Table 1).

Effects of stress and ageing on plasma ACTH and corticosterone

Plasma ACTH concentrations were about 66% higher in resting WKY than in BN rats and were not affected by ageing (Fig. 2). After 2 h of stress, no changes were observed in either young or

Table 1. Effects of age and 2 h restraint stress on hypothalamic monoamines of Wistar-Kyoto and Brown-Norway rats

Monoamine (ng mg^{-1} protein)	Treatment	Wistar-Kyoto rats		Brown-Norway rats	
		Young	Aged	Young	Aged
Noradrenaline	Unhandled	10.7 ± 0.7	8.0 ± 0.6*	10.8 ± 1.2	10.3 ± 1.1
	Stressed	7.0 ± 0.9**	7.6 ± 0.5	7.6 ± 1.6	7.4 ± 0.6**
Dopamine	Unhandled	3.6 ± 0.3	3.1 ± 0.3	4.0 ± 0.4	3.7 ± 0.2
	Stressed	4.0 ± 0.2	4.1 ± 0.5	3.9 ± 0.7	5.1 ± 0.7
Homovanillic acid	Unhandled	0.15 ± 0.05	0.15 ± 0.05	0.15 ± 0.05	0.15 ± 0.05
	Stressed	0.20 ± 0.05	0.15 ± 0.05	0.20 ± 0.05	
DOPAC	Unhandled	0.35 ± 0.05	0.25 ± 0.05	0.40 ± 0.05	0.40 ± 0.05
	Stressed	0.50 ± 0.05	0.50 ± 0.05**	0.60 ± 0.05**	0.65 ± 0.05**
5-HT	Unhandled	4.3 ± 0.2	4.6 ± 0.2	5.1 ± 0.3	6.4 ± 0.3*
	Stressed	4.5 ± 0.2	5.6 ± 0.5	6.5 ± 0.9	6.3 ± 0.6
5-HIAA	Unhandled	5.6 ± 0.4	5.7 ± 0.3	6.4 ± 0.3	6.6 ± 0.6
	Stressed	5.7 ± 0.3	7.9 ± 0.9**	7.4 ± 1.0	7.2 ± 0.8

Results are the mean (±SEM) values of six animals. For homovanillic acid and 3,4-dihydroxyphenylacetic acid (DOPAC), SEM ≤ 0.05. Data were analysed by three-way ANOVA, weighing the effects of rat strain, age and stress.
5-HIAA: 5-hydroxyindoleacetic acid; 5-HT: 5-hydroxytryptamine.
*($P < 0.05$) denotes an age-dependent difference within the same strain.
**($P < 0.05$) denotes a stress-dependent difference within the same age and strain.

aged WKY rats. In contrast, in the BN rats after 2 h of stress, ACTH concentrations were still high in both young (1.292 times higher than normal) and aged (1.524 times higher than normal) BN rats (Fig. 2).

Plasma corticosterone concentrations, in contrast to ACTH levels, were not significantly different between the strains. However, they decreased markedly with ageing in both WKY rats (by 51.3%) and BN rats (by 61.8%) (Fig. 3). After 2 h of stress, while no changes were detected in young rats, corticosterone concentrations were markedly increased in aged rats of both WKY rats (1.678 times as much as normal) and BN rats (2.735 times as much as normal) (Fig. 3).

Discussion

Hypothalamic monoamines and prolactin regulation in stress and ageing

The findings demonstrate that the regulation of plasma prolactin concentrations is strain dependent. In BN rats, prolactin concentrations are lower than in WKY rats and are reduced with ageing, while they remain unchanged in aged WKY rats. Moreover, a profound alteration in the transitory nature of the stress-induced response to prolactin occurs with ageing in both strains, which is apparent by a sustained prolactin increase during longer periods of stressor application. Therefore, these findings indicate that prolactin regulation is genetically influenced and that regulation of the stress-induced response is altered with ageing.

It is well established that the regulation of pituitary prolactin secretion is under the control of hypothalamic dopaminergic neurones (Moore et al., 1985; Mogg & Samson, 1990) (Fig. 4). Yet, in this study, despite large strain- and age-related differences in plasma prolactin, no such differences were detected in hypothalamic dopaminergic indices. Previous studies in female rats have shown an age-associated increase in plasma prolactin concentrations (Parkening et al., 1980; Meites, 1990a; Reymond, 1990; Goya et al., 1991) and a concomitant reduction in hypothalamic dopaminergic neurotransmission (Reymond & Porter, 1981; Demarest et al., 1982; Arita & Kimura, 1986).

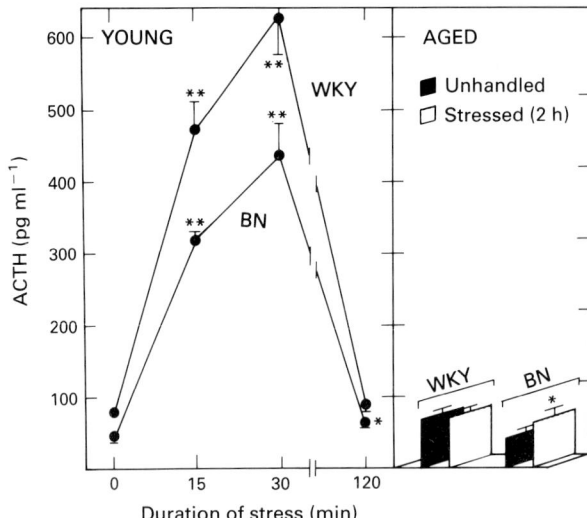

Fig. 2. Effects of restraint stress and age on plasma corticotrophin (adrenocorticotrophic hormone, ACTH) concentrations in Wistar-Kyoto (WKY) and Brown-Norway (BN) rats. Results are the mean ($\pm$ SEM) values of 6–12 animals (some SEM values were smaller than the symbol of their means). For young rats, the data were analysed by two-way ANOVA, weighing the effects of the strain used and of stress. Aged rats were compared with their young counterparts after a single 2 h interval of stress, and data were analysed by the three-way ANOVA, weighing the effects of strain, age and stress. Note the interruption of the abscissa. *($P < 0.05$) and **($P < 0.01$) denote a significant difference in ACTH concentrations induced by stress within the same strain. Values in unhandled rats were significantly different ($P < 0.05$) between the strains.

Therefore, there appears to be an interesting gender difference in prolactin regulation during ageing.

Although the mechanism for this difference has yet to be established, several factors, such as a possible gender-related reduction in pituitary dopamine receptors or in prolactin clearance with ageing, may play a role. Alternatively, interaction between factors controlling prolactin secretion may be altered. In this regard, it should be emphasized that while pituitary prolactin secretion is inhibited by dopamine, it is stimulated by a variety of hypothalamic hormones (Mogg & Samson, 1990), including thyrotrophin-releasing hormone (Koch *et al.*, 1977; Horn *et al.*, 1985), oxytocin (Samson *et al.*, 1986; Sarkar, 1988) and vasoactive intestinal peptide (Oboe *et al.*, 1985), as well as by other neurotransmitter systems (Fig. 4), all of which may also undergo age-related changes. Of further interest is the recent observation that glutamic acid, the concentration of which is increased in the blood after stress (Milakofsky *et al.*, 1985), stimulates prolactin secretion directly (Login, 1990). Age-related changes in the effect of glutamic acid on prolactin and other pituitary hormonal secretions remain to be demonstrated.

Increased prolactin concentrations in aged female rodents have been implicated in the increased incidence of tumour growth (Meites, 1990a, b). Lower prolactin concentrations, as seen in male BN rats, may therefore be advantageous in the ageing process. It would be interesting to examine whether a decrease in prolactin also occurs in aged females of the BN strain.

Interestingly, a sustained increase in prolactin, such as the one occurring in prolactinaemias, has been implicated in the degeneration of hypothalamic dopaminergic neurones (Sarkar *et al.*, 1984b). In this study no changes in dopaminergic indices were observed in the hypothalamus. However, the finding that in aged rats increased prolactin concentrations are sustained during prolonged periods of stress indicates that under chronic stressful conditions degeneration of hypothalamic dopaminergic neurones may occur.

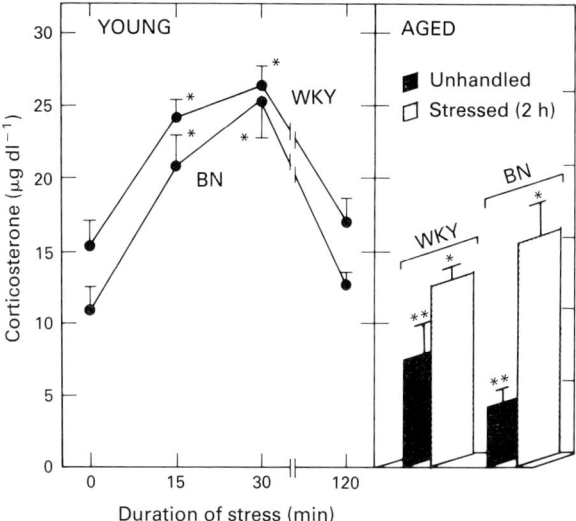

Fig. 3. Effects of restraint stress and age on plasma corticosterone levels in Wistar-Kyoto (WKY) and Brown-Norway (BN) rats. Results are the mean ($\pm$SEM) values of 6–12 animals. For young rats, the data were analysed by two-way ANOVA, weighing the effects of the strain used and of stress. Aged rats were compared with their young counterparts after a single 2 h interval of stress, and data were analysed by three-way ANOVA, weighing the effects of strain, age and stress. Note the interruption of the abscissa. *($P < 0.05$) denotes a significant difference in corticosterone concentrations induced by stress within the same strain. **($P < 0.05$) denotes a significant difference in corticosterone concentrations brought about by ageing within the same strain. Values in unhandled rats did not differ significantly between the strains.

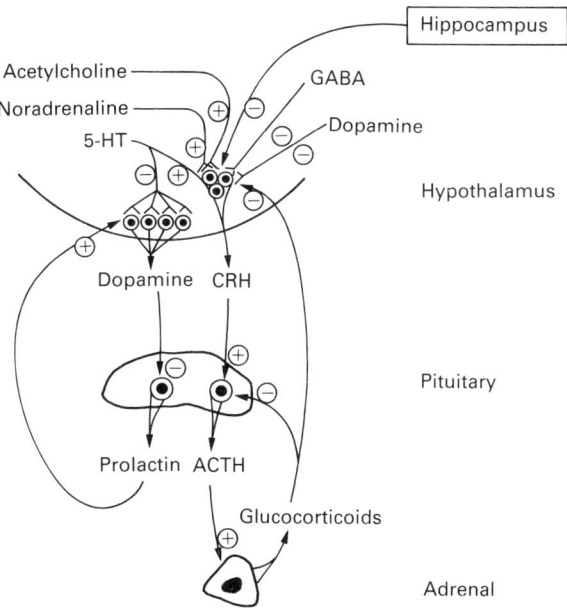

Fig. 4. Illustration of hormonal and neuronal controls of the hypothalamic dopamine–pituitary prolactin system (left side) and the hypothalamic–pituitary–adrenocortical system (right side) of the rat. ACTH: adrenocorticotrophic hormone (corticotrophin); CRH: corticotrophin-releasing hormone: GABA: γ-aminobutyric aid.

The results recorded here corroborate previous observations that the activity of central catecholamine neurones is similar in both strains (Gilad & McCarty, 1981). Furthermore, the findings now indicate that the basal activity of the hypothalamic serotoninergic neurones is also similar in young adults of both strains.

Central catecholamine neurones are activated in response to stressful stimuli (Palkovits et al., 1975; Kvetnansky et al., 1977). Increased reactivity of hypothalamic dopaminergic neurones to stressors was indicated in this study by increased DOPAC concentrations. Increased noradrenergic transmission in response to stressors is generally indicated by a reduction in hypothalamic noradrenaline concentrations (Palkovits et al., 1975; Kvetnansky et al., 1977). In previous studies, hypothalamic noradrenaline was similarly reduced in young rats of both strains (Gilad & McCarty, 1981). However, in this study reduction in noradrenaline concentrations was evident only in the WKY strain – the strain more reactive to stressors. The reason for this discrepancy may be the difference in the types of stressor used. In previous studies, immobilization stress was used (during which the animal's legs were taped to the immobilization platform) – a much more severe stressor than the restraint stress used in the present study (confinement to a narrow space that restricted movement). Therefore, it appears that the noradrenergic system of young BN rats has a higher threshold for stress-induced activation. However, with ageing opposite alterations were noted after stress: in aged WKY rats with reduced basal noradrenaline concentrations, restraint stress did not cause any further reduction, while in aged BN rats, the stress-induced reduction became significant.

The decrease of hypothalamic noradrenaline concentrations in aged WKY rats, the strain with a shorter life span, may be due to degeneration of noradrenergic terminals secondary to degeneration of their parent noradrenergic neurones in the locus coeruleus (Hornykiewicz, 1986). At this age (21 months), WKY rats are approaching their average life expectancy (approximately 24 months) and are, therefore, biologically older than BN rats. It may be assumed that BN rats will show a similar decrease when they approach their average life expectancy of 31 months. This could be verified in future studies by including additional groups of middle-aged WKY rats and older BN rats.

The changes observed in the serotoninergic indices were strain specific. Thus, the significant increase in basal 5-HT concentrations was observed in aged BN, but not in WKY rats. Furthermore, 5-HIAA concentrations increased with stress in aged WKY, but not in BN rats. These findings emphasize the important effect of strain on age-related changes (Simpkins, 1982).

Regulation of the hypothalamic–pituitary–adrenocortical system in stress and ageing

The overall response of the HPA system to stressful stimuli is altered with ageing. This alteration, however, may be confined to specific components of the system. Thus, although basal plasma ACTH concentrations were not altered, basal corticosterone concentrations were markedly reduced in aged rats. Since no change in corticosterone clearance rate during ageing has been detected (Sapolsky et al., 1983), the mechanism responsible for the reduction in corticosterone may involve alterations in adrenal sensitivity to ACTH. Indeed, several studies in vivo and in vitro have demonstrated a decrease in the adrenal response to ACTH in aged rats (Hess & Riegel, 1970; Riegel, 1973; Pritchett et al., 1979; Malamed & Carsia, 1983; Cheng et al., 1990). However, there are inconsistencies in the literature with regard to plasma corticosterone concentrations and adrenal sensitivity to ACTH during ageing. Corticosterone has been reported to be reduced (Wilson et al., 1981; Cizza et al., 1990), unchanged (Tang & Phillips, 1978; Brett et al., 1983; Riegel, 1983; Hylka et al., 1984; Sonntag et al., 1987; Verkhratsky et al., 1988; Brodish & Odio, 1989; van Eekelen et al., 1991) or even increased (Angelucci et al., 1980; Dekosky et al., 1984) during ageing. Similarly, reports of reduction (Hess & Riegel, 1970; Riegel, 1973; Pritchett et al., 1979; Malamed & Carsia, 1983; Cheng et al., 1990), no change (Scaccianoce et al., 1990) or increase (Sonntag et al., 1987) in adrenal sensitivity to ACTH during ageing have appeared. These discrepancies could be due to a variety of factors, including the infliction of varying degrees of stress during blood collection, time of sampling, prior handling, housing conditions and relative age differences, as well as strain and gender differences (DeBoer *et al.*, 1988; Meaney *et al.*, 1988; Mangiacapra & Florini, 1990).

It is intriguing that while basal corticosterone concentrations are reduced in ageing, the stress-induced increase in corticosterone is sustained during longer periods of stress in aged than in young rats. The mechanisms responsible for the increase in corticosterone concentrations during prolonged periods of stress in aged rats remain unclear. In their recent study on BN rats, van Eekelen *et al.* (1991) failed to detect an age-related reduction in basal corticosterone concentrations, a discrepancy that may be explained by the fact that their animals were older (30–33 months old) than the ones used in this study and that in the study described here blood was collected after decapitation, rather than from chronically cannulated animals. However, they did observe a longer-lasting increase in stress-induced corticosterone concentrations (van Eekelen *et al.*, 1991). An additional important finding of their study was a 64% reduction in the binding capacity of the corticosteroid binding protein globulin in aged rats, which may be a contributory mechanism for the observed age-related changes in HPA regulation during stress.

Plasma ACTH concentrations showed no changes with ageing, and the strain differences in the stress-induced ACTH response were maintained in aged rats. Pituitary ACTH secretion is stimulated by corticotrophin-releasing hormone, as well as by a variety of other secretagogues, including arginine-vasopressin, oxytocin, angiotensin, catecholamines (Antoni, 1986) and other neurotransmitters (Fig. 4). On the other hand, ACTH secretion is inhibited by the negative-feedback effects of adrenal glucocorticoids (Antoni, 1986) (Fig. 4). The findings described here do not reveal any apparent age-related correlations between hypothalamic monoamines and plasma ACTH. In contrast, a reduction in pituitary corticotrophin-releasing hormone receptor binding capacity with ageing that is common to both strains (Tizabi *et al.*, 1992) and probably to other rat strains (Heroux *et al.*, 1991) has recently been observed. A reduction in receptors for corticotrophin-releasing hormone is expected to result in reduced stimulation of ACTH secretion and, therefore, lower plasma ACTH. However, the age-related drop in corticosterone concentrations may counterbalance the reduction in this type of receptor, thus providing a mechanism for the maintenance of plasma ACTH during ageing.

Interaction between the neuroendocrine systems

Recent findings indicate that the HPA and pituitary prolactin systems may directly interact with each other. Thus, corticotrophin-releasing hormone can directly enhance pituitary prolactin release (Morel *et al.*, 1989), while prolactin can directly stimulate both hypothalamic corticotrophin-releasing hormone and pituitary ACTH secretions (Kooy *et al.*, 1990; Weber & Calogero, 1991). The significance of these positive interactions during the stress response has yet to be elucidated. As mentioned above, the secretion of both ACTH and prolactin is controlled by multiple regulatory factors. Furthermore, the temporal sequence of action of these factors is unknown. Interestingly, in both strains, the peak of the stress-induced increase in plasma prolactin precedes that of ACTH and corticosterone.

The results demonstrate that the directionality (i.e. reduction) of the age-related changes in the two stress-activated systems studied (i.e. the HPA system and the hypothalamic dopamine–pituitary prolactin system) is similar in *male* rats of both strains. This is intriguing because it suggests that during ageing the two pituitary hormonal systems are influenced similarly by genetic mechanisms.

Strain, stress and longevity

The life spans of the two strains differ under regular laboratory vivarium conditions. The life expectancy of male WKY rats is shorter than their BN counterparts (Gilad & Gilad, 1987).

Therefore, the possible relationship of this difference in longevity to the well-characterized strain differences in behavioural (McCarty & Kopin, 1978; Gilad & Shiller, 1989), neurochemical (Gilad et al., 1979; McCarty et al., 1979; Gilad, 1987; Gilad et al., 1990) and neuroendocrine responses to stressors is intriguing. Two main observations are worth considering in this regard. On the one hand, the shorter-lived male WKY rats are behaviourally more reactive under stressful conditions and are characterized by overall higher basal and stress-induced activities of neuronal and endocrine systems than BN rats. On the other hand, while the reduction in basal concentrations of plasma hormones is more pronounced in aged BN rats, the magnitude of stress-induced increases in these hormones is larger than in aged WKY rats. One implication of these observations is that hyper-reactivity to stressors is inversely related to longevity and that this is genotype dependent. Another important implication is that a relatively robust neuroendocrine response to stressors during ageing is directly related to longevity.

We thank Y. Dodd and R. Singer for their editorial assistance.

References

Angelucci, L., Velour, P., Greasy, E., Veldhuis, H.D., Boohoos, B. & Dekloet, R. (1980) Involvement of hippocampal corticosterone receptors in behavioral phenomena. In *Progress in Psychoneuroendocrinology*, pp. 177–185. Eds F. Brambilla, G. Re-count & D. Dewied. Elsevier, Amsterdam.

Antoni, F.A. (1986) Hypothalamic control of adrenocorticotropin secretion: advances since the discovery of 41-residue corticotropin-releasing factor. *Endocrine Reviews* 7, 351–378.

Arita, J. & Kimura, F. (1986) Effect of aging on in vitro dopamine biosynthesis in the median eminence of rat hypothalamic slices. *Brain Research* 369, 391–394.

Brett, L.P., Chong, K.S., Cool, S. & Levin, S. (1983) The pituitary–adrenal response to novel stimulation and ether stress in young-adult and aged rats. *Neurobiology of Aging* 4, 133–138.

Brodish, A. & Odio, M. (1989) Age-dependent effects of chronic stress on ACTH and corticosterone response to an acute novel stress. *Neuroendocrinology* 49, 496–501.

Cheng, B., Horst, I.A., Mader, S.L. & Kowal, J. (1990) Diminished adrenal steroidogenic activity in ageing rats: new evidence from adrenal cells cultured from young and aged normal and hypoxic animals. *Molecular and Cellular Endocrinology* 73, R7–R12.

Cizza, G., Calogero, A.E., Gold, P.W. & Chrousos, G.P. (1990) Hypothalamic–pituitary–adrenal axis age-related changes in old male 344 Fischer rats. *Age* 12, 156.

DeBoer, S.F., Slangen, J.L. & Van Der Gugten, J. (1988) Adaptation of plasma catecholamine and corticosterone responses to short-term repeated noise stress in rats. *Physiology and Behavior* 44, 273–280.

Dekosky, S.T., Scheff, S.W. & Cotman, C.W. (1984) Elevated corticosterone levels: a possible cause of reduced axon sprouting in aged animals. *Neuroendocrinology* 38, 33–38.

Demarest, K.T., Moore, K.E. & Riegle, G.D. (1982) Dopaminergic neuronal function, anterior pituitary dopamine content, and serum concentrations of prolactin, luteinizing hormone, and progesterone in the aged female rats. *Brain Research* 247, 347–354.

Dilman, V.M., Revskoy, S.Y. & Goluber, A.G. (1986) Neuroendocrine-ontogenetic mechanism of aging: toward an integrated theory of aging. *International Review of Neurobiology* 26, 89–155.

Elm, C.R. (1984) Aging and hypothalamic regulation of metabolic, autonomic and endocrine function. In *Aging and Recovery of Function in the Central Nervous System*, pp. 23–44. Ed. S. W. Scheff. Plenum Press, New York.

Everitt, A.V. & Walton, J.R. (1988) Regulation of aging along the hypothalamic–pituitary–endocrine axis. In *Interdisciplinary Topics in Gerontology*, pp. 1–8. Eds H. P. Von Hahn, A. V. Everitt & J. R. Walton. S. Karger, Basel.

Gilad, G.M. (1987) The stress-induced response of the septohippocampal cholinergic system: a vectorial outcome of psychoneuroendocrinological interactions. *Psychoneuroendocrinology* 12, 167–184.

Gilad, G.M. & Gilad, V.H. (1987) Age-related reductions in brain cholinergic and dopaminergic indices in two rat strains differing in longevity. *Brain Research* 408, 247–250.

Gilad, G.M. & Jimerson, D.C. (1981) Modes of adaptation of peripheral neuroendocrine mechanisms of the sympatho–adrenal system to short-term stress as studied in two inbred rat strains. *Brain Research* 206, 83–93.

Gilad, G.M. & McCarty, R. (1981) Differences in choline acetyltransferase but similarities in catecholamine biosynthetic enzymes in brains of two rat strains differing in their response to stress. *Brain Research* 206, 239–243.

Gilad, G.M. & Shiller, I. (1989) Differences in open field behavior and in learning tasks between two rat strains differing in their reactivity to stressors. *Behavioral Brain Research* 32, 89–93.

Gilad, G.M., McCarty, R., Weise, V.K. & Kopin, I.J. (1979) Strain differences in the regulation of the sympatho–adrenal system. *Brain Research* 176, 380–384.

Gilad, G.M., Rabey, J.M., Tizabi, Y. & Gilad, V.H. (1987) Age-dependent loss and compensatory changes of septohippocampal cholinergic neurons in two rat strains differing in longevity and response to stress. *Brain Research* **436**, 311–322.

Gilad, G.M., Gilad, V.H. & Tizabi, Y. (1990) Aging and stress-induced changes in choline and glutamate uptake in hippocampus and septum of two rat strains differing in longevity and reactivity to stressors. *International Journal of Developmental Neuroscience* **8**, 709–713.

Goya, R.G., Castro, M.G. & Meites, J. (1991) Differential effect of aging on serum levels of prolactin and α-melanotropin in rats. *Proceedings of the Society of Experimental Biology and Medicine* **196**, 218–221.

Hall, M.E., Hoffer, B.J. & Gerhardt, G.A. (1989) Rapid and sensitive determination of catecholamines in small tissue samples by high-performance liquid chromatography coupled with dual-electrode coulometric electrochemical detection. *Liquid Chromatography and Gas Chromatography* **7**, 258–265.

Heroux, J.A., Girigoriadis, D.E. & DeSouza, E.B. (1991) Age-related decreases in corticotropin-releasing factor (CRF) receptors in rat brain and anterior pituitary gland. *Brain Research* **542**, 155–158.

Hess, G.D. & Riegel, G.D. (1970) Adrenocortical responsiveness to stress and ACTH in aging rats. *Journal of Gerontology* **25**, 354–358.

Horn, A.M., Fraser, H.M. & Fink, G. (1985) Effects of antiserum to thyrotrophin-releasing hormone on the concentrations of plasma prolactin, thyrotrophin and LH in the pro-oestrous rat. *Journal of Endocrinology* **104**, 205–209.

Hornykiewicz, O. (1986) Neurotransmitter changes in human brain during aging. In *Modification of Cell-to-Cell Signals During Normal and Pathological Aging*, pp. 169–182. Eds S. Govoni & F. Battaini. Springer-Verlag, Berlin.

Hylka, V.M., Sonntag, W.E. & Meites, J. (1984) Reduced ability of old male rats to release ACTH and corticosterone in response to CRF administration. *Proceedings of the Society of Experimental Biology and Medicine* **175**, 1–4.

Koch, Y., Goldhaber, G., Fireman, I., Zor, U., Shani, J. & Tal, E. (1977) Suppression of prolactin and thyrotropin in the rat by antiserum to thyrotropin-releasing hormone. *Endocrinology* **100**, 1476–1481.

Kooy, A., de Greef, W.J., Vreeburg, J.T.M., Hackeng, W.H.L., Ooms, M.P., Lamberts, S.W.J. & Weber, R.F.A. (1990) Evidence for the involvement of corticotropin-releasing factor in the inhibition of gonadotropin release induced by hyperprolactinemia. *Neuroendocrinology* **51**, 261–266.

Kvetnansky, R., Palkovits, M., Mitro, A., Torda, T. & Mikulaj, L. (1977) Catecholamines in individual hypothalamic nuclei of acutely and repeatedly stressed rats. *Neuroendocrinology* **23**, 257–267.

Landfield, P.W., Waymire, J.C. & Lynch, G. (1978) Hippocampal aging and adrenocorticoids: quantitative correlation. *Science* **202**, 1098–1102.

Login, I.S. (1990) Direct stimulation of pituitary prolactin release by glutamate. *Life Sciences* **47**, 2269–2275.

Malamed, S. & Carsia, R.V. (1983) Aging of the rat adrenocortical cell: response to ACTH and cyclic AMP *in vitro*. *Journal of Gerontology* **38**, 130–136.

Mangiacapra, F.J. & Florini, J.F. (1990) Alterations in hormone syntheses and secretion with age. In *Endocrine Function and Aging*, pp. 13–25. Eds H. J. Ambrecht, R. M. Coe & N. Wongsurawat. Springer-Verlag, New York.

McCarty, R. & Kopin, I.J. (1978) Sympatho–adrenal medullary activity and behavior during exposure to footshock stress: a comparison of seven rat strains. *Physiology and Behavior* **21**, 567–572.

McCarty, R., Gilad, G.M., Weise, V.K. & Kopin, I.J. (1979) Strain differences in rat adrenal biosynthetic enzymes and stress-induced increases in plasma catecholamines. *Life Sciences* **25**, 747–754.

Masoro, E.J. (1991) Biology of aging: facts, thoughts, and experimental approaches. *Laboratory Investigation* **65**, 500–510.

Meaney, M.J., Aitken, D.H., Berkel, C.V., Bhatnagar, S. & Sapolsky, R.N. (1988) Effect of neonatal handling on age-related impairments associated with the hippocampus. *Science* **239**, 766–768.

Meites, J. (1990a) Effects of aging on the hypothalamic–pituitary axis. *Review of Biological Research in Aging* **4**, 253–261.

Meites, J. (1990b) Hypothalamic catecholamines, neuroendocrine–immune interactions, and dietary restriction. *Proceedings of the Society of Experimental Biology and Medicine* **195**, 304–311.

Meites, J., Goya, R. & Takahashi, S. (1987) Why the neuroendocrine system is important in the aging process. *Experimental Gerontology* **22**, 1–15.

Milakofsky, L., Hare, T.A., Miller, J.M. & Vogel, W.H. (1985) Rat plasma levels of amino acids and related compounds during stress. *Life Sciences* **36**, 753–761.

Mogg, R.J. & Samson, W.K. (1990) Interactions of dopaminergic and peptidergic factors in the control of prolactin release. *Endocrinology* **126**, 728–735.

Moore, K.E., Riegel, G.D. & Demarest, K.T. (1985) Regulation of tuberoinfundibular dopaminergic neurons: prolactin and inhibitory neuronal influences. In *Catecholamines as Hormone Regulators*, pp. 31–49. Eds N. Ben-Jonathan, J. M. Bahr & R. I. Weiner. Raven Press, New York.

Morel, G., Enjalbert, A., Proulx, L., Pelletier, G., Barden, N., Gossard, F. & Dubois, P.M. (1989) Effect of corticotropin-releasing factor on the release and synthesis of prolactin. *Neuroendocrinology* **49**, 669–675.

Oboe, I., Angler, D., Mulch, M.E., Bollinger-Ruber, J. & Reichlin, S. (1985) Vasoactive intestinal peptide is a physiological mediator of prolactin release in the rat. *Endocrinology* **116**, 1383–1388.

Palkovits, M., Kobayashi, R.M., Kizer, J.S., Jacobowitz, D.M. & Kopin, I.J. (1975) Effect of stress on catecholamines and tyrosine hydroxylase activity of individual hypothalamic nuclei. *Neuroendocrinology* **18**, 144–153.

Parkening, T.A., Colling, T.J. & Smith, E.R. (1980) A comparative study of prolactin levels in five species of aged female laboratory rodents. *Biology of Reproduction* **22**, 513–518.

Pritchett, J.F., Sartin, J.L., Marple, D.N., Harper, W.L. & Till, M.L. (1979) Interaction of aging with *in vitro* adrenocortical responsiveness to ACTH and cyclic AMP. *Hormone Research* **10**, 96–103.

Reis, D.J. & Ross, R.A. (1973) Dynamic changes in brain dopamine-β-hydroxylase activity during anterograde and retrograde reactions to injury of central noradrenergic neurons. *Brain Research* **57**, 307–320.

Reymond, M.J. (1990) Age-related loss of the responsiveness of the tuberoinfundibular dopaminergic neurons to prolactin in the female rat. *Neuroendocrinology* **52**, 490–496.

Reymond, M.J. & Porter, J.C. (1981) Secretion of hypothalamic dopamine into pituitary stalk blood of aged female rats. *Brain Research Bulletin* **7**, 69–73.

Riegel, G.D. (1973) Chronic stress effects on adrenocortical responsiveness in young and aged rats. *Neuroendocrinology* **11**, 1–10.

Riegel, G.D. (1983) Changes in hypothalamic control of ACTH and adrenal cortical functions during aging. In *Neuroendocrinology of Aging*, pp. 309–332. Ed. J. Meites. Plenum Press, New York.

Samson, W.K., Lumpkin, M.D. & McCann, S.M. (1986) Evidence for a physiological role for oxytocin in the control of prolactin secretion. *Endocrinology* **119**, 554–560.

Sapolsky, R.M., Krey, L.C. & McEwen, B.S. (1983) The adrenocortical stress-response in the aged male rat: impairment of recovery from stress. *Experimental Gerontology* **18**, 55–64.

Sapolsky, R.M., Krey, L.C. & McEwen, B.S. (1986a) The adrenocortical axis in the aged rat: impaired sensitivity to both fast and delayed feedback inhibition. *Neurobiology of Aging* **7**, 331–335.

Sapolsky, R.M., Krey, L.C. & McEwen, B.S. (1986b) The neuroendocrinology of stress and aging: the glucocorticoid cascade hypothesis. *Endocrine Reviews* **7**, 284–301.

Sarkar, D.K. (1988) Immunoneutralization of oxytocin attenuates preovulatory prolactin secretion during proestrus in the rat. *Neuroendocrinology* **42**, 214–219.

Sarkar, D.K., Gottschall, P.E. & Meites, J. (1984a) Decline of tuberoinfundibular dopaminergic function resulting from chronic hyperprolactinemia in rats. *Endocrinology* **115**, 1269–1274.

Sarkar, D.K., Gottschall, P.E., Xie, Q.W. & Meites, J. (1984b) Reduced tuberoinfundibular dopaminergic neuronal function in rats with *in situ* prolactin-secreting pituitary tumors. *Neuroendocrinology* **38**, 498–503.

Scaccianoce, S., DiSciullo, A. & Angelucci, L. (1990) Age-related changes in hypothalamo–pituitary–adrenocortical axis activity in the rat. *Neuroendocrinology* **52**, 150–155.

Selye, H. & Tuchweber, B. (1976) Stress in relation to aging and disease. In *Hypothalamus, Pituitary and Aging*, pp. 553–569. Eds A. V. Everitt & J. A. Burgess. Charles C. Thomas, Springfield, IL.

Simpkins, J. (1982) Regional changes in monoamine metabolism in the aging constant estrous rat. *Neurobiology of Aging* **4**, 3309–3314.

Sonntag, W.E., Goliszek, A.G., Brodish, A. & Eldridge, J.C. (1987) Diminished diurnal secretion of adrenocorticotropin (ACTH), but not corticosterone, in old male rats: posible relation to increased adrenal sensitivity to ACTH *in vivo*. *Endocrinology* **120**, 2308–2315.

Tang, F. & Phillips, J.G. (1978) Some age-related changes in pituitary–adrenal function in the male laboratory rat. *Journal of Gerontology* **33**, 377–382.

Tizabi, Y., Aguilera, G. & Gilad, G.M. (1992) Age-related reduction in pituitary corticotropin-releasing hormone receptors in two rat strains. *Neurobiology of Aging* **13**, 227–230.

van Eekelen, J.A.M., Rots, N.Y., Sutanto, W. & de Kloet, E.R. (1991) The effect of aging on stress responsiveness and central corticosteroid receptors in the Brown Norway rat. *Neurobiology of Aging* **13**, 159–170.

Verkhratsky, M.S., Moroz, E.V., Magdish, L.V., Didenko, S.O. & Kharazi, L.I. (1988) Steroid-hormone-secretion-regulating systems under effect of stress in old age. *Gerontology* **34**, 41–47.

Weber, R.F.A. & Calogero, A.E. (1991) Prolactin stimulates rat hypothalamic corticotropin-releasing hormone and pituitary adrenocorticotropin secretion *in vitro*. *Neuroendocrinology* **54**, 248–253.

Wilson, M.M., Keith, L.D., Levitt, G.R. & Greer, S.E. (1981) Altered regulation of the pituitary–adrenal system of female rats during aging. *Gerontologist* **21**, 238.

Neurotransmitter receptors of rat cortical pyramidal neurones: implications for *in vivo* imaging and therapy

D. M. Bowen, P. T. Francis, M. N. Pangalos and I. P. Chessell

Institute of Neurology, 1 Wakefield Street, London WC1N 1PJ, UK

Summary. Pyramidal neurones of the neocortex have been implicated in a number of neuropsychiatric diseases, such as Alzheimer's disease. Markers that may identify these cells have been investigated using a novel technique. A subpopulation of corticifugal neocortical pyramidal neurones was destroyed by the unilateral striatal injection of volkensin, a toxin that undergoes retrograde suicide transport from the site of injection. Striatal volkensin injections produced significant reductions in the number of large pyramidal neurones of the infragranular cortical layer. The selectivity of the lesion was demonstrated by the preservation of cells containing glutamic acid decarboxylase mRNA, which are considered to be cortical interneurones. Ricin, another toxic lectin, but effective as a suicide transport agent exclusively in the PNS, produced local striatal damage but no cortical cell loss. In autoradiographic binding studies of animals treated with volkensin, binding in deep neocortical layers of [^{3}H]8-hydroxy-2-(n-dipropylamino) tetralin ([^{3}H]8-OH-DPAT) to 5-HT$_{1A}$ but not of [^{3}H]ketanserin to 5-HT$_2$ receptors was significantly reduced. The N-methyl-D-aspartate receptor complex was investigated using the novel glycine site antagonist [^{3}H]L-689,560, and the muscarinic M$_1$ receptor using [^{3}H]pirenzepine. Significant reductions in binding of [^{3}H]L-689,560 and [^{3}H]pirenzepine were observed in the deep neocortical layers of the animals that had been injected with volkensin. The rank order of the ligands as effective markers for this subpopulation of pyramidal neurones was [^{3}H]8-OH-DPAT $\gg$ [^{3}H]pirenzepine > [^{3}H]L-689,560 $\gg$ [^{3}H]ketanserin. These findings are thought to have advanced the understanding of the biology of pyramidal neurones. Implications for *in vivo* imaging treatment of neuropsychiatric conditions such as Alzheimer's disease are discussed.

Keywords: 5-HT receptor; pyramidal neurones; Alzheimer's disease; volkensin; rat

Introduction

The injection of cytotoxins, such as ricin, and their subsequent axonal transport leading to selective destruction of neurones projecting to the injection site ('suicide transport') has proved to be a useful strategy in the study of neurones in the PNS. Ricin, a toxic lectin found in castor beans, binds to oligosaccharides on cell membranes, enters the cells by endocytosis and is axonally transported to the neuronal perikarya. Once in the cell body, ricin inactivates ribosomes, irreversibly inhibiting protein synthesis. However, ricin is ineffective in the CNS. Volkensin, another toxic lectin that comes from the kilyambitti plant *Adenia volkensii*, acts in a similar manner to ricin in the PNS but is also effective in the CNS (Wiley & Stirpe, 1988).

The major cell type of the neocortex is the pyramidal neurone, which accounts for approximately 70% of all neurones in this region. These cells have been implicated in a number of neuropsychiatric diseases, particularly Alzheimer's disease. It has proved impossible to lesion pyramidal neurones selectively and it is difficult to ascribe biochemical changes in some neurodegenerative diseases to loss of specific cellular structures. This study has investigated the use of volkensin to destroy a subpopulation of neocortical neurones. It is proposed that the biochemical investigation into animals with such a neocortical cell loss will advance the understanding of the biology of neocortical pyramidal cells, and, in particular, will address the issue as to whether a specific neurotransmitter receptor(s) is enriched on these cells. This could have important implications for the development of drugs affecting higher mental function and for the development of markers of pyramidal cells for brain-imaging techniques.

Materials and Methods

Lesion and histological procedures

Male Sprague-Dawley rats (200–250 g) were anaesthetized with Hypnorm (0·16 mg fentanylcitrate kg^{-1} and 5·0 mg fluanisone kg^{-1} body weight, i.p.) and Hypnovel (1·0 mg midazolam hydrochloride at kg^{-1}, i.m.). The animals were placed in a stereotactic frame and the scalp reflected to expose the skull. The dura overlying the cortex was exposed by removal of a bone flap, and 6 ng (five rats) or 2 ng (six rats) of volkensin (a gift from F. Stirpe), or 10 ng (four rats) or 2 ng (four rats) of ricin (a gift from P. Thorpe) were stereotactically injected into the striatum on the left side. After the operation the animals were given 0·3 ml Temgesic kg^{-1} (0·09 mg buprenophrine hydrochloride kg^{-1}, i.m.), and allowed to recover.

After a post-operative survival period of 28 days, animals were anaesthetized i.p. with a lethal dose of pentobarbitone, and perfused transcardially with 0·9% saline followed by buffered saline, pH 7·4, containing 30% sucrose. The brains were rapidly frozen (in an isopentane–dry ice mixture at $-40°C$), coated in a layer of a Lipshaw M1 embedding matrix and stored in airtight containers at $-70°C$. Coronal sections 12 µm thick were cut at $-20°C$ and thaw-mounted onto chrome-alum coated slides. These were then stored at $-70°C$ until processed for histology, immunocytochemistry, autoradiography or *in situ* hybridization histochemistry. (All as described by Pangalos *et al.*, 1991.) Sections taken from throughout the brain were fixed with 4% paraformaldehyde and then stained with cresyl violet. In all cases, lamina IV of the cortex was easily recognized. Cells were separately counted both superficial (supragranular) and deep (infragranular) to lamina IV using a Quantimet 570 image analysis system (Leica) set to exclude cells of area $\leqslant 80$ µm². The mean number of cell profiles per field (cell number) and mean size of cell profiles per field (mean cell size) ±SEM from at least five sections were calculated. The differences between the side ipsilateral to the lesion and the side contralateral to the lesion were evaluated using the Student's *t* test ($P < 0.05$ accepted as significant).

Immunocytochemical staining to visualize glial cells, and hence the extent of neocortical gliosis, was performed using a monoclonal antibody against glial fibrillary acidic protein (a gift from J. Newcombe and N. Woodroofe) and on a number of sections an avidin biotin peroxidase technique with a diaminobenzidine chromogen was used.

In situ detection of the mRNA encoding the enzyme glutamic acid decarboxylase (GAD), an enzyme involved in the synthesis of γ-aminobutyric acid (GABA) and thought to be a marker of interneurones, was performed as previously described (Pangalos *et al.*, 1991). Briefly, a synthetic oligonucleotide probe 30 bp long [HPLC pure, Oswell DNA service (Edinburgh University)] directed against bases 1621–1650 of GAD mRNA was 3′end labelled with [^{35}S]dATP. To each section was added 1×10^6 c.p.m. of probe and the sections were incubated in a humidified chamber at 24°C overnight. After hybridization the sections were washed, air-dried and dipped in photographic emulsion. Slides were developed 25 days later and were fixed and counterstained with cresyl violet for the visualization of neuronal cell bodies.

Autoradiography

Anatomical distribution of 5-HT_{1A} receptors using [^{3}H]8-hydroxy-2-(*n*-dipropylamino)tetralin ([^{3}H]8-OH-DPAT), 5-HT_2 receptors using [^{3}H]ketanserin, NMDA receptors using the novel glycine$_b$ site antagonist [^{3}H]L-689,560, and muscarinic M_1 receptors using [^{3}H]pirenzepine was visualized in lesioned animals by autoradiography. Radiochemicals were supplied by NEN/Dupont (Stevenage, UK) except for [^{3}H]L-689,560, which was a gift from Merck, Sharp and Dohme Research Laboratories, Harlow, UK. Incubation conditions were based on previously published conditions and are described in Table 1. In all cases sections were thawed, pre-incubated, and incubated at equilibrium in the presence of the appropriate ^{3}H-labelled ligand. Nonspecific binding was generated in a parallel series of sections by incubation of the ^{3}H-labelled ligand in the presence of a suitable displacer. After incubation, the sections were washed with ice-cold buffer and dried under a stream of cold air. The tissue sections (along with ^{3}H-labelled Micro-scales) were then co-exposed to ^{3}H-Hyperfilm (both Amersham International, Amersham, UK) at 4°C for 9–90 days, depending on the particular ^{3}H-labelled ligand present. The films were developed, fixed, and the autoradiograms were then subjected to colour-coded reconstruction – based on tissue equivalents of the Micro-scale standards – using computerized receptor autoradiography software (Quantimet 570). Specific images were obtained by subtracting the nonspecific image from the total binding image. The mean binding value (±SEM) for each ^{3}H-labelled ligand from at least four autoradiograms were calculated and the differences between the side ipsilateral and contralateral to the lesion were evaluated using the Student's *t* test ($P < 0.05$ accepted as significant).

Table 1. Incubation conditions for the labelling of 5-HT_{1A}, 5-HT_2, NMDA and M_1 receptors

Ligand	Displacer	Buffer	Pre-incubation	Incubation	Wash
^{3}[H]8-OH-DPAT (1 nmol l^{-1})	1 µmol 5-HT l^{-1}	0·17 mol Tris–HCl l^{-1}, 4 mmol CaCl$_2$ l^{-1}, 0·01% ascorbate, pH 7·6	30 min, 25°C	60 min, 25°C	2 × 5 min, 4°C
^{3}[H]Ketanserin (2 nmol l^{-1})	1 µmol methylsergide l^{-1}	0·17 mol Tris–HCl l^{-1}, pH 7·7	15 min, 25°C	120 min, 25°C	2 × 10 min, 4°C
^{3}[H]L-689,560 (5 nmol l^{-1})	1 mmol glycine l^{-1}	50 mmol Tris–acetate l^{-1}, pH 7·0	60 min, 4°C	120 min, 4°C	4 × 1 min, 4°C
^{3}[H]Pirenzepine (2·5 nmol l^{-1})	10 µmol atropine sulphate l^{-1}	Phosphate-buffered saline	20 min, 25°C	90 min, 25°C	1 × 5 min, 4°C

Results

Cell loss as a result of direct spread

In all cases the injection sites were centred on the left striatum. The extent of the damage produced was dependent upon the amount of toxin injected.

In animals in which 6 ng volkensin in 3 µl of vehicle had been injected, most of the striatum was destroyed with considerable collapse of the structure of the hemisphere, substantial ventricular enlargement and associated damage in nuclei surrounding the striatum. In all of these animals injected with high doses, the globus pallidus was completely destroyed, and the lesion had been directly extended in a more ventral direction (e.g. to the ventral striatum and horizontal nucleus of the diagonal band). Additionally, there was cell loss in the anterolateral thalamus in all of these animals. The neocortex overlying the striatum showed evidence of direct damage due to passage of the needle. This damage was more severe in the frontal neocortex of animals receiving 6 ng volkensin than in those receiving either 2 ng volkensin, or 10 ng or 2 ng ricin (in 2 µl of vehicle). However, in the group of animals receiving 6 ng volkensin, more posteriorly the lamina structure of the neocortex was intact and there was no evidence of cell loss in the underlying hippocampus or damage to the corpus callosum, indicating that changes in this area were not due to direct involvement from the injection site.

In the animals receiving 2 ng volkensin, the volume of the striatum destroyed was less, as was the consequent distortion of the hemisphere and damage to the surrounding structures. In four of the six animals, there was substantial direct damage of the globus pallidus, in one there was less damage, and in one animal this nucleus was intact. In four animals there was some suggestion that the anterolateral pole of the thalamus had been damaged as a result of the injection, although this damage was slight, and one animal also showed that the basal forebrain had been affected. In this group of animals, all showed no more damage to the overlying neocortex than was seen in those animals injected with ricin, indicating that only mechanical injury from the passage of the needle had occurred.

Injection of 10 ng ricin caused extensive necrosis in the striatum, producing a lesion similar in volume to that following injection of 2 ng volkensin. Injection of 2 ng ricin caused necrosis within the striatum but to a lesser extent than that caused by 10 ng ricin or 2 ng volkensin.

Cell loss due to retrograde suicide transport

Several neuronal populations known to project to the injection site were examined qualitatively for cell loss and compared with corresponding regions on the contralateral side. There was substantial cell loss in the substantia nigra in both groups of animals injected with volkensin. Some cell loss was also apparent in the intralaminar nuclei of the thalamus, although in some cases this damage may have been caused by diffusion of the toxin.

Neocortical cell loss was clearly visible in the groups of animals treated with 6 ng and 2 ng volkensin. Measurements of cell numbers and cell size were taken posterior to the injection site near to the medial margin (cortical area Fr1/Fr2) and were made from sections where all six laminae of the neocortex were complete and where there were intact subcortical structures (e.g. the hippocampus and the corpus callosum).

After injecting each of five rats with 6 ng of toxin, the number of cells in the infragranular layers counted ipsilaterally was reduced to 57% of those counted in the opposite side ($P < 0.001$, Student's t test; Fig. 1). Injection of six rats with 2 ng volkensin significantly reduced the number

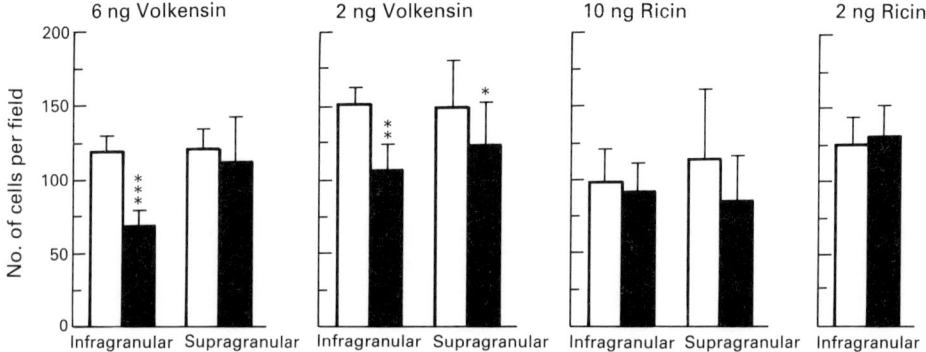

Fig. 1. Neocortical cell loss following injection of the toxic lectins volkensin and ricin into the striatum of rats. Error bars are SEM. The cell counts in the infragranular and supragranular layers of the cortex were significantly different from the corresponding contralateral side where indicated by the significance symbols *($P < 0.02$), **($P < 0.002$), ***($P < 0.001$). No significant cell loss was seen in the supragranular layer of the cortex of the animals into which 2 ng of ricin had been injected (data not shown).

of cells in the infragranular layers on the ipsilateral side to 71% of the cells on the contralateral side ($P < 0.01$), and also significantly reduced the number of cells counted ipsilaterally in the supragranular layers to 84% of the cells on the normal-appearing side ($P < 0.05$; Fig. 1).

After striatal injection of four rats with 2 ng ricin and four rats with 10 ng ricin no significant cell loss was observed (Fig. 1).

The infragranular cell loss in animals treated with 6 ng or 2 ng volkensin was accompanied in all cases by a reduction of 20–25% in mean cell size. No changes in cell size were observed in the supragranular layers (Fig. 2). Frequency histograms of neuronal cell size in the infragranular layers for both the ipsilateral and contralateral sides exhibited quite different population distributions, suggesting that the observed decreases in mean cell size on the side ipsilateral to the injection site are a result of loss of large cells > $180\,\mu m^2$ (Fig. 3). Frequency histograms of cell size in the supragranular layers showed similar distributions irrespective of the side investigated.

Effect of injection of volkensin on interneurones

No significant difference in the number of cells per field that were positive for GAD mRNA were observed between ipsilateral and contralateral sides (Table 2) as determined by *in situ* hybridization.

Binding of ^{3}H-labelled ligands in lesioned rat brain sections

Quantitative analysis of the mean specific binding value ($\pm$ SEM), determined from the autoradiograms, within neocortical areas Fr1/Fr2 and Par1/Par2 are shown in Figs 4 and 5 for

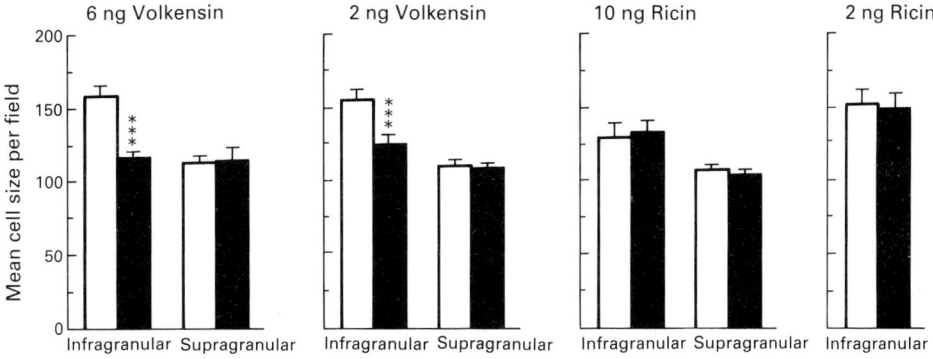

Fig. 2. Changes in neocortical cell size following injection of the toxic lectins volkensin and ricin into the rat striatum. Error bars are SEM. Where indicated by the significance symbol ***($P < 0.001$), the mean cell size in the infragranular layer of the cortex was significantly different from the corresponding contralateral side. No significant cell loss was seen in the supragranular layers of the cortex of the animals into which 2 ng ricin had been injected (data not shown).

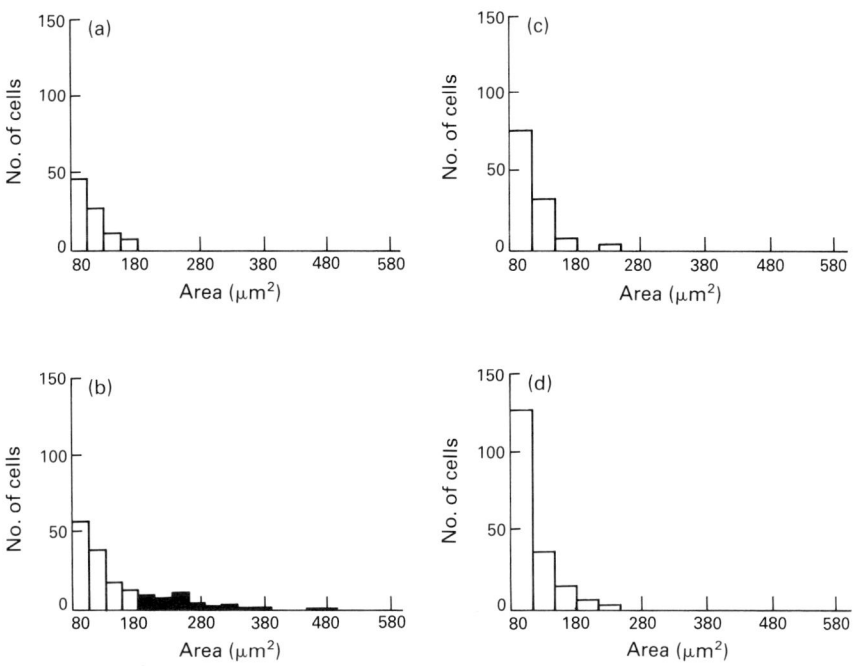

Fig. 3. Cell size distributions in the neocortex of a rat injected with 2 ng volkensin. Representative frequency histograms of cross-sectional area of cell profiles in the cerebral neocortex from a typical animal after 2 ng volkensin had been injected into the striatum 28 days previously. (a) Ipsilateral infragranular layers. (b) Contralateral infragranular layers. (c) Ipsilateral supragranular layers. (d) Contralateral supragranular layers. Solid histobars indicate the cell population most affected by injection of volkensin.

Table 2. Number of cells per field positive for GAD mRNA in groups of rats injected with volkensin

	6 ng Volkensin ($n = 5$)		2 ng Volkensin ($n = 6$)	
	Ipsilateral	Contralateral	Ipsilateral	Contralateral
Supragranular	3·69 ± 0·14	3·63 ± 0·15	3·77 ± 0·31	4·05 ± 0·19
Infragranular	3·40 ± 0·13	3·29 ± 0·19	3·75 ± 0·03	3·93 ± 0·15

Values are mean number of cells per field ± SEM.
No significant difference in the number of cells staining positively for GAD mRNA is observed between ipsilateral and contralateral sides; $P > 0.05$.

[^{3}H]8-OH-DPAT in both volkensin- and ricin-treated animals. The change in distribution of each ligand is summarized in Fig. 6 and Table 3.

Discussion

The histological findings

This study demonstrates that volkensin produces a significant loss of a subpopulation of neocortical pyramidal cells after it has been injected into the striatum. It is not possible in these experiments to exclude the loss of infragranular pyramidal cells in the neocortex, which send their axons to other subcortical nuclei by passing through the striatum without synapsing. However, given the loss of other distant neurones projecting to the injection site, such as, for example, those projecting from the substantia nigra, it is certain that the population of pyramidal cells lost includes cortico-striatal projection neurones.

It is possible that infragranular cell loss occurs as a result of direct thalamic damage (this is more likely when the higher doses are injected) and subsequent retrograde transport from this site. However, the cell loss observed in this study is primarily that of the large pyramidal neurones (predominantly in layer V), whereas the cells of origin of the corticothalamic pathway are typically in layer VI (Crino et al., 1990).

The possibility that volkensin may spread from the injection site directly, or from neurones that initially transport the toxic lectin and then release it into the surrounding neuropil upon cell lysis (from where it may be taken up by adjacent neurones) has been carefully considered. (1) *In situ* hybridization for GAD mRNA, a marker of neocortical interneurones was investigated. Since interneurones do not project to the striatum, any loss of cells positive for GAD mRNA would suggest that cell loss following volkensin injection may have been a consequence of either (i) passive diffusion or (ii) secondary spread from cells that retrogradely transported the toxin and subsequently lysed. No significant differences between the number of neocortical cells staining positively for GAD mRNA were observed between ipsilateral and contralateral sides (Table 2). (2) Injection of the neurotoxic lectin ricin, which is similar in nature to volkensin but is effective as a suicide transport agent only in the PNS, produced local lesions around the injection site but no observable cell loss in other areas or nuclei suggesting that cell loss by diffusion had not occurred. (3) Histological analysis revealed that the cell loss distant to the injection site conformed to known afferent projections to the striatum and was not seen in nuclei or in areas closer to the injection site that had no afferent axons to the striatum.

The occurrence of cell loss from the supragranular layers of the neocortex after injection of 2 ng volkensin where no such loss is seen following larger injections is difficult to interpret (Fig. 1). It is clear that in the infragranular layers of the ipsilateral side the cell loss following volkensin injections is mainly of larger neurones $> 180\ \mu m^2$ in cross-sectional area. Such a loss leads to a change in the cell population distribution (Fig. 3) and in the mean cell size (Fig. 2) that cannot be accounted for

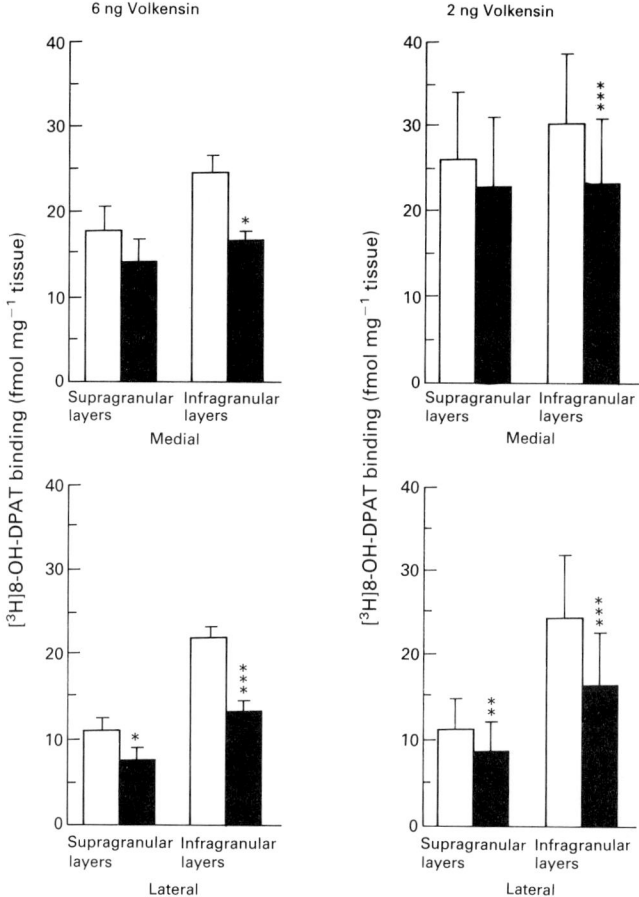

Fig. 4. Binding of [^{3}H]8-OH-DPAT in rats injected with volkensin. Binding was determined from 5–12 autoradiograms taken from each rat in the supragranular and infragranular layers of neocortical areas Fr1/Fr2 (medial) and Par1/Par2 (lateral). Bars represent mean and error bars represent SEM. Where indicated by the significance symbols *($P < 0.05$), **($P < 0.01$), or ***($P < 0.0001$), the binding of [^{3}H]8-OH-DPAT in the ipsilateral side was significantly different from the corresponding contralateral side.

by shrinkage alone. Frequency histograms of the supragranular layers on the ipsilateral and contralateral sides in the rats treated with a lower dose of volkensin show no change in the cell population distributions (Fig. 3), and there is also no significant difference in mean cell size (Fig. 2). These findings suggest that the apparent loss of cells $> 80\,\mu m^2$ could be due to shrinkage below the exclusion criterion (set on the image analyser to exclude glia and smaller neurones), rather than any actual loss of cell numbers. It is not apparent why such a shrinkage should occur only in those experiments in which a lower dose of volkensin was administered. However, the loss is relatively small and a number of technical considerations may contribute to this observation.

The autoradiographic findings

Sections from animals lesioned with volkensin were processed for autoradiographic studies using ^{3}H-labelled ligands binding to various receptors: [^{3}H]8-OH-DPAT binding to 5-HT$_{1A}$ receptors, [^{3}H]ketanserin binding to 5-HT$_2$ receptors, [^{3}H]pirenzepine binding to muscarinic M$_1$ receptors, and [^{3}H]L-689,560 binding to NMDA receptors. The effectiveness of the ^{3}H-labelled ligands

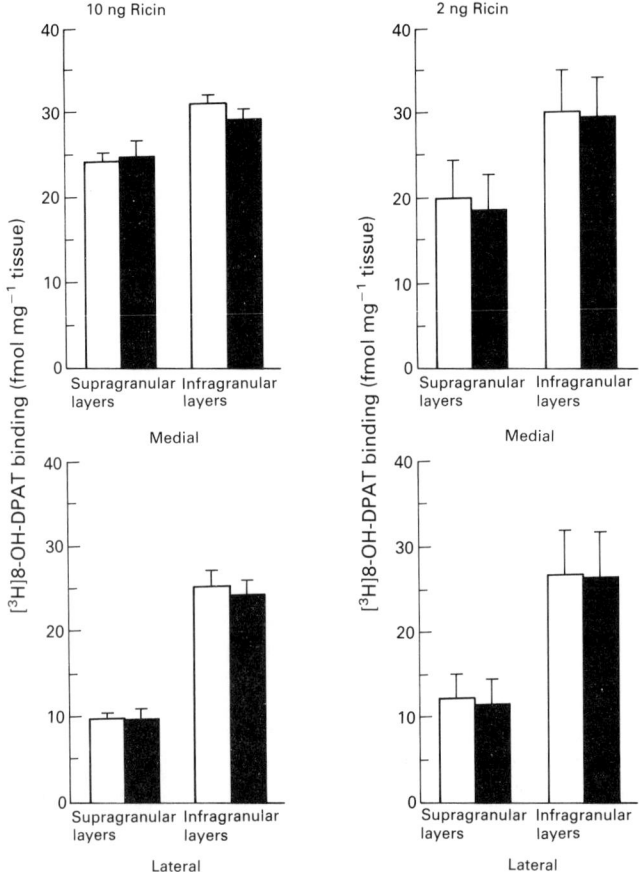

Fig. 5. Binding of [^{3}H]8-OH-DPAT in rats injected with ricin. Binding was determined from 5–12 autoradiograms taken from each rat in the supragranular and infragranular layers of neocortical areas Fr1/Fr2 (medial) and Par1/Par2 (lateral). Bars represent mean and error bars represent SEM.

used, with respect to their use as markers of this subpopulation of pyramidal neurones, was [^{3}H]8-OH-DPAT ≫ [^{3}H]pirenzepine > [^{3}H]L-689,560 ≫ [^{3}H]ketanserin.

The summary of the localization of the receptor changes shown in Fig. 6 shows that except for [^{3}H]ketanserin, binding of all the ^{3}H-labelled ligands was significantly reduced medially (in cortical area Fr1/Fr2) in the infragranular but not the supragranular layers. This suggests that the receptors are associated predominantly with pyramidal cell bodies. In the more lateral area (Par1/Par2), binding of [^{3}H]8-OH-DPAT and [^{3}H]L-689,560 was reduced throughout the depth of the neocortex, suggesting the localization of 5-HT$_{1A}$ and NMDA receptor sites on both cell bodies and apical dendrites. ^{3}H-labelled pirenzepine seemed to be localized on cell bodies only. Since there was no significant loss in the binding of [^{3}H]ketanserin it may be concluded that pyramidal neurones forming the corticostriatal pathway are not enriched in 5-HT$_2$ sites. These data are consistent with the notion that these receptors are predominantly located on neocortical interneurones (Cross et al., 1984; Sheldon & Aghajanian, 1990), which were preserved in this model. The reduction in [^{3}H]ketanserin binding in the most superficial layers of Par1/Par2 in animals receiving 2 ng volkensin is unexplained but the statistical significance ($P = 0.044$) is low. It seems unlikely to be due to diffusion of the toxin, since neocortical layers closer to the injection site were unaffected – as

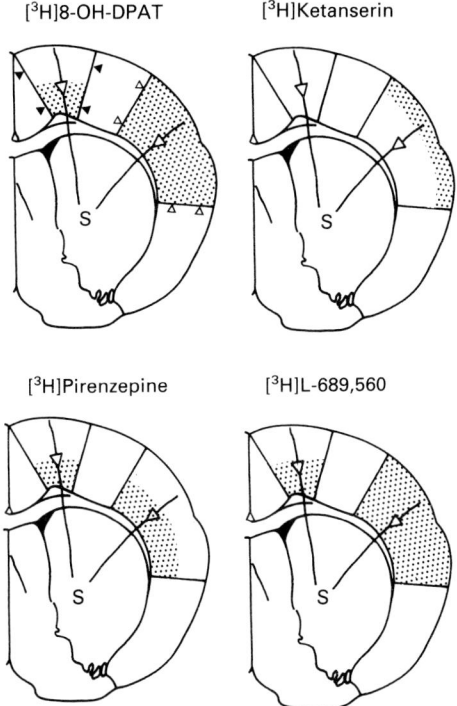

Fig. 6. Overview of receptor loss in rat cortex in the deep (infragranular) and superficial (supragranular) cortical layers following striatal volkensin injections, as determined by autoradiography. A pyramidal neurone is drawn projecting from the infragranular layers to the striatum (S) of each hemisphere in cortical areas Fr1/Fr2 and Par1/Par2. In the top left diagram the boundaries of area Fr1/Fr2 are identified by the filled arrowheads and the boundaries of area Par1/Par2 by the open arrowheads. The pyramidal cells are drawn in such a manner that the cell body of the neurone is represented by a triangle and the apical dendrites by a line protruding from the cell body towards the cortical surface. The shaded areas in each hemisphere represent the regions in which significant reductions in binding occur for each ^{3}H-labelled ligand after unilateral striatal volkensin injection. A reduction in binding of a particular ligand in the deep layers suggests that cells possess these particular receptors on the cell bodies, while a reduction in binding in the superficial layers suggests that the corresponding receptors are present on the apical dendrites (Pangalos, M. N., Francis, P. T. and Bowen, D. M., unpublished data).

were neocortical layers in animals receiving 6 ng volkensin. No functional or anatomical explanation of this reduction is apparent. The most likely interpretation of the observed reduction in [^{3}H]ketanserin ligand binding is that 5-HT$_{1A}$, NMDA and M$_1$ receptor sites are enriched postsynaptically on the pyramidal cells of layer V, forming the corticostriatal pathway. It is also possible that these receptors are found on the terminals of the axon collaterals of these neurones, since local axon collaterals originating from pyramidal cells are one of the most consistently demonstrated features of neocortical circuitry.

It could be argued that the receptors for 5-HT$_{1A}$, NMDA and M$_1$ are located on interneurones destroyed by uptake of toxin released following death of corticostriatal pyramidal neurones. However, cells that stain positively for GAD mRNA, i.e. interneurones, were preserved in the area that showed loss of pyramidal neurones – suggesting that trans-synaptic degeneration or diffusion have not occurred to any great extent.

Another interpretation is that the receptor sites are located presynaptically, either as autoreceptors or heteroreceptors. 5-HT$_{1A}$ autoreceptors are unlikely to be involved since there was no

Table 3. Overview of the effects of unilateral striatal volkensin injections on cortical receptor binding

Receptor	Cortical layers	6 ng Volkensin		2 ng Volkensin	
		Medial	Lateral	Medial	Lateral
5-HT$_{1A}$	Superficial	78	69	85	78*
	Deep	68*	60***	77***	67***
5-HT$_2$	Superficial	86	100	100	91*
	Middle	82	86	94	93
	Deep	85	83	90	91
NMDA	Superficial	90	92	94	100
	Deep	80*	85	100	96
M$_1$	Superficial	90	95	98	98
	Deep	76*	80	89**	83**

Values are the percentage of those values recorded on the contralateral side, and are mean specific binding values determined by autoradiography.
*, $P < 0.05$; **, $P < 0.01$; ***, $P < 0.001$, significantly different from the contralateral side, as determined from mean binding values (Student's t test).
(Pangalos, M. N., Francis, P. T. and Bowen, D. M., unpublished).

reduction in [^{3}H]8-OH-DPAT binding 18–21 days after lesion of the medial forebrain bundle with 5,7 dihydroxytryptamine, although presynaptic markers were markedly reduced (Francis *et al.*, in press). Most evidence to date also suggests that the NMDA receptor complex does not function as an autoreceptor within the neocortex (Barrie, A. P. and Nicholls, D. G., personal communication) or the striatum (Greenamyre & Young, 1989) and the M$_1$ receptor is considered to be primarily a postsynaptic receptor.

Heteroreceptors on the terminals of neurones that project from the injection site to the neocortex are also unlikely to be involved. The striatal area that was lesioned does not project to the neocortex (Heimer *et al.*, 1985), so the only possible corticipetal fibres that might bear such receptors are those of the thalamocortical pathways. In most animals there was some evidence of involvement of the anterior nuclei of the thalamus (due to direct spread from the injection site), but these areas project primarily to the cingulate and retrosplenial cortices and not to the neocortical areas studied here (Faull & Mehler, 1985). Perhaps the most persuasive argument against a corticipetal nerve terminal location is that there was no reduction in ^{3}H-labelled ligand binding following intrastriatal injection of either 2 ng or 10 ng ricin. Thus, if any of the receptor sites were present on thalamocortical (or other corticipetal) projections a reduction in binding in the cingulate and retrosplenial cortices (or other neocortical areas) should have occurred. However, it should not be overlooked that some of these receptors are heteroreceptors on terminals of neurones of the intralaminar nuclei group of the thalamus. Certain cells from these nuclei project to both the striatum and the neocortex. This is a most unlikely explanation of the results analysed here, since the thalamocortical fibres of the intralaminar nuclei terminate sparsely in the neocortex (Faull & Mehler, 1985).

It should also be noted that in animals injected with 6 ng or 2 ng volkensin some direct damage to the anterolateral thalamus was observed. It is therefore possible that retrograde transport from this site may have occurred, resulting in loss of some corticothalamic pyramidal neurones. This is unlikely to explain the reductions in binding observed, since the damage to the anterior thalamus is small and since these neurones project primarily from the cingulate and retrosplenial cortices (Faull & Mehler, 1985).

From this work the most selective marker of this subpopulation of pyramidal neurones is [^{3}H]8-OH-DPAT binding, which marks the 5-HT$_{1A}$ receptor. The connection between 5-HT transmission and glutamatergic transmission has been quite extensively studied in animals. Studies using rats have demonstrated the inhibitory nature of 5-HT on neocortical neurones, probably mediated by

5-HT_{1A} receptors on pyramidal neurones and 5-HT_2 receptors on inhibitory interneurones. It has been reported (in agreement with the finding of others) that in pyramidal cells of layer V of the rat association cortex, 5-HT induces cell hyperpolarization mediated by 5-HT_{1A} receptors (Araneda & Andrade, 1991). Furthermore, 5-HT_{1A} receptor partial agonists have also been observed to mimic the hyperpolarizing action of 5-HT on the resting membrane potential in neurones of the neocortex (Davies et al., 1987).

Studies of fresh human neurosurgical samples have shown that application of 8-OH-DPAT results in the hyperpolarization of cortical and hippocampal pyramidal neurones (McCormick & Williamson, 1989). In addition, receptor autoradiography has also provided further evidence that binding of [^{3}H]8-OH-DPAT is useful for studying 5-HT_{1A} receptors in the neocortex of the human brain (see Bowen et al., 1992). These observations suggest that 5-HT_{1A} receptor sites in the human neocortex are functionally similar to those in the rat and are enriched on a specific structure – probably pyramidal neurones. However, an important species difference should be emphasized: neocortial 5-HT_{1A} receptors in the rodent are predominantly found in the deep layers, while in the primate they are predominantly in the superficial layers. This suggests that in humans the receptor is predominantly present on corticocortical pyramidal neurones and is consistent with the hypothesis that 5-HT_{1A} receptors may be important in the regulation of the activity of these cells.

Implications for treatment of Alzheimer's disease

The data from patients indicate that Alzheimer's disease is characterized by two selective and critical deficits: circumscribed corticocortical glutamatergic and cholinergic degeneration (Bowen et al., 1992). Such a loss of *excitatory* neocortical (glutamatergic) pyramidal neurones in Alzheimer's disease probably results in a reduction of neuronal activity and may underlie the memory loss associated with the disease. Data from this study suggests pharmacological approaches for enhancing glutamatergic transmission using specific 5-HT_{1A} receptor antagonists [which are, by coincidence, now emerging (Bjork et al., 1991; Fletcher et al., 1991; Liau et al., 1991; Millan et al., 1991; Hoyer et al., in press)]. Treatment of patients with Alzheimer's disease with a 5-HT_{1A} antagonist should facilitate the effects of the remaining proportion of the transmitter glutamate by inhibiting the tonic hyperpolarizing action of 5-HT on pyramidal neurones, thereby compensating for the reduced excitatory input caused by the degenerative process.

A further indication of the importance of 5-HT with respect to glutamatergic neurotransmission in Alzheimer's disease is the observation that decreased 5-HT availability can enhance learning and memory, as emphasized by McEntee & Crook (1991). Cortical pyramidal neurones are probably also subject to cholinergic modulation (Halliwell, 1986; McCormick & Williamson, 1989; Geaney et al., 1990; see also Fig. 6). However, no long-lasting and nontoxic acetylcholinesterase inhibitor has been tested with optimal methodology (e.g. no unequivocal diagnostic test for Alzheimer's disease exists, other than neurohistopathology).

Implications for *in vivo* imaging of patients with Alzheimer's disease

This study suggests that the 5-HT_{1A} receptor is a selective marker of pyramidal neurones, and strengthens the inference that the reduction in 5-HT_{1A} receptors observed in Alzheimer's disease (Bowen et al., 1989) indexes loss of pyramidal neurones from the neocortex. Development of ligands specific for the 5-HT_{1A} receptor, the distribution of which can be analysed using positron emission tomography (PET), may therefore provide a specific method for determining the extent of pyramidal cell pathology and this may help in the early diagnosis of the disorder.

Little progress has been made in the development of selective PET ligands for 5-HT_1 receptor subtypes (Hartig & Lever, 1990). Labelling of the 5-HT_{1A} receptor *in vivo* has been approached using an iodinated derivative of 8-OH-DPAT, with visualization by single photon emission computerized tomography (SPECT). This compound displayed similar autoradiographic distributions in the rat brain *in vivo* to those observed *in vitro*, but had the drawback of exceptionally high non-specific binding. Another group of compounds that might target 5-HT$_1$ receptors are the indolealkylamines. These have been reported to cross the blood–brain barrier effectively, although their distribution *in vivo* may reflect active transport sites as well as receptor-specific and non-specific binding sites. While a ligand suitable for analysis *in vivo* has yet to be discovered for the 5-HT$_{1A}$ receptor, substantial advances are being made and new compounds, particularly antagonists such as WAY100135 (Fletcher *et al.*, 1991; Routledge *et al.*, 1992; Dourish *et al.*, in press), are under consideration.

Conclusion

Data from this study, together with work currently in progress in this laboratory, will indicate whether various compounds under investigation in academic and industrial laboratories are likely to be of use either to follow pyramidal cell loss in neurodegenerative diseases *in vivo* or to be of therapeutic value.

Alzheimer's disease has been considered by some to be primarily a genetic disorder involving chromosome 21 and there are those who view with pessimism the idea of pharmacotherapy using drugs that would aim to improve neurotransmission. Alzheimer's disease is a slowly progressing disorder and yet the pessimistic conclusion was based on severely affected subjects at the end-point of the disease. Even if treatment to slow the progression of the pathology ensues as a result of the research centred around chromosome 21 and β-amyloid, traditional pharmacotherapy will still be required for most patients to improve functional activities already lost, as well as for all patients afflicted with the disease during the development of any alternative treatments.

References

Araneda, R. & Andrade, R. (1991) 5-Hydroxytryptamine 2 and 5-hydroxytryptamine 1A receptors mediate opposing responses on membrane excitability in rat association cortex. *Neuroscience* **40**, 399–412.

Bjork, L., Cornfield, L.J., Nelson, D.L., Hillver, S.E., Anden, N.E., Lewander, T. & Hacksell, U. (1991) Pharmacology of the novel 5-hydroxytryptamine 1A receptor antagonist (S)-5-fluoro-8-hydroxy-2-(dipropylamino)tetralin: inhibition of (R)-8-hydroxy-2-(dipropylamino)tetralin-induced effects. *Journal of Pharmacology and Experimental Therapeutics* **258**, 58–65.

Bowen, D.M., Najlerahim, A., Procter, A.W., Francis, P.T. & Murphy, E. (1989) Circumscribed changes of the cerebral cortex in neuropsychiatric disorders of later life. *Proceedings of the National Academy of Sciences USA* **86**, 9504–9508.

Bowen, D.M., Francis, P.T., Pangalos, M.N., Stephens, P.H. & Procter, A.W. (1992) Treatment strategies for Alzheimer's disease. *Lancet* **339**, 132–133.

Crino, P.B., Vogt, B.A., Volicer, L. & Wiley, R.G. (1990) Cellular localization of serotonin 1A, 1B and uptake sites in cingulate cortex in the rat. *Journal of Pharmacology and Experimental Therapeutics* **252**, 651–657.

Cross, A.J., Crow, T.J., Ferrier, I.N., Johnson, J.A., Bloom, S.R. & Corsellis, J.A.N. (1984) Serotonin receptor changes in dementia of the Alzheimer's type. *Journal of Neurochemistry* **43**, 1574–1581.

Davies, M.F., Deisz, R.A., Prince, D.A., Peroutka, S.J. (1987) Two distinct effects of 5-hydroxytryptamine on single cortical neurones. *Brain Research* **423**, 347–352.

Dourish, C.T., Gurling, J., Wright, I. & Routledge, C. Stereospecific effects of the selective and silent 5-HT$_{1A}$ receptor antagonist, WAY100135, on rat hippocampal 5-HT levels: A microdialysis study. *Society for Neuroscience*, (in press).

Faull, R.L.M. & Mehler, W.R. (1985) Thalamus. In *The Rat Nervous System*, pp. 129–168. Ed. G. Paxinos. Academic Press, Sydney.

Fletcher, A., Bill, D.J., Brammer, N.T., Cliffe, I.A., Forster, Y. & Lloyd, G.K. (1991) WAY100135: A novel and highly selective 5-HT$_{1A}$ receptor antagonist. *Society for Neuroscience Abstracts* **17**, 92.

Francis, P.T., Pangalos, M.N., Pearson, R.C.A., Middlemiss, D.N., Stratmann, G.C. & Bowen, D.M. 5-HT$_{1A}$ but not 5-HT$_2$ receptors are enriched on neocortical pyramidal neurones destroyed by intrastriatal volkensin. *Journal of Pharmacology and Experimental Therapeutics* (in press).

Geaney, D.P., Soper, N., Shepstone, B.J. & Cowen, P.J. (1990) Effect of central cholinergic stimulation on regional cerebral blood flow in Alzheimer's disease. *Lancet* **335**, 1484–1487.

Greenamyre, J.T. & Young, A.B. (1989) Synaptic localisation of striatal NMDA, quisqualate and kainate receptors. *Neuroscience Letters* **101**, 133–137.

Halliwell, J.V. (1986) M-Current in human neocortical neurones. *Neuroscience Letters* **67**, 1–6.

Hartig, P.R. & Lever, J.R. (1990) Serotonin receptors. In *Quantitative Imaging: Neurotransmitters and Enzymes*, pp. 153–164. Eds J. J. Frost and H. N. Wagner. Raven Press, New York.

Heimer, L., Alheid, G.F. & Zaborszky, L. (1985) Basal ganglia. In *The Rat Nervous System*, pp. 37–86. Ed. G. Paxinos. Academic Press, Sydney.

Hoyer, D., Schoeffter, P., Palacios, J.M., Kalkman, H.O., Bruinvels, A.T., Fozard, J.R., Siegh, H., Seiler, M.P. & Stoll, A. A selective, potent and silent 5-HT_{1A} receptor antagonist. *British Journal of Pharmacology* (in press).

Liau, L.M., Sleight, A.J., Pitha, J. & Peroutka, S.J. (1991) Characterization of a novel and potent 5-hydroxytryptamine$_{1A}$ receptor antagonist. *Pharmacology, Biochemistry and Behavior* **38**, 555–559.

McCormick, D.A. & Williamson, A. (1989) Convergence and divergence of neurotransmitter action in human cerebral cortex. *Proceedings of the National Academy of Sciences USA* **86**, 8098–8102.

McEntee, W.J. & Crook, T.H. (1991) Serotonin, memory, and the aging brain. *Psychopharmacology* **103**, 143–149.

Millan, M.J., Rivet, J.M., Canton, H., Lejeune, F., Brocco, M., Bervoets, K. & Peglion, J.L. (1991) Benzodioxepiperazine derivatives as novel 5-HT_{1A} antagonists: a pharmacological characterization. *Society for Neuroscience Abstracts* **17**, 92.

Pangalos, M.N., Francis, P.T., Middlemiss, D.N., Pearson, R.C.A. & Bowen, D.M. (1991) Selective destruction of a sub-population of cortical neurones by suicide transport of volkensin, a lectin from *Adenia volkensii*. *Journal of Neuroscience Methods* **40**, 17–29.

Routledge, C., Gurling, J., Foster, E.A., Wright, I., Fletcher, A. & Dourish, C.T. (1992) Antagonism of presynaptic and postsynaptic 5-HT_{1A} receptors *in vivo* by selective 5-HT_{1A} receptor antagonist, WAY100135. *British Journal of Pharmacology* (Abstract).

Sheldon, P.W. & Aghajanian, G.K. (1990) Serotonin (5-HT) induces IPSPs in pyramidal layer cells of the rat piriform cortex: Evidence for the involvement of a 5-HT_2 activated interneurone. *Brain Research* **506**, 62–69.

Wiley, R.G. & Stirpe, F. (1988) Modeccin and volkensin but not abrin are effective suicide transport agents in rat CNS. *Brain Research* **438**, 145–154.

Neuronal nicotinic receptors and their implications in ageing and neurodegenerative disorders in mammals

A. Nordberg

Department of Pharmacology, Uppsala University, Biomedical Center, S-75124 Uppsala, Sweden

Summary. Recent biochemical, molecular biology and pharmacological studies have revealed the existence of multiple functional subtypes of neuronal nicotinic receptor in the rodent as well as in the human CNS. An important goal in this research is to define the physiological role of these receptors and to understand the mechanisms by which these receptors interact with other receptors and neurotransmitters. Nicotinic receptors are detectable in the immature rat brain. Exposition of various agents can change the expression of receptors. Neuronal receptors undergo changes during ageing, the pattern of which is different for various subtypes of nicotinic receptor. Neurodegenerative disorders, such as Alzheimer's disease, are characterized by losses in this type of receptor. An increased understanding of underlying mechanisms leading to this disease will provide pathophysiological knowledge and strategies for treatment. Imaging techniques such as positron emission tomography provide a possible means of tracing the nicotinic receptor *in vivo* in patients with Alzheimer's disease.

Keywords: mammals; ageing; nicotinic receptors; PET; Alzheimer's disease; development

Introduction

The cholinergic system is one of the major transmitter systems with important functions in the brain. It is the neurotransmitter system that best correlates with cognitive function (Drachman 1977, 1978). In 1914 Dale postulated that cholinergic transmission is mediated via two types of receptor: muscarinic and nicotinic receptors. It is now well established that these two types of receptor are members of two distinct receptor families with different properties and functions. The nicotinic receptors are considered to be key molecules in mediating chemical communication between cells in different parts of the body, such as at neuromuscular junctions and autonomic ganglia. The discovery of the existence of nicotinic receptors in the brain and their involvement in higher functions including learning and memory are relatively new phenomena (for reviews see Clementi *et al.*, 1988; Nordberg *et al.*, 1989a; Wonnacott *et al.*, 1990; Lippiello *et al.*, 1992). Recent biochemical and pharmacological studies have revealed multiple functional subtypes of neuronal nicotinic receptor in the CNS. Using molecular biology techniques, a whole family of genes encoding multiple subunits of the nicotinic receptors was isolated (for a recent review, see Deneris *et al.*, 1991). The nicotinic receptor located in the skeletal muscle, which is one of the best-characterized receptors, has proved not to be identical with the neuronal nicotinic receptor – although the two types of receptor are encoded by homologous genes.

The neuronal nicotinic receptors are obvious candidates for transducing the cell surface interaction of the nicotine obtained from tobacco, and as a result are involved in dependence processes that have as yet unknown underlying mechanisms (Nordberg *et al.*, 1989a; Wonnacott *et al.*, 1990). An important goal is to define the physiological role of the neuronal nicotinic receptors. The nicotinic receptors are detectable early in the development of the brain, before the cholinergic innervation; this suggests that the nicotinic receptors might have a trophic action in the brain. Since a better knowledge of normal ageing processes and the involvement of factors that might influence and interact with these processes are of the utmost importance, an investigation into how neuronal nicotinic receptors are altered during ageing is warranted. Consistent losses of nicotinic receptors have been measured in the brain tissue of patients suffering from neurodegenerative disorders such as Alzheimer's disease and Parkinson's disease (for recent review, see Nordberg, in press). These findings suggest that substances that interact with the nicotinic receptors in the brain to improve cognitive functions might be putative drugs in the treatment of Alzheimer's disease and related disorders.

Neuronal nicotinic receptors

Multiple nicotinic binding sites have been characterized in the mammalian brain by receptor binding studies using various radiolabelled agonists such as [^{3}H]nicotine, [^{3}H]acetylcholine, [^{3}H]methylcarbacholine and [^{3}H]cytisine, and antagonists such as [^{3}H]α-bungarotoxin, [^{125}I]-labelled κ-bungarotoxin and [^{3}H]dihydro-β-erythroidine (Nordberg & Larsson, 1980; Larsson & Nordberg, 1985; Nordberg et al., 1988b; Sugaya et al., 1990; Wonnacott, 1987, 1990). Analysis of receptor binding in thin tissue slices by autoradiography has demonstrated a different regional localization in rat brain of the [^{3}H]α-bungarotoxin sites in comparison to that of the nicotinic agonists [^{3}H]nicotine and [^{3}H]acetylcholine (Härfstrand et al., 1988). Although this anatomical divergence has been used as evidence that the bungarotoxin sites are not associated with the cholinergic nicotinic receptors, this assumption must now be modified since bungarotoxin has been found to be sensitive for one nicotinic receptor subunit ($α_7$), at least in chick brain, when expressed in oocytes (Deneris et al., 1991).

The agonists [^{3}H]acetylcholine and [^{3}H]nicotine appear to bind to the same population of agonist binding sites with nanomolar affinity, although [^{3}H]nicotine also binds to low-affinity sites (Adem et al., 1988, 1989; Nordberg, 1988b, c). In the human brain the agonist binding sites occur as superhigh-, high- and low-affinity sites (Nordberg, 1988b, c). The distribution of high-affinity nicotinic agonist binding sites measured in postmortem human brain tissue is compatible with that of the cholinergic innervation of the brain, although some brain regions (e.g. the cerebellum) shows a surprisingly relatively high binding of [^{3}H]nicotine (Table 1). Visualization of nicotinic receptors in vivo by positron emission tomography (PET) and [^{11}C]nicotine in monkeys and humans has revealed a similar pattern of distribution (Nordberg et al., 1989b, 1990b; Nybäck et al., 1989).

The nicotinic receptor is known from studies of the neuromuscular junction to belong to the class of ligand-gated ion channels. The nicotinic receptor found in muscle is composed of four distinct subunits assembled into a heterologous $α_2βγδ$ pentamer (Galzi et al., 1991). Recent molecular cloning has revealed a family of genes encoding a number of neuronal nicotinic receptor subunits. Five α subunits ($α_2$–$α_6$) and four β ($β_2$–$β_5$) subunits have been identified in the rat brain (Deneris et al., 1991). The distribution of subunits has been mapped semiquantitatively in rat brain by in situ hybridization (Wada et al., 1989, 1990). Some of the subunits are expressed strongly in only a few nuclei, while others such as $α_4$ are extensively distributed (Table 2). The distribution of the $α_4$ subunit overlaps that of the $β_2$ subunit and coincides very much with the distribution of high-affinity nicotinic binding sites in rat brain (Härfstrand et al., 1988). Some brain regions show expression of several subunits (Table 2). Such a complex overlapping of subunit expression makes a regional differentiation difficult.

Studies of the expression of nicotinic receptor subunits genes in the human brain are still very limited. The human $α_3$, $α_5$, $β_2$ and $β_4$ subunits have been cloned (Fornasari et al., 1990; Raimondi et al., 1991), but their regional distribution in the brain is as yet unknown. Functional studies of these various subunits in oocytes suggest that differential pairing of α and β subunits may be a mechanism by which different subtypes of neuronal nicotinic receptors are generated (Patrick et al., 1989). Interestingly, various combinations of subunits in the rat are differentially sensitive to

Table 1. Regional distribution of high-affinity nicotinic receptors in the human brain when analysed using 5 nmol [^{3}H]nicotine l^{-1} in human postmortem brain tissue

Brain region	[^{3}]Nicotine binding (pmol g^{-1} protein)
Thalamus	23 ± 2
Putamen	18 ± 2
Caudate nucleus	18 ± 2
Substantia nigra	18 ± 2
Cingulate cortex	14 ± 3
Olfactory tubercle	13 ± 1
Temporal cortex	12 ± 1
Frontal cortex	12 ± 1
Hypothalamus	12 ± 2
Cerebellum	11 ± 1
Occipital cortex	10 ± 1
Hippocampus	9 ± 1
Medulla oblongata	9 ± 2
Amygdala	8 ± 1
Pons	6 ± 1
Globus pallidum	6 ± 1

Values are the mean ± SEM.

Table 2. Detected regional expression of neuronal nicotinic receptor genes in rat brain *in situ* hybridization

Brain region	α_2	α_3	α_4	α_5	β_2	β_3	β_4
Medial habenula		+	+		+	+	+
Thalamus		+	+		+	+	
Substantia nigra		+	+	+	+	+	
Ventral tegmental area		+	+	+	+		
Interpeduncular nucleus	+	+	+	+	+	+	+
Cerebral cortex		+	+	+	+		
Hypothalamus		+	+				
Subiculum			+	+			
Hippocampus	+	+	+	+	+		

various nicotinic agonists (Cachelin & Jaggi, 1991; Luetje & Patrick, 1991). For example, nicotine has been shown to be a potent agonist for $\alpha_2\beta_2$ and $\alpha_4\beta_2$ subunit combinations but a weak agonist for $\alpha_3\beta_2$ (Luetje & Patrick, 1991). By contrast, cytisine is a strong agonist for $\alpha_2\beta_4$ and $\alpha_4\beta_4$. Further research in this field will be of the utmost importance for the development of new selective nicotinic agonists and antagonists for therapeutic purposes.

Development of neuronal nicotinic receptors

Nicotinic receptors are present early in the development of the rat brain. Studies using various labelled ligands for these receptors indicate different timecourses for the development of neuronal nicotinic subtypes (Falkeborn *et al.*, 1983; Larsson *et al.*, 1985; Slotkin *et al.*, 1987; Zhang *et al.*, 1990; Nordberg *et al.*, 1991). Detectable amounts of high-affinity nicotinic receptors are also present in human fetal brain (Cairns & Wonnacott, 1988). In contrast to other receptor systems, nicotinic receptors can be measured in rodents in fairly high amounts pre- and postnatally.

The number of nicotinic binding sites measured in mouse brain prenatally is comparable to the content in adult mouse brain. Interestingly, a drop in the number of nicotinic binding sites has been observed in mouse brain at birth but this is followed by a gradual increase until adulthood (Zhang et al., 1990). During the first postnatal days, only high-affinity nicotinic receptors can be measured in the mouse, while both high- and low-affinity nicotinic receptors can be measured in the adult rodent brain (Table 3). A decrease in the number of nicotinic receptors (mainly that of the low-affinity sites) has been observed between days 17 and 120 (Table 3).

Table 3. Proportion of high- and low-affinity nicotinic binding sites, and their affinity in the cerebral cortex of mice at different ages

Age (days)	K_H (nmol l^{-1})	K_L (nmol l^{-1})	R_H %	R_L %
1	7	—	100	—
5	3	—	100	—
17	0.4	14	55	45
20	0.7	14	69	31
120	4	123	80	20

Values were obtained by analysis of displacement of [^{3}H]nicotine binding by (−)-nicotine.
K_H, K_L: affinity constants of high- and low-affinity binding sites; R_H, R_L: high- and low-affinity receptor binding sites.

Interestingly, it has recently been observed that neonatal exposure to nicotine can prevent the development of low-affinity nicotinic binding sites, with a concomitant change in behaviour in adult mice (Nordberg et al., 1991). It is important now to map the expression of neuronal nicotinic receptor subunits during the development of the brain. Knowledge of the physiological function of high- and low-affinity nicotinic binding is still poor. The high-affinity nicotinic binding sites have been suggested to be mainly presynaptic, mediating release of acetylcholine as well as of other neurotransmitters (Beani et al., 1985; Nordberg et al., 1989c). Impairment of the nicotinic receptors during growth and development of the brain might influence neuronal intercommunications and physiological functions later in life.

Ageing and neural nicotinic receptors

The cholinergic system undergoes changes during ageing (for recent reviews see Giacobini, 1988; Amenta et al., 1991). Age-dependent changes in nicotinic receptors in the rodent and human brain have been reported. A significant reduction in the number of [^{3}H]nicotine binding sites has been found in the cortex and midbrain of rats as a function of age (Zhang et al., 1990) (Fig. 1). Interestingly, differences in receptor properties that are induced during ageing could be deducted from the receptor binding assays. The incubation temperature influenced [^{3}H]nicotine binding differently in the cortex of rats 1 month, 4 months and 14 months old (Fig. 2). In 1-month-old rats the specific [^{3}H]nicotine binding decreased when the incubation temperature increased. The incubation temperature appeared to have no significant effect on the [^{3}H]nicotine binding in 4-month-old cortices. In 14-month-old rats [^{3}H]nicotine binding in the cortex increased with increasing incubation temperature but the binding at 4°C was significantly lower than in 1-month-old rats. These changes in temperature dependence observed for [^{3}H]nicotine binding illustrate that nicotinic receptors undergo dynamic changes during ageing. Changes in receptor properties might be due to variations in lipid composition of membranes or in membrane fluidity, which would lead to more rigid receptor proteins in aged brain membranes and a decrease in receptor plasticity.

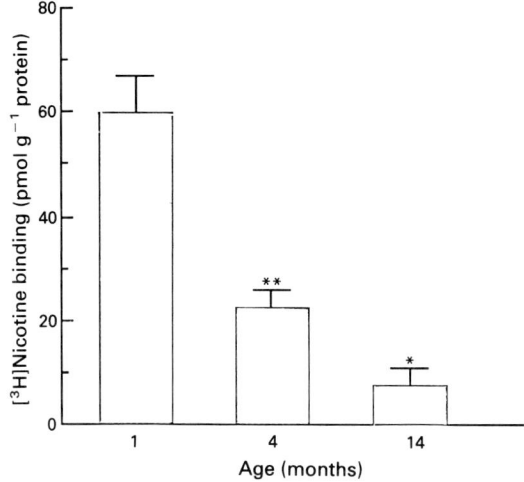

Fig. 1. Effect of ageing on the number of nicotinic receptors in the cerebral cortex of rats. *($P < 0.05$) and **($P < 0.01$) indicate a significant difference between the number of receptors at different ages.

Different effects of ageing on various subtypes of neural nicotinic receptors have been observed in the human brain (Table 4). When the various nicotinic agonists [^{3}H]nicotine and [^{3}H]acetylcholine, and the antagonists [^{3}H]α-bungarotoxin and [^{3}H]tubocurarine were used as labelled ligands, decreases or increases in nicotinic binding sites were observed during ageing depending on the brain area. A significant decrease in [^{3}H]nicotine binding was observed in the frontal cortex (Flynn & Mash, 1986; Nordberg et al., 1992), while it appears to increase during ageing in the thalamus (Nordberg et al., 1992). Perry et al. (1987) reported a decrease in [^{3}H]nicotine binding during ageing in the hippocampus, whereas we observed an increase (Nordberg & Winblad, 1986a). Interestingly, the binding of [^{3}H]acetylcholine appears to be unchanged in the frontal cortex and thalamus (Nordberg et al., 1992), while an age-related reduction in [^{3}H]tubocurarine and [^{3}H]α-bungarotoxin binding is observed in the thalamus (Nordberg et al., 1982; Nordberg & Winblad, 1986a). These findings clearly illustrate that ageing affects various nicotinic binding sites and brain regions in quite different ways. Such differences might indicate different synaptic localizations of the nicotinic binding sites. Hopefully, further investigations using molecular biology techniques will provide valuable information on this topic.

Neural nicotinic receptors in neurodegenerative disorders

Alzheimer's disease is the most common form of dementia, being manifested in 50–60% of all dementia disorders. It has been shown that 2% of the population aged over 65 are affected by the disease. Major signs for the disease are global deterioration of mental function, and a decline in memory and in the ability to think. Early clinical diagnosis of Alzheimer's disease is hampered by the lack of early diagnostic markers. There is still no cure. Among the transmitter systems affected in this disorder the cholinergic system correlates best with the cognitive functions affected (Drachman, 1977). Most of our knowledge about neurochemical changes in Alzheimer's disease is based upon studies of human brain tissues obtained at autopsy.

In contrast to the way in which muscarinic receptors are affected in this disease, a consistent loss of nicotinic receptors in the cortical tissue of brains of patients with Alzheimer's disease was reported by Nordberg & Winblad (1986b) and Whitehouse et al. (1986). A decrease in the number of nicotinic receptors was detected in the brains of affected patients compared with controls (using

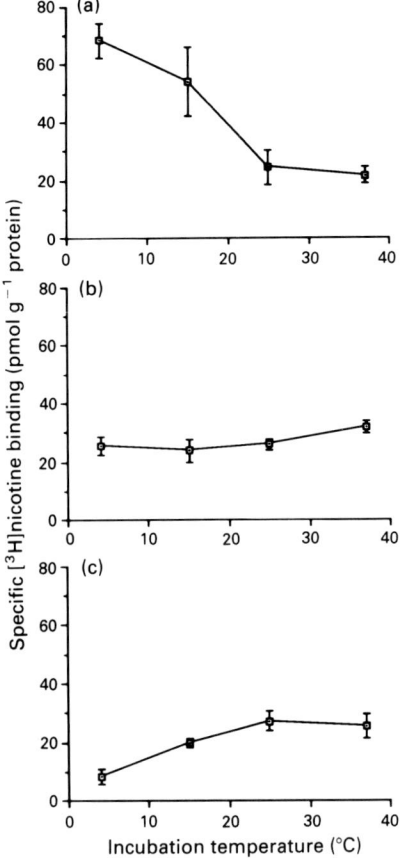

Fig. 2. Effect of incubation temperature on specific [^{3}H]nicotine binding in the cerebral cortex of rats of different ages: (a) 1 month old; (b) 4 months old; (c) 14 months old.

Table 4. Changes in nicotinic binding sites in the human brain during normal ageing

Ligand	Cortex	Hippocampus	Thalamus
[^{3}H]Nicotine	Decrease	Decrease or increase	Increase
[^{3}H]Tubocurarine	n.d.	No change	Decrease
[^{3}H]Acetylcholine	No change	n.d.	No change
[^{3}H]Bungarotoxin	n.d.	No change	Decrease

n.d.: not determined.

nanomolar concentrations of [^{3}H]nicotine or [^{3}H]acetylcholine, in the presence of atropine, to label high-affinity nicotinic receptors in the brain). Flynn & Mash (1986) reported a loss of nicotinic receptors in the temporal cortex but found no change in the number of nicotinic receptors in the frontal cortex of these patients. The consistent loss of nicotinic receptors in Alzheimer's disease has been confirmed by several laboratories (for recent review, see Nordberg, 1992, in press). Similar deficiencies in choline acetyltransferase activity and acetylcholine synthesis suggest that nicotinic receptors presynaptically located in the cholinergic nerve terminals are preferentially lost in Alzheimer's disease.

Further analysis of changes in subtypes of nicotinic receptor in Alzheimer's disease reveal changes in the proportion of high- and low-affinity nicotinic binding sites in cortical regions (Nordberg et al., 1988a). Thus, the proportion of high-affinity sites is decreased, while the proportion of low-affinity sites is increased in competition experiments using either unlabelled nicotine or [^{3}H]nicotine (Nordberg et al., 1988a). Significant losses of both high- and low-affinity nicotinic sites have been reported (Sugaya et al., 1990). Earlier studies using [^{3}H]bungarotoxin and [^{3}H]tubocurarine as ligands for nicotinic receptors have revealed relatively preserved receptors in brains of patients with Alzheimer's disease compared to normal brains (Nordberg & Winblad, 1986a); this was probably due to the fact that these ligands label binding sites not identical to high-affinity nicotinic receptors in the brain (Härfstrand et al., 1988). Binding of [^{125}I]-labelled κ-bungarotoxin, which is a snake toxin supposed to bind to neuronal nicotinic receptors in the brain, is decreased in the frontal cortex of brains of patients with Alzheimer's disease (Sugaya et al., 1990). Muscarinic and nicotinic receptors have been shown to co-localize in cholinoreceptive pyramidal neurones (Schröder et al., 1991). No significant loss of cholinoreceptive neurones per se was found by immunohistochemical techniques, which supports the assumption that the nicotinic receptors are selectively impaired in Alzheimer's disease (Schröder et al., 1991). The different vulnerability of the nicotinic and muscarinic receptors in brains of patients with Alzheimer's disease is quite significant.

In Parkinson's disease also, a reduced number of nicotinic receptors have been found in the hippocampus and cortex (Perry et al., 1987; Whitehouse et al., 1988). Human lymphocytes possess nicotinic receptors (Adem et al., 1986); an increase in the number of nicotinic receptors has been observed during ageing in normal individuals, while patients with Alzheimer's disease and Parkinson's disease show significant losses (Adem et al., 1986; Nordberg et al., 1990a).

Correlations of neurochemical deficits with dementia states and histopathological findings have a limited value since they represent the terminal state of the disease. To obtain insight into early changes in the brain, imaging techniques that can be used in vivo, such as PET, might be useful. PET studies of brain metabolism and blood flow in Alzheimer's disease have been carried out (Rapoport, 1991). Efforts have recently been made to visualize cholinergic markers in patients with this disease by PET. The strategy by which cholinergic activity in the human brain is studied in vivo by PET was initiated using [^{11}C]choline (Gauthier et al., 1985). However, a low penetration of intact [^{11}C]choline into the brain, combined with a rapid conversion into metabolites other than [^{11}C]acetylcholine, hampered this effort. Attempts to visualize nicotinic receptors in the brain using [^{11}C]nicotine and PET were initially performed in monkeys (Nordberg et al., 1989b) and later on in humans (Nybäck et al., 1989; Nordberg et al., 1990b). When [^{11}C]nicotine is injected intravenously into healthy volunteers the regional distribution of ^{11}C radioactivity in the brain measured by PET agrees fairly well with the distribution of nicotinic receptors measured by binding techniques in vitro. Intravenous injections of the two enantiomers ($-$)-s-[^{11}C]nicotine and ($+$)-R-[^{11}C]nicotine into patients with Alzheimer's disease result in a lower uptake of ($+$)-R-[^{11}C]nicotine compared with ($-$)-s-[^{11}C]nicotine into the brain (Nordberg et al., 1990b). The two enantiomers ($-$)(s) and ($+$)(R) nicotine are known from binding studies in vitro to bind preferentially in the brain to high- and low-affinity nicotinic receptors, respectively (Copeland et al., 1991). A significantly lower uptake of ($-$)-s-[^{11}C]nicotine has been observed by PET in the temporal and frontal cortices of patients with Alzheimer's disease in comparison to controls (Nordberg et al., 1990b). The difference in uptake between the two enantiomers can be observed early in the progress of the disease, when the blood flow is still normal (Nordberg et al., in press). The finding might be of diagnostic value.

The advantage of using the PET technique is that the pharmacological effect of drugs can be monitored in patients. PET studies have been performed during treatment of Alzheimer's disease with the cholinesterase inhibitor tacrine (Nordberg et al., in press) or nerve growth factor (Olson et al., 1992). Intraventricular infusion of nerve growth factor for 3 months into a patient with Alzheimer's disease increased the number of cortical nicotinic receptors and the cerebral blood flow (Olson et al., 1992). Tacrine treatment was found to increase the number of nicotinic receptors in the frontal and temporal cortices of brains of patients with Alzheimer's disease and increase the glucose metabolism in the brain (Nordberg et al., in press). Visualization of neuroreceptors and other transmitter activities by PET will be important tools for evaluation of drug therapies in dementia disorders.

Conclusion

Extensive studies with various techniques in vitro and in vivo such as receptor binding, neurophysiology, molecular biology and PET indicate that there are multiple subtypes of nicotinic receptor in the brain. Recent work with receptor cloning has revealed a family of genes encoding a number of neuronal receptor subunits. Some of the subunits show strong expression in only a few brain nuclei whereas others show extensive distribution in the rat brain. Studies of the expression of nicotinic receptor subunits in the human brain are still very limited. The nicotinic receptors undergo dynamic changes during development and ageing. Results obtained clearly illustrate that ageing affects various subtypes of nicotinic receptor and brain regions in a different way. These variations might be signs for different localization of the nicotinic receptors. Consistent losses of nicotinic receptors have been observed in brains of Alzheimer's patients. These observations were initially made on autopsy brain tissue, but have recently been confirmed in vivo by PET studies in patients with Alzheimer's disease. For future therapeutic interventions in Alzheimer's disease drugs that interact with subtypes of neuronal nicotinic receptor might be a fruitful strategy.

This study was supported by the Swedish Medical Research Council, the Swedish Tobacco Company, Loo and Hans Osterman's Foundation, Wiberg's Foundation, Stiftelsen Gamla Tjänarinnor.

References

Adem, A., Nordberg, A., Bucht, G. & Winblad, B. (1986) Extraneural cholinergic markers in Alzheimer's and Parkinson's disease. *Progress in Neuro-Psychopharmacology & Biological Psychiatry* **10**, 247–257.

Adem, A., Singh Jossan, S., d'Argy, R., Brandt, I., Winblad, B. & Nordberg, A. (1988) Distribution of nicotinic receptors in human thalamus as visualized by ^{3}H-nicotine and ^{3}H-acetylcholine receptor autoradiography. *Journal of Neural Transmission* **73**, 77–83.

Adem, A., Nordberg, A., Singh-Jossan, S., Sara, V. & Gillberg, P.G. (1989) Quantitative autoradiography of nicotinic receptors in large cryosections of human brain hemispheres. *Neuroscience Letters* **101**, 247–252.

Amenta, F., Zaccheo, D. & Collier, W.L. (1991) Neurotransmitters, neuroreceptors and aging. *Mechanisms of Ageing and Development* **61**, 249–273.

Beani, L., Bianchi, C., Nilsson, L., Nordberg, A., Romanelli, L. & Sivilotti, L. (1985) The effect of nicotine on ^{3}H-acetylcholine release from cortical slices of guinea pig brain. *Naunyn-Schmiedebergs Archives of Pharmacology* **331**, 293–296.

Cachelin, A.B. & Jaggi, R. (1991) β subunits determine the time course of desensitization in rat α3 neuronal nicotinic acetylcholine receptors. *Pflügers Archiv European Journal of Physiology* **419**, 579–582.

Cairns, N.J. & Wonnacott, S. (1988) [^{3}H](−)nicotine binding sites in fetal human brain. *Brain Research* **475**, 1–7.

Clementi, F., Gotti, C. & Sher, E., eds (1988) *Nicotinic Acetylcholine Receptors in the Nervous System* (NATO ASI Series, Series H: Cell Biology, Vol. H25). Springer-Verlag, Berlin.

Copeland, J.R., Adem, A., Jacob, P. & Nordberg, A. (1991) A comparison of the binding of nicotine and nornicotine stereoisomers to nicotinic binding sites in rat brain cortex. *Naunyn-Schmiedeberg's Archives of Pharmacology* **342**, 123–127.

Dale, H.H. (1914) The action of certain esters and ethers of choline and their relation to muscarine. *Journal of Physiology* **6**, 147–190.

Deneris, E.S., Connolly, J., Rogers, S.W. & Duvoisin, R. (1991) Pharmacological and functional diversity of neuronal nicotinic acetylcholine receptors. *Trends in Pharmacological Sciences* **12**, 34–40.

Drachman, D.A. (1977) Cognitive function in man. Does the cholinergic system have a special role? *Neurology* **27**, 738–790.

Drachman, D.A. (1978) Memory, dementia and the cholinergic system. In *Alzheimer's Disease: Senile Dementia and Related Disorders*, pp. 141–148. Eds R. Katzman, R. D. Terru & K. L. Bick. Raven Press, New York.

Falkeborn, Y., Larsson, C., Nordberg, A. & Slanina, P. (1983) A comparison of the regional ontogenesis of nicotine- and muscarine-like binding sites in mouse brain. *International Journal of Developmental Neuroscience* **1**, 289–296.

Flynn, D.D. & Mash, D.C. (1986) Characterization of L-(^{3}H-nicotine) binding in human cerebral cortex;

comparison between Alzheimer's disease and the normal. *Journal of Neurochemistry* **47**, 1948–1954.

Fornasari, D., Chini, B., Tarroni, P. & Clementi, F. (1990) Molecular cloning of human nicotinic receptor 3 subunit. *Neuroscience Letters* **111**, 351–356.

Galzi, J.L., Revah, F., Bessis, A. & Changeux, J.P. (1991) Functional architecture of the nicotinic acetylcholine receptor: from electric organ to brain. *Annual Review of Pharmacology* **31**, 37–72.

Gauthier, S., Diksic, M., Yamamoto, L., Tyler, J. & Feindel, W. (1985) Positron emission tomography with ^{11}C-choline in human subjects. *Canadian Journal of Neurological Sciences* **12**, 214.

Giacobini, E. (1988) The cholinergic system in aging. In *Handbook of Experimental Pharmacology* (Vol. 86), pp. 665–695. Ed. V. P. Whittaker. Springer-Verlag, Berlin.

Härfstrand, A., Adem, A., Füxe, K., Agnati, L., Andersson, K. & Nordberg, A. (1988) Distribution of nicotinic cholinergic receptors in the rat tel- and diencephalon: a quantitative receptor autoradiographical study using ^{3}H-acetylcholine, α-^{125}I-bungarotoxin and ^{3}H-nicotine. *Acta Physiologica Scandinavica* **132**, 1–14.

Larsson, C. & Nordberg, A. (1985) Comparative analysis of nicotine-like receptor ligand interaction in rodent brain homogenate. *Journal of Neurochemistry* **45**, 24–31.

Larsson, C., Nordberg, A., Falkeborn, Y. & Lundberg, P.Å. (1985) Regional ^{3}H-acetylcholine and ^{3}H-nicotine binding in developing mouse brain. *International Journal of Developmental Neuroscience* **3**, 667–671.

Lippiello, P.M., Collins, A.C., Gray, J.A. & Robinson, J.H. (1992) *The Biology of Nicotine: Current Research Issues*. Raven Press, New York.

Luetje, C.W. & Patrick, J. (1991) Both α- and β-subunits contribute to the agonist sensitivity of neuronal nicotinic acetylcholine receptors. *The Journal of Neuroscience* **11**, 837–850.

Nordberg, A. Neuroreceptor changes in Alzheimer's disease. *Cerebrovascular Brain Metabolism Reviews*, (in press).

Nordberg, A. & Larsson, C. (1980) Studies of muscarinic and nicotinic binding sites in brain. *Acta Physiologica Scandinavica* (Suppl.) **497**, 19–23.

Nordberg, A. & Winblad, B. (1986a) Brain nicotinic and muscarinic receptors in normal aging and dementia. In *Alzheimer's and Parkinson's Disease – Strategies for Research and Development* (Advances in Behavioural Biology, Vol 29), pp. 95–108. Eds A. Fisher & I. Hanin. Plenum Press, New York.

Nordberg, A. & Winblad, A. (1986b) Reduced number of ^{3}H-nicotine and ^{3}H-acetylcholine binding sites in the frontal cortex of Alzheimer brains. *Neuroscience Letters* **72**, 115–119.

Nordberg, A., Adolfsson, R., Marcusson, J. & Winblad, B. (1982) Cholinergic receptors in hippocampus in normal aging and dementia of Alzheimer type. In *The Aging Brain: Cellular and Molecular Mechanisms of Aging in the Nervous System*, pp. 231–246. Eds E. Giacobini, G. Filogamo, G. Giacobini & A. Vernadakis. Raven Press, New York.

Nordberg, A., Adem, A., Hardy, J. & Winblad, B. (1988a) Changes in nicotinic receptor subtypes in temporal cortex of Alzheimer brains. *Neuroscience Letters* **86**, 317–321.

Nordberg, A., Adem, A., Nilsson, L., Romanelli, L. & Zhang, X. (1988b) Heterogeneous cholinergic nicotinic receptors in the CNS. In *Nicotinic Acetylcholine Receptors in the Nervous System* (NATO ASI Series, Series H: Cell Biology, Vol. H25), pp. 331–350. Eds F. Clementi, C. Gotti & E. Sher. Springer-Verlag, New York.

Nordberg, A., Adem, A., Nilsson, L. & Winblad, B. (1988c) Nicotinic and muscarinic cholinergic receptor heterogeneity in the human brain at normal aging and dementia of Alzheimer type. In *New Trends in Aging Research* (Fidia Research Series, Vol. 15), pp. 27–36. Eds B. Tomlinson, G. Pepeu & C. M. Wischik. Liviana Press, Italy.

Nordberg, A., Füxe, K., Holmstedt, B. & Sundwall, A., eds (1989a) *Nicotinic Receptors in the CNS – Their Role in Synaptic Function* (Progress in Brain Research, Vol. 79). Elsevier, Amsterdam.

Nordberg, A., Hartvig, P., Lundqvist, H., Antoni, G., Ulin, J. & Långstrom, B. (1989b) Uptake and regional distribution of (+)-(R)- and (−)-(S)-N-methyl-^{11}C-nicotine in the brains of Rhesus monkey – An attempt to study nicotinic receptors *in vivo*. *Journal of Neural Transmission* **1**, 195–205.

Nordberg, A., Romanelli, L., Sundwall, A., Bianchi, C. & Beani, L. (1989c) Effect of acute, subacute treatment on cortical acetylcholine release and on nicotinic receptors in rats and guinea-pigs. *British Journal of Pharmacology* **98**, 71–78.

Nordberg, A., Adem, A., Bucht, G., Viitanen, M. & Winblad, B. (1990a) Alterations in lymphocyte receptor densities in dementia of Alzheimer type: a possible diagnostic marker. In *Biological Markers in Dementia of Alzheimer Type*, pp. 149–159, Eds C. Fowler, L. A. Carlsson, C. G. Gottfries & B. Winblad. Smith-Gordon, London.

Nordberg, A., Hartvig, P., Lilja, A., Viitanen, M., Amberla, K., Lundqvist H., Andersson, Y., Ulin, J., Winblad, B. & Långström, B. (1990b) Decreased uptake and binding of ^{11}C-nicotine in brain of Alzheimer patients as visualized by positron emission tomography. *Journal of Neural Transmission* **2**, 215–224.

Nordberg, A., Zhang, X., Fredriksson, A. & Eriksson, P. (1991) Neonatal nicotine exposure induces permanent changes in brain nicotinic receptors and behaviour in adult mice. *Developmental Brain Research* **63**, 201–207.

Nordberg, A., Alafuzoff, I. & Winblad, B. (1992a) Nicotinic and muscarinic subtypes in the human brain: Changes with aging and dementia. *Journal of Neuroscience Research* **31**, 103–111.

Nordberg, A., Lilja, A., Lundqvist, H., Hartvig, P., Amberla, K., Viitanen, M., Warpman, U., Johansson, M., Hellström-Lindahl, E., Bjurling, P., Fasth, K.J., Långström, B. & Winblad, B. Tacrine restores cholinergic nicotinic receptors and glucose metabolism in Alzheimer patients as visualized by positron emission tomography. *Neurobiology of Aging* (in press).

Nybäck, H., Nordberg, A., Långström, B., Halldin, C., Hartvig, P., Åhlin, A., Swahn, C-G. & Sedva, G. (1989) Attempts to visualize nicotinic receptors in the brain of monkey and man by positron emission tomography. In *Nicotinic Receptors in the CNS –*

Their Role in Synaptic Function (*Progress in Brain Research*, Vol. 79), pp. 313–319. Eds A. Nordberg, K. Füxe, B. Holmstedt & A. Sundwall. Elsevier, Amsterdam.

Olson, L., Nordberg, A., von Holst, H., Bäckman, L., Ebendahl, T., Alafuzoff, I., Amberla, K., Hartvig, P., Herlitz, A., Lilja, A., Lundqvist, H., Långström, B., Meyersson, B., Persson, A., Viitanen, M. & Winblad, B. (1992) Nerve growth factor affects ^{11}C-nicotine binding, blood flow, EEG and verbal episodic memory in an Alzheimer patient. *Journal of Neural Transmission* **4**, 79–95.

Patrick, J., Deneris, E., Wada, K., Connolly, J., Swanson, L. & Heinemann, S. (1989) Structure and function of neuronal nicotinic acetylcholine receptors deducted from cDNA clones. In *Nicotinic Receptors in the CNS – Their Role in Synaptic Function* (*Progress in Brain Research*, Vol. 79), pp. 27–33. Eds A. Nordberg, K. Füxe, B. Holmstedt & A. Sundwall. Elsevier, Amsterdam.

Perry, E.K., Pery, R., Smith, C.J., Dick, D.J., Candy, J.M., Edwardson, J.A., Fairbairn, A. & Blessed, G. (1987) Nicotinic abnormalities in Alzheimer's and Parkinson's diseases. *Journal of Neurosurgery and Psychiatry* **50**, 806–809.

Raimondi, E., Rubboli, F., Moralli, D., Chini, B., Fornasari, D., Tarroni, P., De Carli, L. & Clementi, F. (1991) Chromosomal localization and physical linkage of the gene encoding the human 3, 5 and β4 neuronal nicotinic receptor subunits. *Genomics* **12**, 849–850.

Rapoport, S.I. (1991) Positron emission tomography in Alzheimer's disease in relation to disease pathogenesis: a critical review. *Cerebrovascular Brain Metabolism Review* **3**, 297–335.

Schröder, H., Giacobini, E., Struble, R.G., Luiten, P.G.M., Van der Zee, E.A., Zilles, K. & Strosberg, A.D. (1991) Muscarinic cholinoreceptive neurons in the frontal cortex in Alzheimer's disease. *Brain Research Bulletin* **27**, 631–636.

Slotkin, T.A., Orband-Miller, L. & Queen, K.L. (1987) Development of ^{3}H-nicotine binding sites in brain. *Journal of Pharmacology and Experimental Therapeutics* **233**, 361–368.

Sugaya, K., Giacobini, E. & Chiappinelli, V.A. (1990) Nicotinic acetylcholine receptor subtypes in human frontal cortex: changes in Alzheimer's disease. *Journal of Neuroscience Research* **27**, 349–359.

Wada, E., McKinnon, D., Heinemann, S., Patrick, J. & Swanson, L.W. (1990) The distribution of mRNA encoded by a new member of the neuronal nicotinic acetylcholine receptor gene family (α_5) in the rat central nervous system. *Brain Research* **526**, 45–53.

Wada, E., Wada, K., Boulter, J., Deneris, E., Heinemann, S., Patrick, J. & Swanson, L.W. (1989) Distribution of alpha2, alpha3, alpha4, and beta2 neuronal nicotinic receptor subunit mRNA in the central nervous system: a hybridization histochemical study in the rat. *Journal of Comparative Neurology* **284**, 314–335.

Whitehouse, P.J., Martino, A.M., Antuono, P.G., Lowenstein, P.R., Coyle, J.T., Price, D.L. & Kellar, K.J. (1986). Nicotinic acetylcholine binding sites in Alzheimer's brain. *Brain Research* **371**, 146–151.

Whitehouse, P.J., Martino, A.M., Wagster, M.V., Price, D.L., Mayeux, R., Attack, J.R. & Kellar, K.J. (1988) Reduction in ^{3}H-nicotinic acetylcholine binding in Alzheimer's and Parkinson's disease: an autoradiographical study. *Neurology* **38**, 720–723.

Wonnacott, S. (1987) Brain nicotine binding sites. *Human Toxicology* **6**, 343–353.

Wonnacott, S. (1990) Characterization of nicotine receptor sites in brain. In *Nicotine Psychopharmacology – Molecular, Cellular, and Behavioural Aspects*, pp. 226–277. Eds S. Wonnacott, M. A. H. Russell & I. P. Stolerman. Oxford University Press, Oxford.

Wonnacott, S., Russell, M.A.H. & Stolerman, I.P., eds (1990) *Nicotinic Psychopharmacology – Molecular, Cellular, and Behavioural Aspects*. Oxford University Press, Oxford.

Zhang, X., Wahlström, G. & Nordberg, A. (1990) Influence of development and aging in nicotinic receptor subtypes in rodent brain. *International Journal of Developmental Neuroscience* **8**, 715–721.

The brain cholinergic system in ageing mammals

G. Pepeu, F. Casamenti, I. Marconcini Pepeu and C. Scali

Department of Preclinical and Clinical Pharmacology, University of Florence, Viale Morgagni, 65, I-50134 Florence, Italy

Summary. The complex picture of age-associated brain cholinergic deficiency in humans and animals, and the possibilities of correcting it, are presented in this article. The changes that occur during ageing and senile dementias in cholinergic neurones and receptors and in the release and synthesis of acetylcholine are described and discussed. The drugs that have so far been administered to humans to correct cholinergic deficiency are listed and the effects of cholinesterase inhibitors, nerve growth factor and phosphatidylserine are discussed in some detail.

Keywords: acetylcholine; ageing brain; Alzheimer's disease; cholinergic therapy; mammals

Introduction

Domino *et al.* (1978) begin their review 'Biochemical and neurotransmitter changes in the ageing brain' with the statement: 'Relatively little is known about the alterations in the cholinergic system in the aged brain'. However, at that time two observations had already called attention to the importance of alterations in brain cholinergic systems in connection with ageing: Davies & Maloney (1976) had shown that in the cerebral cortex and hippocampus of patients affected by the senile dementia Alzheimer's disease there is a marked decrease in choline acetyltransferase (ChAT) activity; while Drachman & Leavitt (1974) had shown that the pattern of cognitive deficit in young subjects receiving scopolamine (which blocks cholinergic receptors) is nearly identical to that observed in untreated ageing subjects.

In the 14 years since Domino's review, much information has been obtained concerning the ageing cholinergic system of the brain, with the aim of understanding the pathogenetic role of cholinergic deficiency in dementia and ageing, and of finding suitable pharmacological treatments. The title of a recent book edited by Becker & Giacobini (*Cholinergic Basis for Alzheimer Therapy*, Birkhauser, Boston, 1991) expresses this heuristic approach well (see also Becker, 1991). Such an approach may also apply to the therapy of age-associated memory impairment – if we accept the hypothesis proposed by Feuerstein *et al.* (1992) that 'the normal ageing process resembles a delayed and attenuated disease process of senile dementia of Alzheimer's type'.

The complex picture of age-associated brain cholinergic deficiency, and the possibilities of correcting it, are discussed below. This overview includes what we believe are the most relevant data, although we make no pretence of being exhaustive.

Age-associated morphological changes of the cholinergic neurones

While senile dementia of Alzheimer's type is characterized by an extensive loss of cholinergic cells in basal forebrain nuclei (Whitehouse *et al.*, 1982) and cholinergic fibres in the cortex (Geula & Mesulam, 1989), the changes in the cholinergic neurones of the forebrain nuclei during normal ageing are more subtle – but nevertheless relevant. In old rats a decrease in body size and the number of dendritic spines was demonstrated by Fischer *et al.* (1989), and the appearance of abnormal neuronal processes with swollen ChAT-positive profiles in these animals was observed by

Armstrong et al. (1988). An age-dependent decrease in the number of neurones containing acetylcholinesterase (AChE) in all forebrain cholinergic nuclei of aged Wistar rats has been reported by Altavista et al. (1990). The decrease in ChAT-positive neurones in the nucleus basalis of 26-month-old Wistar rats appears to be related to the degree of memory impairment (Riekkinen et al., 1990).

The extent of the loss of forebrain cholinergic neurones in normal ageing humans is still a matter of debate (Coleman & Flood, 1987). However, a reduced density of the cortical cholinergic network has been clearly demonstrated (Geula & Mesulam, 1989), and 50% of the total neuronal population of the nucleus basalis, including cholinergic and non-cholinergic neurones, has been found to be lost by 90 years of age, in comparison to the number found between 16 and 29 years (de Lacalle et al., 1991). These findings explain the decline in ChAT and AChE activity observed by McGeer et al. (1971) in the brain of geriatric patients.

Age-associated changes in acetylcholine release

One of the reasons for the decrease in acetylcholine (ACh) release observed both *in vitro* and *in vivo* in several brain regions of ageing rats may be the decrease in the complexity of the cholinergic network and in the number of cholinergic synapses.

From the experiments performed *in vitro* (reviewed by Decker, 1987) it appears that ageing mostly affects evoked ACh release, while basal release is not always reduced. This is presumably because basal ACh release is due partly to neuronal activity and partly to leakage from the cut surfaces.

A marked decrease in ACh release from brain slices that were stimulated using K^+ solution (31 mmol l^{-1}) was observed in old mice by Gibson & Peterson (1981). ACh release from cortical slices elicited by electrical stimulation is approximately half the amount released in 24-month-old as in 3-month-old Wistar rats (Pedata et al., 1983). According to Vannucchi et al. (1987) (who also used electrical stimulation to evoke ACh release) the decrease in cortical ACh release in rats begins almost abruptly between 11 and 14 months of age, with little or no further decrease between 14 and 28 months of age.

Vannucchi et al. (1990) demonstrated that in cortical slices, pre-labelled with [^{3}H]choline and prepared from 4-month-old and 18-month-old rats, both the evoked total ACh release and the amount of [^{3}H]ACh released are approximately 50% less in 18-month-old than in 4-month-old rats. Similarly, Feuerstein et al. (1992) found an age-related decrease in the tritium overflow from electrically stimulated human cortical slices that had been pre-labelled with [^{3}H]choline. A comparison of the specific activity of ACh released in two consecutive electrical stimulation periods indicates that 4-month-old rats synthesize more ACh from endogenous unlabelled choline than do ageing rats (Vannucchi et al., 1990).

A comparison of ACh release that has been evoked by electrical stimulation from cortical, hippocampal and striatal slices shows that a statistically significant decrease of 44% in the cortex, 61% in the hippocampus and 73% in the striatum occurred in 18-month-old rats compared with 4-month-old rats at a stimulation frequency of 10 Hz but not at 1 Hz (Scali, C., Pazzagli, M. & Pepeu, G., unpublished). This finding indicates that the impairment in neurotransmitter availability in ageing rats can be better seen at high-rate neuronal firing. Araujo et al. (1990) found a large decrease in ACh release from K^+-depolarized striatal, hippocampal and cortical slices in 27-month-old rats, with no difference in rats aged between 3 and 9 months.

Using the intracerebral microdialysis technique, Wu et al. (1988) were the first to confirm that an age-related decrease in ACh release occurs *in vivo*. ACh output was found to be 53%, 35% and 37% lower in the striatum, cortex and hippocampus, respectively, of 18-month-old Wistar rats compared with that found in 2-month-old rats. In the striatum a 30% decrease in ACh release could be detected even in 9-month-old rats. A similar decrease in ACh release was found in the cerebral cortex of 19-month-old rats in comparison to 3-month-old rats (Casamenti et al., 1991). The decrease in ACh release was associated with a decrease in choline efflux. In Wistar-Kyoto rats of 6, 12, 18 and 24 months of age, the decrease in ACh release in the cerebral cortex, striatum and hippocampus occurs mainly between 12 and 18 months of age, with a further small reduction occurring during the following 6 months. Choline efflux from the cerebral cortex also shows a statistically significant decrease at 24 months of age (Pepeu et al., 1992).

At variance with our results, and with those of Takei et al. (1989), Fischer et al. (1991b) found no difference in the basal ACh release and in the release following handling, electrical stimulation. K^+ depolarization and muscarinic receptor blockade, as investigated using a microdialysis probe implanted in the CA1 hippocampal area of the dentate girus of 2-month-old and 24-month-old cognitively impaired and non-impaired female Sprague-Dawley rats. In both groups of aged rats, hippocampal ACh release was similar to that found in young rats, even if in the old cognitively impaired animals there was a 20–30% reduction in number and an 8% reduction in the size of the cholinergic neurones of the septal-diagonal band area of the hippocampus. No explanation, except a sex difference, can be offered for this finding, which demonstrates morphological but not functional age-associated cholinergic impairment.

Age-associated impairment in ACh formation

Vannucchi et al. (1987) observed that there is no difference in the ACh content in electrically stimulated and unstimulated cortical slices prepared from young rats. However, in ageing rats the ACh content of stimulated slices was 44% smaller than that of unstimulated slices at the end of the stimulation period. The percentage decrease in ACh content was similar to that of evoked ACh release from the same slices. This finding indicates that in slices prepared from ageing rats, ACh synthesis is unable to compensate for the increasing release and the ACh stores are emptied. Since ACh synthesis depends on high-affinity choline uptake, acetyl CoA supply and ChAT activity, the question arises as to whether one or all of these components of the synthetic machinery are impaired during ageing.

Most of the investigations into age-associated changes in ChAT activity were recently reviewed by Decker (1987), and Sherman & Friedman (1990). Either no change in ChAT activity or only small disparate changes have generally been found in the cerebral cortex and hippocampus of ageing humans and laboratory animals. Recently, Hadjicostantinou et al. (1991) reported a significant decrease in striatal ChAT activity in Sprague-Dawley rats of between 22 and 24 months of age.

It cannot be excluded that the decrease in ChAT activity sometimes observed in normal aged humans might be attributable to undetected cases of Alzheimer's disease. In this pathological condition a marked decrease in cortical and hippocampal ChAT activity has always been found (Hardy et al., 1985). Since there is normally a high level of ChAT activity in the cholinergic neurones, and ChAT does not catalyse a rate-limiting reaction, it is possible that determination of ChAT activity under optimal substrate and co-factor conditions may sometimes mask a small age-associated decrease.

Either no change or only a small decrease in high-affinity choline uptake (HACU) has been found in ageing rats, with remarkable differences in the total uptake between the rat strains used, and the cerebral regions investigated (Decker, 1987; Sherman & Friedman, 1990). A marked decrease in HACU activity was recently detected in the striatum, hippocampus and frontal cortex of old rats by Hadjicostantinou et al. (1991). Since the HACU rate is directly coupled to neuronal activity (Antonelli et al., 1981), the different results found in the literature may depend on the way the rats were handled before killing. That a decrease in HACU activity may actually occur in ageing rats is also supported by the fact that there is a marked reduction in [^{3}H]hemicholinium binding to HACU sites in the brains of aged rats (Forloni & Angeretti, 1992), and, indirectly, by the finding that the total tritium content in slices incubated with [^{3}H]choline is half as great in old as in young rats (Vannucchi et al., 1990).

No change in the steady-state levels of brain ACh have been found in ageing rats (Decker, 1987), with the notable exception of the decrease in striatal ACh levels detected by Hadjicostantinou et al. (1991) in rats aged between 22 and 24 months old.

The conclusion drawn by Decker (1987) and Sherman & Friedman (1990) summarizing the available data on the effect of ageing on ACh synthesis do not concur completely. According to Decker (1987) most evidence indicates that the synthesis of ACh in the brain diminishes with age. Conversely, Sherman & Friedman (1990) conclude that the results on this point are somewhat conflicting and that the decline in ACh synthesis generally reported is modest in comparison to the marked decline of ACh release and turnover. According to Sherman & Friedman it is unlikely that impairment of the intrinsic capacity to synthesize transmitter accounts for the presynaptic cholinergic dysfunction. This conclusion supports our assumption that ageing has only a limited effect on brain ChAT activity. Therefore, the possibility that the decrease in ACh release and turnover might be due to a reduced availability or transport of the precursors for ACh synthesis should be taken into consideration.

Taken together, the investigations into ACh release and the mechanism of ACh formation indicate that in the ageing brain there is a presynaptic cholinergic deficiency. Demonstration of this deficiency can be made difficult because of the way it varies between brain regions and animal strains, and because of the different experimental conditions used.

Age-associated changes in cholinergic receptors

A recent investigation (Nordberg et al., 1992) into how nicotinic and muscarinic receptor subtypes are affected by ageing and dementia demonstrated a significant decrease during normal ageing of the number of cortical M_1 and M_2 receptors and nicotinic receptors, which had been labelled with [^{3}H]nicotine. Conversely, only the number of nicotinic receptors decrease in the cortical tissue of patients with Alzheimer's disease, while the number of M_1 and M_2 receptors increases. The decrease in brain nicotine binding in patients with this disease has been confirmed by positron emission tomography (Nordberg et al., 1990).

In aged rats, there have been conflicting reports of either a decrease or no change in the density of muscarinic binding sites (Sherman & Friedman, 1990). The conflicting results mostly concern the hippocampus; in the cortex and particularly in the striatum most studies in rodents demonstrate a decrease in muscarinic receptor binding. However, in most of these studies in the hippocampus non-selective ligands and the prevalent use of a single concentration of ligand may have caused the discrepancy. In this regard, Araujo et al. (1990) demonstrated that in ageing rats the densities of nicotinic and muscarinic M_2 binding sites were markedly reduced in the striatum, hippocampus, cerebral cortex and thalamus, while muscarinic M_1 receptors were not affected. A recent autoradiographic investigation (Vannucchi & Goldman-Rakic, 1991) in aged monkeys using labelled pirenzepine, a selective M_1 ligand, demonstrated a change in the affinity of muscarinic M_1 receptors for this ligand in cortical areas, without a decrease in the density of these binding sites. The loss of high-affinity agonist binding to M_1 receptors has also been demonstrated in the brain of patients with Alzheimer's disease (Flynn et al., 1991).

In conclusion, it appears that both presynaptic muscarinic and nicotinic autoreceptor function (Araujo et al., 1990) and post-synaptic muscarinic and nicotinic function are impaired in several cerebral areas in ageing animals and humans. The dysfunction of the cholinergic receptors may limit the usefulness of a therapy based on direct and indirect cholinomimetic agents.

Behavioural and cognitive consequences of the age-associated cholinergic deficiency

Memory loss is a common feature of ageing in humans and animals. However, ageing is associated with the impairment not only of the brain cholinergic system but also of other neurotransmitter systems (McEntee & Crook, 1990, 1991). Furthermore, not all types of memory are lost to the same extent. Therefore, it is not easy to establish a relationship between memory deficits and cholinergic hypofunction, although this has been done in patients affected by senile dementia of Alzheimer's type by correlating ChAT levels in the cortical biopsy with the severity of cognitive impairment (Palmer *et al.*, 1987; Rinne *et al.*, 1988). In normally ageing humans and animals the correlation has been established indirectly by creating a cholinergic hypofunction in young and adult subjects by either administering cholinergic antagonists or destroying, in animals, the cholinergic pathways (Beatty *et al.*, 1986; Smith, 1988; Pepeu *et al.*, 1990), and then testing for memory loss. To present the results of these studies is beyond the scope of this article, but they have been reviewed elsewhere (Collerton, 1986; Mesulam, 1990; Fibiger, 1991). Even if there is disagreement on the specific role of the cholinergic system (Fibiger, 1991), it appears that attention, working memory, spatial memory, and part of declarative memory depend on its integrity.

Pharmacological treatment of cholinergic deficiency

From the previous paragraphs it emerges that the deficiency of the brain cholinergic system may be partly responsible for the decline in cognitive function that is the major sign of cerebral ageing and its most severe aspect, senile dementias. As a consequence many attempts have been made, and are still being made, to correct the cholinergic dysfunction, with the hope of improving the cognitive impairment. The different drugs that have been tested in humans are listed in Table 1.

Table 1. Drug treatment of the cholinergic deficiency in the ageing human brain

Type of Agent	Drugs
Cholinomimetic agents	
Acetylcholine precursors	Choline, lecithine, α-glycerophosphorylcholine
Muscarinic agonists	Arecoline, bethanechol, RS-86
Nicotinic agonists	Nicotine
Acetylcholinesterase inhibitors	Physostigmine, tetrahydroaminoacridine, huperzine
Trophic factors	Nerve growth factor, gangliosides
Non-cholinomimetic agents acting on the cholinergic system	
Nootrophic agents	Piracetam, oxiracetam, aniracetam
	Phosphatidylserine, acetylcarnitine

The pharmacological basis of their use, and the clinical results achieved have been repeatedly reviewed. This article mentions some of the recent reviews, and discusses the discrepancy between the recovery of brain cholinergic deficiency and behaviour induced in the rat by cholinesterase inhibitors, nerve growth factor (NGF) and phosphatidylserine, and the therapeutic results in humans.

The most recent analyses of the cholinergic basis of therapy for Alzheimer's disease are made by Becker & Giacobini (1991), Hermann *et al.* (1991) and Kumar & Calache (1991). Kumar & Calache say that '... unfortunately the results have been somewhat disappointing' – a statement that seems to leave little room for hope and casts doubt on the basic tenet of the cholinergic hypothesis of geriatric memory dysfunction (Bartus *et al.*, 1982). With the exception of single cases in which a consistent improvement has been obtained with physostigmine and tetrahydroaminoacridine (THA), therapy using direct and indirect cholinomimetic agents has been unsuccessful. Yet in different species of ageing animals and also in rats with lesions of the nucleus basalis treatment with these drugs results in significant behavioural improvements (Pepeu *et al.*, 1990).

The administration of NGF to ageing rats (so far the best known of the trophic factors) brings about a remarkable improvement in cholinergic function as demonstrated by the increase in the size of the ChAT-containing forebrain neurones (Fischer *et al.*, 1987, 1991a). The recovery of the cholinergic neurones is associated with that of spatial memory. However, the recovery of cognitive functions observed in the only case of Alzheimer's disease that has so far been treated intracerebroventricularly with NGF is not very impressive (Olson *et al.*, 1992).

Phosphatidylserine injected i.p. for at least 7 days can restore ACh release from electrically stimulated cortical slices prepared from ageing rats (Pedata *et al.*, 1985; Vannucchi & Pepeu, 1987), and from the cerebral cortex, hippocampus and striatum in freely moving rats (Casamenti *et al.*, 1991; Pepeu *et al.*, 1992). This effect does not occur after administration of an equimolar dose of phosphatidylcholine (Pedata *et al.*, 1985; Casamenti *et al.*, 1991), and is associated with an improvement in the age-associated cognitive impairment (Vannucchi *et al.*, 1990). A small but consistent improvement has been observed in Alzheimer's patients treated with phosphatidylserine (SMID, 1988). More evident clinical results were obtained after long-term phosphatidylserine administration to subjects affected by age-associated memory impairment (Crook *et al.*, 1991). However, there is a disparity between the therapeutic results in humans and the rapid and remarkable recovery of both behaviour and brain cholinergic function in the rat.

The question arises as to why the excellent therapeutic results observed in ageing rats are not reproduced in humans. It may be that in the rat the cholinergic system plays a more important role in the working and spatial memories, on which drugs for the ageing brain are usually tested, than in humans, in whom cognitive functions are more complex. Therefore, recovery of the cholinergic dysfunction in humans can result only in limited clinical improvement. Furthermore, even if it is important, cholinergic deficiency is presumably only a part of the neurochemical alterations occurring in the ageing brain, particularly in senile dementias in humans.

However, even if the investigations into the cholinergic system have not yet resulted in definite therapeutic agents, they have demonstrated that drugs such as NGF and phosphatidylserine can reverse the ageing of cholinergic neurones. This finding opens the possibility of understanding the mechanism through which age reduces the size of the cholinergic neurones and impairs their function.

Supported by a CNR grant (Target Project on Ageing).

References

Altavista, M.C., Rossi, P., Bentivoglio, A.R., Crociani, P. & Albanese, A. (1990) Aging is associated with a diffuse impairment of forebrain cholinergic neurons. *Brain Research* **508**, 51–59.

Antonelli, T., Beani, L., Bianchi, C., Pedata, F. & Pepeu, G. (1981) Changes in synaptosomal high-affinity choline uptake following electrical stimulation of guinea-pig cortical slices: effect of atropine and physostigmine. *British Journal of Pharmacology* **74**, 525–531.

Araujo, D.M., Lapchak, P.A., Meaney, M.J., Collier, B. & Quirion, R. (1990) Effects of aging on nicotinic and muscarinic autoreceptor function in the rat brain: relationship to presynaptic cholinergic markers and binding sites. *Journal of Neuroscience* **10**, 3069–3078.

Armstrong, D.M., Hersh, L.B. & Gage, F.H. (1988) Morphological alterations of cholinergic processes in the neocortex of aged rats. *Neurobiology of Aging* **9**, 199–205.

Bartus, R.T., Dean, R.L., Beer, B. & Lippa, A.S. (1982) The cholinergic hypothesis of geriatric memory dysfunction. *Science* **217**, 408–410.

Beatty, W.W., Butters, N., Janowsky, D.S. (1986) Patterns of memory failure after scopolamine treatment: implications for cholinergic hypothesis of dementia. *Behavioural and Neural Biology* **45**, 196–211.

Becker, R.E. (1991) Therapy of the cognitive deficit in Alzheimer's disease: the cholinergic system. In *Cholinergic Basis for Alzheimer Therapy*, pp. 1–22. Eds R. E. Becker & E. Giacobini. Birkhauser, Boston.

Becker, R.E. & Giacobini, E., eds (1991) *Cholinergic Basis for Alzheimer Therapy*. Birkhauser, Boston.

Casamenti, F., Scali, C. & Pepeu, G. (1991) Phosphatidylserine reverses the age-dependent decrease in cortical acetylcholine release: a microdialysis study. *European Journal of Pharmacology* **194**, 11–16.

Coleman, P.D. & Flood, D.G. (1987) Neuron number and dendritic extent in normal aging and Alzheimer's disease. *Neurobiology of Aging* **8**, 521–545.

Collerton, D. (1986) Cholinergic function and intellectual decline in Alzheimer's disease. *Neuroscience* **19**, 1–28.

Crook, T.H., Tinkleberg, J., Yesavage, J., Petrie, W., Nunzi, M.G. & Messari, D.C. (1991) Effects of phosphatidylserine in age-associated memory impairment. *Neurology* **41**, 644–649.

Davies, P. & Maloney, A.J.R. (1976) Selective loss of cholinergic neurons in Alzheimer's disease. *Lancet* **2**, 1403.

Decker, M.W. (1987) The effects of aging on hippocampal and cortical projections of the forebrain cholinergic system. *Brain Research Reviews* **12**, 423–438.

de Lacalle, S., Iraizos, I. & Gonzalo, L.M. (1991) Differential changes in cell size and number in topographic subdivisions of human basal nucleus in normal aging. *Neuroscience* **43**, 445–456.

Domino, E.F., Dren, A.T. & Giardina, W.J. (1978) Biochemical and neurotransmitter changes in the aging brain. In *Psychopharmacology: A Generation of Progress*, pp. 1507–1515. Eds M. A. Lipton, A. Di Mascio & K. F. Killam. Raven Press, New York.

Drachman, D.A. & Leavitt, J. (1974) Human memory and the cholinergic system: a relationship to aging? *Archives in Neurology* **30**, 113–121.

Fibiger, H. (1991) Cholinergic mechanisms in learning, memory and dementia: a review of recent evidence. *Trends in Neurosciences* **14**, 220–223.

Fischer, W., Wictorin, K., Björklund, A., William, L.R., Varon, S. & Gage, F.H. (1987) Amelioration of cholinergic neuron atrophy and spatial memory impairment in aged rats by nerve growth factor. *Nature* **329**, 65–68.

Fischer, W., Gage, F.H. & Björklund, A. (1989) Degenerative changes in forebrain cholinergic nuclei correlate with cognitive impairment in aged rats. *European Journal of Neuroscience* **1**, 34–40.

Fischer, W., Björklund, A., Chen, K. & Gage, F.H. (1991a) NGF improves spatial memory in aged rodents as a function of age. *Journal of Neuroscience* **11**, 1889–1906.

Fischer, W., Nilsson, O.G. & Björklund, A. (1991b) In vivo acetylcholine release as measured by microdialysis is unaltered in the hippocampus of cognitively impaired aged rats with degenerative changes in the basal forebrain. *Brain Research* **556**, 44–52.

Feuerstein, T.J., Lehman, J., Sauermann, W., van Velthoven, V. & Jackisch, R. (1992) The autoinhibitory feedback control of acetylcholine release in human neocortex tissue. *Brain Research* **572**, 64–71.

Flynn, D.D., Weinstein, D.A. & Mash, D.C. (1991) Loss of high affinity agonist binding to M_1 muscarinic receptors in Alzheimer's disease: implications for the failure of cholinergic replacement therapies. *Annals of Neurology* **29**, 256–262.

Forloni, G. & Angeretti, N. (1992) Decreased [^{3}H]hemicholinium binding to high-affinity choline uptake sites in aged rat brain. *Brain Research* **570**, 354–357.

Geula, C. & Mesulam, M.M. (1989) Cortical cholinergic fibers in ageing and Alzheimer's disease: a morphometric study. *Neuroscience* **33**, 469–476.

Gibson, G.E. & Peterson, C. (1981) Aging decreases oxidative metabolism and the release and synthesis of acetylcholine. *Journal of Neurochemistry* **37**, 978–984.

Hadjicostantinou, M., Karadshen, N.S., Rattan, A.K., Tejwani, G.A., Fitkin, J.G. & Neff, N.H. (1991) GM1 ganglioside enhances cholinergic parameters in the brain of senescent rats. *Neuroscience* **46**, 681–686.

Hardy, J., Adolfsson, R., Alafuzoff, I., Bucht, G., Marcusson, J., Nyberg, P., Perdahl, E., Wester, P. & Winblad, B. (1985) Transmitter deficits in Alzheimer's disease. *Neurochemistry International* **7**, 345–363.

Hermann, C., Stern, R.G., Losonzcy, M.F., Jaff, S. & Davidson, M. (1991) Diagnostic and pharmacological approaches in Alzheimer's disease. *Drugs & Aging* **1**, 144–162.

Kumar, V. & Calache, M. (1991) Treatment of Alzheimer's disease with cholinergic drugs. *International Journal of Clinical Theurapeutics and Toxicology* **29**, 23–37.

McEntee, W.J. & Crook, H.C. (1990) Age-associated memory impairment: a role for catecholamines. *Neurology* **40**, 648–652.

McEntee, W.J. & Crook, H.C. (1991) Serotonin, memory, and the aging. *Psychopharmacology* **103**, 143–149.

McGeer, E., Fibiger, H.C., McGeer, P.L. & Wickson, V. (1971) Aging and the brain enzymes. *Experimental Gerontology* **6**, 391–396.

Mesulam, M.M. (1990) Human brain cholinergic pathways. In *Cholinergic Neurotransmission: Functional and Clinical Aspects. (Progress in Brain Research*, Vol. 84), pp. 231–241. Eds S. M. Aquilonius & P. G. Gillberg. Elsevier, Amsterdam.

Nordberg, A., Hartvig, P., Lilja, A., Viitanen, M., Amberla, K., Lundqvist, H., Amdersson, Y., Ulin, J., Winblad, B. & Långström, B. (1990) Decreased uptake and binding of 11C-nicotine in brain of Alzheimer patients as visualized by positron emission tomography. *Journal of Neural Transmission* **2**, 215–224.

Nordberg, A., Alafuzoff, I. & Winblad, B. (1992) Nicotinic and muscarinic subtypes in the human brain: changes with aging and dementia. *Journal of Neuroscience Research* **31**, 103–111.

Olson, L., Nordberg, A., von Holst, H., Bäckman, L., Ebendahl, T., Alafuzoff, I. Amberla, K., Hartvig, P., Herlitz, A., Lilja, A., Lundqvist, H., Långström, B., Meyersson, B., Persson, A., Viitanen, M. & Winblad, B. (1992) Nerve growth factor affects ^{11}C-nicotine binding, blood flow, EEG, and verbal episodic memory in an Alzheimer patient. *Journal of Neural Transmission* **4**, 79–95.

Palmer, A.M., Francis, P.T., Benton, J.S., Sims, N.R., Mann, D.M.A., Neary, D., Snowden, S. & Bowen, D.M. (1987) Presynaptic serotoninergic dysfunction in patients with Alzheimer's disease. *Journal of Neurochemistry* **48**, 8–15.

Pedata, F., Slavikova, J., Kotas, A. & Pepeu, G. (1983) Acetylcholine release from rat cortical slices during postnatal development and aging. *Neurobiology of Aging* **4**, 31–34.

Pedata, F., Giovannelli, L., Spignoli, G., Giovannini, M.G. & Pepeu, G. (1985) Phosphatidylserine increases acetylcholine release from cortical slices in aged rats. *Neurobiology of Aging* **6**, 337–339.

Pepeu, G., Marconcini Pepeu, I. & Casamenti, F. (1990) The validity of animal models in the search for drugs of the aging brain. *Drug Design and Development* **7**, 1–10.

Pepeu, G., Casamenti, F., Scali, C. & Jeglinski, J. (1992) Aging of brain cholinergic neurons: pharmacological interventions. *Clinical Neuropharmacology* **15** (Suppl. 1, Part A), 31A–32A.

Riekkinen, P., Miettinen, R., Sirviö, J., Aaltonen, M. and Riekkinen, P. (1990) The correlation of passive avoidance deficit in aged rats with the loss of nucleus basalis choline acetyltransferase-positive neurons. *Brain Research Bulletin* **25**, 415–417.

Rinne, J.O., Sako, E., Paljarvi, L., Molsa, P.K. & Rinne, U.K. (1988) A comparison of brain choline acetyltransferase activity in Alzheimer's disease, multinfarct dementia and combined dementia. *Journal of Neural Transmission* **73**, 121–128.

Sherman, K.A. & Friedman, E. (1990) Pre- and post-synaptic cholinergic dysfunction in aged rodent brain regions: new findings and an interpretative review. *International Journal of Developmental Neuroscience* **8**, 689–708.

SMID Group (1988) Phosphatidylserine in the treatment of Alzheimer's disease: results of a multicenter study. *Psychopharmacology Bulletin* **24**, 130–142.

Smith, G. (1988) Animal models of Alzheimer's disease: experimental cholinergic denervation. *Brain Research Reviews* **13**, 103–118.

Takei, N., Nihonmatsu, I. & Kawamura, H. (1989) Age-related decline of acetylcholine release evoked by depolarizing stimulation. *Neuroscience Letters* **101**, 182–186.

Vannucchi, M.G. & Goldman-Rakic, P.S. (1991) Age-dependent decrease in the affinity of muscarinic M1 receptors in neocortex of rhesus monkeys. *Proceedings of the National Academy of Science USA* **88**, 11475–11479.

Vannucchi, M.G. & Pepeu, G. (1987) Effect of phosphatidylserine on acetylcholine release and content in cortical slices from aging rats. *Neurobiology of Aging* **8**, 403–407.

Vannucchi, M.G., Casamenti, F. & Pepeu, G. (1990) Decrease of acetylcholine release from cortical slices in aged rats: investigations into its reversal by phosphatidylserine. *Journal of Neurochemistry* **55**, 819–825.

Whitehouse, P.J., Price, D.L., Struble, R.G., Clark, A.W., Coyle, J.T. & DeLong, M.L. (1982) Alzheimer's disease and senile dementia: loss of neurons in the basal forebrain. *Science* **215**, 1237–1239.

Wu, C.F., Bertorelli, R., Sacconi, M., Pepeu, G. & Consolo, S. (1988) Decrease of brain acetylcholine release in aging freely moving rats detected by microdialysis. *Neurobiology of Aging* **9**, 357–361.

AUTHOR INDEX

	Page		Page
Bartke, A.	61	Maggi, R.	47
Bowen, D.M.	131	Marconcini Pepeu, I.	155
Butterfield, G.	115	Marcus, R.	115
		Martini, L.	47
Casementi, F.	155	Meites, J.	1
Cecim, M.	61	Messi, E.	47
Cella, S.G.	99	Mode, A.	77
Celotti, F.	47	Motta, M.	47
Chessell, I.P.	131	Müller, E.E.	99
Cocchi, D.	99		
		Negri-Cesi, P.	47
D'Costa, A.P.	87	Nordberg, A.	145
De Gennaro Colonna, V.	99		
Dondi, D.	47	Pangalos, M.N.	131
		Parenti, M.	99
Francis, P.T.	131	Pepeu, G.	155
		Piva, F.	47
Gilad, G.M.	119		
Goya, L.	21	Sahu, A.	11
		Scali, C.	155
Holloway, L.	115	Sonntag, W.E.	87
		Steger, R.W.	61
Ingram, R.L.	87		
Isaeff, M.	21	Timiras, P.S.	21
		Tizabi, Y.	119
Kalra, P.S.	11		
Kalra, S.P.	11	Wise, P.M.	35
		Wyatt, R.J.	119
Lenham, J.E.	87		
Li, R.	119	Zanisi, M.	47
Limonta, P.	47		
Locatelli, V.	99		

SUBJECT INDEX

Acetylcholine
in memory loss 4
formation, age-related impairment 157
release, age-related changes 156
ACTH, plasma, effects of stress and ageing 122
Ageing
anti-ageing interventions and their neuroendocrine aspects in mammals 1–9
effect on growth and protein content of human neuroblastoma cells *in vitro* 21–33
premature, in transgenic mice expressing different growth hormone genes 61–75
Aluminium sulphate
effect on human neuroblastoma cell growth 25
effect on tau protein in neuroblastoma cells 27
Alzheimer's disease 149
brain cholinergic system 155–162
neuronal nicotinic receptors 145–154
role of neocortical pyramidal neurones 141
Anti-ageing interventions 1–9
Antioxidants, role in ageing 3

Behavioural consequences of age-associated cholinergic deficiency 158
Biological clock, and ageing 42
Body composition, human, clinical use of growth hormone 115–118
Bone, ageing, clinical growth hormone therapy 115–118
Brain
cholinergic deficiency, in ageing mammals 155–162
male rat: ageing of neuroendocrine system 47–59

Catecholaminergic neurotransmission 107
Cholinergic
deficiency, brain, in ageing mammals 155–162
hypofunction, pharmacological treatment 159
neurotransmission 107
receptors, age-related changes 158
Circadian rhythm 42
Cognitive consequences of age-associated cholinergic deficiency 158
Cortisone, plasma, effects of stress and ageing 122
Cytochrome P450
enzymes 78
expression in rat liver, regulation by growth hormone 77–86

Dietary restriction 2
importance of growth hormone and IGF-1 92

Exercise, role in ageing process 3

Free radicals 3

Genotype, effects on stress hormones in ageing rats 119–130
Growth hormone
basal and stimulated secretion 100
clinical uses in older people 115–118
diet and ageing, effects 87–98
genes, different, transgenic mice expressing: premature ageing in 61–75
neural regulation of secretion 104

neuroendocrine control of secretion, in ageing mammals 99–114
pituitary sensitivity to 90
receptor 79
recombinant human, administration to elderly humans 116
regulation of cytochrome P450 77–86
regulation of release 89
signalling 80
treatment, effect on ageing 82
Growth hormone-releasing hormone 99–114
pituitary sensitivity to 90

Heat shock, effect on human neuroblastoma cell growth 25
5-HT receptors 132
Hypothalamic–pituitary–adrenocortical system, in stress and ageing 126
Hypothalmus, function, and reproductive ageing 35–46

Immune competence in ageing 4
Insulin-like growth factor 1, during normal ageing 87–98

Liver, rat: growth hormone regulation of cytochrome P450 expression 77–86
Longevity, rat, and stress and strain 127
Luteinizing-hormone-releasing hormone
ageing of male rat brain 48
feedback mechanism 50
and neuropeptidergic signal ageing, in rats 11
receptors, binding characteristics 54

Mammals
ageing, neuroendocrine control of growth hormone secretion 99–114
neuronal nicotinic receptors, implications in ageing and degenerative disorders 145–154
Man. *See also* Alzheimer's disease
growth hormone secretion and ageing 82
neuroblastoma cells, growth and protein content *in vitro* 21–33
Memory loss 4. *See also* Alzheimer's disease
Monoamines, hypothalamic, in stress and ageing 122, 123
Mouse, transgenic, premature ageing 61–75

Nerve growth factor 21, 25
Nervous system, age-related changes 30
Neural regulation of growth hormone secretion 104
Neuroblastoma cells, human: growth and protein content *in vitro* 21–33
Neurodegenerative disorders in mammals: neuronal nicotinic receptors 145–154
Neuroendocrine
ageing, impact on reproductive system of the rat 35–46
ageing, of male rat brain 47–59
aspects of anti-ageing interventions in mammals 1–9
control of growth hormone secretion in ageing mammals 99–114
interventions 5
systems, interaction 127
Neuropeptide Y system and steroids, in rats 15
Neuropeptidergic signals, ageing of, in rats 11–19

Neurotransmitter receptors of rat cortical pyramidal neurones 131–143
Nicotinic receptors, neuronal 145–154

Opioids
  endogenous opioid peptide system 12, 13
  receptors, brain 51
Osteoporosis, growth hormone therapy 117

PET (positron emission tomography), in Alzheimer's disease 151
Pituitary
  aged: somatotroph cells 102
  sensitivity to hypothalamic hormones 90
Positron emission tomography, in Alzheimer's disease 151
Prolactin, plasma, effects of stress and ageing 121, 123
Protein content of human neuroblastoma cells *in vitro* 21–33
Pyramidal neurones, cortical, of the rat: neurotransmitters 131–143

Rat
  brain, of males: ageing of neuroendocrine system 47–59
  genotype, effects on stress hormones 119–130
  liver: growth hormone regulation of cytochrome P450 expression 77–86
  neuropeptidergic signals, ageing of 11–19
  pyramidal neurones, cortical, neurotransmitters 131–143
  reproductive system, effect of neuroendocrine ageing 35–46

Reproductive system, rat, effect of neuroendocrine ageing 35–46

Somatostatin
  dietary restriction, effects on 95
  secretion, and ageing 91
Somatotroph cells, aged pituitary 102
Steroids
  and endogenous opioid peptide system, in rats 13
  and neuropeptide Y system, in rats 15
Stress
  and longevity, in rats 127
  effect on growth and protein content of human neuroblastoma cells *in vitro* 21–33
  hormones, effect of genotype, in ageing rats 119–130

Tau protein, neuroblastoma cell: effect of aluminium sulphate 27
Testosterone, hypothalamic and anterior pituitary metabolism 56
Thyroid hormones, effect on growth and protein content of human neuroblastoma cells *in vitro* 21–33
Transgenic mice expressing different growth hormone genes, premature ageing in 61–75
Triiodothyronine 21
  effect on 'aged' neuroblastoma cells 26

Ubiquitin-tau conjugates in neuroblastoma cells 27

Volkensin 131–143

Journal of Reproduction & Fertility

SUPPLEMENTS

No. 17: **Regnier de Graaf on the Human Reproductive Organs.** An annotated translation of *Tractatus de Virorum Organis Generationi Inservientibus* (1668) and *De Mulierum Organis Generationi Inservientibus Tractatus Novus* (1672) by H. D. JOCELYN and B. P. SETCHELL. 1972. 236 pp. Cloth £6.00 ($17.50)

No. 19: **The Environment and Reproduction in Mammals and Birds.** 1973. Paper £15.00 ($45.00). Cloth £17.00 ($51.00)

No. 25: **Implantation and the Mechanism of Action of IUDs.** 1976. £5.00 ($10.00)

No. 26: **Inhibin, FSH and Spermatogenesis.** 1979. Paper £10.00 ISBN 0 906545 02 1. Cloth £12.00 ($27.00) ISBN 0 906545 01 3

No. 27: **Equine Reproduction II.** 1979. Cloth £27.00 ($60.00) ISBN 0 906545 03 X

No. 28: **The Great Apes of Africa.** 1980. Cloth £19.00 ($45.00) ISBN 0 906545 04 8

No. 29: **Embryonic Diapause in Mammals.** 1981. Cloth £25.00 ($60.00) ISBN 0 906545 05 6

No. 30: **Reproductive Endocrinology of Domestic Ruminants.** 1981. Cloth £30.00 ($65.00) ISBN 0 906545 06 4

No. 31: **Placenta—Structure and Function.** 1982. £25.00 ($55.00) ISBN 0 906545 07 2

No. 32: **Equine Reproduction III.** 1982. Cloth £42.00 ($92.00) ISBN 0 906545 08 0

No. 33: **Control of Pig Reproduction II.** 1985. Cloth £35.00 ($63.00) ISBN 0 906545 10 2

No. 34: **Reproduction in Domestic Ruminants.** 1987. Cloth £35.00 ($67.00) ISBN 0 906545 12 9

No. 35: **Equine Reproduction IV.** 1987. Cloth £50.00 ($95.00) ISBN 0 906545 13 7

No. 36: **The Early Days of Pregnancy.** 1988. Cloth £28.00 ($55.00) ISBN 0 906545 14 5

No. 37: **Maternal Recognition of Pregnancy and Maintenance of the Corpus Luteum.** 1989. Cloth £45.00 ($90.00) ISBN 0 906545 15 3

No. 38: **Cell Biology of Mammalian Egg Manipulation.** 1989. Cloth £25.00 ($47.50) ISBN 0 906545 16 1

No. 39: **Dog and Cat Reproduction, Contraception and Artificial Insemination.** 1989. Cloth £47.00 ($90.00) ISBN 0 906545 17 X

No. 40: **Control of Pig Reproduction III.** 1990. Cloth £48.00 ($93.00) ISBN 0 906545 18 8

No. 41: **Genetic Engineering of Animals.** 1990. Cloth £42.00 ($82.00) ISBN 0 906545 19 6

No. 42: **Cell Messengers at Fertilization.** 1990. Cloth £48.00 ($95.00) ISBN 0 906545 20 X

No. 43: **Reproduction in Domestic Ruminants II.** 1991. Cloth £48.00 ($95.00) ISBN 0 906545 22 6

No. 44: **Equine Reproduction V.** 1991. Cloth £75.00 ($140.00) ISBN 0 906545 21 8

Copies of these supplements (and symposium reports, back issues, cumulative indexes) can be obtained from:

Journal of Reproduction and Fertility
P.O. Box 32, Commerce Way, Colchester, Essex CO2 8HP, UK

Journal of Reproduction & Fertility

Supplement 45

FRONTIERS IN REPRODUCTIVE BIOLOGY

Symposium to honour Professor G. E. Lamming OBE
on the occasion of his 65th Birthday

Edited by N. Brooks, J. Challis, A. McNeilly
and C. Doberska

ISBN 0 906545 23 4: £20 (US$37.50)

FRONTIERS IN REPRODUCTIVE BIOLOGY presents the proceedings of a symposium held in honour of the enormous contribution made to the field of reproductive biology by Professor G E Lamming. The symposium was held at the University of Nottingham Faculty of Agricultural Sciences, Sutton Bonington, in July 1992. This publication contains 15 papers presented at the symposium and covers recent advances in the fields of ovarian function, pregnancy and parturition and the regulation of reproductive processes. Emphasis is given to the future directions that this important field of research will take. *Frontiers in Reproductive Biology* will provide an invaluable reference source to students, research scientists and clinicians.

R.B. Heap. George Eric Lamming: an appreciation
A.S. McNeilly, W. Crow, J. Brooks and G. Evans. Luteinizing hormone pulses, follicle-stimulating hormone and control of follicle selection in sheep
M.G. Hunter, C. Biggs, L.S. Faillace and H.M. Picton. Current concepts of folliculogenesis in monovular and polyovular farm species
D.C. Wathes and P.A. Denning-Kendall. Control of synthesis and secretion of ovarian oxytocin in ruminants
A.P.F. Flint, H.J. Stewart, G.E. Lamming and J.H. Payne. Role of the oxytocin receptor in the choice between cyclicity and gestation in ruminants
H.J. Stewart, F.M.J. Guesdon, J.H. Payne, B. Charleston, J.L. Vallet and A.P.F. Flint. Trophoblast interferons in early pregnancy of domestic ruminants
A.N. Brooks, I.S. Currie, F. Gibson and G.B. Thomas. Neuroendocrine regulation of sheep fetuses
K. Yang. Regulation of gene expression in the ovine fetus
G. Jenkin. Oxytocin and prostaglandin interactions in pregnancy and at parturition
G.R. Foxcroft. Nutritional and lactational regulation of fertility in sows
W. Haresign. Manipulation of reproduction in sheep
R. Webb, J.G. Gong, A.S. Law and S.M. Rusbridge. Control of ovarian function in cattle
I. Wilmut, C.S. Haley, J.P. Simons and R. Webb. The potential role of molecular genetic manipulation in the improvement of reproductive performance
D.W. Lincoln. Human contraception: development of new scientific opportunities
A.R. Peters. Endocrine manipulation—toxicological frontiers
Author and subject indexes

Order directly from the publishers:
Journals of Reproduction & Fertility Ltd., P.O. Box 32, Commerce Way,
Colchester CO2 8HP, Essex, UK
or through any bookseller or agent